CHARLES R. SWINDOLL

SWINDOLL'S
LIVING
INSIGHTS

NEW TESTAMENT COMMENTARY

MARK

Tyndale House Publishers, Inc.
Carol Stream, Illinois

Swindoll's Living Insights New Testament Commentary, Volume 2

Visit Tyndale online at www.tyndale.com.

Insights on Mark copyright © 2016 by Charles R. Swindoll, Inc.

Designed by Nicole Grimes

Published in association with Yates & Yates, LLP (www.yates2.com).

Library of Congress Cataloging-in-Publication Data
Names: Swindoll, Charles R., author.
Title: Insights on Mark / Charles R. Swindoll.
Description: Carol Stream, IL : Tyndale House Publishers, Inc., 2016. |
  Series: Swindoll's living insights New Testament commentary ; 2 | Includes
  bibliographical references.
Identifiers: LCCN 2016033147 | ISBN 9781414393810 (hc : alk. paper)
Subjects: LCSH: Bible. Mark—Commentaries.
Classification: LCC BS2585.53 .S95 2016 | DDC 226.3/07—dc23 LC record available at
  https://lccn.loc.gov/2016033147

Printed in China
25   24   23   22   21
8   7   6   5   4

CONTENTS

Author's Preface v
The Strong's Numbering System vii
Introduction 3
Disciples Called (Mark 1:1–3:35) 11
   Are You Ready for Some Good News? (Mark 1:1-13) 13
   Deciding to Follow Jesus (Mark 1:14-20) 23
   Astonishing Authority (Mark 1:21-28) 37
   A Day in the Life of Jesus (Mark 1:29-39) 42
   Changing a Leper's Spots (Mark 1:40-45) 49
   The Day a Paraplegic Walked Home (Mark 2:1-12) 55
   Look Who Jesus Hung Out With! (Mark 2:13-17) 62
   Battles worth Fighting (Mark 2:18-28) 67
   Mercy under Suspicious Eyes (Mark 3:1-6) 78
   The Perils of Effective Ministry (Mark 3:7-19) 87
   Misunderstood (Mark 3:20-35) 95
Disciples Culled (Mark 4:1–8:38) 104
   Souls in Soil (Mark 4:1-20) 106
   After the Teaching Comes the Testing (Mark 4:21-41) 115
   Restoring a Human Wreck (Mark 5:1-20) 123
   Power over Death and Disease (Mark 5:21-43) 131
   A Prophet without Honor (Mark 6:1-6) 141
   Travel Light, Think Right, Talk Straight (Mark 6:7-13) 149
   Murder at a Stag Party (Mark 6:14-29) 157
   An Unforgettable Dinner on the Grounds (Mark 6:30-44) 164
   Failing to Connect the Dots (Mark 6:45-56) 172
   The Day Jesus Took Off the Gloves (Mark 7:1-13) 179
   Getting to the Heart of Our Defilement (Mark 7:14-23) 186
   Would Jesus Call Your Faith "Great"? (Mark 7:24-30) 194
   Taking Time for Someone in Need (Mark 7:31-37) 201
   Serving Dinner to Four Thousand (Mark 8:1-26) 207
   Crucial Contrasts (Mark 8:27-38) 221
Disciples Cultivated (Mark 9:1–13:37) 231
   A Glimpse of the Glory to Come (Mark 9:1-13) 233
   Confronting an Unclean Spirit (Mark 9:14-29) 241
   A Cross, a Crown, and a Child (Mark 9:30-50) 249
   What about Divorce? (Mark 10:1-12) 259
   Let's Get These Things Straight (Mark 10:13-31) 266
   Prediction, Ambition, Submission (Mark 10:32-45) 277
   What's a King Doing on a Donkey? (Mark 10:46–11:11) 286
   Seeing Another Side of Jesus (Mark 11:12-33) 294
   A Violent and Bloody Parable (Mark 12:1-12) 305

Questions, Questions, Questions (Mark 12:13-44) 311
A Prophet We Can Trust (Mark 13:1-37) 324
Disciples Challenged (Mark 14:1–16:20) 336
Love and Loyalty (Mark 14:1-21) 338
Special Meal, Shocking Temptation (Mark 14:22-42) 347
An Enemy's Deceitful Kiss (Mark 14:43-52) 358
A Rush to Judgment (Mark 14:53-72) 364
The Condemnation of the Innocent (Mark 15:1-15) 372
And They Crucified Him (Mark 15:16-41) 382
A Secret Too Wonderful to Keep (Mark 15:42–16:8) 394
Postscripts and "Mark" 16:9-20 (Mark 16:9-20) 402
Endnotes 407

List of Features and Images
Timeline of Mark 2
Map of Jesus' Life and Ministry 2
The Gospel of Mark at a Glance 4
Jordan River 19
Map of Israel after Herod the Great 25
Excursus: "Easy Believism" and Lordship Salvation 27
First-Century Fishing Boat 29
Synagogue Ruins in Capernaum 39
Map of the Sea of Galilee and the Surrounding Area 40
The Pharisees 70
The Twelve 92
Parables 110
Map of the Cities of the Decapolis 126
Map of Tyre, Sidon, and Capernaum 196
Map of Dalmanutha, Capernaum, and Tiberias 214
Map of the Region of Galilee and Caesarea Philippi 224
"Son of Man" 226
Ancient Millstone 255
The Traditional Route from Galilee to Jerusalem 280
Jericho 288
Map of Jerusalem Area 290
Tiberias Caesar Coin 316
The Sadducees 318
The Jewish Calendar and Festival Cycle 341
Map of Jerusalem 353
Garden of Gethsemane 354
The Trials of Jesus 368
Sanhedrin Hall in Temple 375
Pontius Pilate 376
Fortress of Antonia 379
Flagrum 386
Cross 387
Tomb 398

AUTHOR'S PREFACE

For more than sixty years I have loved the Bible. It was that love for the Scriptures, mixed with a clear call into the gospel ministry during my tour of duty in the Marine Corps, that resulted in my going to Dallas Theological Seminary to prepare for a lifetime of ministry. During those four great years I had the privilege of studying under outstanding men of God, who also loved God's Word. They not only held the inerrant Word of God in high esteem, they taught it carefully, preached it passionately, and modeled it consistently. A week never passes without my giving thanks to God for the grand heritage that has been mine to claim! I am forever indebted to those fine theologians and mentors, who cultivated in me a strong commitment to the understanding, exposition, and application of God's truth.

For more than fifty years I have been engaged in doing just that—*and how I love it!* I confess without hesitation that I am addicted to the examination and the proclamation of the Scriptures. Because of this, books have played a major role in my life for as long as I have been in ministry—especially those volumes that explain the truths and enhance my understanding of what God has written. Through these many years I have collected a large personal library, which has proven invaluable as I have sought to remain a faithful student of the Bible. To the end of my days, my major goal in life is to communicate the Word with accuracy, insight, clarity, and practicality. Without informative and reliable books to turn to, I would have "run dry" decades ago.

Among my favorite and most well-worn volumes are those that have enabled me to get a better grasp of the biblical text. Like most expositors, I am forever searching for literary tools that I can use to hone my gifts and sharpen my skills. For me, that means finding resources that make the complicated simple and easy to understand, that offer insightful comments and word pictures that enable me to see the relevance of sacred truth in light of my twenty-first-century world, and that drive those truths home to my heart in ways I do not easily forget. When I come across such books, they wind up in my hands as I devour them and then place them in my library for further reference . . . and, believe me, I often return to them. What a relief it is to have these resources to turn to when I lack fresh insight, or when I need just the right story or illustration, or when I get stuck in the tangled text and cannot find my way out. For the serious expositor, a library is essential. As a mentor of mine once said, "Where else can you have ten thousand professors at your fingertips?"

In recent years I have discovered there are not nearly enough resources like those I just described. It was such a discovery that prompted me to consider becoming a part of the answer instead of lamenting the problem. But the solution would result in a huge undertaking. A writing project that covers all of the books and letters of the New Testament seemed overwhelming and intimidating. A rush of relief came when I realized that during the past fifty-plus years I've taught and preached through most of the New Testament. In my files were folders filled with notes from those messages that were just lying there, waiting to be brought out of hiding, given a fresh and relevant touch in light of today's needs, and applied to fit into the lives of men and women who long for a fresh word from the Lord. *That did it!* I began to work on plans to turn all of those notes into this commentary on the New Testament.

I must express my gratitude to both Mark Gaither and Mike Svigel for their tireless and devoted efforts, serving as my hands-on, day-to-day editors. They have done superb work as we have walked our way through the verses and chapters of all twenty-seven New Testament books. It has been a pleasure to see how they have taken my original material and helped me shape it into a style that remains true to the text of the Scriptures, at the same time interestingly and creatively developed, and all the while allowing my voice to come through in a natural and easy-to-read manner.

I need to add sincere words of appreciation to the congregations I have served in various parts of these United States for more than five decades. It has been my good fortune to be the recipient of their love, support, encouragement, patience, and frequent words of affirmation as I have fulfilled my calling to stand and deliver God's message year after year. The sheep from all those flocks have endeared themselves to this shepherd in more ways than I can put into words . . . and none more than those I currently serve with delight at Stonebriar Community Church in Frisco, Texas.

Finally, I must thank my wife, Cynthia, for her understanding of my addiction to studying, to preaching, and to writing. Never has she discouraged me from staying at it. Never has she failed to urge me in the pursuit of doing my very best. On the contrary, her affectionate support personally, and her own commitment to excellence in leading Insight for Living for more than three and a half decades, have combined to keep me faithful to my calling "in season and out of season." Without her devotion to me and apart from our mutual partnership throughout our lifetime of ministry together, Swindoll's Living Insights would never have been undertaken.

I am grateful that it has now found its way into your hands and, ultimately, onto the shelves of your library. My continued hope and prayer is that you will find these volumes helpful in your own study and personal application of the Bible. May they help you come to realize, as I have over these many years, that God's Word is as timeless as it is true.

The grass withers, the flower fades,
But the word of our God stands forever. (Isa. 40:8, NASB)

Chuck Swindoll
Frisco, Texas

THE STRONG'S NUMBERING SYSTEM

Swindoll's Living Insights New Testament Commentary uses the Strong's word-study numbering system to give both newer and more advanced Bible students alike quicker, more convenient access to helpful original-language tools (e.g., concordances, lexicons, and theological dictionaries). The Strong's numbering system, made popular by the *Strong's Exhaustive Concordance of the Bible,* is used with the majority of biblical Greek and Hebrew reference works. Those who are unfamiliar with the ancient Hebrew, Aramaic, and Greek alphabets can quickly find information on a given word by looking up the appropriate index number. Advanced students will find the system helpful because it allows them to quickly find the lexical form of obscure conjugations and inflections.

When a Greek word is mentioned in the text, the Strong's number is included in square brackets after the Greek word. So in the example of the Greek word *agapē* [26], "love," the number is used with Greek tools keyed to the Strong's system.

On occasion, a Hebrew word is mentioned in the text. The Strong's Hebrew numbers are completely separate from the Greek numbers, so Hebrew numbers are prefixed with a letter "H." So, for example, the Hebrew word *kapporet* [H3727], "mercy seat," comes from *kopher* [H3722], "to ransom," "to secure favor through a gift."

INSIGHTS ON MARK

Ministry that costs nothing accomplishes nothing. Consequently, faithful discipleship, even in times of hardship, is the theme that dominates Mark's Gospel and may have been the reason he felt compelled to write.

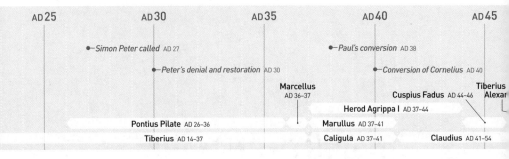

AD 25   AD 30   AD 35   AD 40   AD 45

● Simon Peter called AD 27   ● Paul's conversion AD 38

● Peter's denial and restoration AD 30   ● Conversion of Cornelius AD 40

Marcellus AD 36–37   Tiberius Alexar

Cuspius Fadus AD 44–46

Herod Agrippa I AD 37–44

Pontius Pilate AD 26–36   Marullus AD 37–41

Tiberius AD 14–37   Caligula AD 37–41   Claudius AD 41–54

N

0   5   10   20 miles

0   10   20   30 km

Sidon

Damascus

Mount Hermon

SYRIA

PHOENICIA

Tyre

Caesarea Philippi

Gennesaret

Capernaum

Ptolemais

Bethsaida

GALILEE

Sea of Galilee

Nazareth

Dion

Mount Tabor

Gadara

DECAPOLIS

Caesarea Maritima

Scythopolis

Pella

Sebaste

Gerasa

Jordan River

SAMARIA

PEREA

Joppa

Arimathea

Philadelphia

Lydda

Jericho

Ashdod

Jerusalem

Esbus

Ashkelon

JUDEA

Gaza

Machaerus

Dead Sea

NABATEA

IDUMEA

Mediterranean Sea

Map of Jesus' Life and Ministry. Mark tells the story of Jesus' life by tracing his journey geographically: After his baptism in the Jordan River (1:1-15), Jesus teaches and heals in Galilee (1:16–9:50), and then he journeys down to Judea for more teaching and healing, concluding in his death and resurrection (10:1–16:8).

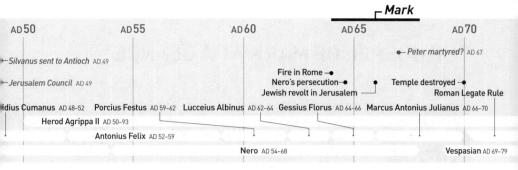

┌Mark

AD50 AD55 AD60 AD65 AD70

●— Peter martyred? AD 67

●—Silvanus sent to Antioch AD 49

Fire in Rome —●
Nero's persecution—●   ● Temple destroyed —●
Jewish revolt in Jerusalem ──┘   Roman Legate Rule

●—Jerusalem Council AD 49

dius Cumanus AD 48–52   Porcius Festus AD 59–62   Lucceius Albinus AD 62–64   Gessius Florus AD 64–66   Marcus Antonius Julianus AD 66–70

Herod Agrippa II AD 50–93

Antonius Felix AD 52–59

Nero AD 54–68   Vespasian AD 69–79

MARK

INTRODUCTION

John Mark was not the kind of man you would expect to record the first account of Jesus' life. Unlike the studious Matthew, the scholarly Luke, the contemplative John, or countless other worthy followers of Christ, Mark had distinguished himself early on as an immature young man . . . impetuous, unreliable, and faltering in his commitment to the gospel. In other words, he was a lot like us.

In the early days of the church, he probably lived in Jerusalem with his mother, Mary, in whose house the first believers met for worship and prayer (Acts 12:12). During this time, he came to know the original apostles, including Simon Peter, as well as several key members of the fledgling band of followers. Then, around AD 46, he was given an opportunity to take a more active role in the church that had grown up there in Jerusalem over the past decade. Mark's cousin Barnabas (Col. 4:10) and an up-and-coming teacher named Paul brought famine relief money to Jerusalem from the church in Antioch. For the past several years, the two men had been leading a flourishing Gentile congregation in Syria, and they invited young Mark to join their ministry (Acts 12:25). The epicenter of Christianity was moving from Jerusalem to Antioch, and as Providence would have it, Mark moved with it.

After a few years of service with Barnabas and Paul, Mark was invited to become a "helper" on their first missionary journey (Acts 13:5). He undoubtedly enjoyed the excitement and probably embraced this new adventure with youthful enthusiasm. Not far into the expedition, however, he abandoned the mission and returned home (Acts 13:13). The New Testament says nothing about his reasons, but we may surmise that the difficulties of ministry and travel proved too demanding for Mark. Paul and Barnabas pressed on without him and

3

THE GOSPEL OF MARK AT A GLANCE

SECTION	DISCIPLES CALLED	DISCIPLES CULLED
PASSAGE	1:1–3:35	4:1–8:38
THEMES	The call to follow Jesus Jesus' ministry begins	Jesus, the emissary of pea Repent and be ready for the kingdom!
KEY TERMS	Follow Forgiveness Arise Immediately Preach	Hear Disciple Parable Encourage Understand

DISCIPLES CULTIVATED	DISCIPLES CHALLENGED
9:1–13:37	14:1–16:20
Jesus pours wisdom into His disciples

Jesus prepares His disciples for ministry | The victory of the kingdom of God over Satan

Challenges of discipleship |
| Kingdom
Gospel
Amazed
Season
Fear | Surrender
Flee
Messiah |

completed their objectives, overcoming incredible hardship and enduring intense persecution along the way. Mark may have been one of several helpers—the New Testament strongly suggests that Titus had been Paul's right-hand man from the very beginning—but he is the only one noted for forsaking his responsibilities during the missionary journey. While the rest of the team pressed on, accepting the difficulties of pioneer missionary work, it seems Mark sought relief in the safety and comforts of home.

After a year or more had passed, the leaders in Antioch made plans to launch a second missionary journey. Barnabas suggested they include John Mark on the team, but Paul would hear nothing of it (Acts 15:37-38). Barnabas, ever the champion of second chances, refused to give up hope that Mark could become a trustworthy, dependable minister of the gospel. Paul—mission-focused and disciplined to the core—couldn't bring himself to recruit a proven deserter, especially when their purpose was to strengthen and encourage Christians living under persecution. When the two couldn't come to terms, Paul chose Silas as a partner and headed off in one direction; Barnabas took Mark and sailed for Cyprus (Acts 15:39-40).

In retrospect, it seems both men were right. Paul's mission was so critical that the team couldn't afford a weak link. Barnabas recognized, however, that some disciples need seasoning, which requires time, experience, the grace of forgiveness, and personal investment.

Years later, the church would reap the benefits of Barnabas's personal investment as Mark served Paul during his first imprisonment in Rome (Col. 4:10) and labored with Timothy in Asia Minor. Several church historians record Mark's service to Peter as an interpreter and personal assistant for many years (Eusebius, *History of the Church*, 1:172-173; cf. 1 Pet. 5:13). Then, near the end of Paul's life, as the apostle languished in prison awaiting execution, he instructed Timothy, "Pick up Mark and bring him with you, for he is useful to me for service" (2 Tim. 4:11).

We don't know specifically what happened after Barnabas took Mark to Cyprus that turned the wavering young disciple into a sturdy pillar of the Christian movement, but two things are clear. First, the personal investment of Barnabas proved crucial. Second, Mark eventually understood that followers of Christ must be servants and that discipleship requires sacrifice. Ministry that costs nothing accomplishes nothing. Consequently, faithful discipleship, even in times of hardship, is the theme that dominates Mark's Gospel and may have been the reason he felt compelled to write.

DISCIPLES UNDER DURESS

While the Holy Spirit prompted Mark to write this Gospel account, several clues within the text and from history suggest that additional influences motivated him and gave his writing focus. The writings of early Christian leaders indicate that Mark wrote while in Rome around the time of Simon Peter's death.[1] Internal evidence supports their testimony; many scholars note Mark's frequent use of "Latinisms" and Latin loan words (e.g., the use of "legion" in 5:9, 15).[2] Moreover, he explained Jewish customs (e.g., 7:2-4; 12:18; 14:12; 15:42) and translated Aramaic terms and names (3:17; 5:41; 7:11, 34; 10:46; 14:36; 15:22, 34), suggesting a western audience largely unfamiliar with eastern culture and the setting of Judea. Most importantly, however, Mark gave special attention—more than the other Gospels—to the issues of persecution, the cost of discipleship, and the possibility of martyrdom (e.g., 8:34-38; 10:28-30; 13:9-13). Taken together, the evidence strongly suggests that Mark wrote this chronicle of Jesus' ministry to encourage and challenge believers during the persecution of Nero (AD 64–68), which claimed the lives of innumerable Christians, including Paul and Simon Peter.

The persecution began shortly after a massive fire consumed large portions of Rome, leaving many homeless and potentially destitute. By then, Emperor Nero's eccentricities had grown more extreme, making him unpopular. Rumors began to circulate that he had arranged the fire himself in order to rebuild the affected sections of Rome to his own liking. According to the historian Tacitus,

> All human efforts, all the lavish gifts of the emperor, and the propitiations of the gods, did not banish the sinister belief that the conflagration was the result of an order. Consequently, to get rid of the report, Nero fastened the guilt and inflicted the most exquisite tortures on a class hated for their abominations, called Christians by the populace. . . . Accordingly, an arrest was first made of all who pleaded guilty; then, upon their information, an immense multitude was convicted, not so much of the crime of firing the city, as of hatred against mankind. Mockery of every sort was added to their deaths. Covered with the skins of beasts, they were torn by dogs and perished, or were nailed to crosses,

or were doomed to the flames and burnt, to serve as a nightly illumination, when daylight had expired.[3]

According to church tradition, Simon Peter was martyred in the early days of this persecution. As these horrors began to decimate the church in Rome—and by extension, the church worldwide—Mark undoubtedly felt compelled to encourage believers to remain faithful in their commitment to Christ and to follow His example to the end.

Because Mark wrote with such a specific purpose in mind, his chronicle of Jesus' earthly life doesn't follow some of the normal conventions of a biography—at least not by modern standards. Mark didn't feel compelled to follow a strictly chronological outline, choosing instead to group episodes by theme or topic. Eusebius, writing in the third century, quotes an early second-century church father, Papias, to explain Mark's literary approach:

> This also the presbyter [probably referring to the apostle John] said: Mark, having become the interpreter of Peter, wrote down accurately, though not indeed in order, whatsoever he remembered of the things said or done by Christ. For he neither heard the Lord nor followed him, but afterward, as I said, he followed Peter, who adapted his teaching to the needs of his hearers, but with no intention of giving a connected account of the Lord's discourses, so that Mark committed no error while he thus wrote some things as he remembered them. For he was careful of one thing, not to omit any of the things which he had heard, and not to state any of them falsely.[4]

The result of Mark's writing is not a biography that records the precise order of events, but an account of Jesus' cultivation of followers in which episodes are arranged to communicate a specific message. The subject of this Gospel is unquestionably Jesus; only two stories feature someone other than the Savior, and those highlight the dedication and faithfulness of John the Baptizer (1:1-8; 6:14-29). But while the subject is Jesus, the point is unquestionably discipleship—its demands, its cost, its impact, and its rewards. While Jesus is central to the story, Mark continually focuses on the disciples, who struggle with a variety of challenges, including selfishness, pettiness, shortsightedness, indecision, fear, and faithlessness. Of course, by the time of his writing, the church had come to know these men as heroes of the gospel—most notably Simon Peter, who may have been martyred shortly before Mark completed his work. Consequently, the story of how Jesus—our ultimate example of sacrifice and service—called and prepared His followers to carry on His mission would have been critical to the morale and faithfulness of persecuted believers.

A GOSPEL FOR TODAY

The style of Mark's writing is not unlike an adventure movie: fast-paced and action-packed. The Gospel of Mark makes for stirring drama—compelling, inspirational, challenging, and sobering—just what believers facing imminent danger would need to help them steel their resolve. While the other Gospel accounts often *explain* the themes and subtext of Jesus' story, Mark tells a vivid story that *shows* us what's important. As one writer stated, "Mark writes with a paintbrush . . . Mark has much more *implicit* major themes, requiring readers to enter into the drama of the Gospel in order to understand its meaning."[5] In the first century, when most Christians were not literate and copies of sacred writings were scarce, believers gathered to hear the reading of Scripture. Mark took full advantage of this and, undoubtedly having seen his fair share of Roman theater drama, brought the very best elements of storytelling to bear on this remarkable piece of literature.

While Mark wrote to a persecuted first-century audience, the Holy Spirit prepared this message for the ages. Throughout the two millennia since Mark's writing, each generation has faced a wide range of challenges to faithful discipleship, and the Gospel of Mark has fulfilled its purpose. Our circumstances and challenges are different today, but this inspired literature is just as much ours. In fact, Mark's style and presentation of Jesus' story is now timelier than ever. The Gospel of Mark conveys its message in a way that our fast-paced, pragmatic generation can appreciate. It is a relatively brief, bottom-line, executive summary of Jesus' life, mission, and ministry depicted in the narrative style today's reader enjoys most. If you enjoy a dynamic page-turner, you'll love Mark's account of the Lord's time on earth. He moves the reader from one action scene to another to show the Savior on the move.

As I stated earlier, Jesus is the central figure of this narrative—it is Jesus who brings the kingdom and redeems humanity from the evil dominion that has asserted itself in the world since Adam and Eve's first sin. God Almighty became the incarnate "God with us" (Matt. 1:23; cf. Isa. 7:14) in the person of Jesus in order to destroy evil, forgive sins, defeat Satan, and reclaim His creation. But Jesus involved His disciples in this endeavor, and Mark especially intended the followers of Jesus to see themselves in his Gospel account. From beginning to end, we will see the Master preparing His disciples and then propelling them forward to encounter challenges they felt ill-prepared to meet.

While the disciples rarely understood what was happening and often lacked confidence in their decisions, they began to realize that following Jesus requires neither great intelligence nor heroic bravery—merely a willingness to do as the Son of God commands. They learned that being a disciple is primarily a matter of faithful obedience.

DISCIPLES CALLED
(MARK 1:1-3:35)

Jesus' earthly ministry—and Mark's Gospel—begins with the long-awaited Messiah's individual baptism in the Jordan (1:9-11) and personal testing and temptation (1:12-13). However, though this commissioning and launch into public ministry was a very personal, individual affair, Jesus never intended to redeem the world from the dominion of Satan all by Himself. Because He is God—all powerful, all knowing, all sufficient—He *could* accomplish this miraculous feat on His own. But He chose not to. For reasons known only among the three persons of the Trinity, God's plan to save humanity and to transform the world involves people. He seeks and invites disciples. He calls ordinary men and women, like you and me, to become students of His person and His work and then, through a lifelong process of internal renovation, to become responsible agents of His redemptive plan.

For this plan to work, however, God's people must be completely dedicated to His cause. A mission this critical requires people ready to offer their complete, undivided devotion without condition, reservation, or hesitation. In the process of discipleship, we become like servants of a great master who teaches and employs us. Most people, however, are ill-prepared to go "all-in" right away. Of course, the Lord knows this. So, in the beginning, He merely issues a call to follow. The disciple's only responsibility is to heed this call. When we say, "Yes, Lord, here am I," God will take the lead.

Discipleship can be stretching. As Jesus took the lead in revealing the kingdom of God—both its message and its power—His disciples undoubtedly found themselves in uncomfortable situations. Their Master took stances that were not always popular. A survey of this section finds Jesus and His followers accused of excessive fraternizing with sinners (2:15-17) and violating rules about the Sabbath (2:23-28). There is even a question about whether Jesus was a messenger of Satan (3:20-30)! The disciples would learn to commit to their Master in spite of such adversity, and they would learn the true teaching of

KEY TERMS IN MARK 1:1–3:35

akoloutheō (ἀκολουθέω) [190] "to come after," "to follow," "to accompany"
Literally, this verb means "to go the same way"; the metaphorical extension of this idea connotes imitating the thoughts, beliefs, actions, or lifestyle of another. Similarly, we might say of a boy adopting his father's occupation, "He's following in the footsteps of his father." The Old Testament doesn't make use of a similar Hebrew term for following after God, but the New Testament favors this term, perhaps because of the accessibility of the human example of Christ and His earthly relationship to his disciples.

aphesis (ἄφεσις) [859] "release," "cancellation," "pardon," "forgiveness"
In the New Testament, this noun nearly always refers to God's forgiveness of human sins. It carries the idea of releasing something or canceling some obligation. In the case of sin, God takes away the penalty for sin. In Mark, this theme is introduced in 1:4 in the ministry of Jesus' forerunner, John the Baptizer.

egeirō (ἐγείρω) [1453] "to arise," "to awaken," "to get up"
This verb depicts lifting or moving upward. Throughout the book of Mark, it has two primary uses. In 1:1–5:43, the primary meaning is simply to "get up." Jesus helps people rise from the ground to stand after healing or commands them to arise after being restored to complete health. In 6:1–16:8, the majority of uses are metaphorical, referring to resurrection or revival.

euthys (εὐθύς) [2117] "straight," "immediately," "proper"
This Greek word is important in the context of a narrative, yet each of the Gospel writers uses the term differently. Mark uses this adverb with the conjunction *kai* ("and" [2532]) to string events together, but without implying that the episodes are necessarily chronological. He uses this adverb in the same way a lecturer lists bullet points to build a case. One might paraphrase Mark's use of *kai euthys* as "And then there was the time . . ."

kēryssō (κηρύσσω) [2784] "to preach," "to proclaim," "to be a herald"
This word generally describes official, public proclamations such as those enjoining royal decrees, public festivals and fasts, or military actions. Such uses appear in the Septuagint (the Greek translation of the Hebrew Old Testament; e.g., Exod. 32:5; 36:6; 2 Chr. 20:3), along with less frequent uses for proclamations of judgment (e.g., Jon. 3:2) and for the

call of Lady Wisdom (Prov. 1:21; 8:1; 9:3). Thus, in the New Testament, we often read of commissioned messengers proclaiming the good news of the Messiah's kingdom. But we also read, especially in Mark, of "proclaiming" that is not strictly attached to official channels. Rather, it is driven by "the inner power and the necessity of proclamation": "Even before the disciples have been commissioned, those who have been healed proclaim, despite being expressly forbidden to do so.... (Mark 1:45...). Their encounter with Jesus, their experience of the mercy of God, their own recognition of the dawn of the new age in this Jesus (7:37 echoes Isa. 35:5) are enough to compel them to tell others."[1]

the kingdom of God. This would prepare them for steadfast ministry at His side when the going really got rough.

This initial period in Jesus' ministry led up to His selection of twelve of His disciples to be the apostles (3:14-19)—those He would send out with the power and message of the kingdom.

Are You Ready for Some Good News?
MARK 1:1-13

NASB

[1] The beginning of the gospel of Jesus Christ, the Son of God.
[2] As it is written in Isaiah the prophet:
"BEHOLD, I SEND MY MESSENGER
[a]AHEAD OF YOU,
WHO WILL PREPARE YOUR WAY;
[3] THE VOICE OF ONE CRYING IN THE WILDERNESS,
'MAKE READY THE WAY OF THE LORD,
MAKE HIS PATHS STRAIGHT.'"

[4] John the Baptist appeared in the wilderness [a]preaching a baptism of repentance for the forgiveness of sins. [5] And all the country of Judea was going out to him, and all the

NLT

[1] This is the Good News about Jesus the Messiah, the Son of God.* It began [2] just as the prophet Isaiah had written:

"Look, I am sending my
messenger ahead of you,
and he will prepare your way.*
[3] He is a voice shouting in the wilderness,
'Prepare the way for the LORD's coming!
Clear the road for him!'*"

[4] This messenger was John the Baptist. He was in the wilderness and preached that people should be baptized to show that they had repented of their sins and turned to God to be forgiven. [5] All of Judea, including all the people of Jerusalem, went out to

NASB

people of Jerusalem; and they were being baptized by him in the Jordan River, confessing their sins. ⁶John was clothed with camel's hair and *wore* a leather belt around his waist, and ªhis diet was locusts and wild honey. ⁷And he was ªpreaching, and saying, "After me One is coming who is mightier than I, and I am not fit to stoop down and untie the thong of His sandals. ⁸I baptized you ªwith water; but He will baptize you ªwith the Holy Spirit."

⁹In those days Jesus came from Nazareth in Galilee and was baptized by John in the Jordan. ¹⁰Immediately coming up out of the water, He saw the heavens ªopening, and the Spirit like a dove descending upon Him; ¹¹and a voice came out of the heavens: "You are My beloved Son, in You I am well-pleased."

¹²Immediately the Spirit impelled Him *to go* out into the wilderness. ¹³And He was in the wilderness forty days being tempted by Satan; and He was with the wild beasts, and the angels were ministering to Him.

1:2 ªLit *before your face*   1:4 ªOr *proclaiming*
1:6 ªLit *he was eating*   1:7 ªOr *proclaiming*
1:8 ªThe Gr here can be translated *in, with* or *by*
1:10 ªOr *being parted*

NLT

see and hear John. And when they confessed their sins, he baptized them in the Jordan River. ⁶His clothes were woven from coarse camel hair, and he wore a leather belt around his waist. For food he ate locusts and wild honey.

⁷John announced: "Someone is coming soon who is greater than I am—so much greater that I'm not even worthy to stoop down like a slave and untie the straps of his sandals. ⁸I baptize you with* water, but he will baptize you with the Holy Spirit!"

⁹One day Jesus came from Nazareth in Galilee, and John baptized him in the Jordan River. ¹⁰As Jesus came up out of the water, he saw the heavens splitting apart and the Holy Spirit descending on him* like a dove. ¹¹And a voice from heaven said, "You are my dearly loved Son, and you bring me great joy."

¹²The Spirit then compelled Jesus to go into the wilderness, ¹³where he was tempted by Satan for forty days. He was out among the wild animals, and angels took care of him.

1:1 Some manuscripts do not include *the Son of God.*   1:2 Mal 3:1.   1:3 Isa 40:3 (Greek version).
1:8 Or *in;* also in 1:8b.   1:10 Or *toward him,* or *into him.*

"Always grab the reader by the throat in the first paragraph, sink your thumbs into his windpipe in the second, and hold him against the wall until the tagline."² That's the advice of Paul O'Neil, an author, playwright, and television producer whose career began in the 1950s. More than sixty years later, his advice is timelier than ever. Today's readers gain much of their information from two- to three-minute television sound bites and three-hundred-word Internet articles. Writers today must understand that reality or risk losing their audience before the tagline.

John Mark, writing two thousand years ago, understood the importance of grabbing the reader by the throat. While we today struggle with a million tiny diversions, the Christians in Rome were driven to distraction by a single ominous prospect: the very real potential of a grisly, agonizing death by torture. Roman officials were rounding up believers by the hundreds and forcing upon them the choice of profaning Christ or suffering torture.

Writing about a later persecution under Emperor Trajan around AD 100, a Roman governor named Pliny the Younger described how he conducted these tribunals:

> The method I have observed towards those who have been brought before me as Christians is this: I asked them whether they were Christians; if they admitted it, I repeated the question twice, and threatened them with punishment; if they persisted, I ordered them to be at once punished: for I was persuaded, whatever the nature of their opinions might be, a contumacious and inflexible obstinacy certainly deserved correction. . . . [Some of the accused] repeated after me an invocation to the gods, and offered religious rites with wine and incense before your statue (which for that purpose I had ordered to be brought, together with those of the gods), and even reviled the name of Christ.[3]

John Mark understood the urgency of his narrative, so he wasted no time getting his readers into the story of Jesus and His disciples, using just a handful of words (twelve in our translation) to set the stage. Compare that to Matthew's Gospel, which begins with a genealogy containing no fewer than forty-seven names (many of them unpronounceable). Luke's account opens with an almost eighty-word sentence in the NASB translation before the action begins. John's readers must wrestle with a philosophical prologue of eighteen verses before he describes the ministry of John the Baptizer. Mark, on the other hand, gets right to business, launching us into the narrative like a pebble from a slingshot.

He quickly establishes the arrival of Jesus as the fulfillment of prophecies given centuries prior by Isaiah and in His own time by John the Baptizer (1:2-3, 7-8). Although Jesus bears the Spirit and is God's beloved Son (1:11), He would be subject to temptation and trial, just as Mark's ancient audience was—and as we are today. Believers under trial can find encouragement as we read about how Jesus would remain faithful and be ministered to by angels (1:13).

— 1:1 —

In the secular sphere, the verb form of the word for "gospel," *euangelizō* [2097], was used to describe the duties of an official messenger bringing news—usually good—concerning the progress of battle, the birth of a royal, the pending arrival of the king, or other matters. The early church borrowed this term, emphasizing the ideas of liberation and victory and applying it specifically to eternal salvation in Jesus Christ.

Though Mark describes his narrative as "beginning" the account of Jesus Christ and the gospel, the plan of God to redeem humanity from evil existed before time, space, the universe, or anything else came into being—including evil itself (cf. Rev. 13:8). The good news of salvation by grace through faith in Jesus Christ existed in the mind of the Trinity even as God fashioned the world, filled it with life, and called His creation good.

Stop for a moment and think about that. God was not shocked by Adam's rebellion in the Garden. The reign of sin and evil didn't take the Creator by surprise. The Lord didn't have to adapt His plan in reaction to the subversion of Satan. He saw it all. Satan's sedition. Adam's rebellion. Cain's murder. My sin. Your sin. God saw everything before the first moment of creation, and He wove His plan of redemption into the fabric of history.

While the gospel existed before creation, God began to accomplish the plan through the work of Jesus on earth. Mark links the appearance of the good news to the official beginning of the Messiah's public ministry. This is not just any official announcement; this good news concerns Jesus, who bears the title "Christ," which is the Greek equivalent of the Hebrew title "Messiah." Moreover, this Christ is "the Son of God," an explicit assertion of His deity. The good news isn't a mystery to be unraveled. The good news isn't a philosophy to comprehend, a perspective to adopt, or a set of life principles to apply. The good news is a person. He is the long-awaited Messiah, God in human flesh, whose name is Jesus.

— 1:2-3 —

Mark didn't write this Gospel narrative primarily to authenticate the identity of Jesus or to convince anyone to embrace Him as Savior, King, or Messiah. He wrote to a predominantly Gentile audience that had already accepted the gift of salvation from sin and identified themselves as Christ-followers. Even so, Mark linked the history of Jesus to God's covenant relationship with Israel. After all, Jesus didn't start a brand-new religion. He didn't suddenly appear on the earthly stage with no prior context. His life and ministry flowed out of a long history of God's interaction with humanity.

Because Mark's original audience was Gentile and Roman, his appeal to Old Testament prophecy might seem out of place. But these Roman Gentiles were followers of Jesus, a Jewish rabbi who claimed to be the Son of God and whose original followers affirmed him as the Messiah. Jesus validated both claims by fulfilling ancient prophecy throughout His earthly ministry and then bodily and miraculously rising from the dead.

Mark's appeal to prophecy begins with a paraphrase of Malachi 3:1 as a preamble to the oracle of Isaiah 40:3. Even Gentile Christians would have been familiar with the Old Testament Scriptures; they would have learned in their gatherings that the good news of Jesus Christ grew from the soil of God's faithfulness to Israel. While Jesus came to save people from all nations, He is the King of Israel, and His future throne on earth will be established in Jerusalem. He will fulfill all of the promises given to Israel, including the promise of land made to Abraham and his progeny.

God promised through Isaiah—as well as other prophets—that a forerunner would prepare the way for the Messiah. The exhortations "Make ready the way of the Lord" and "Make His paths straight" (Mark 1:3) refer to customs no longer familiar, but everyone in the first century would have understood them immediately. In ancient times, construction crews would arrive at a city long before the planned arrival of a king to level hills, fill ditches, clear debris, and remove obstructions in order to prepare a wide, unencumbered, straight road into the heart of town. This work also served as notice to city officials: "Prepare yourselves and your city to receive the king."

— 1:4-6 —

John the Baptizer fulfilled this ancient promise. He was everything you imagine when you think "Old Testament prophet." He was an enigmatic, passionate man who chose to become the very opposite of Israel's religious elite. The Sadducees, Pharisees, chief priests, scribes, and Herodians dined on the best meat and drank the finest wine money could buy. And they had plenty of money, thanks to careful bartering with Rome. John, however, ate from the hand of God, as it were. He depended on no human institution or economy, which left him free from politics and social pressures. His lifestyle choices gave him the freedom to fear no man and to fear God alone.

While the religious elite arrayed themselves in finery, John chose, instead, to wrap himself in a rough garment of camel's hair cinched with a crude leather belt. The image recalls the apparel of Elijah (2 Kgs. 1:8; cf. Zech. 13:4), one of Israel's most courageous and revered prophets. He, too, lived off the land, beyond the reach of kings and culture.

Unlike his wealthy counterparts in Jerusalem, John called his countrymen to a "baptism of repentance" (Mark 1:4). The message proclaimed in the temple assured natural-born Jews that they had a guaranteed place in the kingdom of God by virtue of Abraham's DNA— *as long as* they faithfully kept the Law. Gentiles could receive this assurance by studying the Law, passing an exam, and (for males) submitting to circumcision. To mark their new status as adopted "sons of the covenant," converts were baptized.

John's preaching unsettled natural-born Jews. He proclaimed that sin had separated them from God. He urged Jews to approach the Lord like Gentiles—to repent of their sins and to mark the restart of their relationship with God by submitting to a proselyte's baptism.

Make no mistake, however: The symbol of baptism cannot save sinners any more than circumcision can save Jews. Like circumcision, baptism is supposed to be an outward symbol of one's inner devotion to God (cf. Rom. 2:25-29). Even in the Old Testament, God regarded physical circumcision as worthless apart from obedience, which He described as "circumcision of the heart" (see Lev. 26:41; Deut. 10:16; 30:6; Jer. 4:4; 9:25-26; and Ezek. 44:7, 9). John's baptism, like his ministry, mainly prepared people for the coming of the Christ.

— 1:7-8 —

Later in His ministry among the disciples, Jesus would say of John the Baptizer, "Among those born of women there is no one greater than John" (Luke 7:28). Few people in history have surrendered so much for so long with such intensity to serve God as John had. John was set apart for his role even before God allowed his aging, barren parents to conceive him. From birth, he observed the restrictions of the Nazirite vow (Num. 6:1-21). As an adult, he communed with God in the wilderness, denying himself the creature comforts of civilization in order to remain free of any entanglements of the world that might intrude on his singular devotion.

If good deeds and self-denial could save one's soul, certainly John would have earned his place in heaven. Yet his message shifted the focus away from any goodness he might claim so as to deliberately shine the spotlight on the coming Christ. Take note of his honest spiritual self-assessment: "After me One is coming who is mightier than I, and I am not fit to stoop down and untie the thong of His sandals" (Mark 1:7).

This isn't false modesty. This is authenticity. This is no mere magnanimous gesture. This is true humility. At best, John recognized that his deeds counted for nothing toward salvation. In speaking of one "mightier," John didn't have physical strength in mind; he spoke of spiritual power and moral might. Comparatively, this man—the greatest servant of God up to that time—saw his own moral might as insufficient to qualify him for the lowest form of service then known. The least of household slaves removed shoes and washed feet. (Take note, also, of Mark's subtle message in this episode: Service to Christ is a privilege.)

Having compared his relative moral worth to the coming Messiah, John also contrasted their ministries. Perhaps standing hip deep in the Jordan River, immersing repentant Jews by the hundreds, John said to them, in effect, "I immerse you in water as a symbol of your newly restored relationship with God; the Christ will immerse you *into* God's Spirit." We can be reasonably certain that the implications of John's promise were not lost on his audience. They may not have believed him, but they understood his allusion to Old Testament prophecies describing the world under the Messiah's reign (Isa. 44:3; Ezek. 36:26-27; Joel 2:28-29).

A view from the banks of the **Jordan River**, where Jesus was baptized

— 1:9 —

Mark suddenly turns from the Baptizer's promise of the coming Christ to Jesus of Nazareth. "In those days" marks the general time during which John preached along the Jordan and baptized repentant Jews. Some time after John's prediction, Jesus came to be baptized.

The Son of God didn't need to repent, of course. Unlike the other participants, he would not have confessed any sins (cf. 1:5; Matt. 3:6). So the obvious question becomes, *Why did Jesus have John baptize Him?* Matthew's Gospel records the exchange between John and Jesus, which sheds some light on the Lord's motivation:

> John tried to prevent Him, saying, "I have need to be baptized by You, and do You come to me?" But Jesus answering said to him, "Permit *it* at this time; for in this way it is fitting for us to fulfill all righteousness." (Matt. 3:14-15)

Like proselyte baptism, John's baptism was an outward symbol of inward devotion to God, submission to His will, and identity with the people of Israel. This was the appropriate way for John, the forerunner, to complete his mission: by officially presenting the Messiah and then stepping aside. The fact that this event was located in the desert simultaneously fulfilled the prediction of Isaiah 40:3, mentioned above, and avoided connections with the human institution of the temple, showing that Jesus' authority came directly from the Father (Mark 1:10-11).

Perhaps even more significant to the Lord's plan, Jesus presented Himself for baptism in order to give the symbol of immersion in water a new meaning. Without a doubt, the significance of baptism changed on that day. With that simple ceremony, Jesus officially began a journey that would lead to His ultimate destiny—His atoning sacrifice for sin. He thus made baptism a symbolic doorway to a new kind of life, through which He would be the first to walk. On behalf of the nation, and of all humankind, Jesus received the new covenant (cf. Ezek. 36:25-28. See also Isa. 44:3; 59:21; Jer. 31:31-33; Ezek. 37:14; 39:29; and Joel 2:28-29). By our baptism into Christ, we enter that covenant and partake of all its blessings.

— 1:10-11 —

This is the first of many times (no fewer than forty-one) when Mark will use his favorite Greek adverb, *euthys* [2117], "immediately." Sometimes we should interpret the word literally to mean the given action occurred the very next instant. Other times, however, "immediately" is merely Mark's way of connecting two related stories or infusing a sense of drama or surprise into the narrative. Mark's intention seems to be to show readers that the ministry of Jesus was an exciting time, often punctuated by surprising events.

In this case, the context is relatively clear. The instant Jesus came up out of the water, a physical manifestation of the Holy Spirit descended from the sky. Mark describes the visible form as "like a dove" and notes that "a voice came out of the heavens" addressing Jesus as "My beloved Son." These two verses and their parallels (Matt. 3:16-17; Luke 3:22) feature all three persons of the Trinity. All three persons are God—the Father speaking from heaven, the Spirit descending like a dove, and the Son seeing the Spirit and hearing the voice. Without ceasing to be fully God, the three persons are distinct in that they interact with one another. In other words, God doesn't emerge from the water as the Son, race to heaven from the body of Jesus to utter His affirmation as the Father, and then fly down again as the Holy Spirit to become the Son again. On the contrary, God is shown in this passage to be three and one *simultaneously*. While we see this interchange for a mere instant, the Trinity has always existed this way. As Wayne Grudem so expertly describes the "tri-unity,"

> God eternally exists as three persons,
> Father, Son, and Holy Spirit,
> and each person is fully God,
> and there is one God.[4]

— 1:12-13 —

As in 1:10, the context suggests we take "immediately" at face value. The instant the Holy Spirit descended upon Jesus, the Spirit "impelled" the Son to go out into the wilderness (1:12). "Impelled" represents the Greek word *ekballō* [1544], which is variously rendered "cast out," "throw out," "drive out," or "send out." Though the word lacks the finesse of our English term "impelled," it need not be interpreted so as to leave Jesus without volition. In fact, the Son and the Spirit are one, so "impelled" is appropriate. Still, Mark's depiction is important. The Spirit of God directed the Son to go into the wilderness, and the Son obeyed.

Why is this important? Remember, Jesus is fully human. While He is nonetheless our Savior, He is also our exemplar of humanity in right relationship with God. We are not God, but we do have His Spirit living within us. Therefore, we can follow the impelling of the Spirit to do as He commands, just like Jesus.

Mark briefly described the Lord's experience in the wilderness, where Jesus was confronted by Satan and surrounded by wild beasts.

Without question, his depiction deliberately reflects the experience of Christians in Rome, who faced temptation to renounce Christ or suffer terrifying deaths under Nero's persecution. Writing around AD 100, the Roman historian Tacitus described this terrifying time:

> Mockery of every sort was added to their deaths. Covered with the skins of beasts, they were torn by dogs and perished, or were nailed to crosses, or were doomed to the flames and burnt, to serve as a nightly illumination, when daylight had expired.
>
> Nero offered his gardens for the spectacle, and was exhibiting a show in the circus, while he mingled with the people in the dress of a charioteer or stood aloft on a car.[5]

The overarching purpose of these opening verses of Mark's Gospel is to reaffirm the divine authority of Jesus Christ. Disciples preparing to face the cruel authority of Roman persecutors needed this reminder: *Do not fear Rome; our authority comes from God, who will hold Rome accountable and will minister to those who faithfully endure temptation* (cf. 1:13).

APPLICATION: MARK 1:1-13
Provision for the Wilderness

Many people who read these words understand what it means to enter a spiritual wilderness; chances are good you're one of them. If you haven't suffered the attack of Satan in the form of a distressing moral dilemma, brace yourself. You will doubtless experience one before your life has run its course. To help you endure your crisis, let me offer two simple reminders. These may appear simplistic, but—believe me—in the midst of a distressing spiritual trial, they're helpful. Write them on a card and keep them handy until you emerge victorious.

Number One: *Satan is still the enemy.* When the pain of evil intensifies, the temptation to capitulate can become overwhelming. It's also easy to forget that God is not the enemy. After all, we live in a world corrupted by sin, a world in which good people often suffer punishment for doing what's right while others prosper from doing evil. When that goes on long enough, the decision to remain faithful can begin to feel futile, even counterproductive. It's easy to forget we've chosen to fight for the winning side!

God's Word teaches, "Submit therefore to God. Resist the devil and he will flee from you" (Jas. 4:7). If you don't resist him when times get tough, he will not flee. Rather, he will find ways to take over your life. Unresolved resentments give Satan an opportunity to use you. Extended sexual lust warps the mind, removing one's ability to discern good from bad. Unhealthy or inappropriate relationships drag you down and convince you to hurt the people you love. Cultivating a spirit of entitlement or discontent undermines your ability to trust God.

Satan is looking for channels to find his way in—not to make life better, but to steal, kill, and destroy. Never forget: Satan is the enemy.

Number Two: *The story of Jesus is still good news.* In a spiritual wilderness, when life appears bleak, we must remind ourselves that the gospel is still good news. Our Creator hasn't left us alone. On the contrary, God Almighty became "God with us" (Matt. 1:23; cf. Isa. 7:14) when He took on human flesh in the person of Jesus Christ. He came to earth to redeem humanity, destroy evil, forgive sins, defeat Satan, reclaim creation, and reestablish the rule of God. We have this good news because earlier believers—like Isaiah, Malachi, John the Baptizer, and Mark—remained faithful to the Savior and His gospel.

When evil appears to be gaining the upper hand and you begin to wonder if God will indeed prevail, begin reading the Gospels. Immerse yourself in and be encouraged by the good news of Jesus Christ. Look to the perfect endurance of Jesus Christ—it is both your assurance and your calling. God has given us the same Spirit to drive us to endure, but even if we fail at this calling, Jesus' perfect grace abounds to save us from the enemy.

Deciding to Follow Jesus
MARK 1:14-20

NASB

14 Now after John had been ªtaken into custody, Jesus came into Galilee, ᵇpreaching the gospel of God, 15 and saying, "The time is fulfilled, and the kingdom of God ªis at hand; repent and ᵇbelieve in the gospel."

16 As He was going along by the Sea of Galilee, He saw Simon and

NLT

14 Later on, after John was arrested, Jesus went into Galilee, where he preached God's Good News.* 15 "The time promised by God has come at last!" he announced. "The Kingdom of God is near! Repent of your sins and believe the Good News!"

16 One day as Jesus was walking along the shore of the Sea of Galilee,

NASB

Andrew, the brother of Simon, casting a net in the sea; for they were fishermen. [17] And Jesus said to them, "Follow Me, and I will make you become fishers of men." [18] Immediately they left their nets and followed Him. [19] Going on a little farther, He saw [a] James the son of Zebedee, and John his brother, who were also in the boat mending the nets. [20] Immediately He called them; and they left their father Zebedee in the boat with the hired servants, and went away [a] to follow Him.

1:14 [a] Lit *delivered up* [b] Or *proclaiming* 1:15 [a] Lit *has come near* [b] Or *put your trust in* 1:19 [a] Or *Jacob* 1:20 [a] Lit *after Him*

NLT

he saw Simon* and his brother Andrew throwing a net into the water, for they fished for a living. [17] Jesus called out to them, "Come, follow me, and I will show you how to fish for people!" [18] And they left their nets at once and followed him.

[19] A little farther up the shore Jesus saw Zebedee's sons, James and John, in a boat repairing their nets. [20] He called them at once, and they also followed him, leaving their father, Zebedee, in the boat with the hired men.

1:14 Some manuscripts read *the Good News of the Kingdom of God.* 1:16 *Simon* is called "Peter" in 3:16 and thereafter.

In Dostoyevsky's novel *The Brothers Karamazov*, the middle brother, Ivan, struggles with the idea of a benevolent, personal God because the world appears overrun by evil. In a long lament to his younger brother Alyosha, a novice monk, the disgruntled intellectual offers this penetrating insight concerning human nature:

> The secret of man's being is not only to live but to have something to live for. Without a stable conception of the object of life, man would not consent to go on living, and would rather destroy himself than remain on earth, though he had bread in abundance.[6]

This defines the great struggle of our age. With each passing year, I find fewer people who know who they are and understand what purpose keeps them on planet Earth. Consequently, I find greater numbers of people struggling with aimlessness, hopelessness, loneliness, and depression. My heart aches for them because I can't imagine how I would approach life apart from my calling. Toward the end of 1957, God plucked me from the life I had planned for myself and gave me a very specific and definite purpose: to proclaim the gospel as a shepherd to God's people. This calling has been my internal compass ever since. I shudder to think where I might have ended up or what I might have become if I had not thrown aside all other personal plans and heeded God's call.

While younger generations appear to struggle with aimlessness and despair more often than those of earlier decades, the problem is, in reality, very old. Later in his narrative, Mark describes the Lord's feelings upon seeing the Galilean throngs seeking Him in the wilderness: "He felt compassion for them because they were like sheep without a shepherd" (6:34). Indeed, the first century had taken Israel to a new low point in its long history. Corrupt politician-priests had turned the temple into a virtual Roman outpost while schools of Pharisees quibbled over the details of a "save yourself" religion. The powerful lined their pockets while the rich consolidated their power. Meanwhile, the masses of God's covenant people groped about in spiritual darkness, blind and starving.

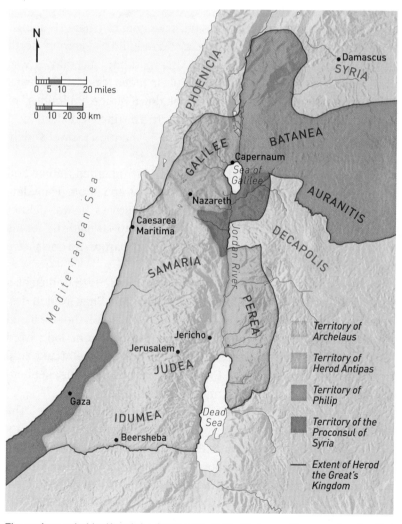

The regions ruled by Herod the Great were divided between his sons when he died in 4 BC.

Then "Jesus came into Galilee" (1:14). Not with merely a proclamation of good news, but a summons to something greater than they'd ever heard.

— 1:14-15 —

Much had already occurred by the time "John had been taken into custody" (1:14). We know from John's Gospel that by now Jesus had encountered John the Baptist, Andrew, Simon Peter, Philip, and Nathanael near Jerusalem (John 1:37-51). Jesus had also conducted ministry in Judea for a time before returning to Galilee. It is at this point that Mark's account picks up the story.

Before we look at what Jesus said, take note of where He ministered. The region known as Galilee lay three full days' journey north of Jerusalem. Politically, Galilee was unimportant; culturally, it was rural and backward. Sophisticated people in Judea regarded Galileans like Manhattan millionaires used to look down on the "hillbillies" of Appalachia. The people of Galilee spoke with a distinctive dialect, lived close to the land like most agrarian people, and didn't travel widely except to attend Jewish festivals.

After Herod the Great died, his son Antipas inherited Galilee and Perea. Although he built some impressive cities and strategically leveraged his relationships in Rome with modest success, he was neither an ambitious politician nor an effective ruler. Antipas made up for his shortcomings as a leader by throwing legendary parties. No one's were bigger, longer, or more frivolous than his.

While Antipas frittered away his opportunities to lead Galilee as a king of the Jews, the people longed for a champion. They lived in desperate anticipation of the Messiah, who wouldn't live off the sweat and tears of His subjects but would take His nourishment from God's Word (Matt. 4:4). They were "looking for the consolation of Israel" (Luke 2:25) by the Christ, who would serve God's covenant people as His shepherd in chief. Instead, they suffered under Herod Antipas.

In this atmosphere of despair, Jesus came preaching the gospel. The Greek term for this, *euangelion* [2098], could describe the favorable report of a messenger from the battlefield, the official proclamation that an heir to the king had been born, or similar kinds of glad tidings. *Kēryssō* [2784] is the Greek term meaning "to preach." It refers to making a proclamation, as a herald would make a public announcement. In those days kings would send out their edicts verbally by their own couriers, who would stand in the marketplace or the public square and

EXCURSUS: "EASY BELIEVISM" AND LORDSHIP SALVATION

MARK 1:15

When Jesus came to Galilee preaching the gospel, He called for people to "repent and believe in the gospel" (1:15). The "good news" was simply this: "The time is fulfilled, and the kingdom of God is at hand." People received the gift of salvation when they chose to repent and to believe.

To repent is to change one's mind regarding a lifestyle of and a tolerance toward sinfulness and to then turn in faith to the Savior. How does one do that? He or she believes. Think of repentance and belief as going together. Don't separate them. Feeling remorse for having done bad things or for being a bad person isn't enough. You haven't really believed in the Lord Jesus until you have repented. You have not really repented (that is, in the full sense—you've not really decided to turn to Christ) until you have chosen to turn away from a lifestyle dominated by selfishness and sinfulness.

Please observe that Mark adds nothing to salvation beyond the word "believe." *Believe.* Don't add one thing to it. The gift of God is a *free* gift. Don't force people to make Jesus the Lord of their lives before they can believe in the Savior. Some people call that "lordship salvation." There are many who teach that people must be sincere, deeply committed, and willing to follow Christ with their whole hearts before God will save them. And if someone doesn't demonstrate a genuine lifestyle transformation, that person didn't really believe and repent the right way. That individual merely *claims* to have believed.

That is problematic on two counts. First, this attitude presumes to know more about what's going on inside a person's heart than any mere human can possibly

know. We are limited to observing an individual's external behavior. The Lord warns, "God *sees* not as man sees, for man looks at the outward appearance, but the LORD looks at the heart" (1 Sam. 16:7; cf. Luke 16:15). I have known many Christians who would have passed the "lordship salvation" litmus test but were in fact ignorant of salvation by grace through faith. On the other hand, I have known many genuine believers whose spiritual journey could be considered as "three steps forward, two steps back." Over the long haul, genuine growth was evident, but day-to-day change was not always easy to perceive.

Second, to say one must do certain things or behave a certain way is to add stipulations to salvation. Do I believe in the lordship of Jesus and our duty to submit to Him as King? With my whole heart! But I don't believe a *sinner* can make Jesus his or her Lord. Sinners have only the capacity to trust in Jesus as Savior: "Jesus died for me. How can I know Jesus? I must believe in Him. That is, I acknowledge before You, God, that I'm a sinner, I know Christ can forgive me of my sins, and I trust in Him—and Him alone—by faith alone because of grace alone. I accept Your gift."

The gospel is a message that calls unworthy people to receive the free gift of righteousness that they cannot possibly earn on their own. The problem with lordship salvation is that one never knows how much good is good enough, both at the moment of choosing to trust in Christ and later, as spiritual maturity develops.

I'm sometimes accused of teaching what critics call "easy believism." That prompts me to ask, *What, exactly, is "hard believism"*? If I must work hard for a gift

(continued on next page)

God wants to give me, what I'd be receiving from Him isn't a gift at all.

I do teach that one must believe in order to be saved. I also teach that the Lord offers the message of "repent and believe." That's the good news. When people trust in the Lord Jesus, a simple prayer puts their belief into words. For example, "Lord, I'm lost, I believe Jesus can save me, and I trust in Him to save me from my sin. Thank You for this priceless gift."

Having seen many people place their trust in Christ, I can assure you that this prayer *never* comes easy for the ones praying. Genuine faith says, "God is now in charge of my life, not me!" That said, however, salvation is truly that simple and that sure. "He who has the Son has the life," wrote the apostle John in his letter to the first-century churches (1 Jn. 5:12). God did not make the path to Himself complicated or uncertain.

"*kēryssō*" the message. They would make authoritative proclamations. These were always bold, and they always captured the attention of the public.

Mark summarizes the Messiah's teaching—familiar to his Christian audience—as a twofold message. The first part announces that "the kingdom of God has drawn close" (my translation of Mark 1:15). Mark's summary uses a literary device known as dramatic irony, in which the reading audience has information not yet known to the people in the story. When Jesus said, "The kingdom of God has drawn close," Mark's readers understood a double entendre. The kingdom of God would soon begin in the theological sense when the Holy Spirit would fill believers, who would then form the first church. But Jesus also referred to the kingdom of God as Himself; the kingdom had come near in the sense that He—the King—was standing right in front of His people!

The second part of His proclamation came in the form of a double imperative: "Repent and believe" this good news. Theologically, "repent" and "believe" describe just one action: the decision to turn away from your old, sinful way of living in order to trust in the Messiah to save you from sin.

— 1:16-18 —

The "Sea" of Galilee is actually a freshwater lake that's nearly 13 miles long, almost 8 miles wide, and ranges from 80 to 160 feet deep. The surface of this lake is roughly 680 feet below the surface of the Mediterranean Sea at the bottom of a deep rift bounded by mountains. This relatively small body of water, and the fish it contained, served the entire northern region of Israel, sustaining many thousands of people with fresh water and a steady diet of fish.

Mark places Jesus somewhere on the shore of the Sea of Galilee. The exact location is not stated, but it couldn't have been far from Capernaum, the home port of James, John, Simon Peter, and Andrew. Fishermen usually cleaned and mended their nets close to home.

Jesus instantly recognized Simon Peter and his brother casting nets as part of their commercial fishing enterprise, which was undoubtedly substantial. According to one expositor,

Berthold Werner/Wikimedia

Pictured is a boat found on the northwest shore of the Sea of Galilee in 1986. It is dated from the first century, and Jesus and his disciples would have sailed across the Sea of Galilee on boats like this one.

Fishing was a thriving industry on the Sea of Galilee, which counted no fewer than sixteen bustling ports on the lake and several towns on the northwest shore, including Bethsaida ("house of the fisher"), Magdala ("fish tower"), and Taricheae ("salted fish"), named for the fishing trade. So numerous were fishing boats that Josephus was able to commandeer 230 of them during the war in Galilee in AD 68 (*War* 2.635). Nor was the catch consumed by local markets alone. It should be remembered that fish, and not meat, was the staple food of the Greco-Roman world. Fish from the Sea of Galilee were exported and prized in distant Alexandria in Egypt and Antioch in Syria. That fishermen in Galilee competed in the larger Mediterranean market testifies to their skill, prosperity, and ingenuity—and probably to their command of Greek, which was the international language of business and culture. The fishermen whom Jesus called were scarcely indigent day laborers. In order to survive in their market league, they needed to be—and doubtlessly were—shrewd and successful businessmen.[7]

Mark makes no reference to the great catch of fish recounted in Luke 5:4-11, preferring to focus on the issue most important to his literary purpose. He cuts right to the chase with the invitation: "Follow Me" (Mark 1:17). According to John 1:35-42, by this time Simon Peter and several others had been introduced to Jesus and were aware of claims that He was the long-awaited Messiah. Many had already become followers of Jesus in the informal sense. Now Jesus asked the men to deepen their commitment, challenging them to go "all in," to set aside all other priorities—including family, vocation, and financial security—to become full-time students of the Christ. That's the essence of the invitation "Follow Me."

We must be careful to interpret this passage as it is, resisting the urge to put words in Jesus' mouth. For example, consider what He *didn't* do. He didn't plan to start a school to train preachers. He didn't announce the founding of a seminary. He didn't invite them to become part of a formal rabbinical course of instruction. The other gospels confirm that He didn't elaborate or explain what He was inviting them to join. His word picture, "I will make you become fishers of men," would not have made much sense at the time; its meaning would only become clear after three-plus years of instruction, a final commissioning (Matt. 28:19-20; Acts 1:8), and the baptism of the Holy Spirit for ministry empowerment (Acts 2). It's important to note that the men were not invited merely to join a program, enter an organization, or even support a movement. They were called to follow a *person*.

Programs, organizations, and movements are fine, as long as they help individuals become more ardent, faithful disciples of God's Son, the Lord Jesus Christ. That's true discipleship.

The call, "Follow Me," represented enormous risk for the first disciples. To follow Christ, the men would have to leave everything familiar and trust God to provide for their families. Moreover, the promise that they would become "fishers of men" would not be fulfilled right away; they would only become qualified to bear this title after an extended process of training and personal transformation.

My Hesitating Yes

MARK 1:17-18

At the ripe age of fifty-nine, I had been casting nets, working the boats, and harvesting the sea in the same ministry for almost twenty-five years. Some retire before they're fifty-nine, but I couldn't see ending something so good. My ministry was fulfilling and exciting. Everything was rolling along great. Then the Lord came along. It wasn't a shout from the shore of the Sea of Galilee; it was an unexpected phone call from Dallas to California. On the other end of the line were two men I knew very well: Dr. Don Campbell, at that time the president of Dallas Theological Seminary, and Jack Turpin, the chairman of the seminary board. Jack and Don, together on the line, called me. My first thought was, Uh-oh. Maybe they know something I don't know.

After we dispensed with the normal pleasantries, they cut straight to the chase: "We'd like you to consider becoming the next president of Dallas Seminary."

My response (in great faith, of course!) was hysterical laughter. I seriously thought they were part of a practical joke. The guys in ministry with me in California had become notorious for their pranks. I wanted to say, "You have got to be kidding! What are you guys smoking?" But I didn't. Instead, I said, "You can't be serious."

"Oh, yes we are. Very serious."

"Look. Come on, you guys. Let me give you the names of five or six qualified people you should consider. I suggest you go to them rather than waste your time with me. Hey, I have . . . many boats, a large sea . . . and the fishin's great where I am. Everything's going great here! Why in the world would I even think of . . . ?"

"Well, we'd like you to think about it."

"No, actually, I don't even need to think about it. I know."

"Would you at least pray about it?"

That gave me pause. What preacher on earth would say, "No, I refuse to pray"? So I agreed. I committed to praying about it.

At supper time, I sat there at the table, still sort of chuckling to myself. I hadn't started praying much. I said to Cynthia, "You will never guess what happened today. I got a phone call from Don Campbell and Jack Turpin from Dallas Seminary. Don has resigned, and a year from now he's retiring from his role. They want a new president, and they thought they'd ask me . . . me, of all people!" I laughed.

(continued on next page)

She didn't laugh. Okay, at that point I knew I wasn't getting out of this easily. I have learned over the years that the voice of the Holy Spirit sounds a lot like Cynthia. (Don't write me letters; that's just a joke.) She responded, "I don't think that's an offer you should take lightly. I think you ought to think about it."

"Are you kidding? Our family is here. Our home is here. It's almost all paid for. Our children and friends are here. We have our ever-growing ministry here."

"I know that. I still think you ought to consider it."

Before an argument started, we decided to sleep on it. The following morning, the first words out of her mouth were, "I seriously think you ought to consider it."

"Honey! I can't wait to tell 'em no."

"Have you prayed about it?"

I wasn't reluctant to pray; I just didn't see the point. I felt certain that I already knew God's answer. But, for the sake of integrity, I began talking to God about the situation. And while I was praying, I was thinking of six or eight other men who were qualified and capable academics who could do the job. So I prayed for the Lord to guide me, to help me think of someone who was qualified to be a seminary president—a leader of people with degrees that I didn't have.

Besides what I considered to be my lack of qualifications, I had it made where I was. Pastors dream of having a church and staff like mine. They work their entire careers hoping to enjoy what I would have to consider leaving. I was comfortable. I had every member of my family nearby. The church was thriving.

When Don and Jack called again, I said, "I've got the names of about five or six . . ." They wouldn't even listen to the names. I won't bore you with the process, but I eventually had to acknowledge that this was a genuine call from God. The move from my ministry in California to that role in Dallas broke all the rules of what we call logic. But the Lord's will isn't constrained by human reasoning. I eventually—gradually and reluctantly—accepted the post.

When I moved into the president's office and later stood on the platform, surrounded by all those brilliant scholars, I was surprised that no one laughed me off the stage. I soon realized that they didn't need another scholar—which I am not—as their president. They had the wisdom to know at that time in the school's history what Dallas Theological Seminary needed most was a shepherd. I didn't know that until several months after I had arrived.

While there, getting acquainted with the students, I began to think it might be wise to remain involved in church ministry and not only train leaders. Rather than causing potential problems in an existing congregation, I began to think of starting a new church in a rapidly growing area north of Dallas, where few churches existed. Meanwhile, we relocated the headquarters of Insight for Living to Plano, where we could utilize the resources offered by the seminary. Within a couple of years, everything I had left behind had been restored—and more. We're still in Texas today, and although I occasionally miss my friends (and the much more comfortable weather) in California, I have no doubt the move was a call from God. That was underscored numerous times!

In a book titled The Call, Os Guinness describes my experience perfectly:

Released from what was "not me," my discovery of my calling enabled me to find what I was. . . . God's call has become a sure beacon ahead of me and a blazing fire within me as I have tried to figure out my way and negotiate the challenges of the extraordinary times in which we live.[8]

For clarity, let me strip the Lord's proposal down to the bare essentials: "Follow Me. I will make you _____." Our responsibility is to trust and follow; He will take care of everything else. So, in a manner of speaking, this was an exchange of trust. The Lord said, in effect, "If I can trust you to follow Me, you can trust Me to equip you."

Simon Peter and Andrew responded immediately. That very moment, the two men made the decision to hand over their fishing operation to others. As we'll see shortly, Mark's depiction indicates that the men left their boats and nets in the capable hands of family members or hired help and then shadowed Jesus as He walked along the shoreline to another grouping of boats.

— 1:19-20 —

Walking a little farther, Jesus approached James and John, who were mending nets with their father, Zebedee. Jesus called them just as He had Simon Peter and Andrew. They, too, turned immediately from their current lives as commercial fishermen. Like Simon Peter and Andrew, they left their boats and equipment in the care of their father and the hired help and shadowed Jesus from that moment forward.

In Mark's quick-paced style, this pivotal moment in the lives of four men has been stripped down to its simplest terms: Jesus called; they followed. If the men harbored doubts or wrestled with angst, we see none of that. If they asked questions or pressed Jesus for details, Mark offers no indication. If they hesitated internally, the men didn't allow misgivings to hold them back. They simply heeded the call of Jesus.

Let me be clear, however. This was not an exercise of blind faith. They would not have followed just any man walking that Galilean shoreline. There was something compelling about Jesus in His words, actions, and character. Having heard His teaching and witnessed His power in action, they had seen in Him many signs that He could be the long-awaited Messiah. Of course, the disciples would spend the next few years wrestling with just what being the Messiah actually entailed. And they would continue to struggle with the deeper reality of Jesus' person as the incarnate God-man. Nevertheless, they knew and believed enough about Jesus that they didn't hesitate to walk away from all things familiar to follow Him.

APPLICATION: MARK 1:14-20

Your Immediate Yes

Mark didn't prepare for us a history lesson or spin a tale for our amusement. This is spiritual direction for all of us. Each disciple of the Lord Jesus has a calling, a purpose for which we must abandon our seemingly aimless "nets" in favor of pursuing focuses and passions given by God. To trust Jesus enough to take the first step, it helps to recognize two unspoken facts in His calling of the first disciples.

First, *Jesus knew much more than He promised.* He told Simon Peter, Andrew, James, and John that they would become fishers of men, and He left it at that. But there was so much more He knew. He knew what their following Him would involve. Beyond the training process of those next three-and-a-half years, they would face privation, endure pain, suffer persecution, and struggle through exhaustion. They would enjoy times of exhilaration and celebration. They would also face circumstances and powers so dark they wouldn't know what to do. They would be attacked, misunderstood, misrepresented, and maligned. Nearly all of them would be killed as a result of their work for Christ.

Jesus knew all of that. Instead of spelling out all the details, He told them what they needed to make the right decision, but no more than they could bear. He said simply, "I will make you become fishers of men."

Second, *Jesus saw in the disciples much more than He revealed.* Simon Peter, for example, saw himself as little more than a rough-and-rugged fisherman. Jesus saw what Simon Peter would become. As John Phillips writes,

Everyone saw Simon Peter or, at least, heard him! Simon was always the center of a crowd. He was always where the action was. At sports, Simon had to bat first. At play, Simon had to be the groom if they were playing weddings, and the rabbi if they were playing funerals—or better still, the corpse! Especially if the game included a resurrection!

"[Jesus] saw Simon." But He saw more than that. He saw "Peter." As Michelangelo saw David in a block of marble, so Jesus saw an apostle in a rugged fisherman. He saw Simon casting his net, but at the same time He saw three thousand souls being saved by a single sermon that Peter would deliver on a coming Pentecost. He saw Peter, and He saw Gentiles being added to the church. He saw Peter, and He saw a man carrying a cross to Execution Hill, faithful unto death, even the death of the cross. He saw Peter, and He saw a name being written down in glory, engraved with an iron pen.[9]

Never doubt it—when Jesus calls you, He sees you as you are *and* as you are to become. The people who see us today would never have believed it if they had known us when God first invited us into His calling and work. That's because the Lord teaches us and transforms us to become His fishers.

I have three searching questions I hope you will ponder deeply. I want them to penetrate your skull and probe your soul. The first question: *Where does the Lord find you today?*

I know where *I* might find you. I can look up the address, I can name the time and the date. But I don't see you like the Lord sees you, and I can't find you the way He finds you. He sees you inside and out. He knows your past as well as your future. He knows your potential, though you are probably blind to most of it.

Next, let's go to your home. Let's go to your family. Where does He find you behind the closed doors of your home? Are things harmonious and satisfying? Or does He find that there are some things that have been dislodged, missing, or perhaps corrupted through acts of omission on your part (or through overt, deliberate acts of sinfulness). Where does He find you in your home?

How about at your work? Are you truly fulfilled in what you do for a living? Are you diligent, faithful, and reliable? How about in this stage of your life in general? Are you changing, or are you stuck? Are you open, or are you closed? Jesus met these men where they were; He saw exactly where they were, and He took them to where only he could take them. Be honest: Where does the Lord find you today?

Second question: *What's the Lord's calling in your life?*

I'm not referring necessarily to a geographical move, though it may include that. I'm not saying that you need to get into some occupation that's different from what you're pursuing now, though you may. I'm asking, "Do you have a reason for being?" Do you have a focused sense of purpose, or do you merely exist each day from dawn to dusk, day after day? Do you have a focused sense of purpose?

Did you notice the new purpose Jesus gave these four men? "You're going to become fishers of men." Once the Lord's calling arrested their attention, they lost virtually all interest in fishing. They left their familiar vocation behind; it was no longer their reason for existence. They sensed the Lord's calling in their lives. What's the Lord's calling in your life? What purpose has He given you that transcends your occupation?

Third question: *How long will it take you to say yes to the Lord's calling?*

Perhaps you are the insecure type. You're waiting until all of your questions are answered. You're weighing each one of the options. Don't waste your time! You'll never say yes if you wait to get all those questions answered. If you're a perfectionist, the Lord's got His work cut out for Him—it'll take you a long time to overcome the drive to make all the details of every part of your future perfect. The same goes for risks. If you want all the risks removed before you consider saying yes to His calling, you're paralyzed to a perpetual no.

If you're willing to take Him at His word and trust Him to lead you as He invites you to follow Him, then your answer is not only yes. It can be an *immediate* yes.

Astonishing Authority
MARK 1:21-28

NASB

21 They went into Capernaum; and immediately on the Sabbath He entered the synagogue and *began* to teach. 22 They were amazed at His teaching; for He was teaching them as *one* having authority, and not as the scribes. 23 Just then there was a man in their synagogue with an unclean spirit; and he cried out, 24 saying, "What ªbusiness do we have with each other, Jesus ᵇof Nazareth? Have You come to destroy us? I know who You are—the Holy One of God!" 25 And Jesus rebuked him, saying, "Be quiet, and come out of him!" 26 Throwing him into convulsions, the unclean spirit cried out with a loud voice and came out of him. 27 They were all amazed, so that they debated among themselves, saying, "What is this? A new teaching with authority! He commands even the unclean spirits, and they obey Him." 28 Immediately the news about Him spread everywhere into all the surrounding district of Galilee.

1:24 ªLit *What to us and to You* (a Heb idiom) ᵇLit *the Nazarene*

NLT

21 Jesus and his companions went to the town of Capernaum. When the Sabbath day came, he went into the synagogue and began to teach. 22 The people were amazed at his teaching, for he taught with real authority—quite unlike the teachers of religious law.

23 Suddenly, a man in the synagogue who was possessed by an evil* spirit cried out, 24 "Why are you interfering with us, Jesus of Nazareth? Have you come to destroy us? I know who you are—the Holy One of God!" 25 But Jesus reprimanded him. "Be quiet! Come out of the man," he ordered. 26 At that, the evil spirit screamed, threw the man into a convulsion, and then came out of him.

27 Amazement gripped the audience, and they began to discuss what had happened. "What sort of new teaching is this?" they asked excitedly. "It has such authority! Even evil spirits obey his orders!" 28 The news about Jesus spread quickly throughout the entire region of Galilee.

1:23 Greek *unclean;* also in 1:26, 27.

Standing in the presence of Jesus Christ must have been a magnificent experience. Try to imagine watching Him in action. Seeing Him as He ministered to people of all types with all kinds of needs would have been altogether unforgettable. Hearing Him preach with His perfect blend of authenticity and authority must have been breathtaking. His audiences must have been thunderstruck. Doing a quick survey in the Gospels, I found their responses in these words:

- "They were amazed" (Luke 4:32; cf. Matt. 7:28).
- "They were astonished" (Matt. 13:54; 22:33; cf. Mark 6:2).
- "No one was able to answer Him a word, nor did anyone dare from that day on to ask Him another question" (Matt. 22:46; cf. Mark 12:34; Luke 14:6; 20:40).
- "Never has a man spoken the way this man speaks" (John 7:46).

His content was reliable, His reasoning irrefutable, His theology impeccable, His presentation flawless, and His insights penetrating. Most of all, His authority was compelling—even astonishing. In every sense of the word, He was *awesome*!

An expositor from the past named George Campbell Morgan was the minister at Westminster Chapel in the heart of London early in the twentieth century. He became a well-known exegetical expositor of the Scriptures and trained several capable men, among them Martyn Lloyd-Jones, an influential leader of British evangelicals during the twentieth century. He taught them that every sermon needed three essential elements: truth, clarity, and passion. Truth gives the message relevance. Clarity allows the audience to grasp the deep truths of Scripture. Passion makes the presentation compelling enough to be remembered and then applied.

Like none other on earth, Jesus preached the truth with clarity and passion. And still more, He demonstrated the authority of His teaching with action. It is an authority that extends even to the supernatural realm. As a result, people were astonished. Multitudes traveled great distances to hear from Him. Some even abandoned their vocations to follow Him, and they made this decision without hesitation. Mark wanted to establish this firmly in the minds of his readers so they would understand why He had such a rapid and profound impact on the region of Galilee. So he chose to include this remarkable episode as an illustration of the ministry Jesus conducted over several months.

— 1:21-22 —

By this time, the Lord was using the sizable village of Capernaum as His home base in Galilee. Not long after calling several disciples to follow Him, Jesus entered the synagogue of Capernaum on a Sabbath, as did most Jews in the town.

For Jews, the synagogue served three primary purposes. First, it was a place of instruction on the Sabbath. Second, it was a center of Jewish culture and literature, where children and proselytes received instruction about the Law and learned to read the *Torah*, the first five books of

These remnants of a third-century **synagogue in Capernaum** stand in the very same place as the first-century synagogue mentioned in the Gospels.

the Hebrew Bible. Third, it was a civil meeting place much like a modern courthouse. Cases were tried and heard, disputes resolved, contracts recorded, marriages conducted, and legal consultations given. Because of the centrality of synagogues in Jewish communities spread throughout the world, they were more directly influential on the hearts and minds of Jews than even the temple in Jerusalem. Therefore, this was the natural starting place for any preacher or teacher with a message for his Jewish countrymen.[10]

By this time, the ministry of Jesus throughout Galilee had generated a huge following. He had become a teacher of great renown. It is no surprise that the synagogue ruler called upon Jesus to read the scroll in the synagogue and exposit the passage.

Mark describes the response of His audience using a Greek term that roughly corresponds to our expression "blown away." *Ekplēssō* [1605] means "to drive out of one's senses by a sudden shock."[11] Mark explains that the teaching of Jesus bore the unmistakable mark of authority, unlike the scribes, who were a kind of attorney in their day. Imagine an attorney explaining the finer points of contract law by appealing to the opinions of judges you don't know who ruled on cases you didn't know existed.

Scribes were forever quoting important rabbis, and what the rabbis said to one another, comparing the two and explaining the tedious

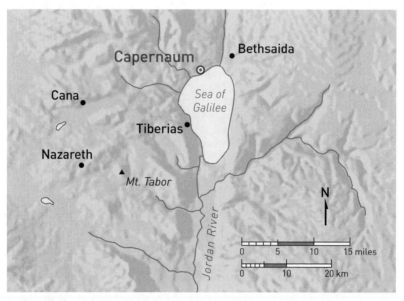

Galilee. Jesus grew up and began his ministry in the region of Galilee near and around the Sea of Galilee. His family lived in Nazareth; He was baptized in the Jordan River, called his first disciples on the shores of the Sea of Galilee, and then journeyed to Capernaum to perform his first miracle as recorded in the Gospel of Mark.

intricacies of what each rabbi meant. Jesus appealed to nothing but the Scriptures; He spoke from His own authority, not the innumerable rabbis of centuries past. What a contrast!

— 1:23-26 —

"Just then" (1:23) is a translation of Mark's signature term, *euthys* [2117], "immediately." During the service, perhaps even in the middle of Jesus' sermon, a demon-possessed man confronted the Son of God. Interestingly, many people in the room struggled to understand Jesus' true identity, but the demon did not (cf. James 2:19). Jesus' closest disciples accepted Him as the Messiah, but the demon took this even further, calling Jesus "the Holy One of God" (Mark 1:24). This wasn't an official title, but it serves to highlight the Lord's stark contrast to the demon's own identity. Whereas holy things are consecrated—that is, set apart for special use in God's service—the demon was unclean and unacceptable, having dedicated himself to the opposition of God's purposes. The literal embodiment of God confronted the literal embodiment of evil.

The rhetorical question, "What business do we have with each other?" translates a Greek expression found in the Septuagint and elsewhere in the New Testament.[12] This was the demon's way of saying,

"Mind your own business." The demon's second question is also rhetorical: "Have You come to destroy us?" This expressed sarcasm and contempt, perhaps as a ploy to turn the people against Jesus.

The Lord responded with two commands, both imperative verbs (1:25). The first was "be quiet," from a Greek verb meaning, literally, "to muzzle." The second was "come out." Jesus exercised His divine authority, and the unclean spirit had no choice but to obey. It did, however, throw a tantrum before leaving, inflicting its human host with a violent shaking fit. Having accused Jesus of coming to destroy, it attempted to destroy the man whom Jesus was setting free.

— 1:27-28 —

Luke's parallel account of this incident (Luke 4:31-37) stresses the power of Jesus in His confrontation of evil. Mark highlights the Lord's authority, both in His preaching and in His command over the spirit realm. In response to His command over the demon, the people were again "amazed" (*thaumazō* [2296]; Mark 1:27). The Greek term here differs from Mark 1:22 and reflects the people's astonishment at seeing Jesus exercise His extraordinary authority.

In our terms today, we'd say that first His preaching "blew them away," and then His authority over demons "put the fear of God in them."

APPLICATION: MARK 1:21-28

Questions on Authority

After preaching, I often field questions immediately following the worship service. As we consider how to apply these verses, let me immediately respond to three of the most common questions I have received over the years.

What makes teaching authoritative?
First of all, its source is the Word of God. The closest you can get to the voice of God is the written Word of God, each and all of the sixty-six books of the Bible. There's no need to ask God for an audible voice, so don't! Don't stay up late hoping for divine writing to appear on your window. Don't expect dreams to yield phenomenal interpretations. Don't waste your time searching for cloud formations that spell out God's message to you. That's nonsense! Devote yourself to studying

and knowing the Holy Scriptures. All the divine revelation you need is written on those pages for you.

Teaching is authoritative when the speaker is empowered by God's Spirit. I don't mean that in some kind of sensational sense. A preacher or teacher is empowered by the Holy Spirit when he or she is consciously and intentionally submitted to God in every area of life, not just teaching.

A sermon or lesson pulsates with authority when it gives witness to the authority of Christ. Great insights are helpful. Clear and accurate exposition of God's truth is essential. But we must never forget that Jesus Christ is the central focus of Scripture, and the same should be true for every sermon, lesson, chapter, or devotional. Authoritative preaching and teaching provide greater knowledge of God and, at the same time, bring people into closer alignment with His will and an intimate relationship with His Son, Jesus Christ.

Do Christians have authority over demons?
No, we don't—not on our own. When we are accomplishing God's will, submitting to His direction, and giving Him glory in the process, we have *God's* authority to confront the forces of evil. Because Christ has the ultimate authority, we must act and speak in His name. It is His name that causes the adversary to retreat. It is the power of His blood that defeats the forces of evil. Those who do not know Christ remain vulnerable before and helpless against Satan and his demons.

Why is submission to God's authority so crucial?
God will not allow His power to be used against His own purposes. We must be submitted to Christ and committed to using divine authority as He would. Without submission, we remain intimidated and helpless against evil forces. Operating under God's authority, however, we have His power within us, which causes us to live in hope.

A Day in the Life of Jesus
MARK 1:29-39

NASB

29 And immediately after they came out of the synagogue, they came into the house of Simon and Andrew, with ᵃJames and John. 30 Now Simon's

NLT

29 After Jesus left the synagogue with James and John, they went to Simon and Andrew's home. 30 Now Simon's mother-in-law was sick in bed with

mother-in-law was lying sick with a fever; and immediately they spoke to [a]Jesus about her. [31]And He came to her and raised her up, taking her by the hand, and the fever left her, and she [a]waited on them.

[32]When evening came, after the sun had set, they *began* bringing to Him all who were ill and those who were demon-possessed. [33]And the whole city had gathered at the door. [34]And He healed many who were ill with various diseases, and cast out many demons; and He was not permitting the demons to speak, because they knew who He was.

[35]In the early morning, while it was still dark, Jesus got up, left *the house,* and went away to a secluded place, and was praying there. [36]Simon and his companions searched for Him; [37]they found Him, and said to Him, "Everyone is looking for You." [38]He said to them, "Let us go somewhere else to the towns nearby, so that I may [a]preach there also; for that is what I came for." [39]And He went into their synagogues throughout all Galilee, [a]preaching and casting out the demons.

1:29 [a]*Or Jacob*   1:30 [a]*Lit Him*   1:31 [a]*Or served*
1:38 [a]*Or proclaim*   1:39 [a]*Or proclaiming*

a high fever. They told Jesus about her right away. [31]So he went to her bedside, took her by the hand, and helped her sit up. Then the fever left her, and she prepared a meal for them.

[32]That evening after sunset, many sick and demon-possessed people were brought to Jesus. [33]The whole town gathered at the door to watch. [34]So Jesus healed many people who were sick with various diseases, and he cast out many demons. But because the demons knew who he was, he did not allow them to speak.

[35]Before daybreak the next morning, Jesus got up and went out to an isolated place to pray. [36]Later Simon and the others went out to find him. [37]When they found him, they said, "Everyone is looking for you."

[38]But Jesus replied, "We must go on to other towns as well, and I will preach to them, too. That is why I came." [39]So he traveled throughout the region of Galilee, preaching in the synagogues and casting out demons.

There's something fascinating, even captivating, about reading the words of another person's journal. This is especially true if they've already gone on before us, having left in their legacy a personal chronicle of their most intimate thoughts. It's even more captivating when you can read their meditations in their own handwriting.

We have that experience when we read a well-written biography. I think especially of two prepared by Doris Kearns Goodwin. In *Team of Rivals* and *No Ordinary Time,* she draws a substantial amount of historical material from personal journals and letters and often weaves the words written by her subjects into the narrative. It's remarkably effective; we invariably feel connected to people we never could have known—people who are long dead. We find ourselves weeping when Abraham Lincoln dies of his head wound, almost as if it had happened yesterday in our own upstairs bedroom. We can feel President Roosevelt's gut-wrenching angst over the suffering of Great Britain as German bombs fall from the night sky. One country after another has fallen, yet the island nation stands firm. We wrestle with indecision alongside Roosevelt as he thinks of every possible way to avoid subjecting Americans to another world war.

Jesus didn't leave a journal. At least not in His own hand. He did, however, through the Holy Spirit, direct the hands of four faithful men to record the significant events of His life. From Mark, we learn that the public ministry of Jesus was never dull. On the contrary, demands on His time were virtually nonstop. While we never get the sense that Jesus rushed from one task to another or felt harried by details, we nevertheless feel the continual burdens of ongoing ministry. Having experienced a thriving ministry myself, reading the Gospel of Mark feels like I'm reading selections from the Savior's diary.

In the previous segment, we watched as Jesus held a congregation in rapt attention with the authority of His preaching in the synagogue of Capernaum. We witnessed a demon-possessed man interrupt the meeting with shouts of derision, and we saw Jesus exercise His divine authority to silence the demon and free the man from its control. We observed the congregation as they marveled at Jesus, yet not without some fear.

Immediately after this encounter with evil personified, the demands of ministry came at Jesus in rapid-fire succession. In the brief passage we're examining now (1:29-39), Mark uses the Greek connective conjunction *kai* ("and" [2532]) no fewer than twenty-two times. Like a child recounting his day at the amusement park, telling about each incident in breathless excitement, Mark strings together several related episodes:

"And immediately after . . ." (1:29)
"And immediately they spoke to Jesus . . ." (1:30)
"And He came to her . . ." (1:31)
"And the whole city had gathered . . ." (1:33)
"And He healed many . . ." (1:34)
"And in the early morning . . ." (1:35, "and" omitted by the NASB for style)
"And they found Him . . ." (1:37, "and" omitted by the NASB for style)
"And He said to them . . ." (1:38, "and" omitted by the NASB for style)
"And He went into their synagogues . . ." (1:39)

I'm wearied just *reading* these eleven verses! Fortunately, we can retrace this segment of Christ's life in slow motion and take time to observe how the Savior managed His priorities in the midst of increasing opportunities for ministry and demands on His time.

— 1:29-31 —

Immediately after His encounter with the demon-possessed man, Jesus left the synagogue with Peter, Andrew, James, and John. It was Saturday, the Sabbath, a sacred day for the Jews. On the Sabbath no one could carry burdens or do work of any kind, including cook meals. Because of this all food was prepared the previous day to enjoy on the Sabbath.

If you will grant some room for imagination: Jesus and His men were probably hungry. (After church, I'm usually the first to say, "I'm starving!") They arrived at Peter's home to find no one enjoying a meal—rather, worried family members were hovering over Peter's mother-in-law, who was "lying sick with a fever" (1:30). In Luke's account, the good doctor uses a Greek expression that equates with our idiom "burning up with fever" (see Luke 4:38). So she wasn't merely struggling with a minor cold; her fever indicated a life-threatening illness. "Immediately" the family members made her condition known to Jesus, obviously with the hope that He would do something to help.

Of course, Jesus responded with compassion. Luke tells us He rebuked the fever, but Mark omits this detail to emphasize the Lord's personal interaction with the woman: "He came to her" and "raised her up," "taking her by the hand" (Mark 1:31). Throughout his Gospel, Mark will draw particular attention to physical touch between Jesus and His patients (1:41; 3:10; 5:27, 41; 6:5, 56; 7:32-34; 8:23-25).

It's worth taking a pause here and realizing that genuine miracles are instantaneous, undeniable, and complete. Although Mark will later record a healing in two stages (8:22-26), even that healing was completed within moments, before the patient departed. Genuine healing miracles—that is, dramatic displays of God's power over illness—do not require a lengthy waiting period. So-called faith healers like to conceal their failures by claiming that healing will occur gradually or sometime later.

In the Bible, authentic healing miracles were intended to authenticate God's representative for the benefit of others, to let them know that the prophet's message did indeed come from God. Therefore, a genuine healing miracle leaves no room to suggest a natural explanation—they are *never* subtle or left incomplete! People born blind receive perfect sight (John 9). Those disabled from birth leap on perfectly function-ing legs (Acts 3:1-10). Deaf people hear words and music and speak with perfect clarity (Mark 7:32-35). Jesus and the apostles never left sick people with lingering symptoms, or blind people needing glasses, or disabled people still walking with a limp.

When Jesus healed Peter's mother-in-law, she was restored to per-fect health immediately. In fact, Matthew, Mark, and Luke note that the woman began to serve the prepared meal as though nothing had slowed her down (1:31; cf. Matt. 8:14-15; Luke 4:38-39)!

— 1:32-34 —

Mark notes that, "after the sun had set," people began to bring Jesus their ailing loved ones (1:32). Unlike the Gentiles, who marked the be-ginning of a new day at midnight, the Jews reckoned days by sunset. Therefore, the Sabbath ended with sunset. Before that time, people were forbidden to travel or carry burdens. After dark on this day, how-ever, they came in multitudes, hoping to see the sick healed of their illnesses and the demonized freed from evil's domination.

Mark expertly crafts this portion of the story to show the rapid spread of Jesus' fame in Galilee. That day, He had freed a demonized man and healed a sick woman. No sooner had the sun set than a long line of people brought their sick and demonized friends to Jesus for help. Mark's hyperbole, "the whole city had gathered at the door" (1:33), vividly describes the pandemonium that overtook the home of Peter and Andrew.

Jesus could have turned the people away; instead, He helped as many as time would allow. The miracles of Jesus authenticated His message; with every healing, more people heard the gospel. With every demonized person set free, multitudes were prompted to seek out this remarkable teacher. Compassion kept Him with His patients long into the night.

Mark notes, as before, that Jesus muzzled the demons—this time before they could speak. "They knew who He was" (1:34), but the Son of God didn't need Satan's minions to be His evangelists—a true message from such a source would be confusing, to say the least.

Some commentators associate Jesus' commands that demons be silent with other instances in which Jesus asked those who had been healed to keep quiet about His work. I discuss this in my comments on 1:43-44; I believe He did this in order to promote His message over His miracles.

— 1:35-39 —

After a full day of preaching, healing, and casting out demons—seeing the last of His patients sometime shortly before daybreak—Jesus apparently got only a few hours of sleep. Deity never gets tired, but humanity can become exhausted. Deity never needs sleep; humanity must rest. In His full humanity, Jesus was exhausted from the day before. Mark notes that Jesus "got up," presumably from bed. Undoubtedly still weary, He nevertheless exercised the wisdom and discipline to slip out of the house to find an isolated place for prayer. Mark's description suggests a time between four and six o'clock in the morning.

Meanwhile, back at the house, Peter and the others arose to find Jesus missing. Another large crowd pressed at the front gate, hoping for an audience with the miracle-working rabbi from Nazareth. So the disciples searched for Jesus and eventually found Him, probably in one of His several customary locations. They announced, "Everyone is looking for You" (1:37), as though the Lord hadn't considered the possibility that He might be in demand.

They probably expected Jesus to say, "Well, then, let's hurry back so I can capitalize on my sudden popularity!" But He brushed off their excited observation and instead refocused their attention on His mission. The pressing physical needs of humanity were not unimportant to the Lord, but neither did they dictate His agenda. He performed miracles to authenticate His message and to set His message apart from others', but personal recognition was never the objective. Rather than return to Peter's house and the never-ending throng of people in need of healing, Jesus set out for other parts of Galilee to reach those who had not yet heard the good news.

Mark briefly summarizes the next several months of Jesus' ministry, which repeated the pattern of the previous two days. Jesus preached in the synagogues and cast out demons throughout the region (1:39). According to Matthew and Luke, in addition to all that, He healed all kinds of illnesses (Matt. 8:16-17; Luke 4:44). Mark doesn't mention healing here, perhaps because the next episode involves Jesus cleansing a man of leprosy.

Mark could have titled this segment of his narrative "A Day in the Life of Jesus." He gives us these details to explain how Jesus' fame spread so quickly and why people thronged from every region in Galilee to see Him. In some respects, His ministry of healing people and casting out demons helped carry the gospel message farther. As we shall see, however, His power to heal could become a hindrance to His primary mission. Jesus would have a delicate balance to manage as His fame continued to spread.

APPLICATION: MARK 1:29-39
How to Succeed in Spite of Your Success

What does all of this say to you and me as we tear this page from the Lord's journal and do a little analysis? Well, I think it says at least four things.

First, *compassion encourages us to care for those who hurt.* A graduate of Denver Seminary once told me about his experience with the compassion of the former president, Dr. Vernon Grounds, who was known for his heart as well as for his mind. Not long into his first year, the student hit an emotional low and experienced one of the darkest days of his life. He stumbled into the chapel and took a seat only to find himself in one of those chapel services where everyone was clapping and singing and smiling and having a great time.

He said, "I didn't feel clappy and happy; I just felt like crying." So he walked out of the chapel and stepped into a kitchen, which was in an old building adjacent to the chapel. He poured himself a cup of hot water to make tea and suddenly burst into tears. He put his back against the kitchen cabinet, slid to the floor, and lay there sobbing. He had come to his emotional end.

"Finally," he said, "I was able to push myself up on one elbow, and I sunk my head in my hands. That's when I felt an arm around me. Another man had been sitting there for some time. He pulled me close and whispered, 'I don't know what it is that's broken you, but I want you to know I care. And I'll stay right here till you get up.'"

When he opened his eyes, he saw Dr. Grounds.

Second, *humility energizes us to remain gracious.* When we are compassionate, we become humble. We don't become the star of the show. There's one star and that's the Savior. When we reach out to other people, humility takes over and energizes us to grow ever more gracious with those in need.

Third, *solitude and prayer empower us to restrain our own ambitions.* Believe me, the crowds won't restrain your ambitions. They'll fan the flame of pride. They'll tell you how great you are, but their praise is fleeting and fickle. When the fans and their cheers disappear, then you'll be wondering what's wrong with you. Without solitude, you'll lose your way. How valuable it is to let solitude and prayer restrain our ambitions.

Fourth, *discipline enables us to continue reaching out to the lost.* Jesus basically said, "Let's go to those in other parts of Galilee" (see 1:38). If we are not careful, we can build our own little world and forget that two blocks away there are people who have never heard the name of Jesus Christ or the gospel of grace. May God remind us that the Christian life isn't supposed to be lived in isolation from the world; may He remind us over and over to take what we gain from Him and release it to the world.

I challenge you this week to share with at least one person the story of Jesus and the good news of salvation by grace through faith in Him. Just one person.

Changing a Leper's Spots
MARK 1:40-45

NASB

⁴⁰And a leper came to Jesus, beseeching Him and falling on his knees before Him, and saying, "If You are willing, You can make me clean." ⁴¹Moved with compassion, Jesus stretched out His hand and touched him, and said to him, "I am willing; be cleansed." ⁴²Immediately the leprosy left him and he was cleansed. ⁴³And He sternly warned him and immediately sent him away, ⁴⁴and He said to him, "See that you say nothing to anyone; but go, show yourself to the priest and offer for your cleansing what Moses commanded, as a testimony to them." ⁴⁵But he went out and began to proclaim it freely and to spread the news around, to such an extent that ªJesus could no longer publicly enter a city, but

NLT

⁴⁰A man with leprosy came and knelt in front of Jesus, begging to be healed. "If you are willing, you can heal me and make me clean," he said. ⁴¹Moved with compassion,* Jesus reached out and touched him. "I am willing," he said. "Be healed!" ⁴²Instantly the leprosy disappeared, and the man was healed. ⁴³Then Jesus sent him on his way with a stern warning: ⁴⁴"Don't tell anyone about this. Instead, go to the priest and let him examine you. Take along the offering required in the law of Moses for those who have been healed of leprosy.* This will be a public testimony that you have been cleansed." ⁴⁵But the man went and spread the word, proclaiming to everyone what had happened. As a result, large crowds soon surrounded Jesus, and he couldn't publicly enter a town

NASB

ᵇstayed out in unpopulated areas; and they were coming to Him from everywhere.

1:45 ᵃLit *He* ᵇLit *was*

NLT

anywhere. He had to stay out in the secluded places, but people from everywhere kept coming to him.

1:41 Some manuscripts read *Moved with anger.*
1:44 See Lev 14:2-32.

Among first-century Jews, a single word could clear a room—the word "unclean."

The Law of Moses required all those afflicted with leprosy to announce themselves by shouting, "Unclean! Unclean!" so others could protect themselves from infection. They were to live alone outside and keep themselves separated from the healthy population to prevent the spread of disease. As a sign of perpetual mourning, they were to leave their heads uncovered and tear their clothing (Lev. 13:45-46).

The word translated "leprosy" in the Old Testament is *tsaraath* [H6883]. This term describes a fairly large range of chronic or malignant skin infections (Lev. 13–14). The Greek translation, which Mark uses here, is *lepros* [3015], which means "scaly" or "scabby" and also describes various skin infections. Some scholars debate whether the lepers in the New Testament suffered from what we know today as "Hansen's Disease." We can't be certain, but I think the correspondences between the biblical description and the modern diagnosis are strong enough to make this association.

Hansen's bacillus, the cause of modern leprosy, has a devastating, dreadful effect on the body. Dr. Paul Brand dedicated much of his life to studying the disease and caring for lepers. He eventually wrote a semiautobiographical book titled *Pain: The Gift Nobody Wants* in which he describes his initial aversion to medicine after watching his father, a medical missionary in the southern hills of India:

> Over time, childhood memories of medicine had distilled into a few scenes of suffering, and I now found these scenes abhorrent. There was the revolting scene of my parents working on a women tormented by guinea worms, including one whose dragon tail poked out of the corner of her eye. And the memory of my father's most challenging patient: a man who survived a mauling by a bear, his scalp torn from ear to ear. There was one more scene, too, perhaps the most haunting of all.
>
> My father would not even let us watch him work on the three strange men who approached the clinic one afternoon. He

confined us to the house, but I sneaked out and peered through the bushes. These men had stiff hands covered with sores. Fingers were missing. Bandages covered their feet, and when Dad removed those bandages I saw that their stumpy feet had no toes.

I watched my father, mystified. Could he actually be afraid? He did not banter with the patients. And he did something I had never before seen: he put on a pair of gloves before dressing their wounds. The men had brought a basket of fruit as a gift, but after they left Mother burned the basket along with my father's gloves, an unheard-of act of waste. We were ordered not to play in that spot. Those men were *lepers*, we were told.[13]

All the way through Scripture, leprosy is never "healed" or "cured." The person is always said to have been "cleansed." It should come as no surprise, then, that ancient cultures regarded leprosy as God's affliction for sin (which cannot be healed, only cleansed.) Many believed that lepers deserved their dreaded disease because their sin had earned God's disdain. Therefore, you can imagine the pang of tension Mark's first-century readers must have felt when the Lord encountered a leper face-to-face somewhere in Galilee.

— 1:40 —

After a long day of healing and casting out demons in Capernaum, the ever-increasing crowds seeking Jesus became a hindrance to His mission, which was to proclaim the good news throughout Israel: "The time is fulfilled, and the kingdom of God is at hand; repent and believe in the gospel" (1:15). Unless Jesus maintained a proper balance between healing and preaching, His ultimate purpose would be compromised. "Repent and believe" offers long-term, permanent freedom from pain and suffering, but people generally want immediate results, even if the relief is temporary. Regardless of what the multitudes wanted, Jesus came to lay an ax at the root of evil, not prune its innumerable branches.

So He led His disciples away from the familiarity of Capernaum to conduct an itinerant ministry throughout Galilee. Somewhere in the countryside, a man with leprosy approached Jesus. The encounter involved two surprises. First, he didn't shout, "Unclean! Unclean!" as the Law dictates. Second, he didn't ask for cleansing in the form of a question; he made a statement of fact: "If You are willing, You can make me clean."

The unusual approach reveals the heart of this leper. He acknowledges his condition—he is unclean. Dr. Luke, in his depiction, states that "the man was full of leprosy" (my literal translation of Luke 5:12). The disease had progressed to advanced stages of decay, perhaps leaving him disfigured. He neither minimized nor denied his need for cleansing. He also displayed remarkable humility. He didn't blame God or possess a spirit of entitlement. "If You are willing" acknowledges the sovereign authority of Jesus—Ruler and Creator of the universe—to do as His own character dictates. The grace of healing is God's to give, not ours to demand.

— 1:41-42 —

The phrase "moved with compassion" (1:41) comes from the vivid Greek verb *splanchnizomai* [4697], which derives from the word for "guts" or "inward parts." It describes the kind of empathy that rises from somewhere deep inside the human body. Jesus experienced intense compassion for the leper's suffering. This prompted Him to do what *no one* did, least of all a man of God: He reached out and actually touched the leper . . . *before he was cleansed*. Still disfigured. His rags still bloody and soaked with puss—the man was thoroughly unclean—yet Jesus touched him. Far from being repulsed, Jesus reached out.

The simplicity of the Lord's response is moving: "I am willing; be cleansed." No lecture. No test of sincerity. No sideshow to draw a crowd (and receive an offering!). No elaboration to impress onlookers. Just a simple healing that forever changed the man's life. Immediately (*euthys* [2117]), the leprosy vanished (1:42). The man was "cleansed" in the ceremonial sense and completely restored to full health in the medical understanding of the word.

— 1:43-44 —

Too many scholars make too much of the Lord's instructions here and elsewhere in the Gospel record (e.g., 1:24-25, 34; 3:12; 5:43; 7:36; 8:29-30; 9:9). Some suggest that Mark (and to a lesser extent, the other Gospel writers) used these commands for silence to explain why the Jewish leadership didn't recognize Jesus as the Messiah. This so-called "messianic secret" prevented them from seeing the whole truth so they would reject Him in accordance with prophecy (cf. 12:10-11; Ps. 118:22-23).

The theory makes little sense for several reasons. First, Jesus presented Himself in the temple as the Messiah, making numerous references to Old Testament prophecy and even laying claim to deity. The religious leaders rejected Him, not because they couldn't believe, but because Jesus didn't conform to their preconception of what the

Messiah should be. They wanted a military politician to become the head of their Jewish world empire.

Second, Jesus didn't need to manipulate events to fulfill prophecy. That would suggest that if everyone had all the facts, they would have immediately "repented and believed," and therefore that Jesus didn't really want them to accept the gospel as truth. The sad fact is, Jesus didn't need to manipulate people into choosing evil over good or dark over light (John 3:19); humanity is already enslaved by evil. We are born with a deep-seated love for our sin. That is precisely what Jesus came to change.

Third, the "messianic secret" hypothesis ignores the context of this passage and others like it. Jesus left Capernaum because the excitement of people seeking healing threatened to overshadow His true purpose for coming to earth. He came to call disciples to Himself and then free them *forever* from their slavery to sin through His atoning death on the cross. He came to destroy evil, not merely trim it back.

Jesus gave the man strict instructions to avoid spreading the word about his cleansing. The Lord didn't want His preaching ministry hampered by sensationalism. He did, however, order the man to follow Old Testament Law by presenting himself to a priest, offering the required sacrifice, and being declared clean so he could rejoin normal society (Lev. 14:1-32).

— 1:45 —

Jesus cleansed the man of leprosy strictly out of compassion, not to advance His mission. But as the old saying goes, "No good deed goes unpunished." Or, as one cynic once noted, "If you want to get the word out, tell someone, 'This is confidential.'"

The man didn't do as Jesus had "sternly warned" (1:43). He announced the news to everyone, with the expected results. Because of the man's disobedience, Jesus could no longer conduct ministry within the city. He had to remain on the outskirts, where He could accommodate the crowds and preach effectively. Of course, this didn't thwart God's plan; it merely created unnecessary complications.

James Edwards offers this intriguing insight: "Mark began this story with Jesus on the inside and the leper on the outside. At the end of the story, Jesus is 'outside in lonely places.' Jesus and the leper have traded places."[14] The image of one bird flying free, bearing the blood of the slain bird in the temple, comes to mind again. Though not explicit, the theme of substitution is highlighted in this short passage.

APPLICATION: MARK 1:40-45

Unclean Within

When we begin to interact with people less fortunate than ourselves, it can be easy to forget that we, too, have needs too great to solve without help. As we reflect on the story of this poor outcast, we must not fail to remember that *our need for relief is as crucial as the leper's need*.

Apart from Christ, we are unclean before God. Though we try to wrap ourselves in good deeds to make ourselves acceptable, our efforts are no more acceptable than the bloody, puss-soaked rags of a leper (Isa. 64:6). As Addison Leitch put it, "If depravity were blue, we'd be blue all over." We might as well shout "Unclean!" when we come into the presence of God and His people. But thanks to the inexplicable love, mercy, and grace of God, He does not reject us. Like Jesus reached out and touched the leper, God's compassion reaches down to heal our sin.

If you're in pain, healing can come only from the living God. If sin has consumed everything good in your life, you can find restoration in a relationship with the living God. If you fear the grief and the tragedy of death, the hope of resurrection can only come from the living God. If you have the stigma of shame in your life, relief and cleansing can only come from the living God. Our need for relief is as crucial as that leper's need.

As I continue to reflect on the plight of this hopeless leper, I learn that *our response to Jesus needs to be the same as the leper's initial response*. He made no demands. He didn't excuse his leprosy or minimize its impact. He didn't come to the Lord with a spirit of entitlement or a "Why me, Lord?" attitude. And He didn't doubt Jesus' ability to cleanse his leprosy. He merely bowed low and acknowledged His sovereignty as King, saying, "If You are willing, You can make me clean" (Mark 1:40).

Anyone who comes to Christ through the Cross can come in the same way: "I acknowledge that I am a sinful person. I acknowledge that deep down inside I am diseased with sinfulness. I am, as the Scripture says, 'dead in trespasses and sins.'[15] And so I come to You, Lord, as a diseased and depraved sinner. I can bring nothing in my own hands that would in any way ingratiate me to You, and I am at Your mercy. Forgive me, cleanse me, take me. I trust in Christ for the cleansing I need."

The Day a Paraplegic Walked Home
MARK 2:1-12

NASB

1 When He had come back to Capernaum several days afterward, it was heard that He was at home. 2 And many were gathered together, so that there was no longer room, not even near the door; and He was speaking the word to them. 3 And they came, bringing to Him a paralytic, carried by four men. 4 Being unable to ªget to Him because of the crowd, they removed the roof ᵇabove Him; and when they had dug an opening, they let down the pallet on which the paralytic was lying. 5 And Jesus seeing their faith said to the paralytic, "ªSon, your sins are forgiven." 6 But some of the scribes were sitting there and reasoning in their hearts, 7 "Why does this man speak that way? He is blaspheming; who can forgive sins ªbut God alone?" 8 Immediately Jesus, aware ªin His spirit that they were reasoning that way within themselves, said to them, "Why are you reasoning about these things in your hearts? 9 Which is easier, to say to the paralytic, 'Your sins are forgiven'; or to say, 'Get up, and pick up your pallet and walk'? 10 But so that you may know that the Son of Man has authority on earth to forgive sins"—He said to the paralytic, 11 "I say to you, get up, pick up your pallet and go home." 12 And he got up and immediately picked up the pallet and went out in the sight of everyone, so that they were all amazed and were glorifying God, saying, "We have never seen anything like this."

2:4 ªLit *bring to* ᵇLit *where He was* 2:5 ªLit *child*
2:7 ªLit *if not one, God* 2:8 ªLit *by*

NLT

1 When Jesus returned to Capernaum several days later, the news spread quickly that he was back home. 2 Soon the house where he was staying was so packed with visitors that there was no more room, even outside the door. While he was preaching God's word to them, 3 four men arrived carrying a paralyzed man on a mat. 4 They couldn't bring him to Jesus because of the crowd, so they dug a hole through the roof above his head. Then they lowered the man on his mat, right down in front of Jesus. 5 Seeing their faith, Jesus said to the paralyzed man, "My child, your sins are forgiven."

6 But some of the teachers of religious law who were sitting there thought to themselves, 7 "What is he saying? This is blasphemy! Only God can forgive sins!"

8 Jesus knew immediately what they were thinking, so he asked them, "Why do you question this in your hearts? 9 Is it easier to say to the paralyzed man 'Your sins are forgiven,' or 'Stand up, pick up your mat, and walk'? 10 So I will prove to you that the Son of Man* has the authority on earth to forgive sins." Then Jesus turned to the paralyzed man and said, 11 "Stand up, pick up your mat, and go home!"

12 And the man jumped up, grabbed his mat, and walked out through the stunned onlookers. They were all amazed and praised God, exclaiming, "We've never seen anything like this before!"

2:10 "Son of Man" is a title Jesus used for himself.

Hoping for a miraculous healing is one thing; experiencing the miracle of healing is something altogether different. Hoping for healing is a human and very natural thing. Experiencing a healing that is immediate is a God thing; it's supernatural, from start to finish. There are no people reading this right now who, deep within their own hearts, don't hope for a healing in their own lives or the life of a friend or loved one. While we hope for a miracle, the fact is, miraculous healings are exceedingly rare. To drive that point home, I have a friend who says, "If miracles were all that common, we'd call them 'regulars.'"

Unfortunately, we toss the word "miracle" around so easily that we tend to forget its true meaning. When we find a parking place at the mall around Christmas time, we call it a "miracle." When, against the odds, we land the job we wanted after looking for many weeks or months, we thank God for the "miracle." Unexpected or unlikely blessings are wonderful, and we are right to thank God for the good things we receive, but we should not call them miracles. A miracle is in a category all by itself.

That is not to say God doesn't intervene supernaturally in the lives of people. He is, in fact, continually involved personally and directly. But there is a big difference between "supernatural" and "miraculous." Miracles achieve a specific purpose in the plan of God. The apostle John repeatedly calls these miraculous acts "signs" (e.g., John 2:11), not merely "wonders," because a genuine miracle points to something. Miracles are dramatic displays of divine power that break the laws of nature and physics in order to validate something or someone that might otherwise be doubted. The passage we are about to examine presents a perfect example.

— 2:1-2 —

Mark opens the scene by establishing the setting, offering three specific details. First, Jesus and His disciples had returned to Capernaum, a fairly large village on the north shore of the Sea of Galilee. You can visit the ruins of the site today, which include the remnants of the synagogue. Second, He was in a private residence—not His own, but a home belonging to someone wealthy enough to own a comparatively large dwelling. Third, the house was full of people. Mark's description could be rendered in today's vernacular, "the house was packed—it was standing room only."

From Luke's description, we discover that the residential dwelling must have been fairly large to accommodate "Pharisees and teachers of the law . . . who had come from every village of Galilee and Judea and from Jerusalem" (Luke 5:17). By this time in Jesus' ministry, he had attracted enough attention from the general population to warrant investigation by the religious authorities. Theological minds from all over Israel came to Capernaum to examine this illness-healing, demon-exorcising, leper-cleansing rabbi from Nazareth. Based on their evaluation, they would either vet His ministry or denounce Him as a heretic.

Mark states that Jesus was speaking "the word" (*logos* [3056]) to them (Mark 2:2). Most likely, this expression had become a technical term for the sum total of Christ's teachings that would ultimately become standard Christian doctrine in the latter-first-century church (cf. 4:14-20; 4:33; 8:32). In other words, Jesus engaged His hearers with doctrine, most likely correcting their erroneous views on the Messiah, the Law, grace, salvation, and the kingdom of God. That kind of challenge to man-made dogmas was bound to get Jesus into trouble with those whose careers depended on maintaining the doctrinal status quo.

— 2:3-4 —

By this time, Jesus' name had become a household word in Galilee. He had been meeting needs by exorcising demons and healing the sick. He had been engaged in a ministry of teaching, sharing the good news of Himself to others. Yet never once did He promote Himself as a healer. He never wanted people to follow Him because of His ability to heal. He healed so that people would realize He was genuinely from God. The healings that Jesus performed—and they were many—were designed to corroborate His authenticity. And then, when the people were ready, He would explain that He is from God because He is, in fact, God in human flesh.

Despite His intentions and lack of self-promotion, people continued to seek Him for healing. But rather than try to dissuade the miracle seekers, Jesus turned their efforts into an opportunity to advance His agenda. While Jesus taught in the house, four men hatched an ingenious plan to bypass the crowd and get their paralyzed friend an audience with Jesus, up close and personal. They climbed on the roof of the house and opened a hole. Kent Hughes describes what was involved:

> The typical Syrian roof was constructed of timbers laid parallel to each other about two or three feet apart. Then crosswise over the timbers, sticks were laid close to each other, thus forming the basic roof. Upon this was laid reeds, branches of trees, and thistles. The whole thing was overlaid with about a foot of earth,

which was then packed down to resist water. All told, the roof was about two feet thick. During the spring, grass flourished on these primitive roofs.[16]

Imagine the scene. As the rabbi taught, debris and dirt began to trickle down His tunic. Then larger chunks of clay fell as a shaft of sunlight poured through the widening hole above. By now, Jesus had abandoned His lesson and everyone was craning their necks and murmuring. Finally, a handmade stretcher descended on four ropes—probably commandeered from the nearby marina—bearing a paralytic. He may have returned Jesus' laughter with a sheepish smile.

— 2:5-7 —

Ever since the paralytic had heard of the healing rabbi in Capernaum, he had dreamed of hearing Him say, "Arise, take up your pallet, and walk." But Jesus saw something lying before Him that others might not. You and I might only see a man with paralysis needing a miracle cure; Jesus saw a man with a sin-sick heart in need of forgiveness. And that is the principal difference between humanity's agenda and God's plan for the world. We place a premium on our present physical bodies, which will someday cease functioning and return to the ground. But our immaterial part—call it a soul or a spirit—will continue after our physical bodies, which will one day be resurrected into eternal torment apart from God or in eternal glory with Him (John 5:28-29). In light of eternity, the physical healing of a present mortal body pales in comparison to the spiritual healing of a sin-sick soul.

While you and I would see a paralytic and his friends seeking a miraculous healing, Jesus saw something far more. He saw their faith (2:5). Many sought Jesus for nothing more than a way to escape their own physical pain, but not these men. They wanted healing for their friend, but they had also apparently heard Jesus preach. The fact that Mark describes them as having "faith" surely means they had repented and believed (1:15). So instead of saying, "Arise, take up your pallet, and walk," the rabbi said for all to hear, "Child, your sins are removed" (2:5, my literal translation). The NASB translation carries the same meaning: "Son, your sins are forgiven."

Surprising words. Outrageous words that reached the ears of the teachers and theologians. They immediately understood the implications of Jesus' declaration. "Why does this man speak that way? He is blaspheming; who can forgive sins but God alone?" (1:7).

C. S. Lewis explains why everyone had good reason to be concerned:

Now unless the speaker is God, [forgiving sins] is really so preposterous as to be comic. We can all understand how a man forgives offences against himself. You tread on my toes and I forgive you, you steal my money and I forgive you. But what should we make of a man, himself unrobbed and untrodden on, who announced that he forgave you for treading on other men's toes and stealing other men's money? Asinine fatuity is the kindest description we should give of his conduct. Yet this is what Jesus did. He told people that their sins were forgiven, and never waited to consult all the other people whom their sins had undoubtedly injured. He unhesitatingly behaved as if He was the party chiefly concerned, the person chiefly offended in all offences. This makes sense only if He really was the God whose laws are broken and whose love is wounded in every sin. In the mouth of any speaker who is not God, these words would imply what I can only regard as a silliness and conceit unrivalled by any other character in history.[17]

— 2:8-9 —

The critics and skeptics had no clue that Jesus was three chess moves ahead in the game. He anticipated their reaction and supernaturally sensed their silent protests. He intended to use this moment to reveal something about Himself to the public for the very first time. He had already been identified as the Messiah by John the Baptizer (1:7-11) and His disciples followed Him in this belief. Now He would personally claim equality with God the Father. The Father called Jesus "My beloved Son" earlier (1:11), but Jesus had not yet affirmed His own deity in public.

Jesus had a point to make, so He seized the opportunity to reason with the scribes and Pharisees, Israel's authorities on all things religious, by asking a profound question (2:9). Take some time now to ponder the question yourself, but don't answer too quickly!

Which is easier, to say to the paralytic, "Your sins are forgiven"; or to say, "Get up, and pick up your pallet and walk"?

I caution you again, don't be too quick to answer. The question is double-edged. Your answer depends upon whether you believe the person can make good on His promise.

Let me illustrate this way: Which is easier for me—writing you a check for one hundred million dollars, or saying, "I will give you the one hundred thousand dollars in my pocket right now"? Your answer depends upon whether you believe I have the funds to cover the check. If the check is good, that would be more difficult for me; I'm out one hundred million dollars instead of just one hundred thousand dollars. If I have no money in the bank, giving up the one hundred thousand dollars in my pocket would be more difficult; writing a bad check would be easier.

On the other hand, it's easier for me to *prove* whether or not I have one hundred thousand dollars in my pocket. Believing I have one hundred million dollars in the bank requires faith! Therefore, the answer to Jesus' question reveals whether one believes in His deity.

— 2:10-12 —

Jesus didn't give the audience long to decide. He already knew that the majority didn't believe He could make good on His promise to forgive sins. So He said to the paralyzed man, "Get up, pick up your pallet and go home" (2:11). Mark's description of the man's response is noteworthy. The man "got up and immediately picked up the pallet and went out" (2:12). Each action corresponds to each of the Lord's commands. The additional clarification "in the sight of everyone" emphasizes the positive effect of the obedience of Christ's followers on those who are watching them.

The fact that Jesus could heal a paralytic made it difficult for the scribes and Pharisees (Luke 5:21) to deny His ability to forgive sins. Both require authority far greater than any mere human possesses. In terms of my illustration, Jesus gave the man a check for one hundred million dollars and then handed over the one hundred thousand dollars in His pocket. Anyone walking around with that sum of money in His pocket is likely to have one hundred million dollars in the bank.

Mark strongly suggests that the majority of the religious experts took a giant step closer to believing Jesus' claim to deity and may have become followers.

APPLICATION: MARK 2:1-12

Lessons from the Great Physician

Three enduring insights emerge from this remarkable display of Jesus' mastery over sin, sickness, and skeptics. One we learn from the paraplegic, a second comes from the skeptics, and a third we glean from the Savior Himself.

First, by focusing on the paraplegic I learn this: *The deepest needs of our lives are not physical; they are spiritual and invisible.* You may think the pain you're suffering right now is the greatest need of your life, but it is not. Your greatest need arises from the dismal condition of your heart. This is true of everyone, which explains why Jesus gave priority to the man's heart before He addressed the hopeless condition of his body. While we tend to invert those priorities, placing physical needs above the spiritual, God continually calls us to reorient our thinking to see things as He does.

We gain a second insight by focusing on the scribes: *The earliest signs of a critical spirit are hidden and unspoken.* This malignancy begins deep down in the hidden recesses of the heart, where it grows unnoticed. Unless it is treated like a cancer—aggressively hunted and eradicated—a critical spirit becomes deadly. As the proverb urges, "Watch over your heart with all diligence, for from it *flow* the springs of life" (Prov. 4:23).

Guard your heart. Examine your motives and keep a close watch on your inner person. Evaluate your attitude to maintain a positive, constructive influence on others. Set a sentry on your thoughts; don't let unhealthy thinking take your mind in destructive or negative directions. These unseen, unspoken, hidden parts of our being have a powerful influence on how we experience life and how we impact others.

When I meet up with a person who has become bitter over something, I know I'm meeting a person who has a long history. That individual didn't become bitter yesterday morning. The bitterness started a long time ago. It festers, it sours, it grows.

When you see cynicism—a bitter, negative, critical, ungracious spirit—call it what it is. When you sense it growing in your own spirit, deal with it. That kind of spirit cannot produce anything good. We grow when we are saying yes to God deep within and when we have relationships that are kept in good repair with other people.

The third insight we gain from focusing on Jesus Himself: *Real miracles are self-evident.* Real miracles are not mere verbal exercises and hopes. They are actual and they are immediate. No person's promise guarantees a miracle. No person stating "You have been healed" guarantees a healing. Don't become distracted by the words of so-called faith healers. If a miraculous healing is genuine, it will speak for itself.

Look Who Jesus Hung Out With!
MARK 2:13-17

NASB

¹³ And He went out again by the seashore; and all the ᵃpeople were coming to Him, and He was teaching them.

¹⁴ As He passed by, He saw ᵃLevi the *son* of Alphaeus sitting in the tax booth, and He said to him, "Follow Me!" And he got up and followed Him.

¹⁵ And it ᵃhappened that He was reclining *at the table* in his house, and many tax collectors and ᵇsinners ᶜwere dining with Jesus and His disciples; for there were many of them, and they were following Him. ¹⁶ When the scribes of the Pharisees saw that He was eating with the sinners and tax collectors, they said to His disciples, "Why is He eating and drinking with tax collectors and ᵃsinners?" ¹⁷ And hearing *this*, Jesus said to them, "*It is* not those who are healthy who need a physician, but those who are sick; I did not come to call the righteous, but sinners."

2:13 ᵃLit *crowd* 2:14 ᵃalso called *Matthew* 2:15 ᵃLit *happens* ᵇI.e. irreligious Jews ᶜLit *were reclining with* 2:16 ᵃI.e. irreligious Jews

NLT

¹³ Then Jesus went out to the lakeshore again and taught the crowds that were coming to him. ¹⁴ As he walked along, he saw Levi son of Alphaeus sitting at his tax collector's booth. "Follow me and be my disciple," Jesus said to him. So Levi got up and followed him.

¹⁵ Later, Levi invited Jesus and his disciples to his home as dinner guests, along with many tax collectors and other disreputable sinners. (There were many people of this kind among Jesus' followers.) ¹⁶ But when the teachers of religious law who were Pharisees* saw him eating with tax collectors and other sinners, they asked his disciples, "Why does he eat with such scum?*"

¹⁷ When Jesus heard this, he told them, "Healthy people don't need a doctor—sick people do. I have come to call not those who think they are righteous, but those who know they are sinners."

2:16a Greek *the scribes of the Pharisees.*
2:16b Greek *with tax collectors and sinners?*

Make no mistake about it: Legalism is an enemy. Legalism isn't a well-meaning but misguided friend, but rather an aggressive opponent to the life of joy, the walk of faith, and the liberty in Christ. Legalism is a thief, stealing our freedom from us and robbing us of spontaneous joy. Legalism is a bully, intimidating all those who don't know how to defend themselves. It is a grim-faced, guilt-giving, self-appointed judge who indicts and pronounces shame and condemnation on all those who refuse to obey its ridiculous lists of nonbiblical rules and man-made regulations.

Legalism cannot tolerate those who are enjoying life. Back in 1963, Dr. S. Lewis Johnson, at that time the chair of the New Testament department at Dallas Seminary, wrote an article that appeared in *Bibliotheca Sacra*, the seminary's theological journal. In that piece, titled "The Paralysis of Legalism," Dr. Johnson wrote,

> One of the most serious problems facing the orthodox Christian church today is the problem of legalism. One of the most serious problems facing the church in *Paul's day* was the problem of legalism. In every day it is the same. Legalism wrenches the joy of the Lord from the Christian believer, and with the joy of the Lord goes his power for vital worship and vibrant service. Nothing is left but cramped, somber, dull and listless profession. The truth is betrayed, and the glorious name of the Lord becomes a synonym for a gloomy kill-joy. The Christian under law is a miserable parody of the real thing.[18]

What is legalism? It is an attitude of authoritarianism. It is a desire to control other people by enforcing an exhaustive list of dos and don'ts that attempts to define which external behavior should be considered acceptable by the circle of legalists. It's playing king of the mountain in other people's lives. Legalists use conformity to an external set of rules as a litmus test to determine one's acceptability, which is the exact opposite of grace. Legalism emphasizes the letter of the law to the exclusion of the spirit or intent of the law. Legalism makes secondary issues primary while making primary matters secondary. Legalism uses manipulation to create blind obedience. Legalism promotes external appearances that seem to be spiritual in nature but that, at the core, represent pride and self-service.

Why on earth would such a thing flourish? How does legalism gain a foothold in so many lives? Why is it ever-present? There are several reasons.

First, *the fear and intimidation from those who are in authority.* People fall in line because they fear the bully who determines the rules and regulations on how to live. What to do and what not to do. What to wear and what not to wear. What to drink and what not to drink. What to eat and what not to eat. Where to go for an evening in a restaurant and which establishments to avoid. How to respond in certain situations and how to behave before the eyes of the ever-watching public. Fear of those people who make the rules gives legalism unassailable power.

Second, *the desire to be accepted by one's peers.* This desire is greater than the determination to honor Christ. It stems from insecurity. Legalists *feed on* insecure, untaught, weak-willed believers.

Third, *ignorance of the Scriptures.* The more a person understands the Word of God—and by that I mean not only the Word itself, but the spirit of the Word—the less that person is inclined to bow to legalists. With ignorance of the principles of Scripture comes a deeper dependence on legalists to direct one's spiritual life.

Fourth, *the hesitation to confront manipulators and to fight for one's freedom.* Jesus refused to allow long-standing traditionalists and legalists to have their way in His life. Now, understand that nothing is wrong with tradition. Paul encourages Timothy to embrace the traditions of the faith (2 Tim. 1:5). But there's something terribly wrong with *traditionalism.* As Jaroslav Pelikan of Yale University put it, "Tradition is the living faith of the dead. Traditionalism is the dead faith of the living."[19]

How did Jesus counter these bullies? He took them on in face-to-face encounters in which He refused to back away. He presented and modeled a grace-oriented message. He refused to be manipulated by those who frowned and criticized. He stood His ground and trained a small group of disciples around Him to do the same. Others ran scared, but not Jesus.

After His teaching session with the religious experts (2:1-12), Jesus would put their theology to the test. God established Israel and gave His covenant people the Law in order to make them a "light on a hill" (see Ps. 43:3; Isa. 42:6-7; 49:6; 60:3), a beacon of truth to bring the lost into a saving relationship with the God of Abraham, Isaac, and Jacob. So how would Israel's foremost Jewish leaders respond when Jesus interacted with sinners? Mark answers that question in this part of his narrative.

— 2:13 —

After forgiving the sins of the paralytic and then healing his body, Jesus remained in Capernaum, teaching the people who journeyed from other parts of Galilee. Mark 2:13 summarizes an unknown period of time that could have been days or weeks in duration.

Capernaum was a large town by Galilean standards, so it had its fair share of religious officials, including Pharisees. In the realm of politics, the Pharisees were nationalistic and exclusive in their foreign policy. They despised Gentiles and wanted to keep Israel for Israelites. Unlike the aristocratic Sadducees, the middle-class Pharisees maintained control over the Jewish masses by becoming conspicuously Jewish. And if obedience to the Law of Moses made someone Jewish, they would remain kings of the moral hill at any cost. They maintained moral superiority—or at least the impression of it—by emphasizing a portion of God's Law that best suited their natural inclinations.

William Barclay observes, "To the Jews, religion was a thing of endless rules. People lived their lives in an endless forest of regulations which dictated every action. They must listen forever to a voice which said, 'You shall not.'"[20] Therefore, ordinary, God-loving Jews in Israel labored under man-made religiosity, enslaved to an endless list of rules that governed virtually every aspect of life. While these rules were derived from laws handed down by God, the requirements were twisted and expanded to serve the desire of one group of people to dominate another.

By the time Jesus came along, the people in the neighborhood of Capernaum had been taught by legalists in the synagogue for decades. I suspect Jesus spent a lot of His teaching time developing His followers' ability to think for themselves. When you follow legalists, you don't have to think; you simply learn the rules and blindly obey them.

— 2:14 —

While in and around Capernaum, Jesus undoubtedly saw Levi regularly. In fact, it's quite possible the tax collector had been listening to Jesus teach out by the seashore. Levi would not have been welcome in the synagogue. Jews in polite society despised tax collectors—and for good reason. By inflating their tax bills and then growing rich on the excess, Levi had betrayed his people, rejected his heritage, despised his temple, and renounced his God. Tax collectors had sold themselves to foreigners, which put Levi on the same level as harlots. So imagine the neighborhood scandal Jesus created when He called Levi to become one of His inner circle of disciples!

— 2:15-16 —

Mark quickly shifts the scene to Levi's house, where Jesus has chosen to dine with people from Levi's social caste—fellow tax collectors and other people that society recognized as immoral. The squint-eyed clerics of Capernaum must have been squirming in their tunics about these sinners because, as Mark notes, "there were many of them, and they were following Him" (2:15).

I would have expected the people of God to rejoice at the repentance of a tax collector. After all, Levi had seen the errors of his ways and turned from his sin. But instead they complained that Jesus was socializing with him and many other tax collectors. It didn't seem to help that Levi was encouraging other tax collectors to hear the same message that convinced him to give up the old lifestyle. The Pharisees still criticized Jesus for His choice of company—not to Jesus directly but to His disciples.

— 2:17 —

When Jesus heard about the Pharisees' question from the disciples, He responded to the complainers Himself. With biting irony, Jesus said, "It is not those who are healthy who need a physician, but those who are sick." How were the sinners going to get the spiritual treatment they needed if the righteous avoided them? Given Jesus' dim view of the genuineness of the Pharisees' "righteousness" (Matt. 5:20), the self-righteous religious leaders could have taken this as a double blow. Not only were they in jeopardy for failing to acknowledge their own sin-sickness and to seek healing from the Physician, but those who insisted on their own righteousness revealed their self-centeredness for also failing to help bring healing to those who needed it most. Once again, Jesus' actions exposed the hypocrisy of the legalists.

APPLICATION: MARK 2:13-17
Laughing at the Expense of Legalism

How do we deal with legalists on the loose? What do we do with them? Let me suggest four simple guidelines. These aren't rules inspired by God—use discernment and apply when appropriate.

Number one: *Learn how to identify a legalist.* If you're not aware that you're dealing with a legalist, his or her warped view of the gospel and spiritual growth can wheedle its way into your mind and start to twist your theology. I'm not referring to the wise counsel of a parent. I'm not referring to the correction of a godly mentor to whom you are account-able. I'm referring to people who make your business their business, and using their influence, start telling you what to keep in or out of your refrigerator, or how to lead your private life, or who your friends ought to be, or what you mustn't watch, read, or listen to. Unless it contravenes Scripture or the behavior is clearly sinful, illegal, or de-structive, those matters are nobody's business but yours as you live in submission to Christ.

Number two: *Ignore the counsel of legalists.* Refuse to allow legalists' advice to affect your decisions, and don't waste your breath arguing against their twisted rules or prohibitions. Legalists feed off superior-ity, so they *love* it when you fall under their spell and adjust your life accordingly. And they delight in the superior feeling of showing you how wrong you were for disagreeing. In Galatians 2, Paul describes the legalists who showed up in Galatia and he says, "We did not yield in subjection to them for even an hour" (Gal. 2:5). I like Eugene Peterson's paraphrase: "We didn't give them the time of day" (MSG).

Number three: *Deliberately stand against legalism.* Sometimes a legalist cannot be ignored and simply will not stop minding your business. You may have to take a firm stand. Avoid arguing; you cannot reason with unreasonable people. Resist the urge to defend or justify your decisions or actions; kindly thank the legalist for his or her concern and firmly state that it is a matter between you and God.

It was a great day in my ministry when I decided I would no longer be a doormat for the whims of every person in the congregation. That is not my task. My task is to answer to God and to live a life that honors Him, which will not please everyone. If God is unhappy with my conduct, His Holy Spirit will be faithful to disrupt my conscience.

Number four: *Enjoy your freedom in spite of legalists.* You have enormous freedom in Christ. Don't be afraid to enjoy this freedom because somebody may not like the way you are, or the way you're becoming, or the things you're doing or saying.

I have found it helpful to maintain a good sense of humor. I don't argue with toddlers about the color of the sky, and I don't sweat the criticism of legalists. In both cases, I simply laugh and let them be.

Battles worth Fighting
MARK 2:18-28

NASB

18 John's disciples and the Pharisees were fasting; and they came and said to Him, "Why do John's disciples and the disciples of the Pharisees fast, but Your disciples do not fast?" 19 And Jesus said to them, "While the bridegroom is with them, ªthe attendants of the bridegroom cannot fast, can they? So long as they have the bridegroom with them, they cannot fast. 20 But the days will come when the bridegroom is taken away from them, and then they will fast in that day.

NLT

18 Once when John's disciples and the Pharisees were fasting, some people came to Jesus and asked, "Why don't your disciples fast like John's disciples and the Pharisees do?" 19 Jesus replied, "Do wedding guests fast while celebrating with the groom? Of course not. They can't fast while the groom is with them. 20 But someday the groom will be taken away from them, and then they will fast.

NASB

21 "No one sews ªa patch of un-shrunk cloth on an old garment; otherwise ᵇthe patch pulls away from it, the new from the old, and a worse tear results. 22 No one puts new wine into old wineskins; other-wise the wine will burst the skins, and the wine is lost and the skins *as well;* but *one puts* new wine into fresh wineskins."

23 And it happened that He was passing through the grainfields on the Sabbath, and His disciples began to make their way along while pick-ing the heads *of grain.* 24 The Phari-sees were saying to Him, "Look, why are they doing what is not lawful on the Sabbath?" 25 And He said to them, "Have you never read what David did when he was in need and he and his companions became hungry; 26 how he entered the house of God in the time of Abiathar *the* high priest, and ate the ªconsecrated bread, which is not lawful for *anyone* to eat except the priests, and he also gave it to those who were with him?" 27 Jesus said to them, "The Sabbath ªwas made ᵇfor man, and not man ᵇfor the Sabbath. 28 So the Son of Man is Lord even of the Sabbath."

2:19 ªLit *sons of the bridal-chamber* 2:21 ªLit *that which is put on* ᵇLit *that which fills up* 2:26 ªOr *showbread;* lit *loaves of presentation* 2:27 ªOr *came into being* ᵇLit *because for the sake of*

NLT

21 "Besides, who would patch old clothing with new cloth? For the new patch would shrink and rip away from the old cloth, leaving an even bigger tear than before.

22 "And no one puts new wine into old wineskins. For the wine would burst the wineskins, and the wine and the skins would both be lost. New wine calls for new wineskins."

23 One Sabbath day as Jesus was walking through some grainfields, his disciples began breaking off heads of grain to eat. 24 But the Phar-isees said to Jesus, "Look, why are they breaking the law by harvesting grain on the Sabbath?"

25 Jesus said to them, "Haven't you ever read in the Scriptures what Da-vid did when he and his companions were hungry? 26 He went into the house of God (during the days when Abiathar was high priest) and broke the law by eating the sacred loaves of bread that only the priests are al-lowed to eat. He also gave some to his companions."

27 Then Jesus said to them, "The Sabbath was made to meet the needs of people, and not people to meet the requirements of the Sabbath. 28 So the Son of Man is Lord, even over the Sabbath!"

I would like to dedicate this segment of *Insights on Mark* to all recover-ing Pharisees. You may not realize that we have Pharisees among us today, but they are very much alive and well.

What is a modern-day Pharisee? A good synonym would be "legal-ist." To review our definition from the preceding section, legalists are individuals who examine the external behavior of others as a means of gauging their spiritual health, when they should give more atten-tion to their own internal thoughts and attitudes in the interest of their own spiritual maturity. Consequently, legalists *appear* more spiritually strong than others but are, in truth, the most spiritually anemic. Rather than finding joy in a relationship with the Almighty, they become grace killers, joy stealers, and freedom destroyers. They *think* they understand grace, but the demands they place on others prove that they haven't the first notion of grace as taught by Jesus.

Eugene Peterson, in his book titled *Traveling Light*, describes legalists well:

> There are people who do not want us to be free. They don't want us to be free before God, accepted just as we are by His grace. They don't want us to be free to express our faith originally and creatively in the world. They want to control us; they want to use us for their own purposes.[21]

I have joined Jesus and the authors of the New Testament as a part of the movement for freedom in grace. My announcement continues to be—despite all the risk that goes with it—that you are free in Christ. Yours is a liberty worth fighting for. There are few causes that I will risk my life to defend, few truths I count worthy of the ultimate sacrifice, but this is one I will die to preserve: *We are free in Christ.*

We can say that today, of course, because we know Christ. We live in the era of the gospel, the age of grace made possible by the Cross. In the first century, however, people lived under the demands of Pharisaism, which turned the Law of God into a binding yoke of the legalists' making. Religionists used the Old Testament as a means to control others. After many decades—perhaps as long as a century—of rigid domination, Jesus arrived on the scene "full of grace and truth" (John 1:14). Sparks were bound to fly.

— 2:18 —

The Old Testament called for only one day of fasting, which occurred on Yom Kippur, the Day of Atonement (Lev. 16:29–17:16). Jews often fasted voluntarily for a variety of reasons, much like people do today. Fasting is a good spiritual discipline that reminds the body that it is not in charge; the Holy Spirit rules the bodily temple. Fasting helps focus the mind on praying and helps the individual remain spiritually attuned to the leading of God. Fasting is even good for the body, assuming it's free of disease and functioning normally. Simply going without food, however, does not impress God. The purpose of fasting is not to earn merit or prove to God that you're serious about your petition. Fasting is a means of aligning our minds with the mind of the Lord, prompting us to submit our wills to His.

THE PHARISEES

MARK 2:18

The most likely meaning of the term "Pharisee" is "separated one." Many trace this sect of Judaism to Daniel and his three friends, who refused to partake of their captors' food (Dan. 1:8-19) or worship the king as a god (Dan. 3:1-30) while exiled in Babylon. Having been taken from the Promised Land and cut off from their temple, they clung to the Law as a means of preserving their identity as distant sons of Abraham. But after more than six hundred years, this admirable loyalty to nationalism and devotion to the Law had taken on a life of its own.

The Pharisees had become a tight-knit brotherhood, a political and religious party that had earned the respect of their fellow Jews. They were meticulous expositors of Scripture and worked tirelessly to apply the general principles of the Law to everyday life. The Law stated, for example, that every Israelite was to set aside the seventh day of the week for resting the body and refreshing the soul (Exod. 20:10-11). So that everyone would know how to apply the Law and to "rest" as they should, the Pharisaic rabbis added a long list of prohibitions. Later, this oral tradition of the Pharisees was preserved in a document called the Mishnah, which contains no fewer than twenty-four chapters *just on how to keep the Sabbath.*

No one rivaled the Pharisees in being religious. No one could!

The Pharisees routinely fasted on Mondays and Thursdays (e.g., Luke 18:12), and they took great pride in this show of their piety (e.g., Matt. 6:16-18). When Jesus dined with tax collectors and other kinds of rabble (Mark 2:15-17), His critics complained about His eating with the wrong people. Now they complained that Jesus and His disciples ate on the wrong days. The Pharisees had elevated their own tradition to the level of scriptural truth. In fact, they also tried to pit the followers of John the Baptist against the followers of Jesus, driving a wedge between allies in ministry.

Legalists do the same today. They tend to believe that everybody has to do everything the same way. This kind of insistence on man-made uniformity crushes the freedom Christians have to worship in spirit and truth (John 4:23). I'm not saying that fasting—even scheduled fasting—was wrong. The fact that John the Baptizer's disciples followed the traditional fast demonstrates this. The problem wasn't in the observance but in the attempt to force the freedom to fast on those who had freedom not to.

— 2:19-20 —

Jesus responded to this Pharisaic legalism with a word-picture that doesn't resonate well today. To make His point, Jesus drew upon a rich body of tradition surrounding the Jewish wedding ceremony. Unlike modern weddings in the West, ancient Near Eastern couples didn't dash away for a honeymoon an hour or two after the ceremony. Jews in Israel gathered in the bridegroom's home to celebrate and feast for as long as a week! The new couple was treated like royalty and sometimes wore crown wreaths.[22] The phrase "attendants of the bridegroom" (2:19) literally means "sons of the bridal chamber." The groom's closest friends took great care to guard the wedding chamber during the feast and otherwise helped the groom's parents make sure everyone had a good time.

The Greek construction of Jesus' question indicates that He anticipated a negative answer, so the NASB correctly adds "can they?" to the end of the sentence. Even Pharisees appreciated the joy of the wedding feast, so they generally relaxed all religious observances, especially fasting (which symbolized mourning).

People in Jesus' day would not have read too deeply into His analogy; He simply meant to say that times of joy call for a relaxed approach to religious rigor. Even Pharisees allowed themselves to have a good time at weddings. For Christians, however, the wedding analogy carries a deeper meaning. Paul would later describe the relationship of Jesus with His church as that of a bridegroom receiving His bride (2 Cor. 11:2-3; Eph. 5:22-33). Jesus may have intended this deeper meaning, recognizing that no one would understand until much later.

The Lord compared His time on earth to the relatively brief time of celebration at a wedding, after which normal life resumes, along with its duties and obligations.

— 2:21-22 —

Having responded to the Pharisees, Jesus drew two quick analogies from everyday life to say, in effect, "Now is the dawn of a new era." Much of what John's disciples and the Pharisees understood about the Law, our relationship with God, and the value of good works would soon be swept aside, replaced by a completely different paradigm.

The first analogy concerns patching an old garment with a new piece of fabric that has not yet been washed and dried (2:21). When the patched garment is later cleaned, the new cloth will shrink, tearing the older fabric. The second illustration is similar (2:22). "New wine" is fresh grape juice. During the process of fermentation, the juice emits carbon dioxide. A brittle, old wineskin would not be supple enough to expand and could burst. In Jesus' day, winemakers always reserved old wineskins for wine that had completed fermentation.

Both analogies illustrate the same point: Pharisaism is incompatible with God's way of salvation. There are two ways to interpret the deeper implications of His double illustration:

1. Any attempt to bind the newness of the gospel to the old religion of Judaism is futile.
2. Your attempt to "fix" the Old Testament way of salvation causes more problems than it attempts to correct.

This may be difficult to accept, but I think Jesus intended both. When people first hear the analogy, they inevitably interpret it as:

Old garment/old wineskin = the religion of the Pharisees
New patch/new wine = the gospel
Application: "Your inflexible, brittle religion cannot tolerate the gospel of grace I bring; you must discard it completely."

And that is entirely correct. However, ponder the Lord's words—as the Pharisees undoubtedly did—and the second message begins to emerge:

Old garment/old wineskin = Old Testament relationship with God
New patch/new wine = the religion of the Pharisees
Application: "Your newfangled, man-made religion of legalism causes more damage than what it attempts to fix."

God originally gave the Law to Israel to give the nation order and to set them apart as His covenant people. His greater purpose, however, was to use the Law as a diagnostic tool to demonstrate their (and our) need for salvation. Paul explains this in Galatians 3:19. Eugene Peterson's paraphrase is helpful: "The purpose of the law was to keep a sinful people in the way of salvation until Christ (the descendant) came, inheriting the promises and distributing them to us" (MSG). The Law was deficient—needing a patch, as it were—because the Law cannot save. The Law can only point out our desperate need for salvation. The religious authorities in Jerusalem—both Pharisees and Sadducees—sought to solve the problem by simply trying harder; in the process, they created a religious system God never intended. When God gave the Law to Israel, He never intended obedience to become a means of salvation. Only a cruel god would demand of its people what they could not hope to achieve.

It's important to note that grace and faith were not new concepts in the first century. Long before Jesus arrived to proclaim the good news of the new covenant, the Old Testament established a meeting place between man and God—at first a tabernacle and, later, a temple. In this special place, God invited His people to repent of their sins and ask for His mercy. And by grace, through faith in God, they received His forgiveness. Following the Law and carrying out sacrifices were old covenant expressions of faith and faithfulness, not the means of salvation. In fact, the rewards for keeping the old covenant Law related specifically to blessings in the Land of Promise, not eternal life in heaven (Deut. 28:1-14). We must never confuse the outward expressions of faith with the inner work of faith that has always been God's means of salvation (Heb. 10). Salvation from sin and the promise of heaven have always been gifts of grace received through faith in God, not by works (our ability to be good or avoid evil).

By the time of Jesus, however, Israel's religious teachers taught that one must be born a descendant of Jacob or be converted through a complicated ceremony and then remain obedient to the Law of Moses in order to safeguard a relationship with God. All legalism stems from the mistaken idea that we can gain or keep God's favor by behaving a certain way—performing certain rituals, keeping specific laws, avoiding forbidden behaviors, meeting an established standard of goodness. If legalism pleased God, the Pharisees would have delighted Him. But Jesus, God in human flesh, clarified their position before the Almighty: "Your way is like a bad patch—like pouring new wine into an old wineskin."

While God is merciful, He is also just. He will forgive sins, but the penalty for sin must be paid—if not by us, then by someone else. Jesus confronted the Pharisees to tell them that their "solution" to the problem created by the Law—the problem of guilt—is defective. The more we try to be good, the more obvious our guilt becomes (see Rom. 7). To divert attention from our guilt, we must either hide it through hypocrisy or shift the attention to the guilt of others through condemnation. Jesus came with a profoundly better solution to the problem of guilt exposed by the Law: "I will pay the penalty of your sin on your behalf; receive this gift by grace through faith . . . like always."

— 2:23-24 —

In keeping with Mark's typical style, the scene suddenly shifts to another day and time while continuing on the same theme. In this case, the theme is legalism.

To divert attention from their moral failures, legalists make a great show of what they naturally do well. For the Pharisees, keeping the Sabbath became their pet cause. In fact, they turned God's gift of rest into a religious fetish. The law they emphasized is the fourth of the Ten Commandments:

> The seventh day is a sabbath of the LORD your God; in it you shall not do any work. . . . For in six days the LORD made the heavens and the earth, the sea and all that is in them, and rested on the seventh day; therefore the LORD blessed the sabbath day and made it holy. (Exod. 20:10-11)

And they no doubt appealed to the incident in Numbers 15:

> Now while the sons of Israel were in the wilderness, they found a man gathering wood on the sabbath day. . . . Then the LORD said to Moses, "The man shall surely be put to death; all the congregation shall stone him with stones outside the camp." So all the congregation brought him outside the camp and stoned him to death with stones, just as the LORD had commanded Moses. (Num. 15:32-36)

Originally, God set aside the seventh day as a weekly holiday to commemorate His creation of the world and to celebrate His provision. In six days, He fashioned the earth and filled it with everything humankind would need. On the seventh day, He stopped. "Sabbath" is based on the Hebrew verb "to cease" (*shabat* [H7673]). God stopped, but not because He was tired or needed rest; He stopped because Creation was complete.

The Sabbath also commemorated the covenant He established with Abraham and, by extension, the nation of Israel. Once He gave His covenant people the Promised Land, Friday at sundown became a time for feasting and singing, a time when families delighted in their God of provision and protection and set aside work to bond with one another. Then, after the armies of Babylon destroyed the temple in 586 BC and carried the Jews away from their land, the Sabbath became something different in the eyes of the Jews. Having been stripped of so much of their distinct Hebrew culture, they clung to the Law of Moses to maintain their identity and to unite them. During this period of exile, the party of the Pharisees rose to prominence, touting a religious system that made legalism king in Israel. And with it, grace began to fade from Jewish faith.

By the time of Jesus, the Pharisees had transformed the Sabbath into something very different from what God had ordained. To the simple command "rest," the Pharisees added a long list of specific prohibitions that, ironically, turned this day of rest into a terrible religious burden. They established thirty-nine categories that constituted "work," all forbidden on the Sabbath: carrying, burning, extinguishing, finishing, writing, erasing, cooking, washing, sewing, tearing, knotting, untying, shaping, plowing, planting, reaping, harvesting, threshing, winnowing, selecting, sifting, grinding, kneading, combing, spinning, dyeing, chain stitching, warping, weaving, unraveling, building, demolishing, trapping, shearing, slaughtering, skinning, tanning, smoothing, and marking.[23]

On this particular Sabbath, Jesus' disciples gleaned grain as they passed through a field (cf. Deut. 23:24-25), but Pharisaic custom identified such activity as work: "Plucking wheat from its stem is reaping, rubbing the wheat heads between one's palms is threshing, and blowing away the chaff is winnowing!"[24]

— 2:25-28 —

The Lord's response to the Pharisees' challenge is wonderfully rich and complex, layered with meaning. He drew a direct correlation between Himself and King David, and between His disciples and David's followers in a familiar Old Testament story (1 Sam. 21:1-6). The passage describes David's encounter with a priest, who set aside a law concerning consecrated bread restricted to the priests (cf. Lev. 24:5-9) in order to feed David's famished men. At that time, David had been anointed king by Samuel the prophet. Furthermore, the Holy Spirit had departed from King Saul and "came mightily upon David from that day forward" (1 Sam. 16:12-14). Therefore, the identity of the true king became the source of a national debate. God had anointed David, but Saul refused to relinquish the crown.

In the first century, the true King of the Jews came to Israel, but the people in power refused to submit to Him.

Jesus' reply also challenged the Pharisees' flawed theology. Using the Sabbath as an object lesson, He appealed to the Scriptures to expose three critical errors in their theology.

First, *the Pharisees placed the customs of men before the Law of God.* Their supposed attempts to obey the Lord more diligently actually had the opposite effect. God ordained the Sabbath as a day to reflect on Him and to rest in His provision and protection; the Pharisees spent their

Sabbath day thinking about themselves and how others didn't keep the Sabbath nearly as well. In their strict obedience, they failed to obey!

Second, *God gave laws to His people to bless them, not to burden them.* Every one of God's laws either elevates the quality of human life or restores one's relationship with God after a sin. He makes no extraneous demands, and He is never capricious. The Lord gave the Israelites one day in seven to cease from work because the human body needs rest. The Pharisees managed to turn this gift into a burden. Only a legalist could spoil a day off from work!

Third, *the Law was given by God; therefore, the Law can never be greater than God.* The Old Testament Scriptures declare, "The LORD blessed the sabbath day and made it holy" (Exod. 20:11, emphasis mine). The Pharisees could quote much of the Law, so they didn't miss the point of Jesus' bold claim, "I (the Son of Man), am the Lord of the Sabbath." In this simple statement, Jesus challenged the authority of the Pharisees, who had stolen the Sabbath from God. He said, in effect, *"The Sabbath is not yours to regulate; it is My gift to My people. Therefore, I am taking it back from you."*

Mark doesn't record a response from the Pharisees. The conversation ended when the legalists couldn't answer Jesus' logic. But that didn't end the conflict. Far from it. Legalists yearn for control like a lion craves raw flesh; they are most dangerous when deprived of what they want.

APPLICATION: MARK 2:18-28

Three Battles for People of Grace

As I observe Jesus in a standoff against the religious power brokers of His day, I see three spiritual battles worth fighting.

Battle #1: The battle for a lifetime of continual joy
Watch out for inflexible killjoys. H. L. Mencken, surely with tongue in cheek, defined a Puritan as someone who lives with "the haunting fear that someone, somewhere, might be happy." That's an unfortunate caricature of most Puritans, but it was certainly true of the legalists among them. So I would build on that statement and borrow from it, saying, "A legalist is someone who lives in a constant search for

anyone, anywhere, who longs to be free in order to shame him or her back under control."

Legalists will steal your joy. They'll find a reason you should never be anything but grim-faced and sober. Their whole lives are spent in a dark tunnel of self-condemnation in desperate search of opportunities to condemn others. They are, nevertheless, limited in their power. They can only steal your joy if you let them.

Battle #2: The battle to maintain ageless flexibility

For some reason, people who are advanced in years tend to grow brittle—not just physically, but mentally and spiritually. They gravitate to the familiar, avoid any source of discomfort, cultivate and nurture a strict routine, and grouse about anything that disrupts their carefully maintained comfort. It is a malignant, self-centered perspective that turns all personal preferences into spiritual mandates, and it sucks the life out of those who want to experience life in abundance.

As you grow older, do your best to stay out of the rut. Travel. *Don't* act your age; do things that are unexpected from people of your generation. Do things that make your kids ask, "Who are you and what have you done with my parents!"

Remain open to considering other opinions. Stay teachable. I love it when professors engage students over a long period of time. Students are right there hammering away with their questions, and fielding those questions keeps them vibrant. Stay in touch with younger people. Learn about the challenges they face without condemning them.

Battle for ageless flexibility.

Battle #3: The battle for meeting real needs

The solution for every need, regardless of the kind, begins with grace. Offer to pray for God's provision, but don't leave it there. Insofar as you are able, become the answer to your own prayer by meeting the needs you see (Jas. 2:15-17). Think of others who might have the resources on hand to meet the need, or find groups who might share the joyous burden together. Grace isn't a feeling; grace is love in action, and it produces observable results.

Believe it or not, legalists will often oppose your efforts to help others in need. Don't waste your time arguing with them; prayerfully do what needs to be done. Put grace into action and meet real needs.

Mercy under Suspicious Eyes
MARK 3:1-6

NASB

¹He entered again into a synagogue; and a man was there whose hand was withered. ²They were watching Him *to see* if He would heal him on the Sabbath, so that they might accuse Him. ³He said to the man with the withered hand, "ᵃGet up and come forward!" ⁴And He said to them, "Is it lawful to do good or to do harm on the Sabbath, to save a life or to kill?" But they kept silent. ⁵After looking around at them with anger, grieved at their hardness of heart, He said to the man, "Stretch out your hand." And he stretched it out, and his hand was restored. ⁶The Pharisees went out and immediately *began* ᵃconspiring with the Herodians against Him, *as to* how they might destroy Him.

3:3 ᵃLit *Arise into the midst*   3:6 ᵃLit *giving counsel*

NLT

¹Jesus went into the synagogue again and noticed a man with a deformed hand. ²Since it was the Sabbath, Jesus' enemies watched him closely. If he healed the man's hand, they planned to accuse him of working on the Sabbath.

³Jesus said to the man with the deformed hand, "Come and stand in front of everyone." ⁴Then he turned to his critics and asked, "Does the law permit good deeds on the Sabbath, or is it a day for doing evil? Is this a day to save life or to destroy it?" But they wouldn't answer him.

⁵He looked around at them angrily and was deeply saddened by their hard hearts. Then he said to the man, "Hold out your hand." So the man held out his hand, and it was restored! ⁶At once the Pharisees went away and met with the supporters of Herod to plot how to kill Jesus.

Living under a cloud of suspicion is, at best, an uneasy existence. Sometimes living under the microscope of distrust can become unbearable. Those who are suspicious of you scrutinize—and sometimes twist—every word you utter and question every deed you perform. Even your good deeds become tainted with the suspicion of evil motives. And, try as hard as you like, you will finally come to the realization that you cannot win—you're not going to change the opinion of those who are suspicious of you. At that point the clouds of suspicion usually burst into a thunderstorm of disastrous proportions that will inevitably lead to serious consequences. At that point, suspicion gives way to outright hostility. An example from history presents itself in the life of Martin Luther.

By 1517, Dr. Luther had been teaching theology in Wittenberg, Germany, for almost a decade when he realized that the doctrine and practices of the established church—of which he was a part—stood in sharp contrast with a commonsense, face-value reading of Scripture.

There were many points at which Roman Catholic Church dogma contradicted Scripture, but it was the selling of indulgences that pushed Luther to the end of his tether. He could remain silent no longer.

His writing, teaching, and preaching conflicted with official Catholic Church doctrine, first in the classroom, where his students and fellow theology faculty members became convinced he was right, and then before his congregation, who saw the validity of his preaching. As greater numbers began to move in his direction, the Church in Rome took notice. Likening Luther to a wild boar destroying a vineyard, the pope sent a "papal bull," an official document bearing the full authority of the Vatican, stating that Luther was to recant his teaching and burn his writings. Luther denounced the document and his following grew even larger. On December 10, 1520, the condemning document from Rome was burned instead of Luther's works.

Luther's defiance threatened the pope's grip on power, and a showdown became inevitable. This took place at an official hearing in Worms, Germany, in 1521 where Luther was commanded to appear and either recant publicly or suffer the wrath of the Church. He stood before the suspicious Holy Roman Emperor, Charles V, along with a host of princes, rulers, and magistrates, and refused to back down. The closing words of his speech are now famous:

> Unless I am convinced by the testimony of the Scriptures or by clear reason (for I do not trust either in the pope or in councils alone, since it is well known that they have often erred and contradicted themselves), I am bound by the Scriptures I have quoted and my conscience is captive to the Word of God. I cannot and will not recant anything, since it is neither safe nor right to go against conscience. May God help me. Amen.[25]

After the hearing, he left for home. Powerful friends feared for his safety, however, and arranged to have him kidnapped and secreted away to a castle in Wartburg. There he immediately began translating the New Testament from Latin into German so that everyone could read the Word of God. The Roman Church, supremely interested in maintaining power and control, suspected Luther of a power grab. When he began his translation—giving power to the people, as it were—the Church's suspicion gave way to open hostility. By the providence of God, the military might of his friend Frederick the Wise kept Luther from an early death.

Hit the historical rewind key on your mental time machine, and you'll find yourself not at a public hearing in Worms, Germany, but at a small synagogue in Galilee. The person conducting ministry under suspicious eyes is not Martin Luther, but a preaching and healing rabbi named Jesus of Nazareth. On the seventh day of the week, a holy day among the Jews, Jesus stands to teach before a congregation of squint-eyed, narrow-thinking, self-righteous Pharisees, who have come for the single purpose of finding fault with him. They suspect Jesus is stealing their influence for the sake of personal gain, and their wariness is teetering on the edge of open hostility. Earlier, Jesus violated their Sabbath customs. What will He do this Sabbath?

— 3:1-2 —

Although editors have inserted a chapter break between 2:28 and 3:1, this story is quite closely connected to the previous episode, in which a group of Pharisees accuse the Lord's disciples of violating the Sabbath. As mentioned earlier, of all the Old Testament laws, the fourth commandment had become the Pharisees' pet concern, and they had turned it into a litmus test of piety. This gave Jesus ample opportunity to challenge their understanding of how the Law fit into God's relationship with His creation. Was the God of Abraham a petty tyrant king, only concerned with perfect obedience and constantly threatening retribution? Or, did this God love His people and seek to help them?

The man-made customs of the Sabbath strictly regarded some medical treatments as forms of work that were forbidden on that day. One may only do what is necessary to keep an injury or illness from getting worse, but the Pharisees prohibited anything beyond that. For example,

> They do not straighten [the limb of] a child or set a broken limb. He whose hand or foot was dislocated should not pour cold water over them. But he washes in the usual way. And if he is healed, he is healed.[26]

When Jesus entered the synagogue, someone with a serious need sat in the congregation: a man whose hand was withered. The Greek term *xērainō* [3583] is variously translated "shriveled," "dried up," and "stiff," but nothing suggests a reason. The injury could have been caused by an accident, disease, or a congenital abnormality. Regardless, the man's hand had been rendered useless, and Jewish theology of the time would have attributed his misfortune to sin (cf. John 9:1-2).

When Jesus walked in, the Pharisees were watching. The Greek term *paratēreō* [3906] describes close or intent observation, like a watchman on a tower or a suspicious customer watching a shady merchant count out money. The imperfect tense adds a strong element of suspense. Suspicious eyes darted between Jesus the divine healer and the disabled man in need of divine mercy. It's quite possible the Pharisees had positioned the man in the synagogue, knowing Jesus would be drawn to him like a magnet to steel. And they waited to see what He would do, looking for a chance to publicly criticize Him (Mark 3:2).

The Pharisees didn't care one whit about the welfare of the man. He became nothing more than their foil against Jesus, whom they "might accuse." In this, Mark highlights the exquisite irony of the scene. Jesus wanted to do good on the Sabbath while the Pharisees conspired to do evil. The evil the Pharisees plotted: to condemn Jesus for doing good.

— 3:3-4 —

When Jesus saw the disabled man and the gallery of suspicious eyes trained on Him, He seized the opportunity to teach. Calling the man forward, perhaps to stand beside Jesus and face the Pharisees together, the Lord asked a penetrating question. The answer would expose their theology—in particular, their view of God's character.

The form of Jesus' question leaves no middle ground between the extremes of good and harm, saving life or killing. This is deliberate. In the mind of God, the failure to do good is nothing short of aiding and abetting evil. It was not merely *permissible* to do good on the Sabbath; it was an *obligation*. Earlier, Jesus established the premise that God gave the Law for the benefit of humanity—a gift of grace—not to burden us (2:27). On this occasion, Jesus carried the principle further. Human need always poses a moral imperative.

It appears that Jesus could have chosen from at least three options. First, Jesus could have delayed the healing until after sundown. That way He could avoid offending anybody. When confronted by the opportunity to do good, we may be tempted to please the legalists in the hope that they'll like us more. After all, Jesus could help the man anytime; he had gone on in this condition this long, so one more day wouldn't matter.

Second, Jesus could have whispered to the man, "Meet Me by the seashore this afternoon when we're alone, and I'll do this in secret. It'll be between you and Me; you'll still get healed, and the synagogue won't be disrupted." In other words, Jesus could have compromised. Many would opt to break the Pharisees' stupid rules in private.

But Jesus chose a third option. He chose to take His stand against His critics then and there. For Him, the issue involved more than a withered hand. As a teacher, He had a responsibility to correct the faulty theology of Israel's religious leaders. He came to reveal God, to be the perfect representation of God in human flesh. Our Creator does not love rules for their own sake; He gave us the Law as an expression of His love.

In taking this stand, Jesus vindicated the character of God and restored His Law to its rightful place.

Note also that Jesus' question is in two parts (3:4). The first highlights His immediate plan: to do good. The second presages the Pharisees' insidious plot to kill Him (3:6). Deeds reveal one's true beliefs, and a litmus test of true versus false religion is its response to injustice (Jas. 1:27). To go further, the primary test of all theology and morality is one's response to the weak and defenseless members of society.

— 3:5-6 —

Mark describes the Lord's response as complex (3:5). Outwardly, He displayed wrath. The Greek term is *orgē* [3709], which depicts a passionate, impulsive expression of intense emotion. When associated with God, the emotion is almost always wrath in response to sin. Jesus' compassion for the disabled man prompted protective anger at those who would deny him help.

Inwardly, however, Jesus felt "grieved." The Greek term is *syllypeō* [4818], which has the sense of "to sorrow with" or "to feel sympathy."[27] This is the only time the term is used in the New Testament. He grieved because of their "hardness of heart." In the first century, to say a person had a "hard heart" didn't mean they were unkind or cruel, but rather that their reasoning and emotions had become resistant to development. We might say the Pharisees were "hard-headed." They were spiritually blind. Jesus grieved for the Pharisees like we would feel sorry for a blind beggar groping aimlessly for food. His compassion for the legalists prompted mourning—deep anguish—for the suffering they would endure for eternity.

He turned from the Pharisees to the disabled man and restored his hand to wholeness.

Imagine your reaction if someone in your neighborhood received miraculous, instantaneous, complete healing. A person born blind or deaf received complete restoration. A paraplegic suddenly leapt from a wheelchair and began walking and running. Everyone I know would rejoice! But not the Pharisees. Hard-hearted and hard-headed, they couldn't see past their hatred for Jesus to congratulate the healed man and celebrate the miracle.

Time to Stand

MARK 3:3-4

In a church I formerly served, we discovered that an elder had molested a child. It was one of the lowest times of my life. I did not know how we would survive the crisis. The threat of a lawsuit loomed over the church like a violent thunderhead—if the matter were to be exposed.

I will be candid; the simplest response would have been to handle everything behind the scenes, say nothing publicly, and simply ask the man to leave. But he would have left our flock to devour lambs in another. As a good friend of mine said to me later, "Molesters will molest, even from a wheelchair."

I remember a long meeting with our elders. After I explained the situation, they sat in dismal silence—mournful for the child and angry at the man they once trusted. One of our elders, an attorney, said, "You realize, Pastor Swindoll, that this has all the makings of a lawsuit." I didn't fault him for saying what we were all thinking. It was his job to be certain we understood the implications of each decision.

I asked the group, "We're not gonna let that stop us from doing what's right, are we?"

They sat in silence a few moments as they blinked and stared, still reeling from the news. Thankfully, each man said firmly, "No, we're not."

We exposed the molester. We dealt with his crime openly. The newspapers and television reporters were on hand, ready for a scandal. We made counselors available for people worried that their children might have been victims. We arranged for the care of the victims we discovered. Civil authorities stood by ready to act on behalf of justice. We did our best to deal with the matter openly, yet with compassion for the victims, and we exposed the molester, exercising church discipline and cooperating with the police.

(continued on next page)

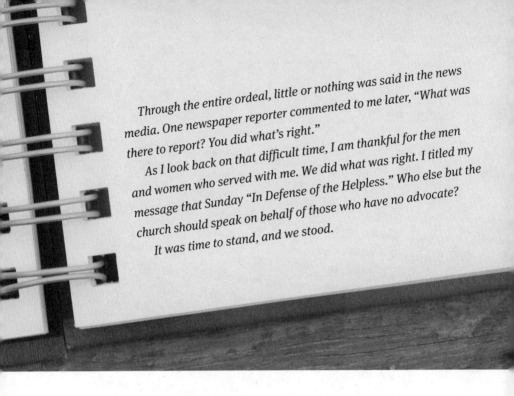

Through the entire ordeal, little or nothing was said in the news media. One newspaper reporter commented to me later, "What was there to report? You did what's right."

As I look back on that difficult time, I am thankful for the men and women who served with me. We did what was right. I titled my message that Sunday "In Defense of the Helpless." Who else but the church should speak on behalf of those who have no advocate? It was time to stand, and we stood.

Of course, the Pharisees were so blinded by their hatred that they couldn't see that their objection made no sense. Strictly speaking, Jesus did no physical labor. He didn't set a bone or apply medicine; He merely issued a verbal command. Furthermore, He accomplished something only possible for God. Even if the legalists objected to Jesus' deed, God obviously affirmed His choice by accomplishing the healing. If the religious authorities had an argument, it was with God.

Mark states that the Pharisees began conspiring to kill Jesus, aligning themselves with the Herodians (3:6). No one knows who the Herodians were; the term isn't used outside the New Testament in ancient literature. The "Herodians" weren't a political party, like the Pharisees, Sadducees, Essenes, or Zealots. The Greek term follows a standard Latin form to indicate the supporters of a leading figure, so the Herodians appear to be people who advocated the dynasty of Herod the Great, perhaps hoping to see one of his sons become emperor. Agrippa I did, in fact, come close before pride led to his early demise (Acts 12:23). And in Galilee at this time, it was Herod Antipas who ruled the tetrarchy (see comments on Mark 1:14-15).

Regardless, the Pharisees and the Herodians made an odd pairing. The Pharisees shunned contact with Gentiles, preferring to remain culturally "clean." The family of Herod, however, carried little or no Jewish DNA, behaved like Gentiles, participated fully in imperial politics, and considered themselves Roman. So the fact that the Pharisees would become allies with supporters of Herod reveals the depth of their loathing for Jesus.

True to form, the Pharisees' suspicion became outright hostility when Jesus refused to compromise the truth. When He stood firm against the power of the religious elite, their true natures emerged and their murderous plot put Jesus on course to fulfill prophecy and complete His mission.

APPLICATION: MARK 3:1-6

Three Encounters, Three Responses

The legalist reduces his or her relationship with God to keeping rules, obeying regulations, and following rituals. The motivation isn't love or devotion, but self-reliance. It is the opposite of the dependent relationship God desires people to have with him. For Jesus, the keeping of rules and rituals takes second place to a spontaneous response to God's unmerited favor toward us. When we live in trusting dependence upon the grace of God, we obey Him as a natural expression of our love for Him.

This spontaneous response to God's grace doesn't end there, however. It has far-reaching and visible implications. The apostle John, in his letter to the churches in Asia, made it clear that we cannot love God without loving the people He made (1 Jn. 4:20). Therefore, our own personal response to God's grace can be seen in our response to those around us who suffer. This particular story in Mark's narrative encourages us to think about how we interact with both legalists and those who suffer.

First, *note that Jesus neither ignored nor shunned the disabled man.* In fact, He looked directly at him, spoke to him, and invited interaction. Oddly enough, very few people ever do that. Show mercy to the disabled by treating them with dignity. Give them the same respect and attention you would give anyone else.

I realize that an encounter with a disabled person can be uncomfortable. We don't know what to say. So it is our tendency to look around people with disabilities. We look past them and through them. We talk to others who are with them. In one church, I observed a man in a wheelchair entering the sanctuary with his wife. The usher never looked at the man. Instead, he asked the woman, "Does he want a bulletin?"

She patiently and kindly replied, "Why don't you ask him?"

"Yes," the man said with a smile, "I would like a bulletin."

I don't think the usher meant to do anything wrong; he simply did what most of us do. Be aware. Stop this trend. Acknowledge and engage disabled men and women as your equals.

Second, *consider the role of mercy-givers in your church body and community.* My daughter and her husband—their whole family, in fact—give 24/7 care to our precious grandson Jonathan. He is autistic and suffers from a broad range of other mental and physical difficulties. We often express our admiration and gratitude for their unrelenting, faithful care for him. Their love for Jonathan never ceases.

Celebrate mercy-givers as heroes. Express gratitude. Find ways to encourage them and support them. Help relieve their burden at times.

At Stonebriar Community Church, we have a night when we ask the parents of special-needs children to let us provide care while they enjoy an evening off. We have volunteers who are trained to meet the particular needs of these kids. This gives the caregivers, usually a mom and dad, a night free of this responsibility so they can enjoy one another and strengthen their marriage.

Third, *be concerned for the hard-hearted.* We need to pray they will allow God to change their darkened minds so that they will come to their senses. We must pray they will realize how blind they have been. Moreover, we must passionately stand strong against their hardness if they're not moved over their sin, even if we must express righteous anger.

And do not forget to grieve over their hardness. Legalists risk God's eternal wrath. When Jesus returns to collect His saints, He will divide the group *claiming* to be His servants into two groups. Like a shepherd, He will separate the sheep from the goats. Jesus explained this judgment:

> "Then [the King] will also say to those on His left, 'Depart from Me, accursed ones, into the eternal fire which has been prepared for the devil and his angels; for I was hungry, and you gave Me nothing to eat; I was thirsty, and you gave Me nothing to drink; I was a stranger, and you did not invite Me in; naked, and you did not clothe Me; sick, and in prison, and you did not visit Me.' Then they themselves also will answer, 'Lord, when did we see You

hungry, or thirsty, or a stranger, or naked, or sick, or in prison, and did not take care of You?' Then He will answer them, 'Truly I say to you, to the extent that you did not do it to one of the least of these, you did not do it to Me.' These will go away into eternal punishment, but the righteous into eternal life." (Matt. 25:41-46)

Jesus mourned the future of the Pharisees, even as He defended the disabled man with righteous anger. Even in our anger, let us be moved with compassion and pray for the redemption of legalists and other modern-day Pharisees.

The Perils of Effective Ministry
MARK 3:7-19

NASB

7 Jesus withdrew to the sea with His disciples; and a great multitude from Galilee followed; and *also* from Judea, 8 and from Jerusalem, and from Idumea, and beyond the Jordan, and the vicinity of Tyre and Sidon, a great number of people heard of all that He was doing and came to Him. 9 And He told His disciples that a boat should stand ready for Him because of the crowd, so that they would not crowd Him; 10 for He had healed many, with the result that all those who had afflictions pressed around Him in order to touch Him. 11 Whenever the unclean spirits saw Him, they would fall down before Him and shout, "You are the Son of God!" 12 And He earnestly warned them not to ᵃtell who He was.

13 And He went up on the mountain and summoned those whom He Himself wanted, and they came to Him. 14 And He appointed twelve, so that they would be with Him and that He *could* send them out to preach, 15 and to have authority to cast out

NLT

7 Jesus went out to the lake with his disciples, and a large crowd followed him. They came from all over Galilee, Judea, 8 Jerusalem, Idumea, from east of the Jordan River, and even from as far north as Tyre and Sidon. The news about his miracles had spread far and wide, and vast numbers of people came to see him. 9 Jesus instructed his disciples to have a boat ready so the crowd would not crush him. 10 He had healed many people that day, so all the sick people eagerly pushed forward to touch him. 11 And whenever those possessed by evil* spirits caught sight of him, the spirits would throw them to the ground in front of him shrieking, "You are the Son of God!" 12 But Jesus sternly commanded the spirits not to reveal who he was.

13 Afterward Jesus went up on a mountain and called out the ones he wanted to go with him. And they came to him. 14 Then he appointed twelve of them and called them his apostles.* They were to accompany him, and he would send them out to preach, 15 giving them authority

NASB

the demons. ¹⁶And He appointed the twelve: Simon (to whom He gave the name Peter), ¹⁷and ªJames, the *son* of Zebedee, and John the brother of ªJames (to them He gave the name Boanerges, which means, "Sons of Thunder"); ¹⁸and Andrew, and Philip, and Bartholomew, and Matthew, and Thomas, and ªJames the son of Alphaeus, and Thaddaeus, and Simon the ᵇZealot; ¹⁹and Judas Iscariot, who betrayed Him.

3:12 ªLit *make Him known*   3:17 ªOr *Jacob*
3:18 ªOr *Jacob*   ᵇOr *Cananaean*

NLT

to cast out demons. ¹⁶These are the twelve he chose:

Simon (whom he named Peter),
¹⁷ James and John (the sons of Zebedee, but Jesus nicknamed them "Sons of Thunder"*),
¹⁸ Andrew,
Philip,
Bartholomew,
Matthew,
Thomas,
James (son of Alphaeus),
Thaddaeus,
Simon (the zealot*),
¹⁹ Judas Iscariot (who later betrayed him).

3:11 Greek *unclean;* also in 3:30.   3:14 Some manuscripts do not include *and called them his apostles.*   3:17 Greek *whom he named Boanerges, which means Sons of Thunder.*   3:18 Greek *the Cananean,* an Aramaic term for Jewish nationalists.

Some people see Jesus as only meek and mild, but most often, in fact, He was courageously bold, characterized by a daring, uncompromising manner that caused many people to be drawn to Him and others to despise Him. His following began to number in the thousands, which often happens when a leader is bold enough to speak the truth at the risk of angering the powerful elite.

I notice that as people get older they become bolder. As the years increase, they begin to realize they have less to lose by speaking the truth. Furthermore, with age comes knowledge and wisdom—for most people, not all—so older people often realize that the consequences of not telling the truth are greater than the downside of telling it. On the upside, smart people want to be around those who boldly speak the truth. We appreciate their courage. We admire them for being willing to stand alone when necessary and to say what other people are too timid to say.

Unfortunately, most people don't know how to handle popularity, and they become less willing to speak the truth for fear of offending followers and losing support. They also fall prey to what J. Oswald Sanders calls "the perils of leadership." In his book *Spiritual Leadership*, Sanders lists the perils of pride, egotism, jealousy, popularity, infallibility, indispensability, elation, depression, and even the potential for disqualification.[28]

Helmut Thielicke, in reflecting upon the work of Charles H. Spurgeon, a great preacher of the nineteenth century, asserted,

> Success exposes a man to the pressure of people and thus tempts him to hold on to his gains by means of "fleshly" methods and practices, and to let himself be ruled wholly by the dictatorial demands of incessant expansion. Success can go to my head, and will unless I remember that it is God who accomplishes his work, that he can continue to do so without my help, and that he will be able to make out with other means whenever he "cuts me down to size."[29]

A quick survey of Jesus' ministry so far reveals a rapidly expanding movement forming behind Him (1:18, 20, 28, 33, 37, 45; 2:2, 13). People from Galilee and far beyond flocked to see the healing rabbi and to hear Him preach with authority. Many brought with them their needs and expectations. He knew that most in the crowd were fickle; they wanted what He could give them to fill their bellies or ease their pain. The pressures mounted, but Jesus was no ordinary leader.

— 3:7-8 —

The Greek term for "withdrew" (3:7; *anachōreō* [402]) also has the sense of "retreated from battle" (as in the *Iliad* and in Josh. 8:15 in the Septuagint). In Mark's narrative, this scene immediately follows the climax of the previous segment, in which Jesus' confrontation with the Pharisees sparked a conspiracy to kill Him. That Mark didn't use the word "immediately" suggests that Jesus withdrew from direct conflict after a period of time. While not afraid of confrontation, Jesus evidently saw direct conflict as counterproductive to His mission at that time. This appears to be the same retreat described in Luke 6:12-13.

Jesus withdrew to "the sea," which is of course the Sea of Galilee. With a lead on the crowds, Jesus and His disciples gained a little solitude there. At this point in Jesus' ministry, the sound of silence would have been rare to these busy men. I often wonder what they talked about, if they spoke at all. This kind of solitude could only last a few hours at most. For real seclusion, Jesus headed for the hill country on the northeastern shore of the sea.

Jesus' fame had spread throughout Israel, and Mark names several regions from which multitudes came to see Him. These regions, when pieced together, comprise all the land that Solomon had acquired when

Israel reached its peak. Some traveled from as far as one hundred miles away, a five-day journey for able-bodied travelers. Who knows how long the infirm journeyed to see Jesus?

— 3:9-10 —

As a practical concern, Jesus instructed His closest disciples to have a boat prepared for launch. While He was moved by compassion to heal the sick, cleanse those with leprosy, and cast out demons, He came for a greater purpose: to proclaim the gospel. As soon as healing began to infringe upon and compromise His preaching ministry, He made adjustments. When the crush around Him became too restrictive, He climbed aboard a boat, pushed out a short distance, and used the shoreline as a natural amphitheater.

Many leaders crave attention and could never have too many followers, but Jesus maintained a careful balance between popularity and effectiveness. His growing popularity aided His ministry, giving Him greater opportunity to spread His message—"The time is fulfilled, and the kingdom of God is at hand; repent and believe in the gospel" (1:15). But there comes a time when popularity begins to hinder effective ministry. Curiosity seekers and courtiers jostle to be close to the famous figure; meanwhile, those with the greatest need to hear the gospel are pushed to the periphery and wander off, not knowing what they're missing.

— 3:11-12 —

While humanity struggled with Jesus' divine identity and was slowly coming to terms with the mounting evidence—miraculous abilities, authoritative teaching, power over demons—the minions of Satan knew exactly who He was. Jesus wanted His followers to receive Him as the Son of God, but not on the testimony of demons. Furthermore, He had a carefully programmed message that progressively revealed truth according to a schedule. Therefore, He wouldn't allow demons to continue calling Him the Son of God. He shut them down (see comments on 1:23-26; 1:32-34; and 1:43-44).

— 3:13-19 —

Mark's narrative shifts scenes, possibly rewinding the chronology between 3:12 and 3:13. In response to the increasing pressure of ministry, Jesus had taken steps to multiply His ministry capacity. First, He withdrew to "the mountain" (3:13). The term is singular, unlike other instances in which the translation would be "mountains" or "hill coun-try." Which particular mountain is unclear. We may therefore conclude that the specific location is not an important detail.

Mark highlights three details that are important. First, Jesus sum-moned those whom He wanted. Being sovereign, He makes decisions based on His own perfect judgment. He need not explain His reasoning to anyone. Second, those whom Jesus called responded and came to Him. The strong implication of choice on the part of the men does not compromise Christ's sovereign control. Third, Jesus appointed those He called.

Mark's use of Greek in 3:14 follows a Semitic idiom, literally saying "He *made* twelve." When one is "made" in this sense, he or she receives authority to carry out a designated role or duty. Robert Coleman puts it well in his work *The Master Plan of Evangelism*.

> His concern was not with programs to reach the multitudes, but with men whom the multitudes would follow. Remarkable as it may seem, Jesus started to gather these men before he ever organized an evangelistic campaign or even preached a sermon in public. Men were to be his method of winning the world to God.
>
> The initial objective of Jesus' plan was to enlist men who could bear witness to his life and carry on his work after he returned to the Father.[30]

He could have called 120 people. He could have called twelve hundred. For those of us impressed with numbers, we might think, *Why didn't He call five thousand or more people?* He selected only twelve because He knew the work could begin with only twelve. Moreover, pouring Himself into more than a dozen men would tax His human limita-tions, given His intense agenda. Having bound the voluntary use of His divine attributes, such as omnipotence and omnipresence, Jesus was constrained by the same twenty-four-hour day that we find so lim-iting today.

Jesus selected twelve ordinary, average men. None came with im-pressive credentials. They were Galileans, many of them fishermen, most from the area surrounding Capernaum. They were literate and well-versed in the Old Testament Scriptures, thanks to the synagogue, but none of them could be called a scholar. By the end of their training under Jesus and the filling of the Holy Spirit, however, these ordinary disciples would become extraordinary apostles.

THE TWELVE			
Matthew 10:2-4	Mark 3:16-19	Luke 6:14-16	Acts 1:13
Simon (Peter)	Simon (Peter)	Simon (Peter)	Peter
Andrew James (son of Zebedee) John	James (son of Zebedee) John Andrew	Andrew James (son of Zebedee) John	John James (son of Zebedee) Andrew
Philip	Philip	Philip	Philip
Bartholomew Thomas Matthew	Bartholomew Matthew Thomas	Bartholomew Matthew Thomas	Thomas Bartholomew Matthew
James (son of Alphaeus)	James (son of Alphaeus)	James (son of Alphaeus)	James (son of Alphaeus)
Thaddaeus Simon (the Zealot) Judas Iscariot	Thaddaeus Simon (the Zealot) Judas Iscariot	Simon (the Zealot) Judas (son of James) Judas Iscariot	Simon (the Zealot) Judas (son of James) ----

Jesus called them, appointed them, empowered them, and then sent them out. Their ministry of preaching and casting out demons mirrored His own activity up to that point. The authority He gave them marks an important milestone in His ministry. It became the first indication that His plan to redeem the world and then rule as its King would not come to completion with His earthly ministry. Somehow, His disciples would factor heavily into His agenda.

APPLICATION: MARK 3:7-19

Radical Responses to Pressure

Let's turn from the first century to the twenty-first. Let's come now to where life crushes in on us. Let's come to where we find people sometimes expecting and demanding more than we have to give, when we find ourselves feeling overwhelmed. What does the Lord say about this?

First, *when life crushes in, that's when we're most often tempted to quit.* My dad used to say to me, "Son, it's always too early to quit. So get that word out of your vocabulary." But when life crushes in, we are tempted to quit. That's when we need to seek quiet solitude.

If you are diligent in your work and you give your best every day, then you should never apologize for taking time off or getting away. Your family and friends know you need the rest—in fact, they would all appreciate it if you'd take a little rest.

When you don't have enough rest you can feel like your life is falling down around you. You may be close to coming apart, and it isn't attractive. God designed our bodies to need rest, and He gave His covenant people one day in seven. In fact, He *commanded* them to lay aside work on a regular basis. In addition to the Sabbath, He built holidays and festivals into the national calendar. God knows you need time to rejuvenate.

Second, *when people expect more, we can become resentful.* It's easy to feel taken for granted when you've met deadlines and satisfied needs and accomplished goals and fulfilled reasonable expectations . . . and the demands keep coming.

When I ministered at a previous church, we held five services each and every Sunday: three in the morning, two at night. It was quite draining. One Sunday, a couple visited from another community, and they looked forward to a personal tour of the church by the pastor. Unfortunately, they came to the second evening service. They waited, and when I finally got to the end of the line, the time was about a quarter or a half past nine. And they said, "Well, we're looking forward to the tour."

I said, "Really? Who's gonna take you?"

"You are! You're the preacher. We've been looking forward to this for a long time."

I kindly replied, "You know what? I'm sorry—I just can't do it."

"You can't do what? You're the preacher here!"

"Actually, I don't do tours at half past nine on Sunday nights."

They left in a huff and wrote an angry letter. In my younger days, I would have taken that personally and probably would have worried what they thought of me or what they might say to their friends. With seasoning in ministry, however, I learned to know my limits and remember that I work for God.

When people expect more than He asks, we need to say, "That's enough." That might sound too simple, but—believe me—it's effective. When you say with gentle respect, "That's enough," most people accept your personal limitations. Those who don't will never be satisfied, no matter how much you labor.

Third, *when feeling overwhelmed, you inevitably start feeling sorry for yourself.* And self-pity rarely helps. In fact, it usually makes life appear worse than it is. There's a better response. When feeling overwhelmed, we need to apply ruthless trust.

After a morning service I had a mother approach me who was very disturbed over a situation at home. My heart went out to her as she described what was going on with a particularly difficult child. She described the situation and then went over it again. And she started from the beginning again, and then she revisited the details several times. Finally, I put my hand on her arm and said, "I cannot give you an answer. No one knows the answer. You want to fix this now-grown child of yours, but you can't. You can continue to exhaust yourself trying to change the situation with your emotions, but churning won't accomplish anything. You must trust God. Ruthlessly trust Him."

This isn't easy. But it's the only way. In fact, the more impossible the situation, the more ruthlessly you must trust God to do what is right—in His time and in His way. Each time a situation begins to churn your emotions, bring it back to the Lord in prayer, and leave it before Him.

I got this idea from Brennan Manning's book titled *Ruthless Trust.* Richard Foster writes in the foreword,

> When our children were young I would sometimes rise early on a Saturday morning and fix them pancakes for breakfast. It was all great fun—the broken eggs, the spilt milk, the batter and the chatter. They loved pancakes—even my pancakes—and they would wolf them down quickly. I would often watch in astonishment at their greedy eating. Not once did I see either of them slipping a few pancakes under the table, or stuffing some in their pockets thinking, "I don't know about Dad. Maybe there won't be any pancakes tomorrow and so I better get myself a little stash just in case." Not once did they ask me about the price of eggs or my ability to secure enough milk for tomorrow. No, as far as they were concerned there was an endless supply of pancakes. They lived, you see, in trust.[31]

You can trust your God with the things you cannot handle. If you could not, He would not be God. You can trust Him. He can handle it.

Misunderstood
MARK 3:20-35

NASB

20 And He came ᵃhome, and the crowd gathered again, to such an extent that they could not even eat ᵇa meal. 21 When His own ᵃpeople heard *of this*, they went out to take custody of Him; for they were saying, "He has lost His senses." 22 The scribes who came down from Jerusalem were saying, "He is possessed by ᵃBeelzebul," and "He casts out the demons by the ruler of the demons." 23 And He called them to Himself and began speaking to them in parables, "How can Satan cast out Satan? 24 If a kingdom is divided against itself, that kingdom cannot stand. 25 If a house is divided against itself, that house will not be able to stand. 26 If Satan has risen up against himself and is divided, he cannot stand, but ᵃhe is finished! 27 But no one can enter the strong man's house and plunder his property unless he first binds the strong man, and then he will plunder his house.

28 "Truly I say to you, all sins shall be forgiven the sons of men, and whatever blasphemies they utter; 29 but whoever blasphemes against the Holy Spirit never has forgiveness, but is guilty of an eternal sin"— 30 because they were saying, "He has an unclean spirit."

31 Then His mother and His brothers arrived, and standing outside they sent *word* to Him and called Him. 32 A crowd was sitting around Him, and they said to Him, "Behold, Your mother and Your brothers are outside looking for You." 33 Answering them, He said, "Who are My mother and My brothers?"

NLT

20 One time Jesus entered a house, and the crowds began to gather again. Soon he and his disciples couldn't even find time to eat. 21 When his family heard what was happening, they tried to take him away. "He's out of his mind," they said.

22 But the teachers of religious law who had arrived from Jerusalem said, "He's possessed by Satan,* the prince of demons. That's where he gets the power to cast out demons." 23 Jesus called them over and responded with an illustration. "How can Satan cast out Satan?" he asked. 24 "A kingdom divided by civil war will collapse. 25 Similarly, a family splintered by feuding will fall apart. 26 And if Satan is divided and fights against himself, how can he stand? He would never survive. 27 Let me illustrate this further. Who is powerful enough to enter the house of a strong man and plunder his goods? Only someone even stronger—someone who could tie him up and then plunder his house.

28 "I tell you the truth, all sin and blasphemy can be forgiven, 29 but anyone who blasphemes the Holy Spirit will never be forgiven. This is a sin with eternal consequences." 30 He told them this because they were saying, "He's possessed by an evil spirit."

31 Then Jesus' mother and brothers came to see him. They stood outside and sent word for him to come out and talk with them. 32 There was a crowd sitting around Jesus, and someone said, "Your mother and your brothers* are outside asking for you."

33 Jesus replied, "Who is my mother? Who are my brothers?"

NASB

³⁴Looking about at those who were sitting around Him, He said, "Behold My mother and My brothers! ³⁵For whoever does the will of God, he is My brother and sister and mother."

3:20 ªLit *into a house* ᵇLit *bread* 3:21 ªOr *kinsmen* 3:22 ªOr *Beezebul;* others read *Beelzebub* 3:26 ªLit *he has an end*

NLT

³⁴Then he looked at those around him and said, "Look, these are my mother and brothers. ³⁵Anyone who does God's will is my brother and sister and mother."

3:22 Greek *Beelzeboul;* other manuscripts read *Beezeboul;* Latin version reads *Beelzebub.* 3:32 Some manuscripts add *and sisters.*

Of all the problems in life, few are more disturbing and distressing than being misunderstood. When you try to defend yourself, you often find that things just get worse. Opinions set like concrete, and no matter what you say or do, nothing can alter others' perspectives. That sad, frustrating difficulty becomes even more grievous when it's in your own family.

If that rings true for you—if that approaches a place of deep pain for you—then this segment of Mark's Gospel will resonate deeply. Jesus experienced this same anguish. The example He set in His response to His immediate family will be helpful as you come to terms with your family and the ways they don't understand you.

Amid the misunderstanding of family and friends, we read of allegations by the highly educated scribes from Jerusalem that Jesus was empowered by the devil. They made Him out to be the very face of evil, come to lead God's people astray. The disciples must have faced mixed emotions when confronted with such false allegations about their Master. By extension, they, too, were being characterized as instruments of evil. Jesus' unequivocal response shows the importance of clear thinking about one's identity and mission as a disciple.

— 3:20-21 —

This segment of the narrative employs a literary structure used often by Mark, a device some call a "story sandwich." Mark often wraps one story within another (see comments on 5:25-27; 6:7-32; 11:12-14). Here is the structure of this segment:

A. Jesus and His Family, Part 1 (3:20-21)
   B. Jesus and the Scribes (3:22-30)
Á. Jesus and His Family, Part 2 (3:31-35)

Very often, the two stories appear unrelated. Mark's structure prompts the reader to consider how each incident informs the other. The question we must ask is, "What do the stories have in common?"

Mark opens the segment with an illustration of how much Jesus' popularity had overtaken the region of Galilee and beyond. Jews from every quarter of Israel had heard of Jesus, and multitudes traveled great distances to have an audience with Him. Mark notes that Jesus and the twelve disciples—His newly formed inner circle—could not even enjoy a meal without interruption from the clamoring crowd (3:20).

"Home" is literally "into a house." Most likely, this was in the Lord's adopted city, Capernaum (cf. 2:1-2), His base of operations in Galilee. The Greek term rendered "again" indicates a return to a normal state or a previous activity. By this time, pressing crowds had become a routine event, no longer a novelty. Moreover, the Lord's fame began to worry His family.

The Greek phrase translated in the NASB as "His own people" (3:21) can be literally translated as "the [ones] from Him." The phrase refers to one's family or clan. For Jesus, this would be His mother, Mary; His brothers, James, Joseph (or Joses), Simon, and Judas (Jude) (Matt. 13:55; Mark 6:3); His unnamed sisters; and possibly His cousins. When His fame reached the tiny, remote outpost of Nazareth, they thought Jesus had lost His mind (cf. John 10:20).

Their attitude is curious. Luke's description of Mary's early experience indicates she knew that her baby would be the Messiah and that His miraculous conception had marked Him as the Son of God. Had her memory faded after the death of her husband? If not, did her testimony carry no weight in the family? Did they expect another kind of Messiah or fear that Jesus had wandered away from His divine mission?

It's a curious fact that we are unable to see greatness in the people we know best yet are most impressed by people we know little or nothing about. Perhaps, like most inhabitants of Jesus' hometown of Nazareth, Jesus' family members were unable to embrace Him as God and Savior after having known Him so long and so well as "Jesus the eldest brother." Mark doesn't elaborate, so we are left to speculate. All we know is that His family came to Capernaum to "take custody" of Him. The word means, as defined in one lexicon, "to take control of someone or something," "seize," or "control."[32] This is what a family does with someone who can no longer care for himself and is too deluded to see the truth. Jesus' family thought that He was crazy!

To be fair, Jesus' movement had all the marks of a personality cult. He gathered around Himself the outcasts and disenfranchised.

He challenged the accepted norms of religious and cultural tradition and called Himself the ultimate authority. He set up headquarters in Capernaum instead of Jerusalem. People were leaving their occupations to follow Him; some even sold all their possessions! From a distance, Jesus showed all the signs of a manic disorder. Unfortunately, His family was neither close enough to Jesus' intentions nor discerning enough to know better.

— 3:22 —

Mark's lens suddenly shifts from Jesus' family to a delegation of scribes from Jerusalem, Israel's religious capital. Scribes were experts in the Law, the first-century-Israel cross between today's attorneys and biblical scholars. As experts in all matters of Jewish custom and religion, they held great influence. These experts traveling from Jerusalem to Capernaum would have been like seminary professors from the city traveling to a rural church 120 miles away to confront an upstart Sunday school teacher who suddenly had a vast following.

No one denied that the supernatural played a central role in Jesus' ministry. So the religious authorities accused Jesus of drawing upon the power of "Beelzebul" to heal physical afflictions and to cast out demons. The phrase "were saying" is conjugated in the imperfect tense, which implies repeated or customary action. The scribes arrived in Capernaum with this charge on their lips, perhaps even before seeing the ministry of Jesus firsthand. They came in their religious garb with the authority of official religion behind them to denounce Jesus as a man possessed by the devil. They claimed that He had within Himself the foul presence of the demons and was Himself an unclean spirit. Interestingly, however, they did not say it to Him directly; they proclaimed this verdict in the court of public opinion.

Beelzebul was a Philistine deity. The name is a combination of *Baal* ("lord" or "master") and *zebul* ("of the height" or "of the house"). Some earlier Jewish literature, including the Old Testament, corrupts the name to *Baal* + *zebub*, which turned the name into a taunt: "Lord of the flies." This Philistine deity was primarily worshiped in the town of Ekron. In the Old Testament, one of Israel's kings, Ahaziah, fell ill and sent messengers to that city to "inquire of Baal-zebub, the god of Ekron, whether I will recover from this sickness" (2 Kgs. 1:2). They were turned back by Elijah, and because the king did not acknowledge the God of Israel, he died of his illness rather than receive the healing that could have been his by faith (2 Kgs. 1:16-17).

In the present passage, the scribes used this false god in a rhetorical device known as *metonymy*. This is a figure of speech in which one refers to a concept or a thing by the name of something intimately associated with it. For example, one might say, "Buckingham Palace issued a statement today," meaning that the queen has authorized a press release. In this case, the scribes used "Beelzebul" to mean Satan.

In saying that Jesus called upon Beelzebul for healing, the scribes accused Him of committing the same error as the faithless king Ahaziah—and implied that He would probably suffer the same fate. They failed, however, to account for the fact that multitudes received undeniable, complete, miraculous, instantaneous healing. Moreover, victims of demon possession had been released from their bondage. The Pharisees unknowingly underscored the nonsense of their own argument, saying, "He casts out the demons by [the agency of] the ruler of the demons."

— 3:23-27 —

Jesus called attention to the illogic of the Pharisees' accusation using three consecutive "if" statements and drawing upon two illustrations. With irrefutable logic, He proved that He could not have cast out demons by the agency of Satan.

Jesus' two word-pictures each call to mind a kind of community: a "kingdom" (3:24) and a "house" (3:25). A "house" refers to the people, property, reputation, and legacy of a family. For example, "the house of Jacob" refers to Jacob, his immediate family, his property, the family's standing in the community, and all of his descendants. When a house is said to fall, it comes to ruin in some irreparable way or becomes extinct. If family members murder one another, their house cannot stand; it will fall.

In the nineteenth century, the United States tore itself apart in civil war. Brothers in the South fought against brothers in the North. If not for the leadership of Abraham Lincoln, the nation would have ceased to exist as "the United States." A kingdom—or a nation—cannot stand if it wars with itself. Satan is certainly evil, but he's not stupid. It makes no sense at all for the devil to cast out himself!

In the final image, Satan is the "strong man" (3:27):

His house is the realm of sin, sickness, demon possession, and death. His possessions are people who are enslaved by one or more of these things, and demons are his agents who carry out his diabolical activity. No one can enter his realm to carry off (*diarpasai,* "plunder") his possessions unless he first binds the strong man (shows he is more powerful).[33]

Jesus claimed to be the one capable of binding this strong man, suggesting that He would now plunder Satan's house.

— 3:28-30 —

The paragraph break between 3:27 and 3:28 is meaningful. The scribes became mute; they had nothing to say in response. Jesus refuted the Pharisees' accusation as soundly and as logically as anyone could expect. Nevertheless, they remained unmoved. Clearly, they were predisposed to finding fault with Jesus, so He did not try to reason with unreasonable people. He instead issued a grave warning, which in their case proved to be a solemn condemnation. This is often referred to as "the unpardonable sin," a declaration that has been the cause of great angst among believers.

Jesus opened with a helpful reassurance: "All sins shall be forgiven the sons of men, and whatever blasphemies they utter" (3:28). This is a relief for those of us who didn't stop sinning the moment we trusted in Christ, and it's especially reassuring for those who have expressed anger against God in the face of deep distress. The apostle John eased the fears of persecuted Christians when he wrote, "If we say that we have no sin, we are deceiving ourselves and the truth is not in us. If we confess our sins, He is faithful and righteous to forgive us our sins and to cleanse us from all unrighteousness" (1 Jn. 1:8-9).

"All" means *all*. In other words, there is no sin that shall not be forgiven. So what do we make of the contrasting conjunction "but" in Mark 3:29? How does the exception stand alongside the "all"? Jesus classified "blasphemy against the Holy Spirit" as an "eternal sin." This is a sin that goes with the guilty person to his or her grave and beyond.

"Blasphemy" can be described as "defiant irreverence." One speaks blasphemy when denigrating another or seeking to do damage to the subject's reputation. This would include insolent language directed against God, defamation, railing, cursing, and reviling. In the case of the scribes, blasphemy included attributing the acts of the Holy Spirit to the work of Satan. Although not in so many words, they said the Spirit of God was an unclean spirit.

If this blasphemy is ever acknowledged as sin, it can be forgiven (3:28). Sin becomes unpardonable when the guilty one rejects the path that leads to pardon, continues in rebellion, and refuses to bow in submission before God. Therefore, a person receiving the penalty of the "unpardonable sin" has condemned himself. This sin is a chronically rebellious and continuing attitude, not a single act. The scribes condemned themselves in this way because, even after Jesus conclusively disproved their allegation, "they were saying, 'He has an unclean spirit'" (3:30). The imperfect tense indicates continuing action; against all reason, they persisted in their blasphemy.

— 3:31-32 —

With the warning of Jesus hanging ominously in the air, Mark shifts the narrative lens back to the Lord's mother and brothers. They traveled to Capernaum intending to "take custody" of Jesus, presuming Him to be deluded by madness (3:21). While they didn't go as far as the rebellious scribes, they came dangerously close to blaspheming the Holy Spirit. When they arrived at the home where Jesus was ministering, they couldn't speak with Him directly. Mark 3:20 suggests that the gathered crowd had become impenetrable.

— 3:33-35 —

Jesus was never antifamily. His remarks should not be interpreted as suggesting that He thought little of family relationships. His ancient Near Eastern audience, who considered the family bond an inviolate sacred trust, understood that the rhetorical question (3:33) was intended to make a point. A decision to believe the gospel and become a citizen of God's kingdom is not a matter of degrees; you're either in God's kingdom or you remain loyal to the earthly dominion of evil. There is no middle ground. To follow Christ requires a willingness to leave all if necessary—even one's family. Today, many in the Middle East make this difficult choice, knowing they will be ostracized by their family and community and quite possibly face physical violence for accepting Jesus as Savior and King.

Jesus looked at the people surrounding Him, many of whom had left everything to follow their Messiah, to become citizens of His kingdom. He regarded them as His true family. They shared the same new birth, born into the family of God through faith in the God-man, Jesus. Eventually, with the coming of the Holy Spirit in the book of Acts, they would receive a common hunger for righteousness, and they would share the mind of God.

Notice, however, that Jesus gave a very specific qualification to identify those He considered true family: "whoever *does* the will of God" (3:35, emphasis added). While trust establishes this kindred bond with

Christ, and faith unites His followers as brothers and sisters, true members of His family share the same birthmark: obedience. It is visible. It is active. It is deliberate. It is distinctive. We may claim to be members of God's family, but *doing* the will of God identifies us without words.

APPLICATION: MARK 3:20-35
Managing Misunderstanding

Those who have struggled to live as disciples of Jesus Christ among unbelieving family and friends know the kind of misunderstanding Jesus Himself experienced. We understand the often excruciating tension we feel as we're pulled in two directions—honoring our natural family on the one hand but honoring our supernatural family on the other. We're born into one, born again into the other. And because we share that common new birth into the family of God, we share spiritual priorities with them that don't always sit well with our natural family and friends. We often find ourselves closer to those who hunger and thirst for righteousness than to our own blood brothers or sisters. We have a greater allegiance to a heavenly Father we've never seen with our eyes than we do to our earthly father and mother. This can quickly lead to conflicting perspectives, priorities, and pursuits.

Managing the misunderstanding that comes from unbelieving (or, in some cases, less committed) family and friends is a delicate issue. On the one hand, we don't want to turn our backs on our natural families, severing earthly relationships and slamming the door to evangelism. On the other hand, we can't disobey our Lord and Savior in a desperate effort to honor our father and mother or please our friends and family. Often, decisions need to be made. Hard decisions that can affect relationships. Decisions that call for supernatural wisdom.

How do we handle this? Let me unpack three simple statements that will give us some guidance as we seek to manage those times when family and friends misunderstand us.

First, *face it*. Realize that not all family members or friends who don't know Christ will be able to understand your devotion to Him. In fact, they will often remain very concerned about you. They'll try to figure you out. Out of genuine—but misguided—love for you, they'll plead their case, trying to win you away from the "cult" you've joined or soften your "extremism." You need to recognize the fact that those who have not experienced new birth in Christ can only come so far in understanding the spiritual relationships you now experience. Face it.

Second, *accept it.* Don't fight it. Don't try to force your perspectives, priorities, and pursuits on them. You can't force them into believing or even accepting your own convictions. That's the work of the Holy Spirit. You're the believer. They're not. Accept the fact that until the Lord turns their hearts around, they won't grasp the joy, the zeal, the delight, and the motivation you have for life. They won't understand your new Christian friends and new spiritual family. They may even begin to be a little jealous of the new company you keep. Their attitude toward you and your faith is out of your control. You can't change it. Accept it.

Third, *adjust to it.* Live your faith, pray for the faithless. Be ready to share Christ with them when the moment is right, but don't do things to push them away. Don't go out of your way to alienate them with a barrage of spiritual emails, gospel-embedded text messages, constant invitations to church events, or hidden gospel tracts under their pillows or taped to the bathroom mirrors. Don't force mealtime prayers on them. Embrace the new reality that you now live with genuine commitments to both your natural family and the supernatural family of God. Adjust to it.

I don't mean to give the impression that managing misunderstanding is easy. It takes a lifetime of negotiating an internal tug-of-war. But that's part of living *in* the world yet not *of* the world (John 17:14-19). We need God's strength to face this reality, to accept it, and to adjust to it. And we need His wisdom to honor our heavenly family without constantly dishonoring our earthly family. We need His help to know where to take a stand that may alienate unbelieving friends and demonstrate our commitment to our true Lord and Savior, Jesus Christ.

DISCIPLES CULLED
(MARK 4:1–8:38)

There are two ways a king of one realm might take control of another: politics or conquest. The first method finds people in positions of power or influence who are dissatisfied with the status quo and have become receptive to change. A clever politician will seek to win their sympathies and cultivate enough popularity to overthrow the existing regime and take over in a bloodless revolution. Jesus Christ is not that kind of king.

People often mistake the Lord for a peaceful politician seeking to mount a bloodless revolution on earth. That's because they misunderstand the current state of affairs in two respects. First, the world is not ruled by humanity; ours is not a democracy in which people hold the reins of power. The world is a dictatorship in which Satan is "the prince of the power of the air" (Eph. 2:2). Fallen humanity is held sway by a delusion that men and women have absolute autonomy to think and act as they desire. The fact is, however, they are unwitting victims of that enemy of God, "the spirit that is now working in the sons of disobedience" (Eph. 2:2).

The first misconception leads to a second: that Jesus came to win our sympathies and cultivate enough popularity to overthrow the existing regime so that He may become our king. Humanity is not in charge of this world; we are held captive in it. It is worth repeating: Jesus didn't come to mount a bloodless revolution; He came to liberate us by force from Satan's dominion. Jesus is not—nor ever has been—a politician; He's a conqueror. When we read about Jesus in the Gospels, we are seeing the first phase of God's conquest of planet Earth. The Son of God came first as an emissary of peace, offering all of humanity the opportunity to defect, to reject Satan's dominion of evil, and to embrace Jesus as our Savior-King. The book of Revelation reveals the second phase—the actual conquest—in which Jesus returns, not as an emissary of peace but as a Warrior-King, defeating and destroying Satan and all who remain loyal to his dark dominion.

When we view the first advent of Jesus Christ from this perspective, it becomes clear why He rejected popularity. He did not want His ministry to be mistaken for a political movement. His message was not, "Join me, and together we will change the world." He proclaimed instead, "The time is fulfilled, and the kingdom of God is at hand; repent and believe in the gospel" (Mark 1:15). His message was a warning: *Repent and be on the right side when My kingdom comes!*

In the first section of Mark's Gospel (1:1–3:35), Jesus called people to become His followers, using His miraculous power strategically to amplify His gospel message. Eventually, He selected from the multitudes twelve men to join an inner circle of disciples, men He would train to advance His ministry and implement phase one of His divine conquest

KEY TERMS IN MARK 4:1-8:38

akouō (ἀκούω) [191] "to hear," "to heed," "to pay attention"
While the Gospel of Mark was written for the benefit of a primarily Gentile audience, the Jewish emphasis on *hearing* the Word of God dominates the narrative. The Shema, Israel's iconic statement of faith, begins "Hear, O Israel! The LORD is our God, the LORD is one!" (Deut. 6:4). Throughout this Gospel, Jesus calls for people to hear, to listen, and to heed His proclamation to repent and to believe the good news. But only those who have willing ears will hear.

mathētēs (μαθητής) [3101] "disciple," "student"
A *mathētēs* subjects oneself to a process of becoming familiarized with experiencing, learning, or receiving direction about something. In early writings, this usually implied the aid of another person; as the term fully developed, it was inconceivable for one to be a learner without a guide or a master. The term is used to refer to the disciples of rabbis and those of John the Baptizer, the Pharisees, and Moses (e.g., Mark 2:18; John 9:28). Although we often refer to the twelve apostles as the "twelve disciples," it is important to recognize that this term often refers to all of Jesus' followers (Mark 2:15).

parabolē (παραβολή) [3850] "parable," "figure," "illustrative comparison"
This word has the basic sense of "set beside" or "stand beside," with the idea that two concepts, stories, or ideas should be placed beside each other to draw out comparisons. In teaching, a parable is a story intended to illustrate a spiritual or moral truth. Usually a parable uses everyday images and scenarios familiar to most listeners and is intended to illustrate a bigger picture. As such, the incidental details are intended to make the story vivid, not to communicate detailed, hidden truths like an allegory.

parakaleō (παρακαλέω) [3870] "to urge," "to implore," "to encourage," "to comfort"

Of all the New Testament writers, Mark's use of this term is the simplest and least adorned with theological meaning. For John, Luke, and Paul, the term takes on a specialized meaning, carrying the idea of standing alongside someone in order to provide counsel, courage, comfort, hope, and positive perspective. For Mark, the word means simply "to implore" or "to beg." Throughout this section especially, Jesus is "implored" by one person after another to exercise His authority in a favorable way.

syniēmi (συνίημι) [4920] "to understand," "to comprehend"

The literal meaning of this verb is "to bring together." A similar term, *symballō* [4820], means "to throw together" or "to bring together." Both words bring to mind the process of arranging the pieces of a jigsaw puzzle. *Syniēmi* suggests that the solution to the puzzle has been found. The results are accurate perception, understanding, and comprehension. In today's terms, we would say someone "gets it." Very often in Mark, the Lord's audience listens, but they fail to understand.

of planet Earth. In this section (4:1–8:38), Jesus begins to winnow the multitudes, deliberately separating true followers from curiosity seekers and revolutionaries-in-waiting. Consequently, His manner of teaching changes, attracting those faithful disciples with "ears to hear" (4:9, 23; 7:16; 8:18) while repelling everyone else. Those remaining would not be called on to carry out tasks that would make them popular and draw accolades from society—rather, they would become targets of the worldly dominion their Master was overthrowing.

Souls in Soil
MARK 4:1-20

NASB

¹He began to teach again by the sea. And such a very large crowd gathered to Him that He got into a boat in the sea and sat down; and the whole crowd was by the sea on the land. ²And He was teaching them many things in parables, and was saying to them in His teaching, ³"Listen *to this!* Behold, the sower went out to

NLT

¹Once again Jesus began teaching by the lakeshore. A very large crowd soon gathered around him, so he got into a boat. Then he sat in the boat while all the people remained on the shore. ²He taught them by telling many stories in the form of parables, such as this one:

³"Listen! A farmer went out to

sow; ⁴as he was sowing, some *seed* fell beside the road, and the birds came and ate it up. ⁵Other *seed* fell on the rocky *ground* where it did not have much soil; and immediately it sprang up because it had no depth of soil. ⁶And after the sun had risen, it was scorched; and because it had no root, it withered away. ⁷Other *seed* fell among the thorns, and the thorns came up and choked it, and it yielded no crop. ⁸Other *seeds* fell into the good soil, and as they grew up and increased, they yielded a crop and produced thirty, sixty, and a hundredfold." ⁹And He was saying, "He who has ears to hear, ᵃlet him hear."

¹⁰As soon as He was alone, ᵃHis followers, along with the twelve, *began* asking Him *about* the parables. ¹¹And He was saying to them, "To you has been given the mystery of the kingdom of God, but those who are outside get everything in parables, ¹²so that WHILE SEEING, THEY MAY SEE AND NOT PERCEIVE, AND WHILE HEARING, THEY MAY HEAR AND NOT UNDERSTAND, OTHERWISE THEY MIGHT RETURN AND BE FORGIVEN."

¹³And He said to them, "Do you not understand this parable? How will you understand all the parables? ¹⁴The sower sows the word. ¹⁵These are the ones who are beside the road where the word is sown; and when they hear, immediately Satan comes and takes away the word which has been sown in them. ¹⁶In a similar way these are the ones on whom seed was sown on the rocky *places,* who, when they hear the word, immediately receive it with joy; ¹⁷and they have no *firm* root in themselves, but are *only* temporary; then, when affliction or persecution

plant some seed. ⁴As he scattered it across his field, some of the seed fell on a footpath, and the birds came and ate it. ⁵Other seed fell on shallow soil with underlying rock. The seed sprouted quickly because the soil was shallow. ⁶But the plant soon wilted under the hot sun, and since it didn't have deep roots, it died. ⁷Other seed fell among thorns that grew up and choked out the tender plants so they produced no grain. ⁸Still other seeds fell on fertile soil, and they sprouted, grew, and produced a crop that was thirty, sixty, and even a hundred times as much as had been planted!" ⁹Then he said, "Anyone with ears to hear should listen and understand."

¹⁰Later, when Jesus was alone with the twelve disciples and with the others who were gathered around, they asked him what the parables meant.

¹¹He replied, "You are permitted to understand the secret* of the Kingdom of God. But I use parables for everything I say to outsiders, ¹²so that the Scriptures might be fulfilled:

'When they see what I do,
    they will learn nothing.
When they hear what I say,
    they will not understand.
Otherwise, they will turn to me
    and be forgiven.'*"

¹³Then Jesus said to them, "If you can't understand the meaning of this parable, how will you understand all the other parables? ¹⁴The farmer plants seed by taking God's word to others. ¹⁵The seed that fell on the footpath represents those who hear the message, only to have Satan come at once and take it away. ¹⁶The seed on the rocky soil represents those who hear the message and immediately receive it with joy. ¹⁷But since they don't have deep roots, they don't last long. They fall away

NASB arises because of the word, immediately they ªfall away. ¹⁸And others are the ones on whom seed was sown among the thorns; these are the ones who have heard the word, ¹⁹but the worries of the ªworld, and the deceitfulness of riches, and the desires for other things enter in and choke the word, and it becomes unfruitful. ²⁰And those are the ones on whom seed was sown on the good soil; and they hear the word and accept it and bear fruit, thirty, sixty, and a hundredfold."

4:9 ªOr *hear!;* or *listen!*   **4:10** ªLit *those about Him*
4:17 ªLit *are caused to stumble*   **4:19** ªOr *age*

NLT as soon as they have problems or are persecuted for believing God's word. ¹⁸The seed that fell among the thorns represents others who hear God's word, ¹⁹but all too quickly the message is crowded out by the worries of this life, the lure of wealth, and the desire for other things, so no fruit is produced. ²⁰And the seed that fell on good soil represents those who hear and accept God's word and produce a harvest of thirty, sixty, or even a hundred times as much as had been planted!"

4:11 Greek *mystery.*   **4:12** Isa 6:9-10 (Greek version).

As a preacher, I must continually find ways to overcome a pervasive spiritual disability. Many who come to hear the preaching of God's Word are "hard of listening." They have healthy hearing, perfectly functioning ears. They can receive the sounds that come from my mouth in the pulpit. Yet they do not *hear*. To help them overcome this disability, I spend many hours honing each message so that it is razor sharp in three respects: It must be accurate, it must be clear, and it must be practical. Even so, there are always some who simply *will not* hear.

As a young preacher, this used to undermine my confidence. I wondered how I had failed. Was it my logic? My use of illustrations? My delivery? These were all worthy questions that needed to be asked and answered, and I became a better preacher as a result. Still, even today, having logged more than ten thousand hours in the pulpit and countless more in preparation, I will not be able to get everyone to hear. I eventually accepted that I must be as accurate, clear, and practical as possible, but I cannot make people hear. It was doubly comforting to see that Jesus encountered the same spiritual disability when He preached. Rather than become preoccupied by this phenomenon, He used it to increase the effectiveness of His ministry.

In this parable about a sower and four kinds of soil, Jesus portrays four states of the human soul that result in a range of responses to the gospel. He did not make people listen, but He closed with a challenge (4:9) to overcome our spiritual disability—to really listen—in humble reliance on Him.

— 4:1 —

The Bay of Parables is a lovely little cove on the northern shore of the Sea of Galilee where tradition says Jesus taught the multitudes. The topography around the bay creates a natural amphitheater with the land sloping gently up to where grass and wildflowers grow in springtime. According to tests conducted by an archaeologist and a sound engineer, a single orator standing in a boat anchored off shore could be heard clearly by an audience of several thousand.[1] Earlier, Jesus had used this method when the crowds pressed in too close for Him to preach (3:9).

The traditional posture for teaching in the ancient Near East was sitting. Jesus took this informal posture when instructing His followers, who were joined by curiosity seekers, people in need of healing or cleansing, zealous troublemakers looking for someone to start a revolution, political malcontents hoping for economic change, and a number of Jesus' enemies. Scribes, Herodians, chief priests, and Sadducees listened to Jesus' teaching hoping to find political and religious ammunition in order to retaliate.

This particular lesson marks a distinct shift in the Gospel narrative. Jesus had used parables before, but His strategy changed. Appropriately, He explained the reason for His new approach in a parable.

— 4:2-4 —

A parable is a pithy story designed to illustrate a truth using familiar images or experiences.

Jesus grabbed the attention of His audience with the command "Listen to this!" (4:3). Parables were never really meant to be read; parables are stories meant to be told. If we listen carefully, the story will put the pieces together, enabling us to assemble a vivid truth in our minds. The Lord's command, "listen," comes from the Greek verb *akouō* [191], which appears in Mark's narrative only four times prior to this. The verb occurs forty times throughout the rest of the Gospel. Obviously, "hearing" becomes a key concept.

This parable concerns a farmer planting seed for a crop. In those days, farmers didn't plant wheat or other grain crops in rows like we see today. They broke the ground and softened the soil with a wooden plow and then scattered the seed by hand. Often they reversed the process, casting seed and then plowing it into the soil. The farmer would tie a bag to his waist and then sling the seed out with his hand. His field might be bordered on one side by a fencerow covered with thickets and

PARABLES

MARK 4:2

Of all the didactic tools available to a teacher, none has greater power to convey deep spiritual truths than the parable. And none has greater potential to confuse. That's why Jesus often chose the art of storytelling when teaching a mixed audience of disciples and detractors. In fact, parables comprise more than one third of Jesus' recorded sayings.[2]

The term "parable" is a cognate of the Greek word *parabolē* [3850]. The meaning has to do with "setting beside," with the intent that two things should be compared and then understood as similar. It therefore means "comparison." Unlike an allegory, in which the figurative people or things have direct, literal counterparts, a parable is intentionally less precise, focusing on a single big idea. Therefore we must avoid two tendencies when interpreting parables. First, we must guard against missing what is important in the hidden truth; second, we must resist the temptation to overanalyze every detail.

A parable is simply the art of teaching through narrative in such a way that the familiar sheds light on the unfamiliar. Common, everyday circumstances are used by the speaker to communicate things that are not familiar and may even be supernatural. They appear simple and obvious, but the truths they convey are neither (see comments on 12:1-12). Two factors make interpretation possible for the hearer.

First, *a willingness to understand.* An unteachable spirit will find it easy to twist a parable into nonsense and then use it to try to prove the teacher a fool. As a result, those who wanted to reject Jesus found more than enough justification in His parables.

Second, *spiritual discernment.* The parables of Jesus reveal truths that exist beyond the natural realm. His lessons cannot be accessed through scientific research. They must be revealed by someone able to transcend the natural world to comprehend the supernatural. Therefore, the listener must have the aid of the Holy Spirit to understand the parables of Jesus. Fortunately, the Lord has promised to teach anyone willing to learn.

Jesus used parables in mixed audiences because this unique form of story accomplished two important objectives: Parables repelled hostile skeptics while equipping serious disciples.

"He who has ears to hear, let him hear" (4:9; cf. 4:23; Luke 8:8; 14:35).

briar bushes and bounded on another by a footpath into town. Even when he tried to conserve seed, some seed landed where it couldn't grow.

Jesus described the fate of the seed using four different circumstances. In the first case, seed fell by the road where the farmer's plow could not soften the soil, leaving the seed vulnerable to birds (4:4). In this case, the seed never stood a chance; it was snatched away before it could germinate. This illustrates the effect of hardened soil.

— 4:5-7 —

Jesus described a second kind of soil as "rocky" (4:5). In such cases, just beneath a thin layer of topsoil was a slab of stone. Perfect for building— lousy for planting. Roots could not find enough depth to draw moisture and anchor the plant. The seeds showed initial promise, but soon succumbed to the scorching sun, withered up, and blew away.

Jesus described a third kind of soil as covered in thorns (4:7). These native plants were normally removed before planting, except along fences or hedges separating one field from another. When a farmer cast seed near the edge, some fell among the weeds, where it could not compete for sunlight and soil. If stalks survived, they would not receive enough nourishment to reproduce.

— 4:8-9 —

Farming is an investment. For each seed dropped into the soil, the sower hopes to receive many more in return. Seed that falls on good soil eventually multiplies the farmer's initial investment. A return of "thirty, sixty, and a hundredfold" (4:8) was considered an abundant harvest. A farmer could expect these returns in the fertile, rain-soaked valleys of Galilee; the return rate was more like tenfold in the dry, high-altitude climate of Judea to the south.

Having opened the parable with the command "Listen!" Jesus closed it with the enigmatic declaration, "He who has ears to hear, let him hear" (4:9). The statement alluded to two passages from Old Testament prophecy:

> Now hear this, O foolish and senseless people,
> Who have eyes but do not see;
> Who have ears but do not hear. (Jer. 5:21)

> Son of man, you live in the midst of the rebellious house, who have eyes to see but do not see, ears to hear but do not hear; for they are a rebellious house. (Ezek. 12:2)

In both cases, God was speaking through a prophet to warn Israel of their impending exile to Babylon. For hundreds of years, they ignored a long line of prophets who begged their nation to turn from idols, repent of sin, and return to the Law. A person who has "ears to hear but [does] not hear" is unwilling to listen to and heed such a message. This is a picture of stubborn rebellion. As the saying goes, "There are none so deaf as those who *will not* hear."

Jesus' warning said, in effect, "Let those who are not rebellious receive this teaching."

— 4:10-12 —

To underscore the fact that volition (the will), not cognition (the intellect), is the primary issue, Mark allows us to eavesdrop on a conversation between Jesus and His true disciples. They failed to understand many of His parables, not just "The Sower and Soils." Jesus gladly answered their questions; after all, He didn't speak in parables to confound those who genuinely wanted to learn.

His explanation of His motive can be unsettling, however. We're surrounded by people who want to do "seeker-friendly" this and "seeker-friendly" that, and I affirm them for the most part. I certainly don't want to make it difficult for people seeking Christ to find Him. I want our churches to be open, welcoming, winsome, attractive places for everyone, especially those who might be uncomfortable with church culture. "Seeker-friendly" sometimes goes too far, however. Some people begin to lose their Christian identity trying to accommodate people who are hostile to Christ, the gospel, and His church. In response to these, Jesus said, though not in so many words, "I deliberately make the truth unfriendly." Jesus used parables as a means of attracting and intriguing seekers while alienating and confusing adversaries.

Those who want to understand will ask questions; those who are predisposed to reject truth will deliberately and consistently misunderstand. Jesus described His adversaries (usually the most learned in the crowd) with an allusion to Isaiah 6:9-10, a reminder that the rebellious misconstrue the Word of God and then miss out on divine blessings.

— 4:13-15 —

Jesus' explanation of His parable provides us with an interpretive key to understand all of His parables. We find a correlation between certain elements of the story and the spiritual truths they symbolize, yet Jesus didn't attribute meaning to every detail. For example, He never identified the sower. It's not important to the story. He revealed, however, that the soil symbolizes people, because He wanted listeners to focus on themselves and to decide what kind of soil they will be.

He explained that the hard soil represents those who do not receive the Word of God, even for a moment. The Word never penetrates, and Satan strips them of the truth before it can germinate. These are the overtly rebellious hearers who are hard of listening.

— 4:16-17 —

The rocky-soil people receive the Word of God gladly but become disillusioned when troubles come their way. The Greek term rendered "fall away" (4:17) is *skandalizō* [4624]. It usually connotes tripping or falling. The shallow followers described by the seeds in the rocky soil stumble over difficult life circumstances. Perhaps they initially embraced Christ because they thought their problems would go away and life would be smooth sailing. When they discover the hardships of real discipleship, however, they fall away from the Word and grasp for some other quick fix. Note how Jesus describes them: "They have no firm root in themselves" (4:17).

— 4:18-19 —

Thorny-ground people are different from the shallow comfort seekers represented by the rocky soil. The Word of God takes root in them and begins to grow, but it cannot compete with their love of wealth. Anxieties steal their attention, and the desire to acquire more and more things distracts them from the Word, which is soon lost in the tangles of materialism. Note that Jesus didn't say the Word dies in them; it merely produces no fruit.

Perhaps this is reading too much into the parable, but it perfectly describes many American Christians, who embrace the Word of God and call themselves followers of Christ but never sacrifice anything significant. They merely add the Bible and Sunday sermons to their cluttered mental storeroom, along with money, possessions, and all the anxieties that accompany wealth. Years pass, and they never progress in their spiritual walk.

The "worries" Jesus had in mind (4:19) are cares associated with losing something we hold too dearly. That's the danger of material wealth: We too easily begin to think in terms of loss prevention. When we begin to fear the loss of money or possessions, our wealth begins to own us. But it doesn't have to be that way. There are many Christians who are fabulously wealthy but have not let their possessions become "worries." In terms of sacrifice, they are more generous than their middle-class peers, and they would be no less happy if God removed all their possessions.

— 4:20 —

Jesus closed His parable with a description of good-soil people. They not only hear the Word—they accept it. The Greek term *paradechomai* [3858], translated "accept," means "to acknowledge something as correct" or "to receive in a hospitable manner." These people receive the truth—even if they don't understand it completely—and give it a welcome place in their hearts. This describes the twelve disciples of Jesus, who didn't comprehend His parables but accepted His truth nonetheless. They welcomed the Word first, then they sought understanding.

• • •

With this episode, Mark sets the stage for this section of His narrative (4:1–8:38). In the first section (1:1–3:35), Jesus called all people to follow Him. Not all people, however, gathered around Jesus for the right reasons. Many wanted someone to keep them well-fed, wealthy, happy, and trouble free. Others hoped to find in Jesus a passionate revolutionary who would drive out the Romans and return Israel to the glory days of David and Solomon. The religious elite followed Jesus hoping to find ways to eliminate a man they considered a rival and a threat to their hold on power. But Jesus would not be fooled. He didn't come to be popular; He came to fulfill a very specific agenda, which He would reveal in the months to come.

APPLICATION: MARK 4:1-20

Choose Your Soil

Where do you find yourself in the Lord's word picture? He gave this illustration to help people determine what kind of soil they represent and then to decide what kind of soil they will be. The application in the first century is the same today: Choose your soil.

Are you a productive, persevering believer? If so, that doesn't mean you're perfect; it means you cling to the truth and seek to apply it consistently. You're open and honest, responsive to Scripture, pliable to the Holy Spirit, grateful for grace, and hungry for righteousness. You are growing toward maturity. This is ideal soil; stay planted here!

Are you a busy, preoccupied believer? When you look at the priorities of your life, do you see thorns choking out the teaching of Scripture? Do you allow the desire for affluence, comfort, power, position, or privilege to keep your relationship with Christ low on your list of priorities? Are you so involved in the pursuit of temporal happiness that anxiety keeps you distracted from spiritual concerns? Does your lack of contentment hinder you from experiencing peace within?

God is ready to hear your prayer. He's ready to transplant you to better soil . . . if you let Him.

Are you in the shallow soil of a superficial seeker? If so, you're rootless and unstable. You responded to an emotional appeal or followed a crowd or did something to please a friend, or you like the company you now keep, but it wouldn't take much to change your mind. You're a hearer, but not a doer. You're not really a believer. You're only slightly better off than the last kind of soil.

Are you the hard-hearted, stubborn one who has no interest in spiritual things? If that's you, a day will come when you'll regret your proud, self-willed attitude. Tragically, it'll be too late.

After the Teaching Comes the Testing
MARK 4:21-41

NASB

21 And He was saying to them, "A lamp is not brought to be put under a ᵃbasket, is it, or under a bed? Is it not *brought* to be put on the lampstand? 22For nothing is hidden, except to be revealed; nor has *anything* been secret, but that it would come to light. 23 If anyone has ears to hear, let him hear." 24 And He was saying to them, "Take care what you listen to. ᵃBy your standard of measure it will be measured to you; and more will be given you besides. 25 For whoever has, to him *more* shall be given; and whoever does not have, even what he has shall be taken away from him."

NLT

21 Then Jesus asked them, "Would anyone light a lamp and then put it under a basket or under a bed? Of course not! A lamp is placed on a stand, where its light will shine. 22For everything that is hidden will eventually be brought into the open, and every secret will be brought to light. 23 Anyone with ears to hear should listen and understand."

24Then he added, "Pay close attention to what you hear. The closer you listen, the more understanding you will be given*—and you will receive even more. 25 To those who listen to my teaching, more understanding will be given. But for those who are not listening, even what little understanding they have will be taken away from them."

NASB

26 And He was saying, "The kingdom of God is like a man who casts seed upon the soil; 27 and he goes to bed at night and gets up by day, and the seed sprouts and grows—how, he himself does not know. 28 The soil produces crops by itself; first the blade, then the head, then the mature grain in the head. 29 But when the crop permits, he immediately a puts in the sickle, because the harvest has come."

30 And He said, "How shall we a picture the kingdom of God, or by what parable shall we present it? 31 It is like a mustard seed, which, when sown upon the soil, though it is smaller than all the seeds that are upon the soil, 32 yet when it is sown, it grows up and becomes larger than all the garden plants and forms large branches; so that THE BIRDS OF THE a AIR can NEST UNDER ITS SHADE."

33 With many such parables He was speaking the word to them, so far as they were able to hear it; 34 and He did not speak to them without a parable; but He was explaining everything privately to His own disciples.

35 On that day, when evening came, He said to them, "Let us go over to the other side." 36a Leaving the crowd, they took Him along with them in the boat, just as He was; and other boats were with Him. 37 And there arose a fierce gale of wind, and the waves were breaking over the boat so much that the boat was already filling up. 38 Jesus Himself was in the stern, asleep on the cushion; and they woke Him and said to Him, "Teacher, do You not care that we are perishing?" 39 And He got up and rebuked the wind and said to the sea, "Hush, be still." And the wind died down and a it became perfectly calm. 40 And He said to them, "Why are you a afraid? Do you still have no faith?"

NLT

26 Jesus also said, "The Kingdom of God is like a farmer who scatters seed on the ground. 27 Night and day, while he's asleep or awake, the seed sprouts and grows, but he does not understand how it happens. 28 The earth produces the crops on its own. First a leaf blade pushes through, then the heads of wheat are formed, and finally the grain ripens. 29 And as soon as the grain is ready, the farmer comes and harvests it with a sickle, for the harvest time has come."

30 Jesus said, "How can I describe the Kingdom of God? What story should I use to illustrate it? 31 It is like a mustard seed planted in the ground. It is the smallest of all seeds, 32 but it becomes the largest of all garden plants; it grows long branches, and birds can make nests in its shade."

33 Jesus used many similar stories and illustrations to teach the people as much as they could understand. 34 In fact, in his public ministry he never taught without using parables; but afterward, when he was alone with his disciples, he explained everything to them.

35 As evening came, Jesus said to his disciples, "Let's cross to the other side of the lake." 36 So they took Jesus in the boat and started out, leaving the crowds behind (although other boats followed). 37 But soon a fierce storm came up. High waves were breaking into the boat, and it began to fill with water.

38 Jesus was sleeping at the back of the boat with his head on a cushion. The disciples woke him up, shouting, "Teacher, don't you care that we're going to drown?"

39 When Jesus woke up, he rebuked the wind and said to the waves, "Silence! Be still!" Suddenly the wind stopped, and there was a great calm. 40 Then he asked them, "Why are you afraid? Do you still have no faith?"

41 They became very much afraid and said to one another, "Who then is this, that even the wind and the sea obey Him?"

4:21 ªOr peck-measure   4:24 ªLit By what measure you measure   4:29 ªLit sends forth
4:30 ªLit compare   4:32 ªOr sky   4:36 ªOr Sending away   4:39 ªLit a great calm occurred
4:40 ªOr cowardly

41 The disciples were absolutely terrified. "Who is this man?" they asked each other. "Even the wind and waves obey him!"

4:24 Or The measure you give will be the measure you get back.

We're all on a learning curve in this thing called "life." Admittedly, some are a little further along than others, but we're all in a learning process. That learning process can be painful. It requires that we learn how to trust in the provision and protection of our heavenly Father rather than depend upon our own intuition, our own strength, our own will, our own way. That's what it means to cultivate faith. At the same time, we must conquer those things that would otherwise frighten us or cause us to act in disobedience. Ultimately, we hope to find such confidence in God that nothing can get the best of us and no fear can shake our trust in God. For that to happen, teaching is vital and testing is necessary.

This isn't popular preaching. Ours is a day of "feel-good theology" that erroneously teaches that God wants everybody happy—that our purpose in life is to find comfort and pleasure. The truth of the matter is that we have been called to a life of submission to the Father's will. In this calling, we will experience deep joy, though not necessarily comfort or happiness. We need strong teaching from the Scriptures, and we must endure severe tests along the way.

The tests of life, however, are not for God's benefit. He already knows what we're made of, where we are strong, and in what areas we need more development. The tests are always for us. Strong teaching followed by severe testing reveals the hard truth of our maturity. Very often we receive an A+ and our confidence grows. Other times, our failure reveals our need for spiritual growth, which the Lord is always faithful to nurture.

What is true for us was certainly true for the original Twelve. He called these men and began training them so they would carry on His ministry after His resurrection and ascension. They needed to be ready for all that life would throw at them, which meant their training would include occasional testing along the way. In this segment of Mark's narrative, the Twelve absorb some of the Lord's most memorable lessons and then face some of their worst fears.

— 4:21-23 —

The phrase "And He was saying to them" (4:21) includes a verb in the imperfect tense, which denotes repetitive or customary action. The pronoun "them" refers to the followers of Jesus, who numbered in the thousands (6:30-44; 8:1-10). As the Lord carried on an itinerant ministry of preaching and teaching, His inner circle of future apostles heard the same lessons over and over. Experts affirm that repetition is an indispensable tool for learning, and the Twelve needed to hear Jesus' message often in order to take it all in.

This first parable in the series concerns a disciple's responsibility to carry the light of divine truth—the gospel message—to the world. In biblical and other ancient literature, truth is often depicted as light. The same is true of the special manifestation of God's presence, which appeared in the form of a supernatural light called the *shekinah* (Exod. 3:1-3; 13:21-22; 19:18; 24:17). The apostle John depicted Jesus Christ as light coming into a dark world, which was his way of declaring that God Himself had come to earth (John 1:1-9). John's description of the new heaven and new earth reveals that those who serve God "will not have need of the light of a lamp nor the light of the sun, because the Lord God will illumine them" (Rev. 22:5). Therefore, Jesus Christ, the new kingdom, and the gospel message are all symbolized by the image of light. Consequently, Mark's Greek is awkward in this parable because he went out of his way to represent Jesus as the Light.

Jesus came to reveal God, to be the image of God in human flesh (2 Cor. 4:4; Col. 1:15). He not only *revealed* divine truth, but in coming to earth, He *embodied* truth as a human being. To see Jesus in the flesh was to see truth.

Having identified true disciples in the parable of the sower and the soils, Jesus illustrated the primary responsibility of a disciple in the parable of the lamp. He didn't call disciples so they would keep the gospel to themselves; Jesus expects His followers to hold high the Son of God so that all might benefit from divine truth. He said, in effect, "Hold Me up before the world so that all may see."

— 4:24-25 —

This saying of Jesus isn't a parable as much as an application. Some have mistakenly applied this saying to the subject of money or material wealth. That's because they completely ignore the context. Jesus had just commanded, "If anyone has ears to hear, let him hear" (4:23). This saying has to do with learning and one's disposition toward truth.

He warns His followers to be intentional in their learning and to be discerning in where they seek knowledge. Mark 4:24 says, literally, "Watch what you hear" (my translation). The Greek word *blepō* [991] can also mean "to observe" or "to pay close attention to." Here, it's the kind of watching a scientist does when running an experiment, or the kind of watching a sentry does when guarding a post. Here's why Jesus wants His followers to be discerning and deliberate in their quest for knowledge: intentional knowledge grows exponentially; the same is true for willful ignorance.

Exponential growth means that new knowledge is multiplied, not merely added. Those who seek truth from the Author of truth will grow very wise, often very rapidly. On the other hand, people who listen to false teachers—men and women who say what people want to hear— remain stupid and, quite frankly, grow dumber by the day!

— 4:26-32 —

Having identified true disciples in the parable of the sower and the soils and having explained their responsibility in the parable of the lamp, Jesus then described how God's kingdom would come to earth. Bear in mind that He described the coming kingdom of God against a backdrop of great expectations. The Jewish people had been waiting for the Messiah, and they expected Him to lead Israel into a Hebrew renaissance in which they would revive the kingdom and restore the golden era of David and Solomon. They dreamed of expelling Rome and hoped the Messiah would bring them the same power and prosperity they once enjoyed, only magnified and multiplied. But that was the old covenant; God had a new covenant in mind. The new kingdom would build upon the old in order to provide God's people more than mere temporal power and material wealth. Moreover, it would not occur overnight.

Jesus compared the kingdom to a farmer's crop that He was planting and over time God would grow. Like a field of wheat, it gradually becomes mature and—at the right time— produces fruit. Eventually the day comes when the farmer gathers in the crop.

He also compared the kingdom to a mustard seed, an extremely tiny germ that produces an unusually large bush. Whereas the previous parable illustrates *gradual* growth, the parable of the mustard seed illustrates *surprising* growth. In the beginning, Jesus began as a movement of one. After His death, resurrection, and ascension, a group of about one hundred became Spirit-filled witnesses who, within a single generation, multiplied and carried the gospel throughout much of the known world.

The question we must answer in light of these parables is this: *Has the kingdom of God come to earth?* The answer is yes . . . and no.

While Jesus brought His kingdom to earth and has been anointed King, He has not yet been crowned, and His literal, earthly, visible kingdom has not yet been established. A good illustration can be found in the Old Testament, which describes the painful rise of one of Jesus' ancestors, King David. Samuel anointed the shepherd boy as King Saul's replacement. Later, the Holy Spirit left the former king to fill David (1 Sam. 16:13-14). Even so, it would be more than a dozen years before David literally wore the crown and actually sat upon the throne, receiving the recognition of the nation. During this waiting period, David lived in the rugged wilderness south of Jerusalem, leading a motley band of outlaws and evading the wrath of Saul, who refused to relinquish a throne that was no longer his to occupy (1 Sam. 22–30).

Though legitimately the king of Israel, and recognized as king by some, David's kingdom had not yet been established.

Jesus came to earth to inaugurate His kingdom, and He is recognized by some as King. His citizens are encouraged to adopt new kingdom culture, though the consummation of His kingdom is yet future. The book of Revelation describes that future time when the King returns in power to obliterate Satan's dominion of evil and then establish His everlasting rule. The kingdom has come in one sense . . . but it has not yet been established and recognized on earth. But do not lose heart. Someday in the future, Jesus will reign as King of kings and Lord of lords!

— 4:33-34 —

Mark closes this segment with a summary of this phase of Jesus' earthly ministry. The Lord continued to speak in parables, thereby winnowing true followers from false disciples. Those with "ears to hear" (4:23) gained spiritual knowledge and grew wise in kingdom living. Those who remained willfully ignorant or were perpetually distracted by temporal concerns eventually drifted away with the wind. Meanwhile, Jesus steadfastly prepared the Twelve for ministry after His ascension.

— 4:35-38 —

As any student knows, teaching always leads to testing. The purpose of a test is to demonstrate mastery of a subject or skill and to reveal areas needing improvement. As Jesus conducted His ministry of teaching and preaching, the Twelve heard the Lord's lessons many times over. After hearing the same discourses repeated dozens of times, they undoubtedly could recite them and convince an audience they understood every word. But had they truly learned anything? A test would tell all.

On one particular day, Jesus, the Twelve, and an unknown number of other followers climbed into a boat and began a journey across the Sea of Galilee. Mark's description suggests they traveled from the Bay of Parables southeast to a region near the southern shore known as Gerasa, of which Gadara was a principal city.

The Sea of Galilee lies 686 feet below sea level at the bottom of a rift between the Arabian Desert and the Mediterranean Sea. Winds unexpectedly whip over the mountains and down the gorge, stirring turbulence so suddenly and violently that modern-day captains of powered vessels keep a close check on weather reports. So we can only imagine the terror felt by people in the crude, small sailboats of the first century.

Mark tells us that several boats crossed the Sea of Galilee, probably indicating that more of the disciples than just the Twelve were crossing with Him. The vessel used by Jesus and at least some of His disciples, however, may have been a large trade vessel rather than one of the small boats regularly used for fishing. The craft seems to have been large enough to allow Jesus relative privacy below deck in the cargo hold. Mark states that He was in the stern, on a cushion (4:38), oblivious to the wind and waves. During their voyage, the waves overwhelmed the crew and began to fill the ship.

In any case, the disciples became terrified, and for good reason. They didn't overreact. Many were seasoned fishermen, accustomed to the violent temper of this particular sea. They understood better than most the gravity of their situation. I have little doubt most of us would have shared their panic. The question they put to the Lord, however, reveals their spiritual immaturity. They understood the sea and its dangers, but they still did not know the man they had been following. Not really. This test exposed their lack of understanding.

— 4:39-40 —

When Jesus emerged from the hold of the ship, He exercised divine power over His creation (cf. Col. 1:16). The word for "rebuke" (see Mark 4:39) means "to express strong disapproval of someone," "reprove," or "censure."[3] Jesus hushed the storm like a parent reprimands a toddler throwing a tantrum. Unlike a rebellious child, however, the wind and waves obeyed. Immediately.

Jesus then gently rebuked His followers with two penetrating questions. "Why are you afraid?" (4:40) suggests that they had behaved unreasonably. In the normal, natural sense, they had every reason to fear. "Do you still have no faith?" indicates that they had neglected to account for the presence of God with them. They failed the test because they had not yet come to terms with Jesus' identity.

Jesus had said, "Let us go over to the other side" (4:35), not "Let us go to the bottom." How could they count on getting to the other side? They had God in the boat. They should have understood that when God is with you, nothing can harm you. Sinking is impossible! This display of divine power, however, gave them a new appreciation for Jesus' presence and power. The disciples had seen His miraculous healing power and His complete command over demonic forces, but this was something more. The Old Testament describes the ability of some prophets to heal the sick, cleanse lepers, and even raise the dead. But Jesus displayed a kind of power reserved for God alone (Pss. 89:8-9; 104:5-9; 106:8-9; 107:23-32). They had just come to know Him as the Messiah—a prophet-king sent by God to lead them. Their fear and His display of power revealed a new facet of His identity. The test also presented them with a new opportunity for spiritual growth.

— 4:41 —

Ironically, after seeing Jesus' power, the disciples became more afraid than when they were battling the wind and waves. Mark's Greek describes the kind of respectful awe people experience when confronted by a manifestation of God. The disciples' rhetorical question reveals their need for growth. They had already learned so much, but their intellectual and spiritual journey had just begun.

APPLICATION: MARK 4:21-41
The Other Side of Life

After teaching His disciples about the kingdom, Jesus led them on a short journey that would test their faith. Testing is never comfortable, but it is crucial for revealing—and shaping—who we are. It might be helpful to think of testing as "the other side" of life. Jesus invited His disciples to join Him in a boat and to travel across the sea to the other side (4:35).

The other side of good health is illness—getting a report from the doctor that you didn't expect. I once read about a professional golfer who had gone in for an exam and learned that he had advanced prostate cancer. He walked out, found the men's room, and threw up. The news was so disturbing to this well-known athlete that it stunned him and turned his stomach.

The other side of the honeymoon is a broken relationship. It's discovering surprises you didn't know you were marrying.

If you are currently experiencing the other side of life, you may quite likely be entertaining the lie that God doesn't care. You might think, *If He cared, He'd change things.* The fact is, He cares enough *not* to change things. It will help to remember instead that He's in control and He's brought you this far. Yes, there are scars. Yes, there are painful memories. Yes, there's brokenness. I've learned in life that anyone who's effective in other people's lives is a broken person. In fact, broken people often resemble Jesus Christ.

To help make sense of how a good God could allow His people to endure pain—to experience the other side of life—imagine God as a heavenly Sculptor who works with marble. He's the Sculptor; you're the block. The fact that you are made of marble represents your stubborn nature. It represents your selfishness, your own self-made rules. The Sculptor starts with a hammer to reshape it. He's not shaping you so that your face looks like Jesus'; He's shaping you so that your life looks like Christ's. It takes a lot of pounding. It's painful. He decides which rough edges need smoothing. But when the masterpiece is complete, you look like His Son.

Restoring a Human Wreck
MARK 5:1-20

NASB

[1] They came to the other side of the sea, into the country of the Gerasenes. [2] When He got out of the boat, immediately a man from the tombs with an unclean spirit met Him, [3] and he had his dwelling among the tombs. And no one was able to bind him anymore, even with a chain; [4] because he had often been bound

NLT

[1] So they arrived at the other side of the lake, in the region of the Gerasenes.* [2] When Jesus climbed out of the boat, a man possessed by an evil* spirit came out from the tombs to meet him. [3] This man lived in the burial caves and could no longer be restrained, even with a chain. [4] Whenever he was put into chains

NASB

with shackles and chains, and the chains had been torn apart by him and the shackles broken in pieces, and no one was strong enough to subdue him. ⁵Constantly, night and day, he was screaming among the tombs and in the mountains, and gashing himself with stones. ⁶Seeing Jesus from a distance, he ran up and bowed down before Him; ⁷and shouting with a loud voice, he said, "ᵃWhat business do we have with each other, Jesus, Son of the Most High God? I implore You by God, do not torment me!" ⁸For He had been saying to him, "Come out of the man, you unclean spirit!" ⁹And He was asking him, "What is your name?" And he said to Him, "My name is Legion; for we are many." ¹⁰And he *began* to implore Him earnestly not to send them out of the country. ¹¹Now there was a large herd of swine feeding ᵃnearby on the mountain. ¹²*The demons* implored Him, saying, "Send us into the swine so that we may enter them." ¹³Jesus gave them permission. And coming out, the unclean spirits entered the swine; and the herd rushed down the steep bank into the sea, about two thousand *of them;* and they were drowned in the sea.

¹⁴Their herdsmen ran away and reported it in the city and in the country. And *the people* came to see what it was that had happened. ¹⁵They came to Jesus and observed the man who had been demon-possessed sitting down, clothed and in his right mind, the very man who had had the "legion"; and they became frightened. ¹⁶Those who had seen it described to them how it had happened to the demon-possessed man, and *all* about the swine. ¹⁷And they

NLT

and shackles—as he often was—he snapped the chains from his wrists and smashed the shackles. No one was strong enough to subdue him. ⁵Day and night he wandered among the burial caves and in the hills, howling and cutting himself with sharp stones.

⁶When Jesus was still some distance away, the man saw him, ran to meet him, and bowed low before him. ⁷With a shriek, he screamed, "Why are you interfering with me, Jesus, Son of the Most High God? In the name of God, I beg you, don't torture me!" ⁸For Jesus had already said to the spirit, "Come out of the man, you evil spirit."

⁹Then Jesus demanded, "What is your name?"

And he replied, "My name is Legion, because there are many of us inside this man." ¹⁰Then the evil spirits begged him again and again not to send them to some distant place.

¹¹There happened to be a large herd of pigs feeding on the hillside nearby. ¹²"Send us into those pigs," the spirits begged. "Let us enter them."

¹³So Jesus gave them permission. The evil spirits came out of the man and entered the pigs, and the entire herd of about 2,000 pigs plunged down the steep hillside into the lake and drowned in the water.

¹⁴The herdsmen fled to the nearby town and the surrounding countryside, spreading the news as they ran. People rushed out to see what had happened. ¹⁵A crowd soon gathered around Jesus, and they saw the man who had been possessed by the legion of demons. He was sitting there fully clothed and perfectly sane, and they were all afraid. ¹⁶Then those who had seen what happened told the others about the demon-possessed man and the pigs. ¹⁷And the

NASB

began to implore Him to leave their region. [18] As He was getting into the boat, the man who had been demon-possessed was imploring Him that he might [a]accompany Him. [19] And He did not let him, but He said to him, "Go home to your people and report to them [a]what great things the Lord has done for you, and *how* He had mercy on you." [20] And he went away and began to proclaim in Decapolis [a]what great things Jesus had done for him; and everyone was amazed.

5:7 [a]Lit *What to me and to you* (a Heb idiom)
5:11 [a]Lit *there*   5:18 [a]Lit *be with Him*   5:19 [a]Or *everything that*   5:20 [a]Or *everything that*

NLT

crowd began pleading with Jesus to go away and leave them alone.
[18] As Jesus was getting into the boat, the man who had been demon possessed begged to go with him. [19] But Jesus said, "No, go home to your family, and tell them everything the Lord has done for you and how merciful he has been." [20] So the man started off to visit the Ten Towns* of that region and began to proclaim the great things Jesus had done for him; and everyone was amazed at what he told them.

5:1 Other manuscripts read *Gadarenes;* still others read *Gergesenes.* See Matt 8:28; Luke 8:26. 5:2 Greek *unclean;* also in 5:8, 13. 5:20 Greek *Decapolis.*

Believe it or not, evil has a face. Evil is not merely a concept or something generally opposite of "good." All evil can be traced back to a single agent: Satan. War, sickness, disease, catastrophes, violence, lust, addictions, pestilence, waste, relational conflicts, selfishness—all sin and all that is wrong in the world is a particular expression of evil, the unending rebellion of Satan against God. The world continues to bear the scars of his mutiny.

This perspective doesn't sit well with our scientific, rationalistic understanding of the universe. Our modern worldview looks to the laws of physics to explain everything, which leaves little room for the spiritual realm. Therefore angels, demons, souls, and even God are dismissed as relics of a bygone mythology, unsuitable for enlightened conversations. It should come as no surprise, then, that few today accept the possibility of another expression of evil: demon possession. Even so, the Bible is clear: Satan not only works through nature to wreak destruction, but he also uses people. And on rare occasions, an individual can become the victim of direct demonic control from within.

Jesus met such a man. According to the Gospels, this time in Israel's history was marked by unprecedented demonic activity; more people than ever had become demonized—personally enslaved by a demonic spirit. This gave Jesus ample opportunity to send a message: He had come to destroy evil. He cleansed leprosy, He healed diseases, He subdued the turmoil of weather, He empowered the helpless, and now He would confront evil personified.

— 5:1 —

Having crossed the Sea of Galilee from the northwestern shore, He and the disciples stepped ashore in "the country of the Gerasenes," which most maps label as "the Decapolis." Literally translated "the ten cities," the Decapolis refers to the ten city-states originally settled after the conquest of Alexander the Great. The historian Pliny, writing in the first century, listed the cities as Canatha, Damascus, Dion, Gadara, Gerasa, Hippos, Pella, Philadelphia, Raphana, and Scythopolis.[4]

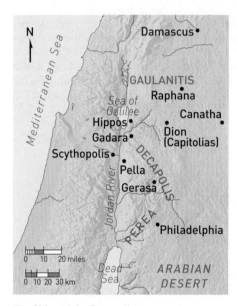

The Cities of the Decapolis

— 5:2-5 —

Jesus probably landed near the beautiful harbor town known today as Ein Gev, where He was met "immediately"—that is, within a very short space of time— by "a man from the tombs" (5:2). Matthew mentions two demon-possessed men (Matt. 8:28), while Luke (Luke 8:27) and Mark focus on one. This one may have been the worse case or was, perhaps, better known by oral tradition at the time.

If the disciples feared the violent storm on the sea, they were about to encounter something far more terrifying. This wild man made his dwelling among the dead, living in the ancient equivalent of a cemetery, a place Jews considered unclean and Gentiles feared as haunted. Mark describes his supernatural strength in graphic terms, explaining that no one could overpower him, no chain could bind him, and no shackle could restrain him (cf. Acts 19:16). He behaved like a savage beast, living outdoors, screaming and howling, gnashing his teeth, and mutilating his flesh.

— 5:6-7 —

While the disciples often struggled to understand Jesus' true identity, demons recognized Him immediately. The evil presence within this man begged for mercy, asking not to be "tormented." Jude 1:6 explains the reason for their fears: "Angels who did not keep their own domain, but abandoned their proper abode, He has kept in eternal bonds under darkness for the judgment of the great day." John explains their fate on that "great day," writing, "The devil who deceived them was thrown into the lake of fire and brimstone, where the beast and the false prophet are also; and they will be tormented day and night forever and ever" (Rev. 20:10).

The expression "What business do we have with each other?" (Mark 5:7) is literally, "What is it to me and to you?" a Hebrew idiom that expresses the incompatibility of two agendas (cf. Josh. 22:24; Judg. 11:12; 2 Sam. 16:10; 19:22).

Then, unable to deny the power of God and the superiority of His redemptive plan for the world, they knelt before Jesus like one would kneel before a king and addressed Him using a title that His followers— members of His kingdom—did not yet fully comprehend. Mark earlier records that demons called Jesus "the Son of God" (Mark 3:11). In the Old Testament, "Most High" and "Most High God" are used by Gentiles who acknowledge the superiority of Israel's God (cf. Gen. 14:18-24; Num. 24:16; Isa. 14:14; Dan. 3:26; 4:2). Here, the demons dare to ask for mercy *in God's name*!

— 5:8-9 —

The verbs "saying" (5:8) and "asking" (5:9) appear in the imperfect tense, which often indicates repeated or ongoing action. The verb *legō* [3004], "to say," is a common exception, however. When describing a historical event in which something is said or asked, the imperfect tense almost always denotes simple past action. Therefore, the translations "He had said" and "He asked" are best. Jesus didn't have to repeat Himself; the demons were compelled to acknowledge His authority and respond despite their resistance.

Jesus wasted no time exercising that authority; without hesitation, He commanded the demons to leave, which prompted them to again beg for mercy. In asking for a name, Jesus used the singular form of "your." He may have intended for the man to answer, but the evil presence within him spoke using the victim's vocal chords. The reply is paradoxical. "My" is singular; "we" is plural. By using the name Legion, the demons referenced a Roman military unit, which in the first century included upwards of six thousand soldiers. Of course, the exact number of demons is unimportant. The point is that virtually nothing of the original man existed. He lived a horrific living death we can only imagine in our worst nightmares.

— 5:10-13 —

Mark's description enhances the unusual nature of the encounter with the odd mixing of singular and plural pronouns ("he" and "them"). Adding to the strangeness, the demons' request appears absurd, almost comical. According to Luke, they wanted to avoid the *abyssos* [12] ("abyss"; Luke 8:31), a word that literally means "bottomless." In the New Testament, this is the place where the unrighteous await final judgment (Rev. 9:1-2, 11; 11:7; 17:8). Mark, however, highlights their desire to remain in the region of the Gerasenes, perhaps to illustrate how evil had overtaken this area. The demons were reluctant to leave the place they found so fertile and hospitable.

The scene becomes even more bizarre when they ask Jesus to allow them passage to a nearby herd of swine. The demons thought this might be a compromise Jesus could accept—the man would be freed and they could remain in the region. Of course, Jesus knew what would happen. He gave permission for them to enter the pigs feeding on a high plateau. If Jesus landed at Ein Gev, the pigs must have been feeding just outside the town of Hippos, which sat on a plateau 1,720 feet above the shore, roughly 2 miles away. When the pigs experienced the evil presence, the massive herd of squealing, writhing animals panicked and rushed down the embankment to their doom in the Sea of Galilee.

The scene must have been terrifying to witness. If you have heard frightened pigs squeal, close your eyes and imagine two thousand of them screaming in terror. Visualize them thrashing in the water in a single mass drowning as unclean spirits drove the unclean animals to suicidal madness. Then try to hear the stunned silence that undoubtedly lingered after the last of the pigs slipped beneath the waves.

The gruesome spectacle sent a clear message to the disciples who witnessed the carnage. The evil manifested in disease, disasters, discord, death, and decay has a name. The agent of darkness who shrouds the earth in despair is none other than Satan. He opposed the work of Jesus in the wilderness (Mark 1:13), in the synagogue (1:23), at home (1:32), and throughout His travels (1:39; 3:11). The author of evil hates God and wants everything God created to be consumed in his self-destructive rebellion.

— 5:14-17 —

The hired hands watching over the pigs reported the incident "in the city and in the country" (5:14). This would have transpired over several days, not a single afternoon. Therefore, Mark's description is a summary of what happened when people from all over the region came to investigate the rumors, to observe the formerly deranged man behaving normally, and to see for themselves the rotting mass of pig carcasses washed onto the shore. The word translated "observed" (5:15) is *theōreō* [2334], from which we get our word "theorize." They gathered the facts in order to understand what had occurred.

They returned to find the man completely cleansed of his unclean spirits, clothed, behaving rationally, and sitting at the feet of the rabbi from Galilee. Jesus had completely restored this wreck of a human being, giving him new life and returning his dignity. The response of these Gentiles of the "ten cities" tells us something about them. Where we might expect gratitude, we find ignorance. They feared the demon-possessed man living among the dead, but they feared Jesus more. However, this kind of fear didn't inspire a respectful awe that prompted worship. Instead of surrendering to their Maker, they shunned Him like darkness rejects the light. And, reminiscent of the demons' initial response, they pushed Him to leave the area. The verb translated "implore" (5:17) is *parakaleō* [3870], which in this context means "to urge strongly," "to appeal to," "to urge," or "to make a strong request."[5]

— 5:18-20 —

Jesus didn't have to leave; He could have remained despite the rejection of the people, but it suited His purposes to go. In a foreshadowing of the near future, Jesus prepared to depart the region. Before crossing over to the other side, He commissioned the man who had been demon-possessed as a witness to tell his salvation story—how he had been enslaved by evil and how a Savior released him from bondage, restored his dignity, renewed his mind, and gave him a divine purpose. Jesus left this believing man to evangelize his unbelieving family and countrymen. His story of redemption would be the means of leading others to find salvation in Christ.

Mark's epilogue is important to note. The man did as Jesus instructed. He obediently proclaimed (*kēryssō* [2784]) the deeds of the Savior, and the people responded with amazement (5:20). The word for "amazed" (*thaumazō* [2296]) means "to be extraordinarily impressed" or "to admire or respect." Mark strongly indicates a favorable response to the man's witness.

This story of restoration, commissioning, and obedience is central to Mark's overarching message in this narrative. The central theme of Mark's Gospel is faithful discipleship: faithful witness to a hostile audience and faithful proclamation of what Jesus said and did. The restored demoniac became the first example of genuine discipleship since Jesus began His ministry—and the man was a *Gentile*.

APPLICATION: MARK 5:1-20
Wrecked, Revived, Restored

The Lord's encounter with the terrifying man from the tombs illustrates three enduring truths that form the outline of our own redemption stories.

First, *we are born hopelessly enslaved to sin.* We emerge from our mothers' wombs as slaves to the evil that rules this world. As members of the human race, we inherit a sin-loving nature that is selfish and rebellious. This sinful nature rules our bodies, twists our minds, and compels us to behave like something subhuman, sacrificing our human dignity with every disobedient choice.

Some reading these words have made such a mess of their lives that they wonder if there is any hope for restoration. If this is you, compare your condition to that of the man from the tombs. Your condition cannot be worse than his. And if Jesus could restore wreckage like that man's, He can restore your life. Any marriage you've ruined, home you've destroyed, lives you've reduced to chaos, people you've harmed—none of that makes your case too hopeless for God. Any wrecked life can be restored.

Second, *any restored soul can be used by God.* Jesus doesn't restore us only to leave us helpless and alone. When He revives us from the living death of sin, He gives us new life. Our restored dignity prepares us to fulfill our divine purpose. After receiving new life from Jesus, the restored man received a great commission to tell his redemption story to everyone.

Third, *anyone used by God can make an amazing difference.* According to Mark, "Everyone was amazed" (5:20). The man's countrymen rejected Jesus and implored Him to leave, but when one of their own proclaimed the good news of the Savior, they responded favorably, presumably in belief. What amazed them? The man's restored life.

Your scars bear witness to the reviving, restoring power of Christ. He turns those shameful marks into emblems of honor. Each can become an opportunity to glorify God and influence others to find the healing and dignity you received. Believe it or not, you could have an amazing impact on the world for the cause of Christ.

Power over Death and Disease
MARK 5:21-43

NASB

21 When Jesus had crossed over again in the boat to the other side, a large crowd gathered around Him; and so He ᵃstayed by the seashore. 22 One of the synagogue ᵃofficials named Jairus came up, and on seeing Him, fell at His feet 23 and implored Him earnestly, saying, "My little daughter is at the point of death; *please* come and lay Your hands on her, so that she will ᵃget well and live." 24 And He went off with him; and a large crowd was following Him and pressing in on Him.

25 A woman who had had a hemorrhage for twelve years, 26 and had endured much at the hands of many physicians, and had spent all that she had and was not helped at all, but rather had grown worse— 27 after hearing about Jesus, she came up in the crowd behind *Him* and touched His ᵃcloak. 28 For she ᵃthought, "If I just touch His garments, I will ᵇget well." 29 Immediately the flow of her blood was dried up; and she felt in her body that she was healed of her affliction. 30 Immediately Jesus, perceiving in Himself that the power *proceeding* from Him had gone forth, turned around in the crowd and said,

NLT

21 Jesus got into the boat again and went back to the other side of the lake, where a large crowd gathered around him on the shore. 22 Then a leader of the local synagogue, whose name was Jairus, arrived. When he saw Jesus, he fell at his feet, 23 pleading fervently with him. "My little daughter is dying," he said. "Please come and lay your hands on her; heal her so she can live."

24 Jesus went with him, and all the people followed, crowding around him. 25 A woman in the crowd had suffered for twelve years with constant bleeding. 26 She had suffered a great deal from many doctors, and over the years she had spent everything she had to pay them, but she had gotten no better. In fact, she had gotten worse. 27 She had heard about Jesus, so she came up behind him through the crowd and touched his robe. 28 For she thought to herself, "If I can just touch his robe, I will be healed." 29 Immediately the bleeding stopped, and she could feel in her body that she had been healed of her terrible condition.

30 Jesus realized at once that healing power had gone out from him, so

NASB

"Who touched My garments?" 31 And His disciples said to Him, "You see the crowd pressing in on You, and You say, 'Who touched Me?'" 32 And He looked around to see the woman who had done this. 33 But the woman fearing and trembling, aware of what had happened to her, came and fell down before Him and told Him the whole truth. 34 And He said to her, "Daughter, your faith has ᵃmade you well; go in peace and be healed of your affliction."

35 While He was still speaking, they came from the *house of* the synagogue official, saying, "Your daughter has died; why trouble the Teacher anymore?" 36 But Jesus, overhearing what was being spoken, said to the synagogue official, "Do not be afraid *any longer,* only ᵃbelieve." 37 And He allowed no one to accompany Him, except Peter and ᵃJames and John the brother of ᵃJames. 38 They came to the house of the synagogue official; and He saw a commotion, and *people* loudly weeping and wailing. 39 And entering in, He said to them, "Why make a commotion and weep? The child has not died, but is asleep." 40 They *began* laughing at Him. But putting them all out, He took along the child's father and mother and His own companions, and entered *the room* where the child was. 41 Taking the child by the hand, He said to her, "Talitha kum!" (which translated means, "Little girl, I say to you, get up!"). 42 Immediately the girl got up and *began* to walk, for she was twelve years old. And immediately they were completely astounded. 43 And He gave them strict orders that no one should know about this, and He said that *something* should be given her to eat.

5:21 ᵃLit *was*   5:22 ᵃOr *rulers*   5:23 ᵃLit *be saved*
5:27 ᵃOr *outer garment*   5:28 ᵃLit *was saying*   ᵇLit
be saved   5:34 ᵃLit *saved you*   5:36 ᵃOr *keep on
believing*   5:37 ᵃOr *Jacob;* James is the Eng form
of Jacob

NLT

he turned around in the crowd and asked, "Who touched my robe?"
31 His disciples said to him, "Look at this crowd pressing around you. How can you ask, 'Who touched me?'"
32 But he kept on looking around to see who had done it. 33 Then the frightened woman, trembling at the realization of what had happened to her, came and fell to her knees in front of him and told him what she had done. 34 And he said to her, "Daughter, your faith has made you well. Go in peace. Your suffering is over."

35 While he was still speaking to her, messengers arrived from the home of Jairus, the leader of the synagogue. They told him, "Your daughter is dead. There's no use troubling the Teacher now."
36 But Jesus overheard* them and said to Jairus, "Don't be afraid. Just have faith."
37 Then Jesus stopped the crowd and wouldn't let anyone go with him except Peter, James, and John (the brother of James). 38 When they came to the home of the synagogue leader, Jesus saw much commotion and weeping and wailing. 39 He went inside and asked, "Why all this commotion and weeping? The child isn't dead; she's only asleep."
40 The crowd laughed at him. But he made them all leave, and he took the girl's father and mother and his three disciples into the room where the girl was lying. 41 Holding her hand, he said to her, "Talitha koum," which means "Little girl, get up!" 42 And the girl, who was twelve years old, immediately stood up and walked around! They were overwhelmed and totally amazed. 43 Jesus gave them strict orders not to tell anyone what had happened, and then he told them to give her something to eat.

5:36 Or *ignored.*

Death is Satan's ultimate affront to God's original creative act. Our Creator didn't make us in His image only to have us endure diseases, fall victim to disasters, suffer death, and then rot in the ground. He created us to live in dignity, to rule with our Savior and Lord as vice-regents over the rest of creation, to enjoy one another, and to share intimate joy with Him . . . *forever*. The world fell victim to evil—disease, disasters, death, and decay—when Satan enticed the first humans to sin (Gen. 3; Rom. 5:12). Now we are all living under the dark shadow of evil, and we are all headed for the grave.

While Satan dealt a deathblow to humanity and all of creation, he did not defeat the Creator, whose power is unequaled. God will not allow His creation to remain under the unholy rule of the devil; He has determined to redeem the world and to bring everything under His sovereign authority again. That is why God became a man in the person of Jesus Christ, through whom He will establish His kingdom on earth.

Mark 4 unveils this theme of "God's kingdom come" with a series of parables revealing several truths:

- The gospel is available to all, but some will not receive it (4:1-25).
- The kingdom is a divine work, but it will come by the agency of people (4:26-29).
- The kingdom begins small, but it will eventually benefit the whole world (4:30-32).

Mark developed the theme of "God's kingdom come" by illustrating Jesus' power and authority over the elements (4:35-41) and over demons (5:1-20). Mark continues this kingdom theme with a demonstration of the Lord's power over disease and death. From Jesus' point of view, these miraculous displays of authority sent a clear message to Satan and all who suffer under his rule: God has come to redeem creation from evil and to establish His kingdom on earth.

— 5:21-24 —

Nothing can bring parents to their knees faster than a critically ill child. When the condition lingers and grows more intense, feelings of helplessness and desperation drive them to consider almost anything. We ignore our own prejudices as we seek advice from complete strangers. We forget our own pride and dignity as we search for anything that will bring relief to our little one. We spend any amount of money necessary, we travel any distance, and we sacrifice any possession for the hope of a cure. Our desperation knows no bounds.

When Jesus docked in Capernaum after returning from the region of the Decapolis, He began ministering to a large crowd. Meanwhile, a couple living near the city had been watching over their daughter, whose condition carried her ever closer to death. Desperate days had given way to anguished nights as her symptoms grew worse. Nothing seemed to keep the young girl from sliding into the sleep of death, never again to wake.

Her father was Jairus, an official in the large synagogue in Capernaum. Jesus now lived in this substantial harbor town and had become a fixture of the community, teaching frequently in the Jewish house of meeting. Any problems the local leaders had with the rabbi from Nazareth were undoubtedly overshadowed by the economic boost they received from the thousands of visitors from all over Israel. Regardless, this particular religious and civic leader gave no thought to theology, politics, or the economy. His daughter—his only daughter, according to Luke 8:42—lay dying, and she had no hope of surviving without the kindness and healing power of Jesus.

None of the Gospels describe the nature of the man's relationship with Jesus. Clearly, he had observed the Lord's healing ability. He asked for Jesus to make the short journey to his home and lay His hands on her "so that" she would receive healing (Mark 5:23). This Greek particle, *hina* [2443] ("so that," "in order that"), makes a logical connection between Jesus touching the child and her recovery. In this case, it's a necessary, causal connection. That is to say, the man recognized that without Jesus the girl would not live. Calling upon Jesus, therefore, represented an exercise of faith.

— 5:25-27 —

Here Mark again sandwiches another story between the beginning and conclusion of this one (see comments on 3:20-21; 6:7-32; 11:12-14). On the brief walk from the shoreline to Jairus's home, Jesus encountered yet another person in need of healing. He had already ministered to a large crowd, teaching and healing in keeping with His custom. But this meeting would be different. In stark contrast to Jairus's bold approach and unhesitating plea for help, a woman tried to sneak a healing. To understand the reason for her shyness, we must appreciate the social complexity of her culture.

In our modern, democratic era, we regard all people as equals in terms of worth. This, however, is a relatively new way of thinking. Throughout all but the last three centuries, societies assigned worth to people based on their family status, then by their usefulness, and then by how well they fit into the mainstream of culture. Similarly, Jews in the first century devalued and marginalized people they considered to be cursed by God. They reasoned that God blesses people who are obedient to the Law and therefore that people suffering from illness or misfortune must be guilty of some sin (cf. John 9:2).

Mark reveals that a woman approached Jesus who had suffered from "a hemorrhage for twelve years" (Mark 5:25). The Greek phrase literally says that she "was in bleeding for twelve years"—a delicate way of stating that she suffered from something like a continuous menstrual flow. As modern Western readers, we immediately think of her physical suffering and how her condition medically affected her quality of life. Ancient readers—especially Jews—understood that her medical condition was only the beginning of her misery; they also understood the social and religious impact of her illness.

According to the Law of Moses, women in menstruation were to remain in relative seclusion as *ritually* unclean (cf. Lev. 15:19-27). The adjective "ritually" is vitally important to understand because it doesn't carry the negative connotations twenty-first-century Westerners imagine. This particular law taught basic hygiene to an ancient people who did not have the knowledge we enjoy today, and it gave menstruating women a break from normal duties in an era when the lack of modern conveniences made a woman's monthly cycle extremely inconvenient. The law also applied to any woman with "a discharge of her blood many days" (Lev. 15:25).

To be ritually unclean meant that a person could not join in normal social activities. A woman in this condition could not enter the temple or a synagogue, she couldn't have physical contact with other people, she couldn't accept invitations to dine with others, she couldn't marry if her condition occurred early in life, and if married, the Law forbade intercourse. Furthermore, her ongoing disease marked her as cursed by God in the eyes of her community. Socially, she might as well have been a leper.

While Jairus enjoyed life from the top of the social ladder (a ruling elder in a prominent synagogue), this woman survived on the crumbs that fell to the bottom, where she eked out a meager existence. Interestingly, she had been struggling with this illness for as long as Jairus's daughter had been alive. While the little girl had been the delight of her father's home, this hopelessly ill woman endured perpetual humiliation and discouragement. The official's daughter enjoyed privileged status in Jewish society; the unnamed woman, on the other hand, existed on the periphery of the community as an outcast. And, while Jairus came to Jesus directly and openly, social custom reduced the diseased, detested woman to groveling for a mere touch of the rabbi's tunic. All this helps us understand why she attempted to "sneak" her healing.

— 5:28-29 —

Mark reveals the woman's inner dialogue. She recognized Jesus as her only hope, though perhaps her attempt at simply touching Jesus' garment indicates some level of superstition. Nevertheless, even this act demonstrated great faith and humility. She likely felt too unworthy to approach Jesus directly, as the synagogue leader had done. So, with a desperate reach through the throng surrounding Jesus, she touched His garment. God honored her faith with healing. A dozen years of chronic bleeding, ineffective medical treatment, and callous exclusion suddenly gave way to a hopeful future. She immediately experienced physical relief.

— 5:30-34 —

Just as quickly as the woman received healing, Jesus perceived a flow of divine power coursing from His body. His question, "Who touched My garments?" (5:30), is His way of reaching out to a woman who desperately wanted to remain anonymous. He could have just let it go, but Jesus wasn't merely interested in dispensing healing power; He wanted to establish a personal relationship with her.

The disciples were incredulous. They asked, as it were, "With this mob of people surrounding You, who *didn't* touch You?" But they could not have been aware of the supernatural flow of power Jesus perceived. Meanwhile, the woman stood back, terrified that she had been called out. With her face to the ground and trembling with fear, she explained everything, undoubtedly expecting a severe rebuke. Instead, Jesus called her "daughter" (5:34).

Custom suggested He should call her "woman," the ancient equivalent of "ma'am," but He used a family term, a tender expression undoubtedly used by Jairus for his own child. He praised the woman for her faith, a factor He rarely found among the religious in Galilee. Ultimately, He declared her "saved." The term translated "made . . . well" is *sōzō* [4982], which literally means "to save," but it has a broad range of uses in addition to spiritual or physical salvation. In this case, Mark emphasizes the spiritual connotation in the first part of Jesus' declaration by giving special attention to the woman's physical healing in the second part. While she received physical healing from Jesus, she also received something far more important: relief from slavery to sin.

— 5:35-36 —

I can picture Jairus standing there, not particularly interested in the woman's story—certainly not as interested in the woman as Jesus was. Perhaps Jairus's sense of urgency was driving him to exasperation. Think about it. While his daughter approached death, Jesus stopped to converse with a social and religious outcast, a woman deemed unworthy by her community, her synagogue, and presumably, her God. If Jesus had been motivated by politics or a desire to advance His social position, He would have put off the bleeding woman, at least temporarily, and hurried to the synagogue ruler's home. But He made time for the outcast; her worth to Jesus was neither less nor more than that of Jairus's little girl.

Jairus wouldn't have known that Jesus didn't have to choose which person to help. He is not restricted by time, distance, or circumstances. His resources have no limitations, so His helping one person doesn't deprive another. Furthermore, He will accomplish His purposes according to His timetable, not ours. Unfortunately, we're selfish and impatient. We think it's all about us . . . and we *hate* delays.

As the anxious father paced with nervous haste and Jesus lingered over the shunned woman, the unthinkable happened. A group of people approached Jairus with terrible news: "Your daughter has died" (5:35). Their next line reveals how little they knew about Jesus: "Why trouble the Teacher anymore?" They were essentially saying, "She's beyond hope now; even Jesus cannot help her."

We shouldn't be too hard on these messengers. They didn't have the benefit of church history or the New Testament. As the Lord's identity unfolded gradually, His friends struggled to understand how the God of Israel could become a man without ceasing to be God. It's a mystery we still cannot fully comprehend today. Besides, death is final. People can recover from diseases . . . unless they die. People rebound from serious injuries . . . unless death takes them. People don't recover from death. The only thing in the universe more final than death is the Word of God saying, "Arise."

Jesus didn't rebuke the messengers; He spoke instead to the shaken father. I imagine Him looking intently at the man and speaking words in the kind of reassuring tone we all need to hear from God: "Do not be afraid, only keep believing" (my rendering of 5:36). The man had exercised remarkable faith in coming to Jesus, believing He could—and would—restore the girl to health. Jesus encouraged Him to keep trusting despite the apparent hopelessness of the situation.

— 5:37-40 —

Jesus realized that dragging a large crowd to Jairus's house would interfere with His freedom to minister as needed, so He left them behind. He took, instead, the three men who would become His closest companions: Peter, James, and John (cf. 9:2; 14:33). Jesus didn't want to create a scene or put on a show, but He did want firsthand witnesses for this and other important events.

In some ancient Near Eastern cultures, families hired mourners to weep and wail over a dead loved one (cf. Jer. 9:17; Amos 5:16), perhaps as an announcement to their neighbors that a death had occurred and the family was in mourning. As Jesus approached Jairus's home, He heard the commotion and effectively fired the mourners. He said, in effect, "Your services aren't needed. There's no place for weeping and wailing where no one has died." They must have been shocked by that statement. He assured everyone present, "The child has not died, but is asleep."

The statement is curious. People in ancient times were well acquainted with death; they had seen it often enough, so it's doubtful they were mistaken. Luke's account adds the comment "and her spirit returned" (Luke 8:55), clearly indicating that the girl had died. So what did Jesus mean?

In this simple statement, Jesus promised a resurrection for all. In saying that she was "asleep" (Mark 5:39), Jesus declared that physical death is not final. Everyone will be awakened from the sleep of death to face judgment. Some will enjoy eternal resurrection in the presence of God; others will suffer a "second death" (Rev. 2:11; 20:6, 14; 21:8), an everlasting existence far worse than dying. At the time, however, few could hear Jesus as He intended. They took His statement literally and scorned Him as a fool.

Jesus didn't defend His statement or try to convince His critics; He focused on the people in need who wanted His help. He dismissed everyone except Jairus, Jairus's wife, and the three disciples.

— 5:41-43 —

Jesus took the young girl's lifeless hand in His, which normally would have rendered Him ritually unclean. He then commanded her to get up.

Mark transliterates the Lord's actual words in Aramaic "Talitha kum!" (5:41). (This is one of many indications that Mark wrote to a Gentile audience unfamiliar with the native languages of Israel.)

"Immediately"—that is, after no passage of time—the girl's parents welcomed her back to the world (5:42). The Greek word for "astounded" is *existēmi* [1839], which literally means "to remove oneself." Figuratively, it means "to lose one's wits" or "to go out of one's mind."[6] Our expression "they were beside themselves" almost captures the full meaning, but *existēmi* is decidedly more colorful.

Unlike when Jesus restored the man in the Decapolis (5:1-20), He instructed the couple to remain silent concerning the girl's resurrection. In the Decapolis, the Gentiles feared Jesus' divine power and sent Him away. In Galilee, by contrast, the Lord's miracles attracted so many people that He couldn't minister effectively. Broadcasting the news about Jesus reviving the girl may have drawn a crowd, but it would not have advanced His mission.

Besides needing to be able to move about freely, Jesus was also guarding against His disciples following Him for the sake of selfish gain. He healed the sick, cleansed demoniacs, and revived the dead because of His compassion. He performed these miracles in public only when validating His message as authentically God-sent. As He culled the crowds, separating true disciples from those attracted to sensationalism, Jesus began to highlight the more sobering aspects of discipleship.

APPLICATION: MARK 5:21-43

God's Gift of Desperation

I can identify with Jairus in his desperate urgency to save his daughter. I've been there many times myself. After experiencing several desperate situations over the years, I have come to accept a difficult truth: Desperation is a gift from God.

If you're feeling desperate, that might seem like a cruel joke. Let me assure you, we do not serve a cruel God. Your circumstances have not escaped His notice. He loves you, and yet your difficulty remains. Therefore, we can accept as a certainty that your desperate situation is something God ultimately intends for good (Rom. 8:26-39).

We typically become desperate when a challenging situation drags on, becomes unbearable, and makes us recognize how helpless we are to avoid the outcome we fear most. It could be joblessness, a painful disease, a broken relationship, a rebellious teenager, upside-down finances—any circumstance headed for disaster that we're powerless to change.

When we arrive at desperation, we're finally prepared to recognize our own powerlessness and to trust in God's sovereign sufficiency. Most of us have become preoccupied with our independence and hardened in our autonomy, leaving the Lord little opportunity to meet our truest, deepest needs. When we become sincerely desperate, we're ready to exchange our autonomy for God's will, in God's way, and on God's schedule—even if we don't get what we want. And that's when we begin to know Him intimately and experientially.

As we reflect on Jairus's story, let me offer three statements that will help you make sense of your desperation.

First, *for humility to displace skepticism, we often must reach the point of desperation.* Many college professors strut around the room spouting all kinds of skeptical comments regarding faith because they've not reached a point of desperation in their own lives. When they do, it's amazing how many of them shrink down to size and become humble before God. When you reach desperation, humility comes naturally.

C. S. Lewis put it this way: "[Pain] plants the flag of truth within the fortress of a rebel soul."[7] This father, no longer a proud official in the synagogue, became a humbled, broken daddy whose daughter lay dying. He became desperate. And when he humbled himself, he found his Savior waiting, willing, and ready to meet all of his needs, including the one that brought him to desperation.

Second, *for trust to eclipse our panic, we must learn the value of delay.* After a while in the process of waiting and waiting and waiting, we relinquish our circumstances to God. When we do, quiet, calm trust rushes in to replace our knee-jerk panic. If you're worried about one of your children, in time you will learn to bathe your worries with prayers. You'll find, bit by bit, year by year, that God is in charge, even when that child has grown up and left the nest. God is not *almost* sovereign. He knows the situation entirely.

I love the fact that Jesus didn't rebuke Jairus for not coming earlier. The man had to get to the place where he, on his own, would come.

Finally, *for faith to replace our fears, we must steer clear of the naysayers.* If you're running with people who keep your faith shallow, tenuous, and weak, you will never learn to trust God. If you maintain relationships that are unhealthy, you will never see beyond your circumstances. You will always wonder, *Why in the world am I not really walking by faith with God?* Look at your friends. When you associate with people who genuinely trust God, your own faith will grow fuller and stronger.

It's amazing how one naysayer can poison an entire group, chipping away at others' trust in God with a list of reasons to show that God doesn't care or doesn't even exist. People like that are not only negative—they're dangerous. They feed on doubt. They know only what cannot be done. They're focused on the horizontal plane and have no concept of the vertical.

Stay away from such people! Remember, Jesus put them all out of the room before He turned Jairus's desperation into joy.

A Prophet without Honor
MARK 6:1-6

NASB

[1] Jesus went out from there and came into [a]His hometown; and His disciples followed Him. [2] When the Sabbath came, He began to teach in the synagogue; and the many listeners were astonished, saying, "Where did this man *get* these things, and what is *this* wisdom given to Him, and such [a]miracles as these performed by His hands? [3] Is not this the carpenter, the son of Mary, and brother of [a]James and Joses and Judas and Simon? Are not His sisters here with us?" And they took offense at Him. [4] Jesus said to them, "A prophet is not without honor except in [a]his hometown and among his *own* relatives and in his *own* household." [5] And He could do no [a]miracle there except that He laid His hands on a few sick

NLT

[1] Jesus left that part of the country and returned with his disciples to Nazareth, his hometown. [2] The next Sabbath he began teaching in the synagogue, and many who heard him were amazed. They asked, "Where did he get all this wisdom and the power to perform such miracles?" [3] Then they scoffed, "He's just a carpenter, the son of Mary* and the brother of James, Joseph,* Judas, and Simon. And his sisters live right here among us." They were deeply offended and refused to believe in him.

[4] Then Jesus told them, "A prophet is honored everywhere except in his own hometown and among his relatives and his own family." [5] And because of their unbelief, he couldn't do any miracles among them except to place his hands on a few sick

NASB

people and healed them. [6]And He wondered at their unbelief.

And He was going around the villages teaching.

6:1 [a]Or *His own part of the country*   6:2 [a]Or *works of power*   6:3 [a]Or *Jacob*   6:4 [a]Or *his own part of the country*   6:5 [a]Or *work of power*

people and heal them. [6]And he was amazed at their unbelief.

Then Jesus went from village to village, teaching the people.

6:3a Some manuscripts read *He's just the son of the carpenter and of Mary.*   6:3b Most manuscripts read *Joses;* see Matt 13:55.

NLT

"I knew you back when . . . " Statements beginning with those words typically make me cringe. That declaration usually leads to a story I'd prefer to forget, and the person speaking those words usually wears a devilish smile or is shaking his or her head—or both. One thing's for sure: The people who knew us "back when" aren't impressed with who we are or what we have become *now*. They remember when we were young, vulnerable, ignorant, or foolish, overtaken by flaws and shortcomings. They witnessed our foolish childhood years, our irresponsible teenage years, our most humbling learning experiences. Interestingly, they are never asking for our autograph! That's why returning to your childhood home can be difficult—even for Jesus, who didn't have an embarrassing past. He didn't do things wrong—not even once. He simply grew up. Unfortunately, people are unwilling to see greatness in the people they know best. Consequently, hometown people are less likely to applaud someone they knew "back when."

Through a series of vignettes, Mark's narrative has revealed the undeniable power and authority of Jesus. Any reasonable person reading this literature would begin to see that Jesus is more than a rabbi, more than a dynamic speaker, and more than a charismatic leader. Jesus healed diseases, cleansed lepers, gave sight to the blind, cast out demons, commanded the elements, and revived the dead. With all of that as background, Mark now allows us to see how the people from Jesus' hometown would respond to His call to follow Him.

— 6:1-2 —

Jesus considered Nazareth His hometown. After His birth in Bethlehem and a sojourn of two years or more in Egypt, His parents settled in this tiny Jewish town, where the inhabitants of Nazareth—no more than a couple hundred of them—watched Him grow up. When He began His public ministry, however, He chose to minister out of Capernaum, about 21 miles northeast. This location gave Him greater access to Galilee, allowing Him to travel faster and farther via ships in the local

Me, Back When

MARK 6:3-4

If I tell you about my early years, you will understand why no people in El Campo, Texas, have my picture hanging on their walls (except maybe down at the local post office).

For example, take my fourth-grade year. We sat in alphabetical order, so I sat behind a very bright student with the most boring report card you could imagine: straight As. And she had these long pigtails that hung down to her waist. She was so proud of those pigtails. And just before she got up to get the blue-ribbon award for winning the spelling bee, I tied her pigtails to her desk chair. When she stood up to get her blue ribbon, she dragged the chair halfway up to the front. Sort of like Samson dragging the gates of Gaza (Judg. 16:1-3). What a great sight!

A few years later, I became a burden to our eleventh grade English literature teacher—God bless her—who took everything very seriously and couldn't understand why my hooligan friends and I didn't. Bored with guys like Chaucer, Browning, Coleridge, and Shakespeare, one student thought it would be a great idea to ride his British James motorcycle down the center aisle of that dull class . . . with me riding on the back yelling, "Yee-haw!"

Yep, we did it. Through the hall, down the aisle, and then bump, bump, bump, right down the steps. The last view I had of our teacher was her rummaging through her desk for nitroglycerin tablets.

When we got to the bottom of the stairs, the principal was there to greet us. The other guy took off on his own. The principal told me to go sit in my chair. (I had my own chair in his office.) That's when he brought down the shame. Just a month earlier, I had won "Junior Rotarian of the Month" and received a nice trophy. He said, "You should give the trophy back."

I said, "I can't. I already pawned it." That was true. I had used the money to buy cigars for all the guys in the room who cheered us on as we roared down the aisle in English class.

Then there was our band and orchestra teacher, who not only had to endure my sister, Luci, playing cello like a guitar, but suffered through having me as a clarinet player in the same orchestra.

(continued on next page)

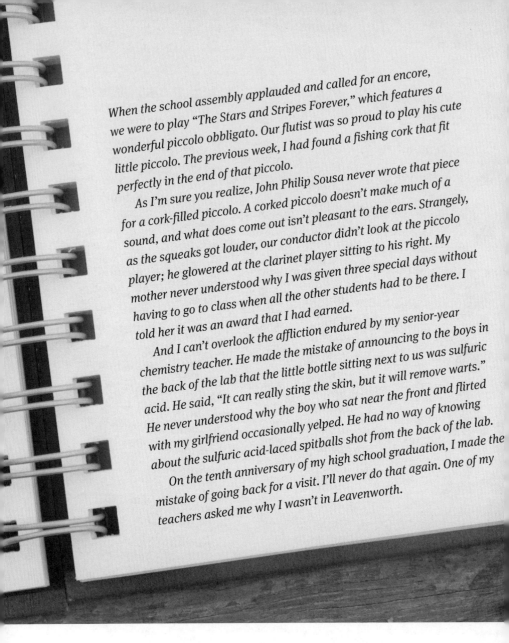

When the school assembly applauded and called for an encore, we were to play "The Stars and Stripes Forever," which features a wonderful piccolo obbligato. Our flutist was so proud to play his cute little piccolo. The previous week, I had found a fishing cork that fit perfectly in the end of that piccolo.

As I'm sure you realize, John Philip Sousa never wrote that piece for a cork-filled piccolo. A corked piccolo doesn't make much of a sound, and what does come out isn't pleasant to the ears. Strangely, as the squeaks got louder, our conductor didn't look at the piccolo player; he glowered at the clarinet player sitting to his right. My mother never understood why I was given three special days without having to go to class when all the other students had to be there. I told her it was an award that I had earned.

And I can't overlook the affliction endured by my senior-year chemistry teacher. He made the mistake of announcing to the boys in the back of the lab that the little bottle sitting next to us was sulfuric acid. He said, "It can really sting the skin, but it will remove warts." He never understood why the boy who sat near the front and flirted with my girlfriend occasionally yelped. He had no way of knowing about the sulfuric acid-laced spitballs shot from the back of the lab.

On the tenth anniversary of my high school graduation, I made the mistake of going back for a visit. I'll never do that again. One of my teachers asked me why I wasn't in Leavenworth.

harbor. Having visited much of the region, the time had come to bring the gospel home to Nazareth.

News generally carried quickly throughout Galilee, usually on the tongues of merchants whose routes took them from one urban center to the next. Nazareth, however, remained cut off from the mainstream of Jewish gossip in Galilee. For one thing, it sat in a bowl-shaped depression 1,150 feet above the Jezreel Valley—too inconveniently located for a casual visit. Additionally, it was the site of a Roman garrison, complete with a bathhouse. Jews generally kept to themselves, especially in Israel, where Gentiles were shunned like household pests. As a result, the people of Nazareth were more likely to hear news from Caesarea and Rome than from their neighboring towns below. Still, reports of Jesus' deeds reached His former playmates and their parents.

The people of Nazareth extended a warm welcome to Jesus and His disciples. They even invited Him to teach in their little synagogue. Luke adds that "all were speaking well of Him, and wondering at the gracious words which were falling from His lips" (Luke 4:22). Likewise, Mark records the initial response of the Nazarenes as delightfully surprised. They wondered how this homegrown young man, Jesus, had gained such great wisdom and how He—of all people!—could perform genuine miracles.

Soon, however, their delightful surprise turned to spiteful resentment.

— 6:3 —

Notably, the people who knew Jesus "back when" didn't object to the content of His teaching—they called it wise. Their question concerning His miracles, however, suggests something sinister. They didn't deny that the miracles had taken place; instead, their rhetorical question leaned in the direction of Satan giving Him "these things" (6:2). Then they settled on the reason for their doubt.

Jesus had been a carpenter. The Greek word for this refers to "one who constructs," "a builder," or "a wood joiner." Some Greek writers used the term to describe men who made plows and yokes. In other words, Jesus didn't come from the right class of people to be a teacher. As a lowly, blue-collar handyman, He didn't have the education other rabbis received through years of rigorous training in Jerusalem.

The people of Nazareth drew even greater ammunition from Jesus' parentage. The phrase "son of Mary" was deliberately derogatory. In first-century Israel, "it was the common practice among the Jews to use the father's name, whether he were alive or dead. A man was called the son of his mother only when his father was unknown."[8] When Mary and Joseph had settled back in Nazareth, the story of her unusual pregnancy had undoubtedly given their neighbors plenty of gossip. These rumors followed Jesus for the rest of His life (cf. John 8:41; 9:29).

The mention of Jesus' brothers and sisters may be a reference to their attitude toward Him. Earlier, they had judged Him to have "lost His senses" (Mark 3:21), an opinion the other people of Nazareth undoubtedly shared. So, when they heard His wise teaching and saw His miraculous deeds—and then considered His origins—they "took offense at Him." The Greek term is *skandalizō* [4624], appearing in a middle/passive voice. It can describe being brought to one's downfall. Beyond bringing to mind the idea of being offended, this verb was the word of choice for deliberately placing a hazard in the path of another to cause injury or even death.

The people of Nazareth weren't merely "offended" in the sense that their feelings were hurt or they became angry. They stumbled over the issue of Jesus' identity. Their unwillingness to set aside their prejudice to accept Him as the Son of God brought them to their spiritual end. Mark's use of *skandalizō* indicates that they made the moral decision to reject Jesus as the Christ.

— 6:4-5 —

Jesus commented on their disbelief with a proverb. The word translated "honor" (6:4) could mean "deference," "reverence," or "respect," depending on the context. A prophet receives honor, except among those who know Him best. Note the progression: "hometown," "relatives," "household."

Jesus may have been quoting another teacher, but it is more likely that He originated this saying right then. Of course, He was more than a mere prophet; He undoubtedly said this in memory of the many Old Testament prophets who had been rejected by the religious authorities, ignored by the common people, and martyred by Israel's kings (cf. Matt. 5:12; 23:29-37; Luke 11:47-50; 13:34; 16:31).

As we examine this passage, keep Mark's original audience in mind. Imagine how the Lord's example would have applied to them during the persecution of Nero.

The next statement is intriguing: "He could do no miracle there except that He laid His hands on a few sick people and healed them" (Mark 6:5). Clearly, Mark means that in a general way the Lord's miracle-working ministry was limited, not completely absent. Even so, the text appears to suggest that God's power was limited by something in Nazareth.

Because God is omnipotent, He is able to do anything He determines to do. The fact that so few in Nazareth chose to set aside their prejudice points to their lack of faith—their lack of trust in Jesus as Messiah and Savior—as the limitation. Consequently, the Lord's power was not limited; His *purpose* was limited. Jesus could not perform miracles in the same way that a wise parent cannot give a disobedient child gifts until the rebellious behavior has been corrected.

— **6:6** —

The Nazarenes' lack of faith caused Jesus to "wonder." The term is *thaumazō* [2296], which appears in the Septuagint (the Greek translation of the Hebrew Old Testament) most often to describe someone's response to God's supernatural activity. Mark turns the word around to show God wondering at faithlessness so rigid that miracles became impractical. Unfortunately, the people of Nazareth and their refusal to believe in Christ represented the kind of spiritual dullness that had overtaken Israel.

Despite this widespread faithlessness, Jesus pressed on. He refused to curtail His ministry of preaching and healing; He continued to travel around Galilee, teaching anyone who would listen. All the same, He also began to focus more on His true followers while the general population became more cynical and combative.

APPLICATION: MARK 6:1-6

The Cynical, the Curious, and the Committed

I don't know if you've seen yourself in this story, but I see those I've encountered in my years of ministry there. I see three different settings featuring three different groups of people. First, I see disciples. In each of Mark's stories, I see genuine followers listening without debating anything. They truly drank in Jesus' teaching like parched souls at a well. While they failed to understand a great many things, they nonetheless accepted His Word as truth from God's lips.

To the disciples reading these words today—to the genuinely committed—I commend you. I'm grateful for you. You make your pastor's work a delight. You keep the wheels of ministry turning wherever you serve. You give preachers and teachers the courage to overcome difficulties, to power through opposition, and to remain faithful in their callings. Your response is seen in your face and heard in your words. You're saying, "Stand and deliver! We thank you for it. We're listening. We're grateful. We see the truth." You're "the company of the committed."[9]

There's a second group. Not quite committed, but curious. You haven't rejected the gospel because you're still reflecting, still undecided about all of this. You have honest doubts. Questions need answering, and your ears are attentive. I commend you as well. Stay with it.

Let me caution you, however. Don't wait to have every question answered, all your curiosity sated, every doubt dispelled. Even when you're born again, you won't have all the answers you seek. In fact, you'll discover that God delights to reveal many of His mysteries along your spiritual journey—an expedition you must choose to begin first. In the meantime, you may need more convincing proof. You may need time. But you're someone He still can heal.

The largest group consists of those who are cynical and closed. Cynics think all the problems rest with the people who believe or with the object of the believers' faith. They rarely, if ever, stop to consider that the problem with belief may lie within themselves. You cannot reason with a cynic because he or she has only questions to ask, never answers to risk. If you adequately address one supposed concern, the cynic quickly changes the subject by raising another "gotcha" question. I will not try to convince you of the truth; instead, I leave you to God. You're in His hands, and I pray He is merciful with you.

Years ago, I was traveling across South Texas and I heard a radio preacher near Del Rio on one of those "screamer stations"—the kind where the preachers think their point will only be understood based on the volume of their voice. The preacher at the microphone unloaded the truck on somebody who had opposed him publicly. He said, "I just want to say to some of you folks, I talked to God about you last night. And I said to God, 'Sic 'em. Just sic 'em.'"

Believe it or not, that's not bad theology. When I meet a stubborn skeptic, I often say under my breath, "Lord, sic 'em." And I don't mean for Him to be cruel or vindictive. The thought is, "Break down this person's resistance to Your truth; make Your Word irresistible." Only as the person's cynicism is crushed can saving faith begin to take its place. That's not to suggest that God takes delight in hurting people; it is only to say that spiritual surgery is usually needed, and it can be painful. If you're a cynic, I pray—for your sake—you will be crushed.

Travel Light, Think Right, Talk Straight
MARK 6:7-13

NASB

⁷ And He summoned the twelve and began to send them out in pairs, and gave them authority over the unclean spirits; ⁸ and He instructed them that they should take nothing for *their* journey, except a mere staff—no bread, no ᵃbag, no money in their belt— ⁹ but ᵃ*to* wear sandals; and *He added,* "Do not put on two ᵇtunics." ¹⁰ And He said to them, "Wherever you enter a house, stay there until you ᵃleave town. ¹¹ Any place that does not receive you or listen to you, as you go out from there, shake the dust ᵃoff the soles of your feet for a testimony against them." ¹² They went out and ᵃpreached that *men* should repent. ¹³ And they were casting out many demons and were anointing with oil many sick people and healing them.

6:8 ᵃOr *knapsack* or *beggar's bag* 6:9 ᵃLit *being shod with* ᵇOr *inner garments* 6:10 ᵃLit *go out from there* 6:11 ᵃLit *under your feet* 6:12 ᵃOr *proclaimed as a herald*

NLT

⁷ And he called his twelve disciples together and began sending them out two by two, giving them authority to cast out evil* spirits. ⁸ He told them to take nothing for their journey except a walking stick—no food, no traveler's bag, no money.* ⁹ He allowed them to wear sandals but not to take a change of clothes.

¹⁰ "Wherever you go," he said, "stay in the same house until you leave town. ¹¹ But if any place refuses to welcome you or listen to you, shake its dust from your feet as you leave to show that you have abandoned those people to their fate."

¹² So the disciples went out, telling everyone they met to repent of their sins and turn to God. ¹³ And they cast out many demons and healed many sick people, anointing them with olive oil.

6:7 Greek *unclean.* 6:8 Greek *no copper coins in their money belts.*

A handful of men turned the world upside down. Unlettered, unknown men from the region of Galilee—then considered a rural, backwater home to the first-century equivalent of rednecks—changed planet Earth as never before. They were successful because of their Master and His training. His game plan can be summarized in two words: "Follow Me." His strategy can be condensed into one sentence: "If I can trust you to follow Me, then you can trust Me to lead you." His first disciples trusted, He faithfully led them, and the world has never been the same.

Having selected the Twelve, Jesus spent time with them, modeled for them how they should conduct ministry, clarified His expectations, and then released them. There was no formal curriculum, no audition process, no lecture to attend, no tuition to pay, no established course of study, no written examination. They had only the Old Testament Scriptures to read and the divine Author of those writings to teach them.

149

How extravagantly simple. Amazing as it may seem with this high-tech, sophisticated, corporate mentality of ours—where business seminars are expensive and corporate training programs are complicated—Jesus prepared these men by drawing them close to Himself, remaining authentic and transparent in their company, and allowing them to experience ministry at His side. He didn't merely give His followers knowledge and skills; He transformed them. And this transformation didn't take place through dogmas and laws and rituals, but rather in relationship with a living person who walked among them—in acquaintance with His personality, style, and methods. They saw Him up close and personal, and as a result, these ordinary men went on to accomplish extraordinary things.

After the Twelve had accompanied Jesus in His ministry for a while, He sent them out to begin to do the same miracles He had been doing, and more importantly, to spread the same teaching by His authority. They had learned with Him and now they would learn in pairs as an independent study of ministry. As Jesus sent them out, He gave practical instructions that reflect some important principles for ministry.

— 6:7 —

A subtle shift takes place between 6:6 and 6:7. Mark's emphasis transitions from Jesus and His disciples to focus on the disciples and their ministry. During the Lord's itinerant ministry of preaching, teaching, healing, and casting out demons in Galilee, He summoned the Twelve to delegate these ministry duties to them. When delegating a task to a subordinate, a leader initiates a transaction. Instructions and authority are handed down; in return, the leader expects accountability.

In 6:7-32, Mark again begins one story, breaks away to tell another, and then returns to conclude the first story (see comments on 3:20-21; 5:25-27; 11:12-14):

A. The Twelve are delegated the responsibility to go out and preach the gospel. (6:7-13)
B. John the Baptizer is martyred for his faithful witness. (6:14-29)
Á. The Twelve give account of their activities. (6:30-32)

Rather than attempt to devour the entire sandwich in one sitting, I have elected to give attention to the first two components in their own segments of this commentary. This one will examine the Lord's delegation of responsibility to the Twelve.

The Dynamics of Two by Two

MARK 6:7

During the early days of my training at Dallas Seminary, I met a wonderful young man named Swede Anderson. Swede went on to serve with Campus Crusade for Christ and has had a marvelous ministry over many years. From the very beginning of His ministry career, even during seminary, Swede involved himself in campus ministry. On one occasion, he said to me, "Why don't you go with me up to the Oklahoma campus in Norman this weekend to preach on the free-speech platforms?"

Back in the 1960s, anybody could "stand and deliver" on these platforms and speak his or her mind on any subject. I said, "Great! Sounds wonderful."

He warned, "Just be ready for anything."

I braced myself for rejection. I expected hecklers as I took my place on the platform and began to preach about Christ. While I preached, Swede stood about 15 or 20 yards from me, pouring his heart out to people gathering around him. As I proclaimed the truth about sin and Christ's gift of His life in exchange for our punishment, splat! I looked down to see the guts of a tomato oozing down my chest.

That doesn't usually happen in church services. As I stared blankly at the organic residue of rejection dripping from my shirt, Swede looked over at me and yelled out, "Exciting, isn't it?"

That helped put my circumstances into perspective. It was a tomato, not a stone or a hand grenade. He laughed, I laughed, and we pressed on. Later, the words of Winston Churchill came to mind: "Nothing in life is so exhilarating as to be shot at without result."

You go out in pairs so that you know how to be "shot at without result." If you're alone, you'll probably turn and run. Or you'll try to fight the enemy in your own strength. A faithful partner will say, "Don't run. Don't let your mind go there." A steadfast companion in ministry will offer wisdom when you're out of ideas. Or when you get discouraged, your partner will say, "Come on, we can make it through this."

"Two are better than one," wrote Solomon (Eccl. 4:9). It's true. Going out in pairs is very wise. I've rarely seen lone rangers survive long.

Jesus didn't tell the disciples where to go; He apparently allowed them to decide where they would proclaim the good news. The Gospel of Luke says they went "throughout the villages . . . everywhere" (Luke 9:6). Matthew, however, includes a few additional details. The disciples could travel anywhere except Samaria, and wherever they did go, they were to evangelize "the lost sheep of the house of Israel" (Matt. 10:5-6). This is not surprising, given the Jewish orientation of Matthew's Gospel. While Matthew's account highlights the continuity of the new covenant as proceeding from the old covenant, Mark wrote his Gospel to encourage a faithful witness among believers facing persecution—a theme needed by the church throughout its two-thousand-year history.

Mark gives special attention to the transaction between the Master and His trainees. He sent them out in pairs—the Greek wording (apparently reflecting a Hebrew or an Aramaic idiom) is *dyo dyo* [1417], which means "two by two"—armed with His authority over evil and a specific set of instructions. This early method of ministering features two important elements: companionship (cf. Eccl. 4:9) and authority. Let's examine each element independently.

Jesus granted His disciples the advantage of *companionship* because He understood the power of discouragement. Were it not for His continual, uninhibited fellowship with His Father and the indwelling of the Holy Spirit, Jesus would have ministered alone. While He cherished the companionship of His closest students, Peter, James, and John, no humans fully understood Him—not until His ascension and the arrival of the Holy Spirit within believers.

In my early days of training in the Marine Corps, we were taught to dig a hole in the ground large enough for two. During the heat of battle, fellow warriors must bear equally the duties of fighting; during the terrifying silence between enemy attacks, when imagination runs wild, survival depends upon mutual encouragement. Two-by-two still works!

Jesus also delegated His *authority* over evil, which included—but was not limited to—the authority to command demons to release individuals from bondage. The word for this authority is *exousia* [1849], which refers to more than mere power. Unlike Luke (Luke 9:1), Mark omits *dynamis* [1411] from the dialogue to focus on the Lord's delegated authority. The distinction between *exousia* and *dynamis* is subtle yet important.

Exousia is an intrinsic influence that comes from another source. The other source in the case of a police officer standing in an intersection directing traffic is a government agency. A city or state government stands behind the officer, who uses this authority to stop traffic by holding up a hand. The officer cannot possibly stop a two-ton vehicle using personal might or "power" (*dynamis*). Rather, the officer depends upon the authority of a judge, who will say to violators, "By the authority vested in me by the people of this state, I hereby declare you are guilty as charged and subject to fines or imprisonment." That's authority.

— 6:8-9 —

Having delegated His authority, Jesus gave the Twelve specific instructions. While they were replicating His ministry of proclaiming the gospel, casting out demons, and healing the sick, they were to forego the normal preparations of a journey. Instead, they were to follow a model we might call "functional simplicity." A good motto for functional simplicity would be "Travel light."

Obviously, traveling in the first century was very different from our modern methods. Today, we can pile into a car and start out with nothing more than a few possessions, a plastic card, and a GPS. We have a highway system filled with choices for lodging and dining, as well as hundreds of fuel stations to keep us moving. If you have money, you can travel indefinitely, no preparation needed.

In the first century, travelers either carried everything they needed on their backs or in a cart, or they depended upon the hospitality of strangers. Carrying large sums of cash to pay for lodging and food was not advisable; some stretches of road teemed with robbers preying upon travelers in small groups. Fortunately, the ancient Near Eastern culture made hospitality to strangers a sacred duty. So the Lord's instructions were not a call to be foolhardy. The disciples were, however, expected to depend upon God's provision along the way rather than load up a cart with several weeks' worth of necessities.

Their provisions were to include little more than a staff, which shepherds and travelers would use to steady their gait and as a means of self-defense, and sandals. No food, no change of clothes, no money, not even a change of undergarments. At this time, a tunic was a plain garment worn next to the skin, over which one wore a decorative outer garment. A change of tunics would be needed if a traveler didn't have access to both water for washing and privacy. In other words, the disciples should expect God to supply all of their needs, including lodging. He wanted them unencumbered by the distractions of *too much* preparation and unburdened from the stresses of provision so they could focus on their mission.

— 6:10-11 —

At first glance, the Lord's advice looks like a quote from Yogi Berra: "Wherever you are, stay 'til you leave." In truth, Jesus meant for His disciples to remain in one household while evangelizing a given population center. They were not to move from house to house but to receive the hospitality of a single host until they had completed their work in that city. He didn't want them to move into one guest quarters only to entertain more attractive offers of hospitality. He didn't want them to gain a reputation for freeloading like many false teachers of the day. He wanted them unencumbered and focused.

Jesus also encouraged the Twelve to use their time wisely. He didn't charge them with the responsibility to convince people without "ears to hear" or to plead with the obstinate to surrender to Jesus as Messiah (see comments on 4:8-9). He told them to proclaim the truth boldly and effectively only to those ready to receive the gospel message. If His men encountered resistance to the Word of God, they were to "shake the dust from under [their] feet" (my literal translation) as a witness to those people's eventual judgment before God. Devout Jews typically used this gesture when leaving Gentile or Samaritan territory to symbolize their dissociation from people outside God's covenant with Abraham. In this context, the Twelve symbolically said to rebellious Jews, "By rejecting Jesus as your Messiah, you are not one of God's covenant people, and you're no better than a pagan."

— 6:12-13 —

Mark's brevity here is deliberate. Jesus commanded and the Twelve obeyed. Jesus sent and the disciples went. Jesus told His followers to testify, so the Twelve scattered across Israel and the surrounding areas to wherever they could find their fellow Jews. And they replicated the ministry of Jesus as they had witnessed it for many months. They preached repentance (6:12; cf. 1:15). That is, they proclaimed the good news of Jesus Christ and called individuals to turn away from their old, sinful ways of living in order to trust in the Messiah as their Savior from sin.

Repentance is not merely feeling sorry for sin. Repentance is a deliberate, radical, life-changing decision to turn away from the wrong direction and to turn toward the right direction. When you come to Christ, you deliberately leave your old way of living behind. You change your mind about the direction which is wrong, and you turn in the direction which is right. You make the decision to trust Christ alone and to trust yourself no longer.

A quote from the novel *Quo Vadis* vividly expresses the idea of repentance. In this story set in Rome during the persecution of Nero, a character named Vinicius reflects on the gospel message he had heard: "He felt that if he wished . . . to follow that teaching, he would have to place on a burning pile all his thoughts, habits, and character, his whole nature up to that moment, burn them into ashes, and then fill himself with a life altogether different, and an entirely new soul."[10]

In addition to preaching the gospel, the Twelve used their delegated authority to cast out demons and to heal the sick. Mark mentions the disciples' use of oil in their ministry, writing that they were "anointing" the sick (6:13). The Greek language has two words for the application of oil: *aleiphō* [218] and *chriō* [5548]. The latter most commonly refers to the ceremonial anointing used to signify God's special blessing upon someone. The term *aleiphō*—the one Mark uses here—is quite different. It describes the pragmatic, therapeutic use of oil, such as rubbing or massaging with it for medicinal purposes. Various herbs and extracts were added to olive oil to aid with a number of afflictions.

Throughout Jesus' ministry, it's clear that all four Gospels have miraculous healing in mind. And Luke's description of Jesus sending out the disciples would lead us to assume their healing of the sick was by supernatural means as well. Mark's mention of medicinal oil, therefore, does not suggest that they merely practiced medicine on the evangelism trail. The fact that they cast out demons argues against that view. They apparently applied a combination of natural therapies and supernatural healing.

Mark compares the deeds of the Twelve to the activities of Jesus. They became imitators of their Master and multiplied His ministry six times over, going out two by two. Mark's description also highlights their success. Their obedience accomplished much in Israel. In fact, they created such an impact that Herod Antipas began to fear the movement he thought he had ended by killing John the Baptizer (6:14-16).

APPLICATION: MARK 6:7-13

Success in Ministry

Let's examine the ministry of the Twelve to see what we might learn from their example.

First, *keep your life simple and free from distractions.* If you want to maintain an effective ministry—regardless of your vocation—and present a faithful witness, then simplify. Keep your life uncomplicated and free of distractions. You have to determine whether what you possess is too much or just enough. You have to make that determination— no one can give you a list. As you cultivate an authentic relationship with the Lord, maintaining a sensitivity to the Holy Spirit's prompting, determine to live above the downward drag of possessions, position, money, or any other encumbrance. Learn to say no. Train yourself to think, *Enough.* Practice the words, "I am content with what I have, so that's enough."

Second, *stay where you should and leave when you must.* Just because the going gets tough where you are doesn't mean you should cut your losses and move on. Sometimes you need to tough it out to be a faithful witness to Jesus Christ and the gospel. Don't let a loud minority speak for the whole group; hang in there. When you sense it is no longer right or best for you to stay, then make a graceful, dignified exit. Leave and never look back. You served faithfully, regardless of the results, but it's time to move on.

Third, *tell the truth.* Just admit the truth that if there's any success in ministry, God is responsible, often in spite of us. Even so, He delights to share His victories with those who answer His call and say, "Yes, Lord, send me."

Cynthia and I led a group of people on a Reformation tour in Europe. While in Martin Luther's part of the world, we encountered a number of the great Reformer's quotes. When asked about launching the Protestant Reformation, he replied, "I simply taught, preached, wrote God's Word. Otherwise I did nothing. And then, while I slept, or drank Wittenberg beer with my Philip and my Amsdorf, the Word so greatly weakened the Papacy that never a Prince or Emperor inflicted such damage upon it. I did nothing. The Word did it all."[11]

If ministers don't rely upon the Word, it's because they don't trust the Word. They trust entertainment. They trust the strategies of our times. They trust that their own creativity and cleverness will keep people coming back. Wrong. The truth is this: God's Word—and God's Word alone—lives forever.

For years in my ministry, I worried about whether congregations grew or declined. My Sundays were miserable. I'd focus on how many people were there. I'd go over my sermon and I'd rewrite lines that I knew weren't clear and accurate, sometimes obsessing over them. Fortunately, I have learned a lot since then. I'm not worried about how many are present and who hears what and which person will respond. I'm not in charge of people's response; I'm responsible to proclaim the Word faithfully, clearly, correctly, compellingly, and passionately. Now after I preach the Word, I relax. I go home and doze in front of the Sunday football games. If I sow faithfully, God will give the increase.

Murder at a Stag Party
MARK 6:14-29

NASB

¹⁴And King Herod heard *of it*, for His name had become well known; and *people* were saying, "John the Baptist has risen from the dead, and that is why these miraculous powers are at work in Him." ¹⁵But others were saying, "He is Elijah." And others were saying, "*He is* a prophet, like one of the prophets *of old*." ¹⁶But when Herod heard *of it*, he kept saying, "John, whom I beheaded, has risen!"

¹⁷For Herod himself had sent and had John arrested and bound in prison on account of Herodias, the wife of his brother Philip, because he had married her. ¹⁸For John had been saying to Herod, "It is not lawful for you to have your brother's wife." ¹⁹Herodias had a grudge against him and wanted to put him to death and could not *do so;* ²⁰for Herod was afraid of John, knowing that he was a righteous and holy man, and he kept him safe. And when he heard him, he

NLT

¹⁴Herod Antipas, the king, soon heard about Jesus, because everyone was talking about him. Some were saying,* "This must be John the Baptist raised from the dead. That is why he can do such miracles." ¹⁵Others said, "He's the prophet Elijah." Still others said, "He's a prophet like the other great prophets of the past."

¹⁶When Herod heard about Jesus, he said, "John, the man I beheaded, has come back from the dead."

¹⁷For Herod had sent soldiers to arrest and imprison John as a favor to Herodias. She had been his brother Philip's wife, but Herod had married her. ¹⁸John had been telling Herod, "It is against God's law for you to marry your brother's wife." ¹⁹So Herodias bore a grudge against John and wanted to kill him. But without Herod's approval she was powerless, ²⁰for Herod respected John; and knowing that he was a good and holy man, he protected him. Herod

NASB

was very perplexed; [a]but he [b]used to enjoy listening to him. [21]A strategic day came when Herod on his birthday gave a banquet for his lords and [a]military commanders and the leading men of Galilee; [22]and when the daughter of Herodias herself came in and danced, she pleased Herod and [a]his dinner guests; and the king said to the girl, "Ask me for whatever you want and I will give it to you." [23]And he swore to her, "Whatever you ask of me, I will give it to you; up to half of my kingdom." [24]And she went out and said to her mother, "What shall I ask for?" And she said, "The head of John the Baptist." [25]Immediately she came in a hurry to the king and asked, saying, "I want you to give me at once the head of John the Baptist on a platter." [26]And although the king was very sorry, *yet* because of his oaths and because of [a]his dinner guests, he was unwilling to refuse her. [27]Immediately the king sent an executioner and commanded *him* to bring *back* his head. And he went and had him beheaded in the prison, [28]and brought his head on a platter, and gave it to the girl; and the girl gave it to her mother. [29]When his disciples heard *about this*, they came and took away his body and laid it in a tomb.

6:20 [a]Lit *and* [b]Lit *was hearing him gladly*
6:21 [a]I.e. chiliarchs, in command of a thousand troops 6:22 [a]Lit *those who reclined at the table with him* 6:26 [a]Lit *those reclining at the table*

NLT

was greatly disturbed whenever he talked with John, but even so, he liked to listen to him.

[21]Herodias's chance finally came on Herod's birthday. He gave a party for his high government officials, army officers, and the leading citizens of Galilee. [22]Then his daughter, also named Herodias,* came in and performed a dance that greatly pleased Herod and his guests. "Ask me for anything you like," the king said to the girl, "and I will give it to you." [23]He even vowed, "I will give you whatever you ask, up to half my kingdom!"

[24]She went out and asked her mother, "What should I ask for?"

Her mother told her, "Ask for the head of John the Baptist!"

[25]So the girl hurried back to the king and told him, "I want the head of John the Baptist, right now, on a tray!"

[26]Then the king deeply regretted what he had said; but because of the vows he had made in front of his guests, he couldn't refuse her. [27]So he immediately sent an executioner to the prison to cut off John's head and bring it to him. The soldier beheaded John in the prison, [28]brought his head on a tray, and gave it to the girl, who took it to her mother. [29]When John's disciples heard what had happened, they came to get his body and buried it in a tomb.

6:14 Some manuscripts read *He was saying.*
6:22 Some manuscripts read *the daughter of Herodias herself.*

Some stories in the Bible are so heartbreaking that they almost make us weep. Others are so filled with adventure that we find ourselves transported to faraway places with strange-sounding names, places we will never see. And then there are stories filled with heroism and courage, tales that give us strength to go on as we see the faith of godly men and women triumph over evil. And then there are stories so shocking, shameless, and scandalous, it's hard to believe they appear in the pages of God's inspired book. They read like lurid pieces of pulp fiction, things you'd see on the supermarket checkout stand. Scenes that raw and vulgar just don't seem to fit the Bible.

This segment of Mark's Gospel is like that. With vivid storytelling, he transports us from our sanitized world of comfort and stability to a time when rulers did as they pleased. He rips us from our homes to place us into a sleazy setting of pulsating music, filthy jokes, sensual dancing, too much alcohol, and too little moral restraint. For sixteen verses, we must observe the shameful inner court of Herod Antipas, the son of Herod the Great and tetrarch of Galilee and Perea.

— 6:14-16 —

Herod the Great had dreamed of becoming the emperor of Israel. He so jealously guarded the title "king of the Jews" that he ordered the slaughter of male toddlers in and around Bethlehem in an attempt to kill the Messiah, the rightful bearer of the title (Matt. 2:16). He even had two of his own sons, Alexander and Aristobulus, killed after suspecting they wanted his throne too soon. Caesar Augustus reportedly blurted out, "I'd rather be Herod's pig than Herod's son!"[12]

When Herod the Great died around 4 BC, his wealth and lands were divided among his wicked sons (see map on page 25). Galilee and Perea went to Herod Antipas, who followed his father's example of using building projects to gain political favor in Rome but lacked the intelligence and self-discipline to use it well. His appetite for women—usually other men's wives—undermined any hope of expanding his territory. He evidently made up for his lack of political savvy by throwing lavish and wild parties.

Jesus' fame continued to spread throughout Galilee, and it eventually reached Herod's palace. As often happens, the rumor mill blended truth with folklore to concoct a story that was certain to shake Antipas to his core. Some rumors suggested that Elijah had returned to Israel as promised in Old Testament prophecy (Mark 6:15; cf. Mal. 3:1; 4:5-6). Others claimed Jesus was merely a prophet (cf. Matt. 21:11). But Antipas, plagued by his guilty conscience, latched onto his worst fear—that John the Baptizer had returned from the dead to claim his vengeance.

— 6:17-18 —

To explain the reason for Antipas's fear, Mark inserted a flashback story of how the tetrarch of Galilee had killed the most revered man in all of Israel. Even John's political and religious enemies in Jerusalem had refused to touch him for fear of the people and the potential of angering God (Matt. 14:5; 21:26).

Herod's feud with the Baptizer began when Herod drove his own wife into exile in order to consummate an adulterous liaison with his sister-in-law and niece, Herodias. By marrying his brother's wife, he not only violated an important marriage treaty, causing political unrest, but he also violated Jewish Law (Lev. 18:16; 20:21). John, of course, didn't care about politics or treaties; he objected to the shameless disregard for God, His Law, and the covenant Antipas supposedly upheld as a ruler of Jews. Consequently, Antipas locked him away in a dungeon near his palace.

— 6:19-20 —

The wife Herod had banished was the daughter of his rival, King Aretas IV of Nabatea, who ruled from Damascus. The woman he stole had been the wife of his half brother Philip, whose territory bordered his own in the north. Consequently, he needed to keep Rome happy. To satisfy Rome, he needed to keep the Galileans happy—no easy task considering his open disdain for Jewish Law. So although Herodias wanted John executed, Antipas couldn't bring himself to do it. He not only feared John's power, which he didn't understand, but he also feared losing the support of the people, which he needed desperately.

John languished in prison for two full years. Mark explains an additional reason Antipas kept John alive: He respected the Baptizer as "a righteous and holy man" (6:20). Moreover, he found John oddly fascinating, such that "gladly he was listening to him" (my literal translation). This phrase might also be translated as "he was listening to him fondly." This detail has invited all kinds of speculation through the centuries, so I won't hold back mine. I believe he saw in John a kind of integrity he knew he didn't have the spine to maintain. He saw an earnest devotion to God that he longed to experience but didn't have the faintest idea how to have it. He kept John around like a talisman and protected him from harm because the man in his dungeon was his last and only connection with anything good.

— 6:21-23 —

Herod's wife had been looking for the right opportunity to maneuver him into executing John. Her waiting paid off on Antipas's birthday, during which he threw another infamous party with all the rulers, military leaders, and leading citizens of Galilee. Women were typically not allowed to attend this kind of party except as servers or entertainers. This was truly what past generations would have called a "stag party." Normally, the dancers would be highly educated, sophisticated courtesans whose role in society stood somewhere above simple prostitutes but below concubines. Their dancing promised to end with sex before morning. No doubt as the alcohol flowed freely and the festivities grew to a crescendo, Herodias sent in her daughter to dance in place of the courtesans.

History tells us that the daughter in question was Salome, Herodias's child by Philip, Antipas's brother. Of course, Herodias was the niece of both men, which made the girl Antipas's blood relative as well as stepdaughter. (At this point, the Herodian family tree becomes a twisted vine.) The Greek term rendered "girl" (6:22) indicates that she was a teenager of marriageable age.

Herodias knew her husband well. Her daughter's seductive dance aroused Antipas so much that he blurted out a rash promise to reward the girl with a request. The expression "up to half of my kingdom" (6:23) was hyperbole, of course, but it bound him by oath to grant her wish (cf. Esth. 5:6; 7:2). Mark stated earlier that every notable man in Galilee attended, which put Antipas on the spot. He couldn't renege without losing the respect and admiration of his peers.

— 6:24-25 —

Interestingly, Salome knew the kind of performance to give—nothing a woman of her social standing needed to know—but she didn't know the purpose. When Antipas made his promise, she had to leave the room to ask her mother what to request. This was the moment Herodias had been waiting for, and she didn't hesitate. Salome appeared unmoved by her mother's gruesome demand: the head of John the Baptizer. In fact, she embellished the order by asking for it "at once" and for it to be delivered on a platter (6:25), an added element of derision against the man her mother hated. Furthermore, she heightened the drama of her request by putting John's name at the end of her sentence. (She most likely spoke Greek.) A literal translation would be, "I want, at once, you to give me on a platter the head of John the Baptizer."

— 6:26-28 —

Antipas suddenly found himself in a dilemma. He had to "put up or shut up." Mark describes him as "very sorry" upon hearing the request (6:26), either because he genuinely hated the idea of killing John or because he had been outwitted by his own lust. As John Phillips states,

Herod was sorry that his drunken tongue had landed him in such an awkward situation. But he was not sorry enough to do what was right. He was not sorry about his sin; he went on to commit worse ones. He was only sorry that he had said what he had said and that he had no way out of his predicament, except to confess himself in the wrong. But with the curious eyes of his guests upon him, and the implacable eye of Herodias in his thoughts, and the mocking eye of Salome challenging him, he forgot all about the all-seeing eye of God.[13]

Sorry for the rash promise but bound by pride and vanity to follow through, he "immediately" (6:27) ordered the executioner to carry out the beheading and to return with John's head on a platter as the girl had instructed. To indicate the executioner, Mark uses a Latin loanword his audience knew all too well. The man would have been a bodyguard to Herod, not unlike the Praetorians who acted as Caesar's secret police, doing his dirty work whenever called upon.

When the blood-filled platter—literally, "large dish"—arrived, Salome gave it to her mother.

— 6:29 —

When John's students heard about his death, they came to request his body for burial. We have no indication of whether this included the Baptizer's head. Regardless, the task would have been heart wrenching for the men who had loved and served their teacher during previous years.

Mark draws a clear parallel between John's death and burial and that of Jesus, no doubt to make a point. Jesus' first faithful witness had endured the hostility of the religious elite, and from a godless, amoral ruler he had received persecution, ridicule, imprisonment, and finally death. He died like his Lord eventually would. Faithful witnesses could take comfort in knowing that they, too, suffered like Jesus. And if they faced death, they could do so with honor. As Paul would later write, they would "know Him and the power of His resurrection and the fellowship of His sufferings, being conformed to His death" (Phil. 3:10).

I don't want to suffer persecution, and I don't long for a painful martyr's death. I will accept them if they come, however. My great hope is that, regardless of how I die, my last breath brings glory to my Savior. May it be so for all of us.

APPLICATION: MARK 6:14-29
Character Studies

Narrative literature like the Gospels offers us a unique opportunity to gain spiritual wisdom, because stories invite us to see ourselves in the characters. Herodias teaches us something. Herod offers us insight. Salome presents a vital lesson we cannot afford to ignore. Here are some timeless lessons I find in the players of this Gospel drama.

Herodias teaches us about the danger of revenge. If you're nurturing a grudge, you're courting disaster. You don't think so because your resentment hasn't yet bloomed into hatred and Satan hasn't yet baited his trap with a vicious plan for revenge. But keep massaging that grudge, and you'll soon find a tantalizing opportunity to get your own justice. When Herodias discovered that her "strategic day" had arrived (cf. 6:21), her hunger for revenge sealed the eternal doom of three souls: her own, her husband's, and her daughter's.

Herod teaches us about the power of peer pressure. As the sovereign of Galilee, he wielded more political and military power than any other person in the region. He answered to no one but the emperor of Rome, yet his personal weakness made him the puppet of his wife and a servant to the opinion of the court. He didn't want John dead; his wife did. He wanted to renege on the outrageous request of his stepdaughter, but his need for public acceptance forced his hand. Herod warns us to examine our need for the approval of others and to be guided by conscience, not pride.

Salome teaches us about the deceptiveness of rationalization. According to one dictionary, "rationalize" means "to attribute (one's actions) to rational and creditable motives without analysis of true and especially unconscious motives."[14] Some have called this behavior "the Eichmann syndrome." Adolf Eichman was Adolf Hitler's commandant in charge of the death camps, ordering the slaughter of millions of Jews. When made to stand trial for such unconscionable acts of murder, he calmly defended himself with these five words: "I was only following orders."

Salome didn't know John the Baptizer, and she had no personal quarrel with him. When her mother decided to pimp her out as entertainment at her stepfather's stag party, she mindlessly followed orders. When urged to ask for the head of an innocent man she did not even know, she blindly followed orders. She didn't push back or ask any questions; she did as she was told. She rationalized that obedience to her mother overshadowed what she undoubtedly knew to be wrong. (By the way, never forget that parents have a powerful influence over their children, teaching them right from wrong and good from evil. Our children watch us and learn, whether we know we're teaching or not.)

Finally, *the whole story teaches us about the extent of sin*. One of my sources has given me a wonderful word-picture; these words are a blend of what he wrote and what I have thought:

> Sin is like a spider weaving its web. Beginning with a single filament, thread after thread is spun and interconnected until the filmy structure forms a sticky world of its own.

Herod's web of foolish lusts and Herodias's web of vengeful bitterness caught Salome in their sticky tangles. At first, she knew nothing of the murderous plot. She began to dance, and before long, she became culpable in a senseless, helter-skelter act of murder!

If only we would stop and consider how many innocent lives could be drawn into our own sinful webs. Unfortunately, the webs we spin have a powerful self-deluding power that we ourselves become helpless to see.

Before we cluck our tongues and point our fingers or blame anyone in this tragic story, we must pause and take a critical look at ourselves.

An Unforgettable Dinner on the Grounds
MARK 6:30-44

NASB

30 The apostles gathered together with Jesus; and they reported to Him all that they had done and taught. 31 And He said to them, "Come away by yourselves to a secluded place and rest a while." (For there were many *people* coming and going, and they did not even have time to eat.) 32 They went away in the boat to a secluded place by themselves.

33 *The people* saw them going, and

NLT

30 The apostles returned to Jesus from their ministry tour and told him all they had done and taught. 31 Then Jesus said, "Let's go off by ourselves to a quiet place and rest awhile." He said this because there were so many people coming and going that Jesus and his apostles didn't even have time to eat.

32 So they left by boat for a quiet place, where they could be alone. 33 But many people recognized them

many recognized *them* and ran there together on foot from all the cities, and got there ahead of them. ³⁴When Jesus went ªashore, He saw a large crowd, and He felt compassion for them because they were like sheep without a shepherd; and He began to teach them many things. ³⁵When it was already quite late, His disciples came to Him and said, "ªThis place is desolate and it is already quite late; ³⁶send them away so that they may go into the surrounding countryside and villages and buy themselves ªsomething to eat." ³⁷But He answered them, "You give them *something* to eat!" And they said to Him, "Shall we go and spend two hundred ªdenarii on bread and give them *something* to eat?" ³⁸And He said to them, "How many loaves do you have? Go look!" And when they found out, they said, "Five, and two fish." ³⁹And He commanded them all to ªsit down by groups on the green grass. ⁴⁰They ªsat down in groups of hundreds and of fifties. ⁴¹And He took the five loaves and the two fish, and looking up toward heaven, He blessed *the food* and broke the loaves and He kept giving *them* to the disciples to set before them; and He divided up the two fish among them all. ⁴²They all ate and were satisfied, ⁴³and they picked up twelve full baskets of the broken pieces, and also of the fish. ⁴⁴There were five thousand men who ate the loaves.

6:34 ªLit *out*   6:35 ªLit *The*   6:36 ªLit *what they may eat*   6:37 ªThe denarius was equivalent to one day's wage   6:39 ªLit *recline*   6:40 ªLit *reclined*

and saw them leaving, and people from many towns ran ahead along the shore and got there ahead of them. ³⁴Jesus saw the huge crowd as he stepped from the boat, and he had compassion on them because they were like sheep without a shepherd. So he began teaching them many things.

³⁵Late in the afternoon his disciples came to him and said, "This is a remote place, and it's already getting late. ³⁶Send the crowds away so they can go to the nearby farms and villages and buy something to eat."

³⁷But Jesus said, "You feed them."

"With what?" they asked. "We'd have to work for months to earn enough money* to buy food for all these people!"

³⁸"How much bread do you have?" he asked. "Go and find out."

They came back and reported, "We have five loaves of bread and two fish."

³⁹Then Jesus told the disciples to have the people sit down in groups on the green grass. ⁴⁰So they sat down in groups of fifty or a hundred. ⁴¹Jesus took the five loaves and two fish, looked up toward heaven, and blessed them. Then, breaking the loaves into pieces, he kept giving the bread to the disciples so they could distribute it to the people. He also divided the fish for everyone to share. ⁴²They all ate as much as they wanted, ⁴³and afterward, the disciples picked up twelve baskets of leftover bread and fish. ⁴⁴A total of 5,000 men and their families were fed.*

6:37 Greek *It would take 200 denarii.* A denarius was equivalent to a laborer's full day's wage.
6:44 Some manuscripts read *fed from the loaves.*

As we look back over the last five, eight, or even ten years of our own lives, who among us would have anticipated years like that? I suspect very few. Not only is our God filled with surprises, but He puts us in situations that are humanly impossible. Every one of us could put together a list of impossibilities we have faced over the past few years. In fact, at this very moment, you may be living with a situation that is impossible. Not merely difficult. More than just worrisome. Deeper than troubling. From your vantage point, the predicament is humanly impossible. You can't fix it, and you're having a difficult time tolerating it. Unless God comes through, your impossible situation will remain an impossibility.

Before we examine this segment of Mark's Gospel, let me ask you to ponder three questions.

First, what is an impossibility? What do we mean by the expression "impossible situation"? A situation becomes "impossible" when it is insuperably difficult—hopeless from our point of view, extremely undesirable, beyond any normal human ability to resolve.

Second, what is *your* impossibility? It might be something that you have caused. Or maybe it's an impossible situation in which you are an innocent victim. It may be the consequence of a foolish decision, or several foolish decisions back-to-back. You may have violated one of God's long-standing principles of life and are suffering for it.

Third, what does God's Word teach us about impossibilities? You may be interested to know that the Bible addresses the topic directly in at least three places. I will simply list a couple of key verses, but I encourage you to read them in context:

> Ah Lord God! Behold, You have made the heavens and the earth by Your great power and by Your outstretched arm! Nothing is too difficult for You. (Jer. 32:17)

> But He said, "The things that are impossible with people are possible with God." (Luke 18:27)

Of course, a third passage is Mark 6:30-44 (along with the parallel accounts in Matt. 14:13-21, Luke 9:10-17, and John 6:1-14).

Like the disciples, we live and make decisions in a realm governed by two opposing points of view. Every conscious moment from the time you awaken until you fall asleep each day, you operate your life from one of two viewpoints: the human viewpoint or the divine viewpoint. Every day, as you observe life and interpret what you see, you perceive circumstances from either the horizontal plane or from the vertical.

What do I mean by the human, horizontal viewpoint? That is our own limited perspective and plan. It revolves around ourselves—how *we* feel, what *we* expect, the things *we* think, *our* assumptions. The human, egocentric, people-power viewpoint dominates every news broadcast, every news article, every self-help book, and every get-rich-quick scheme. This perspective seeps from every pore of Hollywood's elite and drives the rich and famous to want more, more, always more.

The divine viewpoint is the exact opposite. The one who operates his or her life in this way views the world from a vertical, unlimited perspective and plan. This divine orientation observes life in terms of how *God* operates, what He has in mind, and what He has planned on our behalf. If I operate my life from the divine viewpoint, I interpret every circumstance as God's opportunity to accomplish His agenda.

As we begin our examination of this pivotal event in the disciples' education, bear in mind that we are like they were. Jesus used this incident to teach His followers something that would impact their understanding of ministry for the rest of their lives.

— 6:30 —

This verse concludes the story Mark began in 6:7-13, in which Jesus sent the Twelve out to minister in Galilee two by two. He had delegated to them the tasks of preaching, healing, and casting out demons—in imitation of His own ministry—and granted them His divine authority to carry out their mission. According to Mark and the other Gospel writers, their ministry saw amazing success; they accomplished through the Lord's authority what no mere human could apart from God. In fact, their success poured fuel on Herod's burning conscience; he feared the return of John the Baptizer from the grave (6:16).

Having recounted the unjust imprisonment and gruesome martyrdom of Jesus' first faithful witness, Mark returns to the story he began. The excited disciples returned to Capernaum with stories to tell their Master.

— 6:31-33 —

Crowds seeking an audience with Jesus continued to flow into Capernaum, keeping Him from attending to His disciples. They needed His guidance more than ever after their exhilarating time of ministry in Galilee. So He took the men on a retreat, first to Bethsaida (according to Luke 9:10), and then by boat to the wilderness northeast of the Sea of Galilee. He and the disciples frequently disappeared into the relatively fertile hill country to recover, to rest, and to prepare for further ministry. As often happens, though, escape from the demands of ministry proved difficult. By the time they arrived, the ever-present multitude greeted them with a host of expectations.

— 6:34 —

From a horizontal, human viewpoint, the mass of people looked like a multitude of burdens. No doubt a few of the disciples said, "Let's keep sailing. If we go to the other side, they won't find us." But Jesus saw something different. The Good Shepherd saw aimless, vulnerable sheep. This word picture may have come from Jesus Himself, recalling the words of Moses: "May the LORD, the God of the spirits of all flesh, appoint a man over the congregation, who will go out and come in before them, and who will lead them out and bring them in, so that the congregation of the LORD will not be like sheep which have no shepherd" (Num. 27:16-17).

The men reluctantly pulled ashore and Jesus quickly went to work, beginning to "teach them many things."

— 6:35-36 —

As Jesus ministered to the spiritual needs of the multitude, their physical needs became an issue. While "man does not live by bread alone" (Deut. 8:3), bread is essential nonetheless. The weary disciples suggested the Lord conclude His teaching and send the people on their way before hunger became a concern. To be fair, it was a reasonable suggestion. Jesus could use a break while the people saw to their needs. Moreover, the disciples by now had reached their own limits. They had been traveling, preaching, healing, and casting out demons, and they needed rest. The teaching could resume later.

But Jesus had other plans.

— 6:37 —

Jesus surprised the Twelve with an unusual command: "You give them something to eat!" The verb is imperative and the pronoun "you" is emphasized. According to John's Gospel, "This He was saying to test [them], for He Himself knew what He was intending to do" (John 6:6). He knew from the beginning how unreasonable feeding so many people appeared from a strictly human point of view.

The Twelve responded by pointing out the logistical and monetary problems they faced. Two hundred denarii represented six to eight months' wages for an unskilled worker. While that sum of money *might* have been sufficient to purchase barely enough food, the disciples were miles from the nearest town, and they probably didn't have twelve denarii among them. They had just returned from several weeks or months of ministering in Galilee with no money and no provisions other than their walking sticks.

Ministry Takes a Holiday

MARK 6:31-33

A number of years ago, when our children were all smaller, Cynthia and I planned a wonderful time away with just the family in Hawaii. Our favorite island is Kauai, "The Garden Island," because it is small and the most remote. If you go due north from Kauai, you don't get to anything until Alaska. If you go due west from the center of Kauai, there's nothing but water until you see Taiwan. It's a nice place to go to get away.

One morning the boys and I decided we would fish together. We chartered a boat and went out off the north shore of Kauai. It was delightful. We caught a few fish and decided to bring them back to the hotel and ask the chef to cook them for us. All the way back to shore, we talked about how much fun we had and how good the fish would taste that evening. As our boat pulled into the shallows, we hopped out and waded ashore. It was simply idyllic.

Until I looked up and I saw a row of people waving on the beach. At that moment, the boys said, "Okay, Dad, this is your crowd. We're gone," and left me! They both forsook me and fled!

I got to the shore and the leader said, "Hey, Chuck. We have a Bible study here, and we heard you were on our island, and I've brought all of these people here so you can teach us."

I hope I wasn't too rude when I said, "You know, my family and I are here for a little time away." Their faces fell, and I said, "I'm really not prepared to . . ."

"Oh, well, we've got a Bible," he said. As the dialogue continued, they countered my every response. They had great expectations, but I'm afraid I disappointed them that day. Fortunately, by that time in my vocation, I had learned that every ministry request isn't necessarily a ministry need. Taking time to rest can be as important as being actively engaged in ministry.

— 6:38 —

Jesus sent the men on a scavenger hunt for food, undoubtedly to prove what they had already accepted as fact: They were broke, and no one had any food. All they could find were five loaves of bread, each probably about the size of a man's fist if made with yeast, and two small fish, likely dried with salt. These were pathetic provisions compared to the needs of the people gathered on the hillside—some five thousand men (6:44). Including their wives and children, the crowd could have been as many as twelve to fifteen thousand people. Imagine the possibility of feeding all these people!

Notably, the disciples accepted their own human limitations, but not one thought to ask Jesus for help. They had just returned from an amazing ministry in which they accomplished the impossible—healing and casting out demons—using authority received from Jesus, but they didn't think to ask for His authority or power to complete their divine mandate. How great it would have been if Andrew or Peter or John had replied, "But Lord, You're the Lord of bread. You're the Lord of fish. This is *nothing* to You. There is nothing You *cannot* do."

That's the divine, vertical viewpoint.

— 6:39-41 —

I sometimes imagine a twinkle in Jesus' eye when He ordered the disciples to seat the people and to prepare them for a meal. The disciples divided the multitude into manageable groups, most likely divisible by twelve, and then waited for Jesus to act.

Jesus didn't speak any longer; instead, He did what only God can do. After giving thanks to the Father for His provision, He broke the loaves into pieces along with the two fish. So far, nothing surprising there. But then from those few insufficient fragments, Jesus supplied the disciples with more than enough food so they could indeed "give them something to eat" (6:37) as originally instructed.

— 6:42-44 —

Who knows how long it took to distribute enough bread and fish for more than ten thousand people. But in the end everyone's hunger had been satisfied (including all the teenagers!). As the men carried the Lord's miraculous provision to the people and returned to have their empty baskets refilled all afternoon, His object lesson could not have been lost on them. Years after His departure, with the burdens of ministry—and all its impossible demands—falling upon the apostles, they undoubtedly thought back to the day Jesus challenged them with the impossible and then provided them the means to accomplish it. Years later, when confronted with the unfathomable depth of human need all around them, the apostles must have remembered the Lord's paradigm for ministry: We are responsible to apply what we have, regardless of how insignificant it is. He will then multiply our sacrifice to meet the need, and together we will accomplish His plans.

With all the people satisfied, Jesus put the disciples to work on another task. He sent them to gather the excess food. Each of the Twelve took a basket called a *kophinos* [2894], which, according to one Greek dictionary "was proverbially the Jewish traveling basket. . . . The Jews carried their food in these wicker baskets while traveling in Gentile countries to avoid defilement."[15] In other words, each man collected enough leftover food to keep his stomach satisfied while on a long journey. They had participated in a miracle. The impossible need had been met.

Today, the Lord's message is the same. We all face impossible challenges. His answer? *You take care of the addition; I'll be in charge of the multiplication. And the mission I've called you to fulfill will be abundantly accomplished. You have My Word on it.*

APPLICATION: MARK 6:30-44
Impossible Situations and Magnificent Opportunities

If you have come to an impasse in your life, it may be looming before you and seem as impossible as trying to feed fifteen thousand people with a handful of bread and a few fish. You absolutely do not know how to meet the demand, or solve the problem, or overcome the challenge, or address the issue. It has, perhaps, come as close to unbearable as you ever thought possible. Impossibilities, by their very nature, cannot be tolerated indefinitely. Their intensity mounts, and soon the odds multiply against us, and our minds begin to play tricks. Panic sets in. We lose sleep as our stomachs churn, we lose all desire to eat (or we can't stop eating), we struggle to concentrate . . . and the list goes on.

When an impossible situation drags on, our whole lives become consumed by our human, horizontal perspective of the world. If this describes you today, then you have encountered this story at this time by no mere coincidence. So I challenge you to place yourself in this passage as one of the disciples and to make your impossible situation the crisis of the story. If you are like most, you will identify with the disciples more than you can identify with the Savior. That's because you're plagued with the same earthbound viewpoint they struggled to overcome.

Jesus saw the hunger of the multitude completely different from the way the Twelve did. Where they saw an impossible situation, Jesus saw a magnificent opportunity. We would do well to keep this reminder close at hand when a situation becomes unbearable: We face magnificent opportunities throughout our lives, each one brilliantly disguised as an impossible situation.

Your dilemma may be a domestic problem—maybe you and your spouse have reached an impossible stage in your relationship. It may be a seemingly impossible employment situation. It may be financial upheaval. It may be a medical issue or a relational conflict between you and another individual. It may be some sort of personal disaster you are enduring. In any case, you're at an end. It's a human impossibility. God must come through.

From our limited human viewpoint, we cannot see the magnificent opportunity God sees. If we truly believe God, we must accept this fact: Nothing is impossible with Him. This is His magnificent opportunity to come through.

So how can we find relief from the pressure? We put our bread and our fish in His hands. Then we follow His orders.

Failing to Connect the Dots
MARK 6:45-56

NASB

⁴⁵ Immediately Jesus made His disciples get into the boat and go ahead of *Him* to the other side to Bethsaida, while He Himself was sending the crowd away. ⁴⁶ After bidding them farewell, He left for the mountain to pray.

⁴⁷ When it was evening, the boat was in the middle of the sea, and He was alone on the land. ⁴⁸ Seeing them ªstraining at the oars, for the wind was against them, at about the ᵇfourth watch of the night He came to them, walking on the sea; and He

NLT

⁴⁵ Immediately after this, Jesus insisted that his disciples get back into the boat and head across the lake to Bethsaida, while he sent the people home. ⁴⁶ After telling everyone goodbye, he went up into the hills by himself to pray.

⁴⁷ Late that night, the disciples were in their boat in the middle of the lake, and Jesus was alone on land. ⁴⁸ He saw that they were in serious trouble, rowing hard and struggling against the wind and waves. About three o'clock in the morning* Jesus

intended to pass by them. ⁴⁹But when they saw Him walking on the sea, they supposed that it was a ghost, and cried out; ⁵⁰for they all saw Him and were ^aterrified. But immediately He spoke with them and said to them, "Take courage; it is I, do not be afraid." ⁵¹Then He got into the boat with them, and the wind stopped; and they were utterly astonished, ⁵²for they ^ahad not gained any insight from the *incident of* the loaves, but ^btheir heart was hardened.

⁵³When they had crossed over they came to land at Gennesaret, and moored to the shore. ⁵⁴When they got out of the boat, immediately *the people* recognized Him, ⁵⁵and ran about that whole country and began to carry here and there on their pallets those who were sick, to ^athe place they heard He was. ⁵⁶Wherever He entered villages, or cities, or countryside, they were laying the sick in the market places, and imploring Him that they might just touch the fringe of His cloak; and as many as touched it were being cured.

6:48 ^aLit *harassed in rowing* ^bI.e. 3-6 a.m.
6:50 ^aOr *troubled* 6:52 ^aLit *had not understood on the basis of* ^bOr *their mind was closed, made dull,* or *insensible* 6:55 ^aLit *where they were hearing that He was*

came toward them, walking on the water. He intended to go past them, ⁴⁹but when they saw him walking on the water, they cried out in terror, thinking he was a ghost. ⁵⁰They were all terrified when they saw him.

But Jesus spoke to them at once. "Don't be afraid," he said. "Take courage! I am here!*" ⁵¹Then he climbed into the boat, and the wind stopped. They were totally amazed, ⁵²for they still didn't understand the significance of the miracle of the loaves. Their hearts were too hard to take it in.

⁵³After they had crossed the lake, they landed at Gennesaret. They brought the boat to shore ⁵⁴and climbed out. The people recognized Jesus at once, ⁵⁵and they ran throughout the whole area, carrying sick people on mats to wherever they heard he was. ⁵⁶Wherever he went—in villages, cities, or the countryside—they brought the sick out to the marketplaces. They begged him to let the sick touch at least the fringe of his robe, and all who touched him were healed.

6:48 Greek *About the fourth watch of the night.*
6:50 Or *The 'I AM' is here;* Greek reads *I am.* See Exod 3:14.

Even in the simple things in life, we can miss the point. In my home, we call this "failing to connect the dots." Some use the expression "miss the forest for the trees." It isn't that we don't hear what's being said or we don't see what's happening; we just fail to put everything together to see the primary issue as a whole.

Let's take a few moments to note a couple of individual dots recently drawn by Mark in his narrative. In 6:7-13, Jesus delegated His authority to the Twelve, who then spread out across Israel preaching, healing, and casting out demons—performing incredible supernatural deeds—just as they had seen Jesus do from the beginning. Then in 6:33-44, Jesus challenged the Twelve to feed a multitude, only to provide the means by His own divine power. They carried food to the hungry masses, but only as they received it from their Master.

In each instance, the disciples were given an opportunity to reach a logical conclusion about their role in ministry: With Jesus' authority and power, they could accomplish what is humanly impossible. Without Jesus' provision, they could do nothing. Simple—unless you fail to connect the dots.

— 6:45-46 —

After feeding the multitude, gathering the leftovers, and dismissing the assembly, Jesus instructed His disciples to go ahead of Him by boat. The Gospel of John tells us that He wanted to distance Himself from the crowd because they were ready to take Him by force and put Him forward as their king (John 6:15). Rather than submit to their agenda, Jesus retreated to the hill country rising above the northeastern shore of the Sea of Galilee. He planned to meet them in Bethsaida, the hometown of Andrew, Peter, and Philip (cf. John 1:44; 12:21).

He evidently planned to spend some downtime with them at last. Bethsaida had been a small village until Philip the tetrarch, the brother of Antipas, enlarged it to support a private residence. Even so, the town lay near the bank of the Jordan River north of the sea and offered a quiet retreat from the constant bustle of Capernaum.

— 6:47-48 —

Sometime during the evening, the Twelve had rowed part of the way to their destination. As the sun dipped below the Mediterranean horizon, a fierce squall descended upon the Sea of Galilee, an event that occurs frequently to this day. The surface lies 686 feet below sea level in a deep rift between the Arabian Desert and the Mediterranean Sea. Winds frequently whip down through the gorge and churn the Sea of Galilee into a choppy nightmare for small craft. One commentator states, "Even today the situation is similar. Power boats periodically are warned to remain docked as the winds whip the water into foamy white caps."[16]

Mark states that Jesus could see the disciples struggling against the wind. During daylight, He could easily watch them from His vantage point on a plateau several hundred feet above the water, but as night and storms darkened the sea, Jesus must have seen them supernaturally. He began watching them struggle at the oars before darkness fell, but He didn't start after them until "the fourth watch of the night" (6:48), which was between three and six in the morning. That means they rowed diagonally against the wind and waves for nearly twelve hours! Finally, enough was enough. He had to rescue His men from themselves.

While the Twelve struggled against the elements, Jesus walked across the surface of the sea, stepping on and over the waves to where the boat was. He intended to "pass by them" in the manner of God in the Old Testament, who sometimes allowed His people to glimpse His presence as a means of reassuring them (e.g., Exod. 33:19-22; 1 Kgs. 19:11). In the Old Testament, only God could tread upon the waves (cf. Job 9:8; 38:16; Ps. 77:19; Isa. 43:16).

— 6:49-50 —

What Jesus intended as reassurance, the disciples perceived in terror. They mistook Jesus for a *phantasma* [5326], a rare term in the New Testament. It doesn't necessarily mean "ghost" in the sense of the disembodied spirit of a dead person. In Hebrews 12:18-21, the term is used to describe visual manifestations of God's supernatural presence—fiery smoke and thunderous darkness. Good Jews were not typically given to superstition, but they did have a healthy appreciation for the spiritual and supernatural realm. Bear in mind that these men had earned their living on the Sea of Galilee most of their lives, so they didn't fear much. They saw something they perceived as a supernatural unknown presence coming toward them, and the sight drove them to screaming terror.

Jesus reassured them with the exhortation *tharseō* [2293], which means "to be firm or resolute in the face of danger or adverse circumstances."[17] This is the kind of encouragement a commander on the battlefield would shout to his men so they would stand their ground and refuse to retreat. Jesus then announced Himself with a statement full of meaning *egō eimi* [1473 + 1510], "I am." The rendering "it is I" (Mark 6:50) doesn't capture the theological implications of the phrase, which Jews understood as the classic self-designation of God (see Exod. 3:14). Then finally, He commanded them, "Do not be afraid."

Literally rendered, here is what the Lord said: "Be courageous. I am. Don't fear."

— 6:51-52 —

When Jesus stepped off the waves, over the side of the boat, and onto the deck, nature's fury dissipated like a vapor. The storm ceased, the winds died down, and the whitecaps melted into ripples as the boat righted itself and obeyed the till. Finally, the sea was as smooth as slick silk. Again, the authority of Jesus came to the rescue of the inadequacy of humans, turning their impossible situation into His magnificent opportunity to teach them.

The Twelve were again beside themselves with astonishment. In the recent past, they had seen Jesus calm an earlier storm (4:39-41), cast out demons (5:8-13), raise the dead (5:41-42), and feed a multitude with a small lunch (6:41-42); yet they marveled at this latest demonstration of His power. Why would they? Mark explains in simple terms: "They had not gained any insight from the incident of the loaves" (6:52). The ESV renders the Greek well: "They did not understand about the loaves."

Look at that! Their horizontal perspective took over. They missed the point. They failed to connect the dots.

Let's not be too hard on the disciples. They didn't have a complete understanding of the incarnation. They didn't expect God to become human. They never considered that their Messiah might be divinity in human flesh. We, on the other hand, have a completed New Testament and two thousand years of brilliant theological minds to explain and clarify what we're reading. Furthermore, we aren't in that boat, dripping wet from the storm.

The Gospel writer describes the source of their astonishment: "their heart was hardened." This idiom doesn't mean they were unkind or cruel, as it does in English. Rather, their reasoning and emotions remained hardened against—resistant to—development. We would say they were "thick-headed." (Dare I say it, just like many of us?!)

— 6:53 —

The next four verses frequently fall through the cracks of many commentaries. The verses don't seem all that important when you read through them. You won't find a single word spoken by Jesus. You won't find one person named, though there are many in the narrative. You won't even know for certain where the incidents took place; no one can say for sure where Gennesaret was. No major event transpires in these verses. There's no dialogue between Jesus and His disciples, no profound lessons taught to the crowds, no parables to ponder, no miracles to witness. These four verses, in fact, appear devoid of all significance.

While the passage may lack theological implications—on an intellectual level, at least—Mark takes care to highlight a profoundly important divine attribute in Jesus. He possessed the nonsensical, irrational, unjust, and costly character trait we call *compassion*.

— 6:54-55 —

Gennesaret most likely lay alongside the northwestern shore of the Sea of Galilee. At some point during the Lord's travels, He and the disciples pulled their boats into shore, intending to minister in that region. While they had been rejected in some places and ignored in others, the people here received them eagerly. They even ran with great expectations to gather their sick and disabled friends, bringing them to Jesus on pallets, knowing He would have compassion and heal them with a mere touch. Mark's description indicates that Jesus moved from place to place, carrying out His itinerant ministry as He had always done, and that people tracked Him down to have their loved ones restored by Him.

What a contrast to the apathy and faithlessness of His own people back in Nazareth.

— 6:56 —

In the first century, towns were built around a public area called an agora. Often the agora featured a well or some other communal resource. This is where news was traded, goods were sold, politics discussed, disputes resolved, agreements struck, and speeches given. If you arrived in town and hoped to find a familiar face, this was the place to look. Most likely, Jesus headed straight for the *agora* of a new town before going anywhere else. Because people knew this, they brought their sick friends to the marketplace to gain an audience with the healing rabbi from Nazareth.

Like the diseased, outcast woman in Capernaum (5:25-34), the sick in Gennesaret begged for the opportunity to touch a tassel of Jesus' outer garment (cf. Num. 15:37-40; Deut. 22:12), and like her, they were immediately relieved of all disease or deformity. Picture the scene: roads in cities and throughout the countryside lined with the sick. As He walked along there was no fanfare, no announcement, no public crusade meeting; they just touched His garment as He passed by. And following Him were those standing to their feet, now instantly whole.

APPLICATION: MARK 6:45-56

Impossible People

I know that having faith is often caricatured by unbelievers as blindly embracing things that are contrary to reason simply because they make us feel better. Faith is often contrasted with reason, religion with science, belief with fact. But that's not how the Bible portrays faith. It's true that faith is "the assurance of things hoped for, the conviction of things not seen" (Heb. 11:1). But believers can have assurance of hope and certainty of the invisible dimensions of life because of the supreme, proven trustworthiness of the object of our faith: God Almighty. Our faith—or trust—in something that has proven itself trustworthy allows us to move beyond what we see in order to experience what cannot yet be seen.

Throughout the Lord's ministry, He proved Himself trustworthy to the disciples. Time and again, they saw their Master turn impossible situations into divine victories. And they also learned that they were powerless apart from His delegated authority or power. He used these experiences to help them cultivate an abiding trust in Him. And He gave them multiple opportunities to put their faith into action. Unfortunately, they frequently failed.

We know from the book of Acts that the disciples eventually learned to trust in Christ completely and became immensely powerful witnesses for Him. Their hearts softened, and they became models of unswerving faith. Sadly, however, many people never make this eternally significant decision, despite God's repeated demonstrations of His trustworthiness. Therefore, they die in their rebellion.

Why? There are at least two primary reasons.

First, *their minds refuse to believe that God is who He says He is.* Put bluntly, they are thick-headed. Insensitive. Unyielding in their dedication to a horizontal, human perspective. They're so stiff-necked in their rebellion that they will not look up to acknowledge God's existence. Despite their supposed dependence upon logic, they ignore every evidence of God's involvement in their lives and behave very unreasonably.

Second, *their hearts refuse to trust that God will do what He says He will do.* In my experience, most atheists don't really disbelieve in the existence of God; they simply do not trust His character. Most deny His existence because they're angry at Him for what they perceive to be His character flaws or His failures to behave as they would expect Him to. This is hard-heartedness—a refusal to submit to Him.

It's not likely that you're an atheist, or you probably wouldn't be reading a Bible commentary. So how does this information apply to you? Because you (and I) are, at times, guilty of the atheist's sin of unbelief. Despite God's many demonstrations of His faithfulness, we fail to connect the dots and trust that He is alive, active, and able to address our impossible situations. And like some atheists, we do not trust His character to handle our difficulties righteously.

This is a dangerous mindset for the Christian. The book of Hebrews declares, "Without faith it is impossible to please Him, for he who comes to God must believe that He is and that He is a rewarder of those who seek Him" (Heb. 11:6). If you truly trust in Christ, your life should show evidence of that faith. You not only trust Him with your eternal soul, but you also trust Him with your temporal concerns—everyday needs and problems—here on earth.

If you're not an atheist, it's time to prove it!

The Day Jesus Took Off the Gloves
MARK 7:1-13

NASB

¹The Pharisees and some of the scribes gathered around Him when they had come from Jerusalem, ²and had seen that some of His disciples were eating their bread with impure hands, that is, unwashed. ³(For the Pharisees and all the Jews do not eat unless they ªcarefully wash their hands, *thus* observing the traditions of the elders; ⁴and *when they come* from the market place, they do not eat unless they ªcleanse themselves; and there are many other things which they have received in order to observe, such as the ᵇwashing of cups and pitchers and copper pots.) ⁵The Pharisees and the scribes asked Him, "Why do Your disciples not walk according to the tradition of the elders, but eat their bread with impure hands?" ⁶And He said to them, "Rightly did Isaiah prophesy of you hypocrites, as it is written:

'THIS PEOPLE HONORS ME WITH
    THEIR LIPS,
BUT THEIR HEART IS FAR AWAY
    FROM ME.

NLT

¹One day some Pharisees and teachers of religious law arrived from Jerusalem to see Jesus. ²They noticed that some of his disciples failed to follow the Jewish ritual of hand washing before eating. ³(The Jews, especially the Pharisees, do not eat until they have poured water over their cupped hands,* as required by their ancient traditions. ⁴Similarly, they don't eat anything from the market until they immerse their hands* in water. This is but one of many traditions they have clung to—such as their ceremonial washing of cups, pitchers, and kettles.*)

⁵So the Pharisees and teachers of religious law asked him, "Why don't your disciples follow our age-old tradition? They eat without first performing the hand-washing ceremony."

⁶Jesus replied, "You hypocrites! Isaiah was right when he prophesied about you, for he wrote,

'These people honor me with
    their lips,
but their hearts are far from me.

7 'But in vain do they worship
Me,

Teaching as doctrines the
precepts of men.'

8 Neglecting the commandment of
God, you hold to the tradition of
men."

9 He was also saying to them, "You
are experts at setting aside the commandment of God in order to keep
your tradition. **10** For Moses said,
'Honor your father and your
mother'; and, 'He who speaks evil
of father or mother, is to ªbe
put to death'; **11** but you say, 'If a
man says to *his* father or *his* mother,
whatever I have that would help
you is Corban (that is to say, ªgiven
to God),' **12** you no longer permit
him to do anything for *his* father or
his mother; **13** *thus* invalidating the
word of God by your tradition which
you have handed down; and you do
many things such as that."

7:3 ªLit *with the fist* 7:4 ªOr *sprinkle* ᵇLit
baptizing 7:10 ªLit *die the death* 7:11 ªOr *a gift*,
i.e. *an offering*

7 Their worship is a farce,
for they teach man-made ideas
as commands from God.'*

8 For you ignore God's law and substitute your own tradition."

9 Then he said, "You skillfully side-
step God's law in order to hold on to
your own tradition. **10** For instance,
Moses gave you this law from God:
'Honor your father and mother,'*
and 'Anyone who speaks disrespect-
fully of father or mother must be put
to death.'* **11** But you say it is all right
for people to say to their parents,
'Sorry, I can't help you. For I have
vowed to give to God what I would
have given to you.'* **12** In this way,
you let them disregard their needy
parents. **13** And so you cancel the
word of God in order to hand down
your own tradition. And this is only
one example among many others."

7:3 Greek *have washed with the fist.* 7:4a Some
manuscripts read *sprinkle themselves.*
7:4b Some manuscripts add *and dining couches.*
7:7 Isa 29:13 (Greek version). 7:10a Exod 20:12;
Deut 5:16. 7:10b Exod 21:17 (Greek version); Lev
20:9 (Greek version). 7:11 Greek *'What I would
have given to you is Corban' (that is, a gift).*

It is a sad fact that our culture now favors wimps and weaklings and
punishes people of strong conviction. If you hold to certain beliefs or
defend a particular set of principles, you're considered ignorant, arrogant, and bigoted. If you hold strongly to your own opinions, you're
intolerant, unbending, and narrow. If you confront someone who is in
error, you're rude and unloving. If you believe there are times it is right
to fight or to resist, you're labeled as contentious or hateful.

Even though we know in our hearts that the truth sets us free,
something within us recoils a little when someone has the guts to
state the truth without apology, especially publicly, to those who
need to hear it. But if someone doesn't stand up to challenge those
in authority who have departed from the truth, every playground will
be run by bullies. Every nation will be controlled by tyrants. Every
church will be intimidated by legalists. The truth must be spoken, or
error will run amok and we'll all suffer. Every culture and generation

needs someone who publicly challenges the directors of groupthink and dares to speak the truth.

In first-century Israel, Jesus was just that kind of man, although you wouldn't know it from the early days of His ministry in Galilee. In the beginning, He took a gentle approach to opposition, choosing to speak softly—despite feeling intense anger—and to counter falsehood with reasoning. For the most part, He steered clear of conflict, choosing instead to spend His time proclaiming the truth throughout the land, concentrating on those who wished to hear the gospel. He simply brushed aside those who resisted the truth as He pressed on with His agenda.

Jesus wasn't afraid of conflict; the rich and powerful didn't intimidate Him. Confronting the imposing religious elite of Israel simply didn't fit into His program . . . yet. Having completed several tours around Galilee, and after sending His disciples to preach the good news, the time had come to turn His attention southward toward Jerusalem, the stronghold of theological and religious error. He didn't take His ministry there at this point; that journey would come later (10:1). Instead, He began to confront various factions from Jerusalem as part of His agenda, becoming increasingly assertive in His approach.

Up to this point, He had countered the religious authorities with clear reasoning from the Scriptures, but the time for that had come to an end. When a delegation from Jerusalem came to Capernaum to pick a fight with Jesus, the gloves came off. The men who had perverted the Lord's covenant with Abraham and turned Judaism into a legalistic cult needed to feel the wrath of God.

— 7:1-2 —

The delegation of religious authorities from Jerusalem included Pharisees. By Jesus' time, the Pharisees' once admirable loyalty to nationalism and devotion to the Law had taken on a life of its own. These meticulous expositors of Scripture worked tirelessly to preserve an oral tradition about how to apply the Law of Moses to everyday life. The Pharisaic rabbis added a long lists of specific duties and prohibitions to the Law. No one rivaled the Pharisees in being religious. (See "The Pharisees" at Mark 2:18.)

Scribes were men of letters—those who were highly skilled at reading and writing, especially when it came to scouring the Hebrew Scriptures. They were likely the ones primarily responsible for meticulously copying the Old Testament to preserve it from decay or corruption. In any case, their constant contact with God's Word made them extremely knowledgeable; these were the men called upon to explain and apply the Law.

Mark's telling of the story strongly suggests that the Pharisees and scribes had arrived with a mission to trap Jesus. We last saw the Pharisees in a Galilean synagogue, where Jesus defied their rules against healing on the Sabbath (3:1-6). Afterward, they "went out and immediately began conspiring with the Herodians against Him, as to how they might destroy Him" (3:6). Obviously, they wanted to discredit Him publicly before disposing of Him physically. That's Conspiracy 101. If you kill a beloved populist leader, you risk turning him into a symbol around which opposition forms. Dishonor Him first, and then no one will care when he's murdered.

In boxing, experienced fighters often take the first round to feel out their opponents. After taking a few minutes to get a sense of the opponent's range, speed, and style, a seasoned fighter will attack where the opponent appears weak. The local Pharisees were unable to match wits with Jesus, so they brought in the heavy hitters from Jerusalem. These highly trained theological debaters most likely took their time, blending with the crowds, observing the habits of Jesus and the Twelve, taking copious notes. Then, when the time came to engage Jesus, they started with a relatively minor issue: ceremonial hand washing.

— 7:3-5 —

For the benefit of his Gentile readers, Mark explains the peculiar issues involved in this ritual. His brief description of ceremonial hand washing barely does justice to the practice. He probably wanted to avoid ridiculing his Jewish brothers and sisters. For the benefit of readers like us, Alfred Edersheim summarized the tradition this way:

> As the purifications were so frequent, and care had to be taken that the water had not been used for other purposes, or something fallen into it that might discolour or defile it, large vessels or jars were generally kept for the purpose. These might be of any material, although stone is specially mentioned. It was the practice to draw water out of these with what was called a natla, antila, or antelaya, very often of glass, which must hold (at least) a quarter of a log—a measure equal to one and a half 'egg-shells.' For, no less quantity than this might be used for affusion. The water was poured on both hands, which must be free of anything covering them, such as gravel, mortar, etc. The hands were lifted up, so as to make the water run to the wrist, in order to ensure

that the whole hand was washed, and that the water polluted by the hand did not again run down the fingers. Similarly, each hand was rubbed with the other (the fist), provided the hand that rubbed had been affused; otherwise, the rubbing might be done against the head, or even against a wall. But there was one point on which special stress was laid. In the 'first affusion,' which was all that originally was required when the hands were not Levitically 'defiled,' the water had to run down to the wrist. . . . If the water remained short of the wrist . . . the hands were not clean. Accordingly, the words of St. Mark can only mean that the Pharisees eat not 'except they wash their hands to the wrist.'[18]

This excessively detailed, tedious process became highly symbolic for the Pharisees, who saw this as an expression of love for God's Law. Pharisees gladly endured this and other similar rituals every day, in every sphere of life, all for the sake of pleasing God. And what they expected of themselves, they expected of anyone who dared call himself a "son of the covenant."

— 7:6-8 —

The Pharisees challenged Jesus on something relatively minor but still serious enough to discredit Him in their culture. For them, this was merely the opening round of a calculated strategy ending with a murdered Jesus. But, as experienced boxers know, you cannot let your opponent dictate the fight. The Pharisees had prepared to dispose of an insignificant, untrained, upstart rabbi from the discredited town of Nazareth. They didn't expect to match wits with the Author of Truth in human flesh!

In His rebuke, Jesus called the men "hypocrites" (7:6), a word used often of actors or pretenders. Secular Greek writers used the term both positively and negatively, depending upon the situation. In a positive sense, it was used to describe one dutifully portraying a character on the stage. It could also be used negatively if one viewed the stage as a sham world and actors as deceivers.[19]

Jesus then appealed to Scripture to identify the Pharisees as the contemporary version of the detractors that Isaiah wrote about. To clarify what He meant by the word "hypocrite," He quoted Isaiah 29:13. As recorded by Mark, the Lord's quote closely matches the Septuagint (the Greek translation of the Hebrew Bible).

Here's a comparison of how we see the passages in the NASB:

MARK'S ACCOUNT (GREEK)	ISAIAH'S WRITING (HEBREW)
This people honors Me with their lips, But their heart is far away from Me. But in vain do they worship Me, Teaching as doctrines the precepts of men.	This people draw near with their words And honor Me with their lip service, But they remove their hearts far from Me, And their reverence for Me consists of tradition learned by rote.
Hebrew → Septuagint → Mark → English	Hebrew → English

It's important to note that the work of translation is not merely a process of decoding. Languages do not match up word for word, so there is sometimes a need to render a *thought* faithfully at the expense of being verbatim. In this case, the meaning comes through clearly. Isaiah mourned the loss of true devotion to God as His people exchanged relationship for ritual. The Pharisees merely repeated the error Isaiah lamented. In their misguided sense of devotion to God, they set aside His inerrant Word in favor of man-made religiosity. In fact, they had strayed so far from the truth that when Truth incarnate stood before them, they condemned Him as a heretic!

— 7:9-13 —

To make His point plain, Jesus compared one of their traditions to the fifth commandment: "Honor your father and your mother, that your days may be prolonged in the land which the LORD your God gives you" (Exod. 20:12). The motivation to obey this commandment should have resonated with the Pharisees, who longed to rid Israel of Roman interlopers and return to the glory days of David's reign.

Jesus also cited Exodus 21:17 (cf. Lev. 20:9) in which God forbids disrespecting parents upon penalty of death. Let's not forget the Pharisees' ultimate goal: to destroy Jesus (cf. Mark 3:6). In this way, Jesus turned the tables around to show that they, not He, deserved death.

The Lord then cited a well-known tradition among the Pharisees, to which they assigned the technical term *korban* [2878]. This is a Greek transliteration of a Hebrew word (e.g., Lev. 1:2-3) that describes something that is set aside and reserved for God's exclusive use. This could include people, money, land, possessions, inheritance—anything. Using Numbers 30:2-4 as a pretext, the Pharisees claimed that a vow of dedication takes precedence over other normal obligations, including the Ten Commandments. Based on this tradition, one could dedicate all his possessions to God, dedicate himself completely to God, and then excuse himself from all other duties, such as caring for mom and dad in their old age. The Pharisees had cleverly turned the Law against itself, finding in one law a pretext for disobeying many other laws.

Jesus claimed that the Pharisees did "many things such as that." This last word not only shut down the scribes' attack, but it also repudiated their entire manner of living and condemned their supposed piety as heresy.

In the next verse, Mark shifts to another scene, but the Lord's conflict with the corrupt religious experts of Jerusalem was far from over. In fact, this was merely round one.

APPLICATION: MARK 7:1-13

Stop. Look. Listen.

Years ago, railroad crossings prominently featured signs that read, "Stop, Look, and Listen." Let's do that now.

Stop before you criticize first-century legalists.

You may very well be a twenty-first-century legalist. Do you add shame to other people's lives, or do you set them free? Do you cultivate trust with your children, or do you try to control them? Do you release others who are younger in the faith, or do you try to saddle them with rules? Do you find sin in other people's lives and then go after them for it?

If so, stop.

Look in a mirror before naming the sins or failures of others.

You know why Jesus was qualified to call the Pharisees hypocrites? He was living a perfect life. He knew perfection. He knew no sin, did no sin, had no sin. He was qualified to speak this way and to name the sins of others. Before you do that, take a look in the mirror. By the way, it takes guts to pull the mask off and say the whole truth—even to yourself.

You may be wearing a mask around your non-Christian friends. Truth be told, they can already see through you. One of the ways of winning them is to tell them the truth. I don't mean that you need to confess all your sins to them; I mean that you should be transparent about your own struggles and then point them to the Cross.

Listen to what the Bible says about freedom.

Even though Jesus didn't use the word "free" in this story, He freed His disciples from the condemning, self-made rules of the Pharisees. Jesus stood against the legalists, saying about His disciples, "These men are okay. You leave them alone. They're free."

I want to suggest an assignment. This week—and each week for the rest of your life—seek to set somebody free.

Getting to the Heart
of Our Defilement
MARK 7:14-23

NASB

14 After He called the crowd to Him again, He *began* saying to them, "Listen to Me, all of you, and understand: 15 there is nothing outside the man which can defile him if it goes into him; but the things which proceed out of the man are what defile the man. 16 [aIf anyone has ears to hear, let him hear."]

17 When he had left the crowd *and* entered the house, His disciples questioned Him about the parable. 18 And He said to them, "Are you so lacking in understanding also? Do you not understand that whatever goes into the man from outside cannot defile him, 19 because it does not go into his heart, but into his stomach, and ais eliminated?" (*Thus He* declared all foods clean.) 20 And He was saying, "That which proceeds out of the man, that is what defiles the man. 21 For from within, out of the heart of men, proceed the evil thoughts, afornications, thefts, murders, adulteries, 22 deeds of coveting *and* wickedness, *as well as* deceit,

NLT

14 Then Jesus called to the crowd to come and hear. "All of you listen," he said, "and try to understand. 15 It's not what goes into your body that defiles you; you are defiled by what comes from your heart.*"

17 Then Jesus went into a house to get away from the crowd, and his disciples asked him what he meant by the parable he had just used. 18 "Don't you understand either?" he asked. "Can't you see that the food you put into your body cannot defile you? 19 Food doesn't go into your heart, but only passes through the stomach and then goes into the sewer." (By saying this, he declared that every kind of food is acceptable in God's eyes.)

20 And then he added, "It is what comes from inside that defiles you. 21 For from within, out of a person's heart, come evil thoughts, sexual immorality, theft, murder, 22 adultery, greed, wickedness, deceit, lustful desires, envy, slander, pride, and

sensuality, [a]envy, slander, [b]pride *and* foolishness. [23] All these evil things proceed from within and defile the man."

7:16 [a]Early mss do not contain this verse
7:19 [a]Lit *goes out into the latrine* 7:21 [a]I.e. acts of sexual immorality 7:22 [a]Lit *an evil eye* [b]Or *arrogance*

foolishness. [23] All these vile things come from within; they are what defile you."

7:15 Some manuscripts add verse 16, *Anyone with ears to hear should listen and understand.* Compare 4:9, 23.

If you ask the average Christian about his or her impression of the Old Testament, the word "rules" will enter the conversation before long. To be fair, the Old Testament does indeed spell out many rules and commandments, rituals and rites. Even so, the Lord didn't emphasize rules and regulations when relating with His covenant people. He gave Israel a detailed set of laws for the same reason the Founding Fathers of the United States wrote a constitution to govern the new nation: *The rule of law makes societies safe and prosperous.*

While the Old Testament—the first five books in particular, known as the Pentateuch—helped guide the nation, God never intended the Law to become a measure of righteousness. He knew from the beginning that rules do not make people righteous; rules can only expose our unrighteousness. He instead wanted His people to let love for Him inspire obedience. While God ordered men to be circumcised as a symbol of their obedience to Him, He greatly desired for them to have "circumcised hearts" (cf. Deut. 10:16; 30:6; Jer. 4:4; Rom. 2:29). Sometime in history, however, the nation of Israel lost its way and forgot that "God sees not as man sees, for man looks at the outward appearance, but the Lord looks at the heart" (1 Sam. 16:7).

We shouldn't be too hard on the Hebrews, however. We are no better. Everything within us desires to hide what is on the inside and dress up what is on the outside so we might appear better than we are when, in fact, we are a moral mess. We look holy (we think) when we keep certain rules and regulations, but down deep inside all kinds of unholy, shameful thoughts reside, and desires run amok. We simply keep our depravity under wraps; we become masters at cover-up. We camouflage the truth by adding to the rules and regulations that will (we think) cause other people to admire us as godly, righteous, and truly separated unto God. The thought is this: *If I keep enough rules and practice sufficient, rigid regulations, I will become spiritual.*

That kind of thinking is taught as truth in legalistic settings, not all of which are churches. Sometimes they are schools. Philip Yancey describes his experience as a student at a Bible college located in the South during the 1960s:

The Sixties' sexual revolution did not penetrate the Bible college's hermetically sealed environment. "Students must absolutely avoid holding hands, embracing, kissing, and other physical contacts," read the 66-page rule book, which students had to sign each year. To limit temptation, underclassmen were allotted just two dates a week (though not both with the same person)—double-dates, of course, and on Sunday evenings only to church. Freshman women had to apply to the dean of women in advance for each date. Apart from those dates, even students engaged to be married could only "socialize" one hour a day, during the evening meal with the entire student body. Telephone contact was forbidden.

Standing too close to your date in the cafeteria line could subject you to a dean's inquisition. *Have you ever held hands? Did you kiss? Why are you flirting with temptation?* Eyes were always watching and spies reported infractions of the rules. The bus driver on a school outing confronted a friend of mine: "It's my obligation to talk to you as a Christian. In the rear view mirror I saw you and that girl touching noses. Don't you know the Bible verse, 'It is good for a man not to touch a woman'?"

One revered professor, a bald senior citizen, insisted that in his own car his wife must sit over by the door handle lest someone who didn't know they were married draw the wrong conclusion if they sat too close. He sold his stock in the local Belk Gallant department store because it sold swimsuits, which went against his beliefs on "mixed bathing." "When you wear lipstick," he would balefully warn the virginal girls in his classroom, "you are saying to the world, 'Kiss me! Kiss me!'"[20]

I am convinced that Flannery O'Connor was thinking of good ol' fashioned Southern legalism when she wrote in a letter, "You shall know the truth, and the truth shall make you odd."

The fact is, the perspective that righteous living will make one righteous goes on all the time and in every setting. The additional fact is, this kind of thinking isn't limited to our time and culture; legalism goes back at least to the first century. Legalists back then, just like legalists today, sincerely believed that to break with traditional norms was to become defiled. This was Jesus' challenge when confronted by the scribes and Pharisees. Having rebuked these religious experts for their hypocrisy and upside-down theology, Jesus turned to his disciples to explain the truth about the Law, righteousness, depravity, and our need for something greater than our own willpower.

— 7:14-15 —

Jesus stood before a mixed crowd—some were close followers, some were seeking to know more, others were enemies. He determined to set straight what the religious experts had perverted for many generations. He answered the twofold question, "What is the purpose of the Law, and what role does tradition play in my relationship with God?" Because the topic created such a sharp divide between Jesus and the Jewish authorities, and because the answer to this question affected everyone in Israel, Jesus opened with the exhortation, "Listen to Me, all of you, and understand" (7:14).

What He said next appeared to fly in the face of God's Word and repudiate a thousand years of religious tradition. Throughout the Old Testament, God told His covenant people what they were permitted to eat and which foods to avoid as "unclean." God declared that exposure to certain things rendered a person ceremonially unclean, a condition that must be remedied before a person could intermingle with the community or enter the temple for worship and sacrifice. He determined that some behaviors also rendered one ceremonially unclean and required specific rituals to restore one's status as ceremonially pure.

Until the Jews were carried into exile by the Babylonians around 586 BC, they seemed to have understood that becoming "unclean" after handling a dead carcass didn't automatically render a person sinful or immoral. They certainly didn't think themselves morally pristine after ceremonial washing restored their "clean" status. The confusion seems to have begun with a misunderstanding of Daniel's decision to reject King Nebuchadnezzar's "choice food or . . . the wine which he drank" (Dan. 1:8).

Concerned about eating meat that had been offered to idols—a repulsive thought to any good Jew—Daniel and his friends chose a diet of vegetables and water. This personal conviction also guided the exiled nation. Having been taken from the Promised Land and cut off from their temple, they clung to the Law as a means of preserving their identity as heirs to God's covenant with Abraham. More than six hundred years later, however, this admirable loyalty to nationalism and strict devotion to the Law had become a fetish. The Pharisees equated ceremonial cleanliness with moral righteousness—and the cleaner the better!

Of course, the Pharisees might have taken Jesus too literally when He clarified that "the things which proceed out of the man are what defile the man" (Mark 7:15). He wasn't saying that excrement would make a person physically and ceremonially unclean; He had in mind sinful behavior. Some deeds rendered one ceremonially unclean; others put one at moral odds with God. To touch a dead carcass was one matter; to commit murder was another. Deeds done from a corrupt heart are what make a person unrighteous, not what one eats, drinks, or touches.

— 7:16 —

The earliest manuscripts do not contain this verse, which appears to have been a note written by a scribe in the margin or above the line. Sometime later, a scribe inserted these words into the main text (see the section on postscripts on page 402).

— 7:17 —

Having concluded this discourse with His audience of Jewish followers, seekers, and enemies, Jesus returned to "the house," most likely His temporary quarters in Capernaum. The Twelve and perhaps a handful of other disciples asked the Lord to explain His teaching further. His sermon, as reported by Mark, didn't use a parable in the strict sense of the word. He used a picturesque metaphor to lay one concept beside another for the sake of comparison.

The disciples appear dull-witted to some commentators, who write that Jesus' meaning is so obvious that the disciples should have understood immediately. But those who make this suggestion fail to appreciate the power of a paradigm to shape one's perception so completely that it makes one miss the obvious. In this case, the Jews had been told for generations that obeying rules and observing rituals could make them righteous. They had been trained from birth to regard equally God's dietary rules and His moral laws—to the first-century Jew, these had become one and the same. It's helpful to remember this. It clarifies why Jesus' followers couldn't believe their ears. He appeared to declare God's moral code null and void, something the Messiah could never do. So they asked for an explanation.

— 7:18-19 —

The form of Jesus' rhetorical question (7:18) leans toward a positive reply. Literally rendered, the question is, "So then, you also are without understanding?" The disciples were a product of the same foolish, hypocritical theological tradition as the Pharisees. Even so, Jesus appreciated a crucial difference in them. The disciples—like many earnest, untrained Jews—suffered from ignorance. The scribes and Pharisees did not; they held on to their tradition because it gave them power over others and underscored a strong sense of righteousness for themselves. They liked the system, and they knew how to leverage it to their political and economic advantage. Pride fueled their position.

Jesus returned to His earlier illustration, this time emphasizing the inability of anything eaten to render someone morally guilty. Food—even ceremonially unclean food—goes down the throat, bypasses the heart, moves into the stomach, and then finally "goes out into the latrine" (7:19, NASB note). It's Anatomy 101. The GI tract and the heart are not connected. To this declaration, Mark adds the parenthetical statement that Jesus thus "declared all foods clean." He includes this for the benefit of his Gentile readers, assuring them that Christians are not bound by the dietary restrictions of the old covenant (cf. Rom. 14:14; Gal. 2:11-17; Col. 2:20-22). The Mosaic Law no longer applied as a rule of life to regulate all of society as it had for the nation of Israel (cf. Rom. 10:4).

— 7:20-23 —

Jesus repeated His earlier statement, this time confirming that He was using the illustration to describe sinful behavior. Sins originate in the "heart" (Mark 7:21), a person's intellectual and emotional center. He then lists several deeds that render an individual morally corrupt and, therefore, unacceptable to God.

While this is not an exhaustive list of sinful behaviors (see chart on next page), it nonetheless bears a strong Old Testament influence. The first seven items name activities that represent prohibited behaviors; the last six describe attitudes that lead to sin. The Lord's catalogue of evil behavior accomplished two important objectives. First, while setting aside ceremonial guidelines, He upheld God's moral law. His act of declaring all foods ceremonially clean did not nullify God's standard of righteousness. Second, Jesus condemned evil thoughts and intentions as equally reprehensible to evil deeds. The Pharisees obsessed over outward behavior to the exclusion of actually combatting the inner disposition toward sin.

dialogismos kakos [1261 + 2556]	"evil reasoning"	fantasizing about and/or planning evil deeds
porneia [4202]	"sexual immorality"	any sexual activity involving someone other than one's spouse and, particularly, prostitution and fornication
klopē [2829]	"stealing"	taking money or possessions against the owner's will
phonos [5408]	"murder"	deliberately ending an innocent life
moicheia [3430]	"adultery"	having sexual intercourse in violation of the marriage covenant
pleonexia [4124]	"avarice"	desiring to gain more than one's due
poneria [4189]	"malignancy"	in the moral sense, a cultivated disposition toward sin
dolos [1388]	"treachery"	contriving to deceive
aselgeia [766]	"debauchery"	showing a lack of self-constraint involving socially unacceptable behavior, including excessive violence, wanton sexual activity, and gluttony
ophthalmos poneros [3788 + 4190]	"evil eye"	desiring what one sees despite moral restrictions against possessing it
blasphēmia [988]	"denigration"	reviling, disrespecting, or defaming another
hyperēphania [5243]	"arrogance"	thinking too highly of oneself
aphrosynē [877]	"foolishness"	willfully failing to use one's capacity for reasoning

APPLICATION: MARK 7:14-23

A Cure for the Common Depravity

In reflecting on Jesus' teaching about the source of impurity in the human heart, I am reminded that the Old Testament prophet Jeremiah wrote, "The heart is more deceitful than all else and is desperately sick; who can understand it?" (Jer. 17:9).

Spiritually, we cannot heal ourselves or anyone else. You can't love your baby enough to take away his or her built-in, natural impulse to do wrong. You can help that child learn restraint, but you can't change that child's nature. As a pig's nature is to roll in mud, ours is that we cannot stay away from sin. You can take a pig out of the slop, scrub him, put a nice pink ribbon around his neck, dust him up with baby powder, spray perfume behind his ears, and dress him in silk. But as soon as you let him out, right back to the slop he'll run. Why? Because he has a pig's nature.

Fortunately, the Bible doesn't leave us in the pigsty. We can be freed from the grip of our depravity and rescued from our sin if we accept three crucial truths.

First, *facing the ugly truth of your sin is a painful but necessary process*. Acknowledge your past sins. Stop denying your out-of-control desire for more sin. Give up any hope that willpower alone will keep you from doing more wrong or causing further harm. Your struggle to avoid sin is futile apart from the strength offered through Jesus Christ. When you finally accept the ugly reality of your depraved nature, you're ready to receive the remedy—but not before.

Second, *understanding the full extent of your depravity is a helpful necessity*. Everyone, even the worst criminal, is capable of good. All of us periodically do good things. We can convince ourselves that the good we do makes us good people—perhaps even good enough for heaven. We can rack up an impressive list of good deeds. We can immerse ourselves in the most genteel culture—listen to fine music, surround ourselves with great art, associate with quality people—but that's only slightly better than giving a pig a makeover. Our depravity remains.

Third, *Jesus Christ is the only cure for the disease of sin*. God sent us a cure for our depraved sinful nature. The Father sent His Son, Jesus Christ, to free us from our bondage to sin. By His death, He paid the penalty for sin that we deserve. Through His resurrection, we receive a new kind of life—abundant and eternal. After His ascension, we were given the gift of God's Spirit, a new nature to free us from the grip of our slop-loving nature. It's encouraging to remember that there's no nature too sinful for God to remedy.

After a church service one Sunday, a man shook my hand and, like many people, told me about the first time he heard a broadcast of *Insight for Living*. It happened several years ago. He was in a prison cell, locked behind iron bars, several steel doors, concrete walls, and fences topped with razor wire. He fought back tears as he described the hopelessness he felt. How could someone who committed multiple felonies change? He felt like the worst human being on earth, and his worst sins were a matter of public record.

The gospel gave him hope. He learned from the Bible that all people stand equally guilty before the Judge of heaven. While his rap sheet told of his crimes, he discovered from the Bible that all people deserve a punishment worse than prison. But most encouraging of all, he learned that his disease of sin could be cured by the Great Physician.

If you're anything like that former felon, wondering if you're too sinful to save, let me assure you that every Christian has come to terms with these truths as part of his or her spiritual journey. Take heart. Give these things serious thought. Trust that God is big enough to save anyone—even you.

Would Jesus Call Your Faith "Great"?
MARK 7:24-30

NASB

24 Jesus got up and went away from there to the region of Tyre[a]. And when He had entered a house, He wanted no one to know of it; [b]yet He could not escape notice. 25 But after hearing of Him, a woman whose little daughter had an unclean spirit immediately came and fell at His feet. 26 Now the woman was a [a]Gentile, of the Syrophoenician race. And she kept asking Him to cast the demon out of her daughter. 27 And He was saying to her, "Let the children be satisfied first, for it is not [a]good to take the children's bread and throw it to the dogs." 28 But she answered and said to Him, "Yes, Lord, *but* even the dogs under the table feed on the children's crumbs." 29 And He said to her, "Because of this [a]answer go; the demon has gone out of your

NLT

24 Then Jesus left Galilee and went north to the region of Tyre.* He didn't want anyone to know which house he was staying in, but he couldn't keep it a secret. 25 Right away a woman who had heard about him came and fell at his feet. Her little girl was possessed by an evil* spirit, 26 and she begged him to cast out the demon from her daughter.

Since she was a Gentile, born in Syrian Phoenicia, 27 Jesus told her, "First I should feed the children—my own family, the Jews.* It isn't right to take food from the children and throw it to the dogs."

28 She replied, "That's true, Lord, but even the dogs under the table are allowed to eat the scraps from the children's plates."

29 "Good answer!" he said. "Now

daughter." [30] And going back to her home, she found the child [a]lying on the bed, the demon having left.

7:24 [a]Two early mss add *and Sidon* [b]Lit *and*
7:26 [a]Lit *Greek*   7:27 [a]Or *proper*   7:29 [a]Lit *word*
7:30 [a]Lit *thrown*

go home, for the demon has left your daughter." [30] And when she arrived home, she found her little girl lying quietly in bed, and the demon was gone.

7:24 Some manuscripts add *and Sidon.*
7:25 Greek *unclean.*   7:27 Greek *Let the children eat first.*

It's easy to be fooled when it comes to faith. Some things seem to represent faith, but they don't show faith at all. Often what passes for trust in God is actually presumption. In fact, our culture is filled with people who presume on God. Many televangelists tell us, "Name it and claim it. You've got a life of prosperity ahead of you. Give to my ministry, then count on God to make you rich. Just claim the riches you desire." That's presumption. Or, "You're sick, but God wants you well. Claim your wellness." Scripture tells us to pray in belief, with a strong confidence in God's ability to heal, but He is bound by no obligation to do what we say.

These days, some of my pastoral ministry involves dealing with those who weren't made rich after sending what little they had to a "Word of Faith" huckster. Furthermore, I'm forced to answer the anguished questions of those who didn't find healing and who would have benefited from the care of a good physician. Now they're sick, poor, and confused because they named it and claimed it but "God didn't come through." What disillusionment!

Presumption is not faith, and neither is wishful thinking. Many people offer prayers like children wishing upon a star. They worry about saying the right words and hope they have repeated them often enough to be effective. They lace their requests with promises and augment their supplications with good deeds. They repeat the same words again and again. Their prayers sound more like incantations than genuine petitions. But that's not faith—it's superstition. They hold on to God like He's a lucky charm.

Faith is neither presumptuous nor tentative. Having faith is believing that God is who He says He is, trusting in His integrity to do what He says He will do. It is being confident that He will always do what is right for our good and for His glory.

The story we have come to in our study in Mark highlights a woman who came upon a situation that left her helpless. She, like many of us today, found herself at the mercy of someone who could do something about her difficulty. Her example is worth noting and then emulating. She didn't presume upon God to give her what she asked, yet she didn't treat Him like a rabbit's foot. In fact, she got it just right, and Jesus said so.

— 7:24 —

Sometime after His confrontation with the religious authorities in Capernaum, Jesus journeyed to the region surrounding the Gentile city of Tyre. The territory was called Phoenicia, but it had been annexed to the Roman province of Syria for more than a century. By this time, Tyre was a Roman colony.

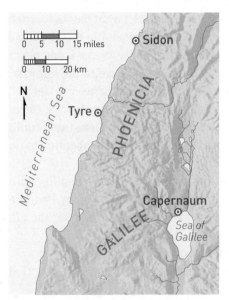

The land God had promised to Abraham and his descendants included this fortified port city with its excellent natural defenses. Unfortunately, the Israelites failed to take it, so Tyre became a perpetual neighbor and sometimes ally (cf. 2 Sam. 5:11; 1 Kgs. 5:1-11; 1 Chr. 14:1; 2 Chr. 2:3-16). Later, however, the people of Tyre betrayed Israel, earning some of the strongest prophetic denunciations ever written (cf. Isa. 23:1-18; Jer. 25:22; 27:1-11; Ezek. 26:1–28:19; Joel 3:4-8; Amos 1:9-10). Ezekiel described the arrogance of Tyre as emblematic of Satan's hubris against God (Ezek. 28:2).

Jesus left the region of Galilee to visit **Tyre** and **Sidon**, where he healed both a Gentile woman's daughter (from a demon) and a deaf man.

Jesus didn't intend to minister publicly in Phoenicia; He may have taken the disciples there for private instruction. As often happened, however, someone recognized Him, and word spread quickly.

— 7:25-26 —

The residents who heard about Jesus' arrival and came to Him for healing included a Gentile woman whose ethnic roots ran deep in Tyre. She undoubtedly had ancestors who had deserved the demise predicted by the Hebrew prophets and then had suffered as a result. Regardless, she had heard of Jesus and, like any parent, desperately wanted healing for her daughter, who suffered the awful agony inflicted by demons.

According to Mark, she "immediately" prostrated herself at Jesus' feet (7:25), a sign of both respect and deep sorrow. Moreover, she "kept asking" (7:26), a verb appearing in the imperfect tense, indicating repetitive action. Matthew writes that she "began to cry out" (again, imperfect tense) from a distance, asking for mercy on her daughter. He also states that Jesus chose not to acknowledge her (Matt. 15:22-23).

Putting the two accounts together, it appears that the woman initially prostrated herself but didn't receive the answer she had hoped to hear. So she remained a short distance away, crying out for mercy loud enough and long enough to annoy the Twelve. They wanted to send her away but, notably, Jesus did not. Although He didn't grant her request immediately, He had a plan for this Gentile woman.

Mark emphasizes her gender and heritage. Matthew describes her as a "Canaanite woman" (Matt. 15:22). Jewish culture at the time treated women remarkably well relative to other cultures of the day, but Hebrew men did not esteem women as equals. The fact that she was not Jewish reduced her personal value to almost nothing in the first-century Jewish mind. No one would have blamed Jesus for continuing to ignore her. Nevertheless, He responded to her persistence.

— 7:27-28 —

The fact that Jesus welcomed the woman's persistence should be a significant factor when interpreting His initial response. Remember also that He had spent significant time teaching, healing, and casting out demons among the Gentiles of the Decapolis, and would again soon. He loved Gentiles—they, too, are His creation made in His image—and He wanted to save them.

The face-value reading is shocking to the modern, Gentile reader, but it would have been quite in line with the predominant Jewish mindset toward non-Jews. Hebrews frequently referred to Gentiles as dogs, using a term describing dirty (and ceremonially unclean) street mongrels. Presumably, Jesus spoke to this woman in Greek, and He softened the image by using the word *kynarion* [2952], which means "little dog" or "puppy," perhaps referring to a house pet. Even so, it's unsettling to think of God's Son referring to any person as a dog. But as Jesus begins to respond to the woman's persistent appeals for help, we can be sure that something else lies beneath the surface of His apparent rebuff.

Jesus, the Hebrew Messiah, came to the Jews first because they were God's covenant people, chosen centuries earlier to be His instrument in reaching the world. They were to be His light on a hill (see Ps. 43:3) and become His means of world evangelism (Isa. 43:10; 44:8). Jesus came to redeem Israel and then, while ruling from the throne of David, call all people everywhere to bow before Him as Savior and King (Isa. 45:23). It would be wrong for Him to neglect these "children" and give what is due them to their pets (Mark 7:27).

The woman's response is both insightful and prophetic. Extending the Lord's metaphor, she noted that "even the dogs under the table feed on the children's crumbs" (7:28).

What insight. What determination. What humility. What faith! When initially ignored (Matt. 15:23), she didn't doubt God's ability to heal, and she didn't doubt His goodness or His desire to do what is best for everyone concerned. Instead, she persisted. Even when rebuffed, she didn't sulk or storm off, declaring God uncaring and cruel. Moreover, she showed no sense of entitlement, no expectation that Jesus *should* heal her daughter. On the contrary, she appealed for mercy. And owing her nothing, Jesus extended grace.

— 7:29-30 —

As He had intended all along, Jesus granted the woman's request, cleansing her demonized daughter and setting her free. This interaction between the Jewish Messiah and the Gentile woman is profoundly important to all Gentile Christians. He had come to the Jews first, intending to redeem the world as the Hebrew King. While the world will indeed bow before Him and declare Him sovereign (Phil. 2:9-11), the plan now unfolds differently. God will set aside the rebellious "sons of the covenant" and will allow Gentiles to receive the gospel as it falls like crumbs from the children's table.

Jesus confirmed that, because of her insightful, humble, persistent trust in Him, the woman would receive healing for her daughter. Matthew's account includes the Lord's additional affirmation, "O woman, your faith is great" (Matt. 15:28). And upon returning home, this persistent, believing mother found her daughter well.

APPLICATION: MARK 7:24-30
What Is Great about Your Faith?

Let's return from the ancient city of Tyre, where we watched a woman plead for the release of her daughter. In that scene, we observed the attitude of the disciples, we listened to Jesus use this encounter with the woman as an object lesson, and we saw Jesus fulfill one of His promises. Now, let's pull from the original account some timeless principles and apply them.

It's very likely you have a pressing need right now. It may be as near to impossible as any you have ever faced. What should you do when you have a situation like this woman's? How should you deal with it? How can you rise above it or live through it? How do you cope? How do you find relief?

I do not know God's plan for your life; when it comes to your particular future, I don't know what He has in mind for you. So I'm not offering an airtight "yes" answer to your request. No one can. And I can't give you a method that's sure to accomplish what you want. I simply urge you to take that need to our Savior and Lord in prayer. Not in a spirit of wishful thinking. Not with a spirit of entitlement. But with a confidence in God's power and goodness to do what is right by you and the people you love—no matter what the outcome. That's putting genuine faith into action.

Having faith is coming to our God, believing that He is who He says He is, and believing that He will do what He says He will do. It's trusting Him completely. It's refusing to attempt to manipulate Him or try to change things without His clear direction or to rush something He plans to accomplish on His timetable. Faith is a relentless dependence upon Him. The woman described in this passage would have stayed for days if Jesus hadn't answered her right away, and I find in her the four characteristics of great faith.

First, *she had persistence.* The woman spoke boldly, pleaded repeatedly, and intensified her request to the point of shouting (Matt. 15:21-23). That's what the disciples were complaining about. (For those of you who love music: It's like when a crescendo mark gets larger and larger and you play with greater intensity until you've reached double and triple fortissimo.)

We are given the liberty to "bother" the Lord with our prayers. He's infinitely patient. If you're not seeing results and the situation remains impossible, keep coming to Him. Don't stop. Don't back off. He loves it when His children come to Him. He isn't deaf. He's hearing everyone. He isn't cruel to make you wait; He's accomplishing something wonderful in you. He's cultivating in you a great faith. Keep at it. Remain persistent. Deliberately wait for God to work.

Second, *she had humility.* This was a woman who was truly humble. Her society considered her less than human; Pharisees considered her no more valuable or worthy than a dog. Even so, the woman came to Jesus and said, in effect, "I have no racial claim to the promises of God. I have no righteousness worthy of divine rewards. I have only my need and my faith in Your mercy." Her humility left no room for a spirit of entitlement.

If there's a curse in the twenty-first century, it's an attitude growing among younger generations that the universe owes them success and comfort. The painful, sad truth is that God owes us nothing but eternal punishment! We all deserve nothing except hell. When our expectations begin with the truth of what we are really entitled to, everything else becomes a gift.

A humble heart also avoids blaming and bears no grudges. Undoubtedly, the woman had been marginalized and ignored much of her life, yet she did not let a negative attitude keep her from seeking mercy from God.

Third, *she had focus.* The woman sought out one person and no one else. The fact that there is no mention of a husband or other family suggests that she was alone, or at least that she had a family that remained distant and aloof. The evil presence in her home probably affected everyone with whom she had contact. She was likely shunned by her neighbors—just think of the implications of rearing a demonized child. With no one else capable of helping her, she focused on Christ, her one true hope.

Fourth, *she had confidence.* Despite her past experiences, irrespective of the disciples' discouragement (Matt. 15:23), and regardless of the Lord's apparent disinterest, the woman continued to ask Jesus for help. And when He declared the girl free of her demon, the woman went home. She didn't hesitate or ask for assurance. She didn't require a sign of proof. Without a doubt plaguing her mind, she set out for home to see her daughter cleansed.

As you review the woman's qualities, ask yourself this question: Would Jesus assess your faith as great?

Taking Time for Someone in Need
MARK 7:31-37

NASB

³¹Again He went out from the region of Tyre, and came through Sidon to the Sea of Galilee, within the region of Decapolis. ³²They brought to Him one who was deaf and spoke with difficulty, and they implored Him to lay His hand on him. ³³Jesus took him aside from the crowd, by himself, and put His fingers into his ears, and after spitting, He touched his tongue *with the saliva;* ³⁴and looking up to heaven with a deep sigh, He said to him, "Ephphatha!" that is, "Be opened!" ³⁵And his ears were opened, and the ªimpediment of his tongue ᵇwas removed, and he *began* speaking plainly. ³⁶And He gave them orders not to tell anyone; but the more He ordered them, the more widely they continued to proclaim it. ³⁷They were utterly astonished, saying, "He has done all things well; He makes even the deaf to hear and the mute to speak."

7:35 ªOr *bond* ᵇLit *was loosed*

NLT

³¹Jesus left Tyre and went up to Sidon before going back to the Sea of Galilee and the region of the Ten Towns.* ³²A deaf man with a speech impediment was brought to him, and the people begged Jesus to lay his hands on the man to heal him. ³³Jesus led him away from the crowd so they could be alone. He put his fingers into the man's ears. Then, spitting on his own fingers, he touched the man's tongue. ³⁴Looking up to heaven, he sighed and said, *"Ephphatha,"* which means, "Be opened!" ³⁵Instantly the man could hear perfectly, and his tongue was freed so he could speak plainly! ³⁶Jesus told the crowd not to tell anyone, but the more he told them not to, the more they spread the news. ³⁷They were completely amazed and said again and again, "Everything he does is wonderful. He even makes the deaf to hear and gives speech to those who cannot speak."

7:31 Greek *Decapolis.*

My heart goes out to anyone who struggles with stuttering. Along with facing the difficulty of trying to get words out, a person with a speech impediment can be left feeling embarrassed and excluded. The fear of talking in front of a group can be absolutely debilitating. Add to that the loss of hearing, and you have a person who is truly cut off from others. Unable to hear and incapable of communicating, someone in this situation would feel desperately lonely even while surrounded by people. I know this because my ears and my tongue conspired against me earlier in life.

I had a slight stammer as a young boy, but it had become a debilitating stutter by the time I entered high school. To make things worse, I had a very bright older brother who set scholastic records and an older sister who was extremely popular. Both were immensely gifted and articulate, so this set an impossible standard for me with my teachers. My siblings made their respective marks on the high school scene. But not me. At least, not in that way.

I struggled with a congenital hole in one of my eardrums. It frequently became infected, so my mother would take me to "Dr. Frankenstein," a doctor who used a long wire with a swab to pierce the eardrum and drain the fluid. My poor hearing made blending in even more difficult. It's hard to pass yourself off as normal when you're constantly saying, "Huh?"

Between my speech impediment and my hearing loss, I should have been doomed to float through school with all the personal presence of a ghost. And I was—until Richard Nieme, the drama teacher and debate coach, tapped me on the shoulder and said, "You need to take one of my courses."

"M-m-me? You want to t-t-t-a-a-alk to me?"

"That's right," he said. "You've got what it takes. If you spend time with me, I can teach you how to speak. In fact, you'll speak well enough to take the lead in our senior play."

True to his word, he worked with me daily until I overcame my stuttering and, in my senior year, I played the lead role in our major theatrical production. At the end of the third act, the curtains closed. Right in the center of the front row of the balcony, the first man on his feet, screaming and whistling and applauding with all his might, was Richard Nieme, the mentor who invested in my life like no one ever had. Regaining the ability to speak opened the world to me and I became a full member of the high school community. My high school experience then prepared me for a life of preaching and teaching I could never have imagined for myself.

I offer that personal background to help prepare us for the Lord's encounter with a man in the region of the Decapolis. Deafness isolated him and a speech impediment kept him from relating with his family, friends, and community. He, too, needed someone to see his potential and invest a little personal time in him.

— 7:31-32 —

Mark places this incident directly after the Lord's encounter with the Gentile woman in Tyre. Jesus journeyed farther north to Sidon before turning southeast and then crossing the Sea of Galilee to visit the Decapolis again. Earlier, Jesus had cleansed a demonized man of a host of demons, allowing them to enter a massive heard of swine, who went berserk, ran into the sea, and drowned en masse. The spectacle so frightened the man's Gentile community that they urged Jesus to leave the region (5:1-20).

We don't know exactly where Jesus visited; the Decapolis spans an extremely large area. If it was the same region as the one in 5:1-20, certainly Mark would have said so. Regardless, the people in this story responded to Jesus' ministry very differently. When a group in the area heard of His arrival, they brought the deaf man for healing. James Moffatt's quaint rendering describes him as, "a deaf man who stammered."[21] Immediately, I identify with him. This was the *last* place he wanted to be, and he loathed becoming the center of attention. But his neighbors insisted.

These Gentiles, far removed from Jewish society in Galilee, had heard of Jesus' healing power. In fact, they may have heard about Him from the formerly demonized man, whom Jesus had instructed to tell everyone about his experience. The people of the Decapolis clearly knew about His custom of laying hands on a person when healing (7:32).

— 7:33-34 —

Before we rush to examine the Lord's process of healing the man, let's slow down to observe His "bedside manner." The man was undoubtedly embarrassed to be singled out for his disability and then made to stand before everyone. Jesus did something different with the man than what He normally did with those He healed. Instead of healing him before the watching community, He took the man aside to deal with him privately. Jesus respected the man's privacy and gave him the rare gift of courtesy.

When the two were all alone, Jesus pantomimed the process of healing so the man could understand what was happening. Jesus placed His fingers in the man's ears to indicate that He would restore his hearing. He then spit a little saliva onto His finger and touched the man's tongue to signify that his speech would be restored. Jesus touched the places of the man's need. Then He looked up to heaven with a groan. The Greek word translated "with a deep sigh" (*stenazō* [4727]) is a verb that means "to express oneself involuntarily in the face of an undesirable circumstance" or "to express discontent."[22]

Jesus hates what His creation has done to itself. He groans over the pain that humanity has brought upon itself through sin, just as He grieves over the sorrow we experience because of our sinful behavior. He most likely looked to heaven and groaned at this moment as an expression of His deep compassion for the man and out of longing to see him freed from his misery.

Mark transliterates the Lord's actual command, which was a single Aramaic verb meaning "be opened" (*ephphatha*). The form of the word gives it extra emphasis, so the best rendering is, "Be completely opened!"

— 7:35 —

When Jesus ordered the man's ears and speech to be completely opened, his ears received sound and his tongue moved without restriction. Mark declares that he spoke *orthōs* [3723]. It's one of the Greek words from which we derive the terms "orthodox" ("correct belief") and "orthodontics" ("straight teeth"). He spoke correctly, without obstruction or defect. The verb meaning "to speak" (*laleō* [2980]) appears in the imperfect tense, which is not uncommon when a narrative describes someone making a statement. In this case, it is safe to assume that the verb describes action that began and then continued uninterrupted for some time!

In that epochal moment, the man's life completely changed. No longer cut off from communication, he was free. He probably had *years'* worth of stories to tell. Everything he'd had to keep to himself before this all-important day he undoubtedly unloaded in a nonstop verbal stream. He had a lot to say!

— 7:36-37 —

The Lord's instructions to the man's neighbors took an ironic turn. He had commanded the demonized man in the Decapolis, "Go home to your people and report to them what great things the Lord has done for you, and how He had mercy on you" (5:19). He charged this man and his people, however, "not to tell anyone" (7:36). The man could finally hear his loved ones speak and could express himself freely for the first time—yet he was forbidden to share the news with anyone! Apparently, Jesus' fame had started to impede His ability to minister, so He had to curtail reports of His miraculous healings.

Mark states, however, that the more Jesus requested discretion, the more people talked. The expression "utterly astonished" (7:37) combines two Greek words and conveys the idea of being beside oneself with amazement. The people couldn't believe their eyes, and they told everyone they knew about the wonder-working Jew from the other side of the Jordan.

Their reaction to Jesus was quite different from that of His own countrymen. Earlier, instead of marveling and celebrating, the Jews had accused Jesus of using Satan's power to heal people and cast out demons (3:22). But these pagan Gentiles received His miracles as a gift from God and affirmed, "He has done all things well." Their final declaration alludes to the Old Testament prophecy in Isaiah 35:3-6:

Encourage the exhausted, and strengthen the feeble.
Say to those with anxious heart,
"Take courage, fear not.
Behold, your God will come with vengeance;
The recompense of God will come,
But He will save you."
Then the eyes of the blind will be opened
And the ears of the deaf will be unstopped.
Then the lame will leap like a deer,
And the tongue of the mute will shout for joy.

APPLICATION: MARK 7:31-37
Words to Live By

Taking time for someone in need doesn't require miraculous abilities or special talents. It requires awareness and attention to the present moment and to the impact of the Lord's presence on each moment. In that vein, I want to pass along three very simple statements that will change your life. I mean that with my whole heart. These simple statements hold the power to your life. Furthermore, they will change others' lives.

Treat everyone with courtesy.
I think in concentric circles, so I'll begin with family. Too many people give the gift of courtesy to complete strangers while treating their closest family members and friends with disrespect and outright hostility. Why would we be more polite to people we don't know than to the people who love us? Treat your spouse with the kind of courtesy you would offer royalty. Do the same for the other members of your household. Start there. Tell them how much they mean to you and how

deeply you love them. When you're wrong, tell them you're wrong, and ask their forgiveness. When they do something nice, thank them. And always add those all-important words, "I love you."

Promote liberty everywhere.

Most people are bound up too tightly. You may be one of them. For whatever reason, you have restrained yourself. Scars from the past. Memories that are heartbreaking. Failures. A moral tumble. A series of foolish or sinful decisions. Brokenhearted disappointments. Fractured romances. You may have a prison sentence in your past. You may be going through the difficulty of mental illness. Past wounds can bind you and restrict your freedom to live as joyfully as Christ intends. Consequently, you might be restricting others because of your past struggles.

A great way to enjoy your own freedom is to be a person who sets other people free. Affirm others. Give others room to fail and the dignity of cleaning up their own messes. Release others from your expectations.

When I was in seminary, I took courses from many great teachers. One of them was Dr. Howard Hendricks. Every once in a while, he would write an affirming note at the top of my paper. One time he wrote, "This is great, Chuck. Someday you will write." Years later, as I put together my first book, those words fueled my drive to get the manuscript done. Those words—"Someday you will write"—freed me to write.

Your words have the power to free people. Use them to promote liberty. Let grace awaken!

Do everything well.

By now, you might be yawning, perhaps expecting something unusually profound. This may sound elementary, but don't overlook it!

Where do you work? Have you determined to do your job well? Believe it or not, doing your job with excellence can create a more effective impact for Christ than words alone. Undergird your spoken testimony of Christ's gift of salvation with quality work. As Paul urged first-century believers, "Whatever you do, do your work heartily, as for the Lord rather than for men, knowing that from the Lord you will receive the reward of the inheritance. It is the Lord Christ whom you serve" (Col. 3:23-24).

Serving Dinner to Four Thousand
MARK 8:1-26

¹In those days, when there was again a large crowd and they had nothing to eat, Jesus called His disciples and said to them, ²"I feel compassion for the ᵃpeople because they have remained with Me now three days and have nothing to eat. ³If I send them away hungry to their homes, they will faint on the way; and some of them have come from a great distance." ⁴And His disciples answered Him, "Where will anyone be able *to find enough* ᵃbread here in *this* desolate place to satisfy these people?" ⁵And He was asking them, "How many loaves do you have?" And they said, "Seven." ⁶And He directed the ᵃpeople to ᵇsit down on the ground; and taking the seven loaves, He gave thanks and broke them, and started giving them to His disciples to ᶜserve to them, and they served them to the ᵃpeople. ⁷They also had a few small fish; and after He had blessed them, He ordered these to be ᵃserved as well. ⁸And they ate and were satisfied; and they picked up seven large baskets full of what was left over of the broken pieces. ⁹About four thousand were *there;* and He sent them away. ¹⁰And immediately He entered the boat with His disciples and came to the district of Dalmanutha.

¹¹The Pharisees came out and began to argue with Him, seeking from Him a ᵃsign from heaven, ᵇto test Him. ¹²Sighing deeply ᵃin His spirit, He said, "Why does this generation seek for a ᵇsign? Truly I say to you, ᶜno ᵇsign will be given to this

¹About this time another large crowd had gathered, and the people ran out of food again. Jesus called his disciples and told them, ²"I feel sorry for these people. They have been here with me for three days, and they have nothing left to eat. ³If I send them home hungry, they will faint along the way. For some of them have come a long distance."

⁴His disciples replied, "How are we supposed to find enough food to feed them out here in the wilderness?"

⁵Jesus asked, "How much bread do you have?"

"Seven loaves," they replied.

⁶So Jesus told all the people to sit down on the ground. Then he took the seven loaves, thanked God for them, and broke them into pieces. He gave them to his disciples, who distributed the bread to the crowd. ⁷A few small fish were found, too, so Jesus also blessed these and told the disciples to distribute them.

⁸They ate as much as they wanted. Afterward, the disciples picked up seven large baskets of leftover food. ⁹There were about 4,000 men in the crowd that day, and Jesus sent them home after they had eaten. ¹⁰Immediately after this, he got into a boat with his disciples and crossed over to the region of Dalmanutha.

¹¹When the Pharisees heard that Jesus had arrived, they came and started to argue with him. Testing him, they demanded that he show them a miraculous sign from heaven to prove his authority.

¹²When he heard this, he sighed deeply in his spirit and said, "Why do these people keep demanding a miraculous sign? I tell you the truth, I will not give this generation any

NASB

generation." [13] Leaving them, He again embarked and went away to the other side.

[14] And they had forgotten to take bread, and did not have more than one loaf in the boat with them. [15] And He was giving orders to them, saying, "Watch out! Beware of the leaven of the Pharisees and the leaven of Herod." [16] They *began* to discuss with one another *the fact* that they had no bread. [17] And Jesus, aware of this, said to them, "Why do you discuss *the fact* that you have no bread? Do you not yet see or understand? Do you have a [a]hardened heart? [18] HAVING EYES, DO YOU NOT SEE? AND HAVING EARS, DO YOU NOT HEAR? And do you not remember, [19] when I broke the five loaves for the five thousand, how many baskets full of broken pieces you picked up?" They said to Him, "Twelve." [20] "When *I broke* the seven for the four thousand, how many large baskets full of broken pieces did you pick up?" And they said to Him, "Seven." [21] And He was saying to them, "Do you not yet understand?"

[22] And they came to Bethsaida. And they brought a blind man to Jesus and implored Him to touch him. [23] Taking the blind man by the hand, He brought him out of the village; and after spitting on his eyes and laying His hands on him, He asked him, "Do you see anything?" [24] And he [a]looked up and said, "I see men, for [b]I see *them* like trees, walking around." [25] Then again He laid His hands on his eyes; and he looked intently and was restored, and *began* to see everything clearly. [26] And He

NLT

such sign." [13] So he got back into the boat and left them, and he crossed to the other side of the lake.

[14] But the disciples had forgotten to bring any food. They had only one loaf of bread with them in the boat. [15] As they were crossing the lake, Jesus warned them, "Watch out! Beware of the yeast of the Pharisees and of Herod."

[16] At this they began to argue with each other because they hadn't brought any bread. [17] Jesus knew what they were saying, so he said, "Why are you arguing about having no bread? Don't you know or understand even yet? Are your hearts too hard to take it in? [18] 'You have eyes—can't you see? You have ears—can't you hear?'* Don't you remember anything at all? [19] When I fed the 5,000 with five loaves of bread, how many baskets of leftovers did you pick up afterward?"

"Twelve," they said.

[20] "And when I fed the 4,000 with seven loaves, how many large baskets of leftovers did you pick up?"

"Seven," they said.

[21] "Don't you understand yet?" he asked them.

[22] When they arrived at Bethsaida, some people brought a blind man to Jesus, and they begged him to touch the man and heal him. [23] Jesus took the blind man by the hand and led him out of the village. Then, spitting on the man's eyes, he laid his hands on him and asked, "Can you see anything now?"

[24] The man looked around. "Yes," he said, "I see people, but I can't see them very clearly. They look like trees walking around."

[25] Then Jesus placed his hands on the man's eyes again, and his eyes were opened. His sight was completely restored, and he could see everything clearly. [26] Jesus sent him

sent him to his home, saying, "Do not even enter the village."

away, saying, "Don't go back into the village on your way home."

8:2 ªLit crowd 8:4 ªLit loaves 8:6 ªLit crowd ᵇLit recline ᶜLit set before 8:7 ªLit set before them 8:11 ªOr attesting miracle ᵇLit testing Him 8:12 ªOr to Himself ᵇOr attesting miracle ᶜLit if a sign shall be given 8:17 ªOr dull, insensible 8:24 ªOr gained sight ᵇOr they look to me

8:18 Jer 5:21.

John Milton Gregory loved education. He lived at a time in America when universities were just beginning to proliferate. In fact, he was a founder of the University of Illinois and served as its first president. Gregory loved teaching and the whole process of education. That's because he loved learning. When he reached the end of his productive life, he was buried, at his request, near the main quadrangle of the campus that he had enjoyed and served with such devotion and diligence.

If you're a teacher, if you're a coach, or if you're someone who loves to learn, you owe it to yourself to get a copy of his classic book, *The Seven Laws of Teaching*. While expressed in archaic language, each law is as timeless as it is true. In the introduction to his educators' manual, he writes, "These two great branches of educational art,—training and teaching,—though separable in thought, are not separable in practice. We can only train by teaching, and we teach best when we train best."[23]

Teaching is communicating information so that truth is passed from one who knows it to one who needs to learn it. Teaching stretches the learner's mind; training challenges the student's life. Teaching leads to training, which provides opportunity for practical, hands-on application. Only as the head and hands—knowledge and application— synchronize can the student gain mastery of a particular discipline. Naturally, this involves a fair amount of failing before success becomes the norm.

The last of Gregory's seven laws highlights the need for review and application: "The completion, test, and confirmation of teaching must be made by reviews."[24] As an old Latin proverb states, "Repetition is the mother of learning." Our brains require repeated exposure to information. As neural pathways are stimulated over and over by the same ideas, the concepts become a part of us. When I was engaged in the Scripture memory program of The Navigators, my mentor said, "Chuck, the secret of memory is really no secret at all; it's review, review, review, review."

One reason I journal is to have opportunities to review the life lessons God has taught me. If I don't review events in my life, I will forget how He has met my needs in days past and then fail to trust Him for today's needs. The principles I discover through great pain and sorrow will slip from my conscious mind, and I will have gained no lasting wisdom. It's amazing how quickly we can forget what He teaches.

Our greatest example is the Lord Jesus, who "appointed twelve, so that they would be with Him"—that's teaching—"and that He could send them out to preach"—that's training (3:14). And throughout their period of teaching and training, Jesus put these men to the test, knowing that one day He would be gone, they would remain, and they would be responsible to continue the mission He had begun.

As He trained and taught, Jesus also used repetition. This episode in Jesus' ministry will be familiar (cf. 6:34-44). Jesus was teaching a large number of people in the wilderness. The people had no food but needed to be fed. There was only a small amount of loaves and fish available, the staple lunch diet near the Sea of Galilee. And, again, the Lord turned the insufficiency of the disciples into abundance for ministry. As that great baseball sage Yogi Berra once said, "It's like déjà vu all over again."

As Kent Hughes points out, skeptics have "outdone themselves in attempting to prove that Mark is really explaining the same event twice." He continues,

> The main argument is that the disciples' dialogue regarding where they were going to get enough food to feed the 4,000 (v. 4) does not make any sense if they have already seen Jesus previously feed 5,000. In the words of one critic: "the stupid repetition of the question is psychologically impossible!"[25]

But think about it. If this is the same event, Mark inserted the same story twice—by hand, with pen and ink on papyrus—without realizing it, read the finished product, and still failed to notice the duplication. Moreover, if Peter was the authority behind the account as I suggested in the introduction, then he—an eyewitness—didn't question the retelling, despite conflicting details between two accounts of the same event on the same scroll! And to make matters even worse, Jesus mentioned both stories along with their conflicting details (8:19-20).

Either Mark and Peter were laughably incompetent, or else Jesus was taking an opportunity to reinforce one of the most important lessons a minister must learn: *We can only succeed in ministering to others when Jesus turns our inadequacy into abundance.*

— 8:1-3 —

Mark usually mentions when there is a change of geography, as in 8:10, 13; therefore, the opening phrase "in those days" places Jesus (still) in the Gentile region of the Decapolis. The ten cities of the Decapolis were spread out over a very large territory, as I mentioned earlier, so He could have been almost anywhere. Because few cities could accommodate large crowds in a single venue, Jesus found natural amphitheaters in the wilderness. Mark describes this particular place as "desolate" (8:4), a term that would typically describe an "uninhabited or lonely region, normally with sparse vegetation."[26]

Jesus had been teaching the multitude for three days, and they finally ran out of food. When their provisions ran low, they chose not to leave His teaching, which we should take as evidence of their faith (cf. Deut. 8:3). The Lord wanted to honor their trust in Him by providing for their need.

Jesus said He felt "compassion" for His audience (Mark 8:2). The word *splanchnizomai* [4697] denotes an emotional reaction so deep that one feels moved at what we would call a "gut level." We might even say Jesus felt "gut-wrenching" empathy for the needs of these faithful listeners.

By the way, that's some pretty effective teaching! Few preachers can keep an audience's attention for more than an hour, to say nothing of holding the rapt concentration of several thousand for three days straight! They didn't even break away to eat!

While Jesus wants us to give priority to kingdom issues, He remains completely aware that our physical needs do matter (Matt. 6:33). He is our creator. He knows what we need. So Jesus understood the implications of sending His audience away with no food for the journey home, which was quite long for many of them.

— 8:4 —

The disciples asked a question that undoubtedly exasperated Jesus. My grandson would call this a "face-palm moment." Who could have forgotten the day Jesus multiplied a small lunch to feed ten to fifteen thousand people? An event like that had to have burned itself into the memories of the Twelve, who had spent hours shuttling baskets of food from the Lord to their Jewish kinsmen gathered in a similar circumstance.

On the one hand, I don't want to be too hard on the disciples. As I pause to recall some of my own times of testing and learning, I'm embarrassed to say that I haven't always learned all that I should on the first go-around. In some cases, I've struggled more the second time around, doubting the faithfulness of God, or wondering if He's forgotten about my needs, or thinking He might not care about me very much this time. I sometimes fail to "get it." I need a second and third review. And I'm sure it's the same with you.

On the other hand, we have to marvel at their hardheaded response. They ask, "Where will *anyone* be able to find enough bread?" (emphasis mine). Anyone? Including the Son of God? Including the man who proved Himself "able" before? Their response should have been, "Lord, here are seven loaves of bread; we'll go get some baskets to haul the food. You are more than able. You are YHWH-jireh, the God who provides (see NASB note at Gen. 22:14). We believe what You said at the last feeding of the multitude: You are the Bread of Life (John 6:35). You're the great I Am. We will trust You, and we will follow Your instructions. Just as You were able to do this before, You are able to feed this multitude today."

— 8:5-7 —

Both Mark and Matthew describe this event (cf. Matt. 15:32-38). Neither of them records a negative response from Jesus. He didn't lecture. He didn't scold. He didn't expel them from His apostleship training program. He merely clarified the number of loaves they had on hand, undoubtedly to underscore their inadequacy against the overwhelming human need before them. He then issued familiar instructions: Seat the people. The disciples knew the drill. They seated the people in groups and then facilitated the distribution of food.

— 8:8-9 —

As before, the people received the food and were satisfied. And again the disciples gathered up the leftovers. This time they collected seven full baskets. Earlier, they had used a relatively small *kophinos* [2894], which travelers would use to carry their provisions. In this case, the type of basket was a *spyris* [4711], a hamper-like basket used to store grain or transport produce to the market. There is no real significance to the number seven in this case; the point is that Jesus used inadequate resources to provide abundantly.

If the Twelve didn't "get it" earlier, and if they missed the point on this day, they would eventually understand what Jesus was trying to teach them. It's a lesson we followers—this means you!—must learn, or we'll flame out like a shooting star and fall to earth stone cold. God has called us to join Him in an enterprise too great for all of us combined. The sheer volume of human need is so overwhelming that it boggles the mind. Yet He has called each one of us to His side and said, as it were, "You give them something to eat!" (6:37). In other words, *I give you the responsibility to address the needs of a world oppressed by evil.*

When we respond, "Lord, the need is too great for me!" we fail to understand His command. God already knows that the size of the task is beyond the scope of human ability. Besides, He doesn't *need* you or me. Truth be told, He doesn't need anyone in order to accomplish His mission. He's God! He's all powerful, all knowing, and all sufficient. Nevertheless, He calls His disciples to join Him in ministering to the world, not because He can't get the job done on His own, but to let us share in His victory. The fact that He delegates responsibility to us is a gift of grace. At the end of this particular day, as four-thousand-plus people went home with full bellies, the disciples could legitimately say, "By God's grace and power, *we* fed the multitude!" And Jesus wants it that way.

— **8:10-11** —

Mark shifts the narrative to a new scene, but he has not abandoned the theme of bread. He will return to it in 8:14, so we must discern how 8:10-13 fit.

Having sent away the four thousand, Jesus led His disciples west again, back across the Sea of Galilee to Dalmanutha, a place Matthew calls Magadan (Matt. 15:39) that was also known as Magdala. The exact location is not known, but New Testament scholars agree that it lay on the west side of the lake in a valley south of Capernaum called Gennesaret.[27]

There were no large or important towns nearby. Mark probably mentions the location to demonstrate how persistent the Pharisees had become in harassing Jesus. He visited the first-century-Galilee equivalent of a backwoods region of America, only to find a contingent of religious experts waiting to challenge Him.

The Pharisees didn't attack the Lord's theology in this encounter; they wanted Him to prove His identity and legitimacy with a sign.

The Greek term for "sign" is *sēmeion* [4592]. Its most basic meaning is "something that gives a true indication of something else." A road

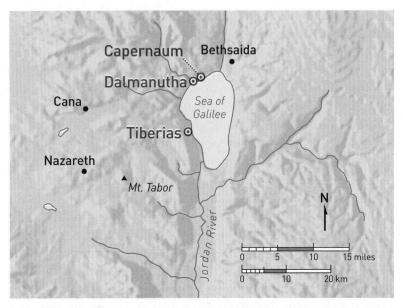

Jesus was in the region of the Decapolis on the east side of the Sea of Galilee. To escape the crowds, Jesus and his disciples crossed the Sea to Dalmanutha.

sign accurately indicates what lies ahead for the traveler. The Greeks gave the term special meaning as a physical indication of divine will or a supernatural omen. For example, lightning was thought to indicate the will of Zeus, and thunder was a foreboding indication that he was about to speak through a "sign." For the Jews, a "sign" was a visual confirmation that a prophet was authentically from God. This word also referred to a physical manifestation of God's glory.

— 8:12-13 —

Jesus expressed a mixture of weary exasperation and empathetic sorrow for the people He called "this generation" (8:12), an indirect reference to His immediate audience as well as Israel at large. He lamented two difficulties among the Jews: the inability to see the truth on the part of some (most notably His own disciples), and the unwillingness to see the truth on the part of others. We might separate them into these two categories: those who *did* not see and those who *would* not see.

The fact that the Pharisees asked for a sign follows the pattern set by the disciples in 8:1-9. When confronted with the challenge of feeding the four thousand, the Twelve failed to connect the dots. The feeding of the five thousand should have prepared them to respond positively to this new, almost identical challenge. The disciples wanted to see, but

What's Your Point?

MARK 8:17-21

A young seminary student was given the responsibility to fulfill an assignment for his preaching class at school. He was to preach to a group of people. He didn't have any experience in this, so he was already a little uneasy about it. When the opportunity came for him to preach, to his surprise, it was to a group of men at the Gospel Mission, down in the sleazy part of town. These men pretty much existed in the gutter and lived on cheap wine. Because they were cold during the day, were half-starved, and needed shelter at night, the only reason they would come into the Gospel Mission was to get a hot meal, which they could smell from the street. To receive a meal, however, they had to sit through the sermon.

Rev. Clean (who had never had a drink in his life) showed up in his three-piece suit to preach on the evils of alcohol. What he lacked in experience he made up for in creativity. He brought with him an object lesson consisting of two large mason jars of liquid. One was filled to the brim with fresh water; the other was filled with distilled "bathtub gin." During his sermon, he pulled from his pocket a very healthy earthworm. "I want all you men to watch," he said, and he dropped the worm into the water.

They watched for a few moments as the worm swam around, wriggled to the side, and began to inch his way back up over the top. Rev. Clean plucked it off the rim and said, "Now watch!" Immediately after being dropped into the gin, the worm began to quiver, started to disintegrate, and finally dropped to the bottom in pieces.

"Now, what have you learned from what you've seen?"

Silence fell, and pangs of guilt covered the room as the men glanced at one another. Finally, a grizzled old man in the back said, "Well, Sonny, I learned that if you drink enough booze, you'll never have worms."

Clarity and precision are an important part of communication, but they do not guarantee that the message will be received. The hearer bears a part of that responsibility. And some people simply will not "get it" because they have a strong desire to remain in their ignorance. In that case, you have no choice but to let them.

they had—as it were—scales over their eyes. They were hindered by a spiritual dullness.

The Pharisees, however, had a different kind of blindness. They had already seen Jesus heal diseases, cast out demons, and even raise the dead! In fact, they had dismissed His earlier miracles, not as tricks or illusions, but as genuinely supernatural acts done with the help of Satan (3:22). They had already seen all the evidence they needed to make a logical deduction about the identity of Jesus, yet they remained blinded to the truth.

Jesus' point in refusing the Pharisees' request was this: "If what I have done and what you have seen thus far in My earthly ministry have not convinced you that God is evident in and through My life, something spectacular blazing across the sky will not convince you. You must soften your hearts." Besides, both Jesus and the Pharisees knew that false prophets traffic in the sensational. More miraculous signs would only begin to undermine His credibility.

Jesus discontinued the dialogue and simply carried on with His ministry.

— 8:14-16 —

Jesus and His men sailed the Sea of Galilee to another destination. We learn from 8:22 that they eventually reached Bethsaida, although they may have ministered somewhere else first.

Regardless, they hadn't been on the water very long when Jesus began to debrief His encounter with the Pharisees. He wanted to prepare the future apostles for their eventual clash with the religious authorities in Jerusalem. Using the image of leaven (yeast) and bread, He warned about the subtle, corrupting influence of the Pharisees and their political opposites, the Herodians. During His object lesson, someone evidently thought, *Leaven. That makes bread rise. Speaking of bread, I'm getting hungry, and there's only one loaf of bread on board.* While Jesus was driving home a crucial spiritual lesson, the disciples began to discuss lunch plans. They became especially concerned with the fact that one loaf of bread couldn't possibly satisfy the appetites of thirteen men.

— 8:17-21 —

This became another "face-palm moment" for Jesus. He asked, "Do you not yet see or understand?" (8:17). The Greek word translated "see," *noeō* [3539], means "to perceive by the mind," "to apprehend," or "to observe with reflection or comprehension." The term for "understand," *syniēmi* [4920], has the literal sense of bringing separated things together; metaphorically, it denotes the process of assembling data or clues to arrive at a reasonable conclusion. I would paraphrase Jesus this way: "Don't you get it? Can't you connect the dots? The clues make the conclusion self-evident; how can you fail to see it?"

Jesus then reviewed their experiences, walking them through the evidence while highlighting important facts:

EXPERIENCES	FACTS
Jesus cared about the needs of the five thousand in the Galilean wilderness.	Jesus multiplied insufficient supplies to provide for His people an abundance.
Jesus cared about the needs of the four thousand in the wilderness of the Decapolis.	Jesus multiplied insufficient supplies to provide for His people an abundance.

The pattern had been established. Logic demanded that the disciples consider the present situation. Jesus cared about their needs. They held a loaf of bread in their hands. The man responsible for those two earlier miracles sat in the boat with them. So . . .

Let me be clear. The disciples were not stupid. They struggled to overcome two difficulties that plague us to this day. The first is the dulling influence of old paradigms. Like wagon wheels in a rut, we follow the patterns of thinking traced across the spiritual landscape by previous generations. The world system would have us think that if we don't provide for ourselves, we will not eat. Jesus called twelve men to blaze a new trail of grace so that succeeding generations would learn the foundational principle of the new kingdom: "Seek first His kingdom and His righteousness, and all these [fundamental provisions] will be added to you" (Matt. 6:33).

At times, the disciples also struggled with what I call "the hothouse syndrome." They had been around the Miracle Worker for many months. The supernatural had become second nature. Jesus gave sight to the blind. He restored withered hands. Cleansed hopeless lepers. Opened deaf ears and loosened mute tongues. He cast out demons, changed the weather, and raised the dead. The Twelve witnessed His power so often they began to regard His miracles as commonplace.

We face this danger as well. We can be around spiritual things and scriptural teaching and Bible studies and verse memorization so long and so often that the revolutionary message of the gospel can become ho-hum. Like the disciples, we can forget that the mission and vision of Christ apply to us.

— 8:22 —

Mark again shifts the scene from the boat on the Sea of Galilee to the beautiful village of Bethsaida. Located about 4 miles northeast of Capernaum, this small hunting village was beautified by Philip the tetrarch when he built his private residence there. Jesus took His disciples there on occasion to escape the relentless pull of ministry for a little R & R (cf. Luke 9:10). While there, Jesus encountered a blind man in need of healing. "They"—most likely referring to the disciples—brought the man to the Lord and urged Him to restore the man's sight.

The placement of this miracle in Mark's narrative is no accident. Mark alone records it as the conclusion of a short series of stories woven together by the unifying theme of seeing. It happens to be the only miracle that occurred in stages—partial sight followed by a repeat application of miraculous touch, which then produced complete sight. It is also a rare instance in which the disciples brought to Jesus a person in need of healing.

— 8:23-24 —

Jesus led the blind man out of the city, most likely to avoid a spectacle. In Galilee, miraculous signs had become a hindrance to effective ministry. The crowds not only restricted His movement, but they became enamored with the short-term solution to sickness when Jesus wanted to redeem the world from the source of its troubles—sin.

The English translation of Mark's description sounds disgusting. The Greek allows for a little more subtle of an image than "spitting on his eyes" (8:23). Jesus likely applied saliva to His fingers and then touched them to the man's eyes before placing His hands on him. The symbolism is unclear. The use of spittle in healing was not unknown in Greek literature. Perhaps Jesus used a familiar symbol of healing to be clear about His actions.

Rather than commanding the miracle to be accomplished or declaring it as completed, Jesus asked the man, "Do you see anything?" Nowhere else did He ask about the efficacy of His healing power. He did so here to illustrate a point that will become clearer as the story unfolds.

In response, the man described blurry, unfocused vision. It was better than complete darkness, but not yet sufficient for independent living.

— 8:25-26 —

To complete the man's restoration of sight, Jesus touched his eyes again. This time, as the man strained to see, the world came into focus, and twenty-twenty vision became his once more.

Why the repetition in Jesus' healing of this man? Why was it not instant? I will point out that the disciples' spiritual blindness gradually gave way to effective sight only after repetition. As they remained in the Lord's presence and He continued to invest Himself, they began to understand Him. In this story, they knew enough to bring the blind man to Jesus; they believed in His ability to heal, and they trusted that His compassion would prompt His mercy. They were just beginning to "get it."

The seventh law of teaching—repetition—had begun to accomplish its work.

APPLICATION: MARK 8:1-26
A Cheat Sheet for Your Next Spiritual Exam

I don't like repeating lessons. Especially painful ones. Since I'm sure you're the same way, let me give you four statements to keep handy when challenged by life. You might call this a "cheat sheet" for your next test. I pray that the statements help you learn your spiritual lesson early so that you pass the test with as little sorrow as possible.

Statement #1: There is no need too great for God to hear. I was once stopped by a woman just before a Sunday-morning worship service. As she wept, she told me about how she had been abandoned. I felt gut-wrenching compassion for her. The more her story went on, the more complicated it became, and the stronger my feelings of empathy grew. As she described her situation, every detail seemed increasingly outrageous. We discussed some practical options but concluded with this reassurance and challenge: "This is not too great for God. I urge you to tell Him everything."

I highly recommend finding trained, competent help for situations that become unmanageable, but I always remind people in pain that they have a direct line to their heavenly Father. We all have direct, immediate access to the throne room of the Ruler of the universe. He will never say, "My, that's a tough problem you have there. Frankly, you're on your own. That is beyond My ability to solve."

Statement #2: There is no reason for us ever to forget. When the people of Israel experienced great suffering, they rehearsed God's faithfulness to them in the past. He had called Abraham to follow Him and had established an unconditional covenant of blessing with him. When oppressed by enemies or afflicted by famine, the Hebrews recalled how God had delivered them from Egypt, cared for them in the wilderness, settled them in the Land of Promise, and guaranteed them a future of shalom.

Never forget God's past provision and protection. He has met your needs before; He can meet your needs now.

Statement #3: There is no limit to what God can provide. God's supply always exceeds our need. He owns the whole universe, so He's never without resources. That's not to say He will give you exactly what you ask for. But He will hear your prayer, and He will provide what you need.

We have to be careful not to turn this principle into a theology of prosperity. Health and wealth are not God's obligation to us. Furthermore, He never promised to make us comfortable. That's not theology; that's nonsense. In the upper room, on the eve of His crucifixion, Jesus promised His disciples that the world would hate them, persecute them, and seek their destruction (John 15:18-27). Jesus promised suffering! Even so, the Bible assures us that even the evil intended by the world will be used for our good (Rom. 8:28).

We may not receive what we want, but God will faithfully provide what we need.

Statement #4: There is no way God will give up on us when we don't get it. While training the Twelve to become apostles, Jesus experienced many exasperating moments. A lesser man would have expelled the entire school and started over with more promising men. But Mark 8:10 states, "Immediately He entered the boat with His disciples." Their failures notwithstanding, Jesus never gave up on them. And He won't give up on you, either.

The apostle Paul assures us,

For those whom He foreknew, He also predestined to become conformed to the image of His Son, so that He would be the firstborn among many brethren; and these whom He predestined, He also called; and these whom He called, He also justified; and these whom He justified, He also glorified. What then shall we say to these things? If God is for us, who is against us? (Rom. 8:29-31)

Crucial Contrasts
MARK 8:27-38

NASB

27 Jesus went out, along with His disciples, to the villages of Caesarea Philippi; and on the way He questioned His disciples, saying to them, "Who do people say that I am?" 28 They told Him, saying, "John the Baptist; and others *say* Elijah; but others, one of the prophets." 29 And He *continued* by questioning them, "But who do you say that I am?" Peter answered and said to Him, "You are ªthe Christ." 30 And He ªwarned them to tell no one about Him.

31 And He began to teach them that the Son of Man must suffer many things and be rejected by the elders and the chief priests and the scribes, and be killed, and after three days rise again. 32 And He was stating the matter plainly. And Peter took Him aside and began to rebuke Him. 33 But turning around and seeing His disciples, He rebuked Peter and said, "Get behind Me, Satan; for you are not setting your mind on ªGod's interests, but man's."

34 And He summoned the crowd with His disciples, and said to them, "If anyone wishes to come after Me, he must deny himself, and take up his cross and follow Me. 35 For whoever wishes to save his ªlife will lose it, but whoever loses his ªlife for

NLT

27 Jesus and his disciples left Galilee and went up to the villages near Caesarea Philippi. As they were walking along, he asked them, "Who do people say I am?"

28 "Well," they replied, "some say John the Baptist, some say Elijah, and others say you are one of the other prophets."

29 Then he asked them, "But who do you say I am?"

Peter replied, "You are the Messiah.*"

30 But Jesus warned them not to tell anyone about him.

31 Then Jesus began to tell them that the Son of Man* must suffer many terrible things and be rejected by the elders, the leading priests, and the teachers of religious law. He would be killed, but three days later he would rise from the dead. 32 As he talked about this openly with his disciples, Peter took him aside and began to reprimand him for saying such things.*

33 Jesus turned around and looked at his disciples, then reprimanded Peter. "Get away from me, Satan!" he said. "You are seeing things merely from a human point of view, not from God's."

34 Then, calling the crowd to join his disciples, he said, "If any of you wants to be my follower, you must give up your own way, take up your cross, and follow me. 35 If you try to hang on to your life, you will lose it. But if you give up your life for my

NASB

My sake and the gospel's will save it. ³⁶ For what does it profit a man to gain the whole world, and forfeit his soul? ³⁷ For what will a man give in exchange for his soul? ³⁸ For whoever is ashamed of Me and My words in this adulterous and sinful generation, the Son of Man will also be ashamed of him when He comes in the glory of His Father with the holy angels."

8:29 ªI.e. the Messiah   8:30 ªOr *strictly admonished*
8:33 ªLit *the things of God*   8:35 ªOr *soul*

NLT

sake and for the sake of the Good News, you will save it. ³⁶ And what do you benefit if you gain the whole world but lose your own soul?* ³⁷ Is anything worth more than your soul? ³⁸ If anyone is ashamed of me and my message in these adulterous and sinful days, the Son of Man will be ashamed of that person when he returns in the glory of his Father with the holy angels."

8:29 Or *the Christ. Messiah* (a Hebrew term) and *Christ* (a Greek term) both mean "anointed one."
8:31 "Son of Man" is a title Jesus used for himself.
8:32 Or *began to correct him.*   8:36 Or *your self?* also in 8:37.

One of the staff members of our church took a video camera to the local mall and asked passersby a simple question: "Who is Jesus?" I remember sitting in a small room, watching the clip with several other members of our staff and feeling sickened by what I saw and heard. Here's a small sample of people's actual words:

MAN 1. That's a trick question. (*Laughs.*) I don't know how to answer that.

WOMAN. I mean, I believe that He was a real person and that He died on the cross, but I don't believe that He was God's Son.

MAN 2. He was, you know . . . He was just another person that found religion and all that, so it's . . . I mean . . . He's nothing like . . . He's, of course, a good person and all that, and He's a really big part of religion, so . . . You know . . . All people that find religion are, you know, important. So people have different views.

MAN 3. He is . . . uh . . . (*Turns to younger man.*) Help me out here. (*Young man shrugs.*) Jesus Christ is, uh . . . the Son of God? (*Looks again to the younger man.*)

This took place less than 2 miles from the church where I serve as senior pastor. That little video haunted me for weeks.

On another occasion, I sat outside a rug shop near ancient Ephesus, talking with a Turkish gentleman whose English sounded better than mine. He asked, "Why are all of you here?"

I replied, "We came to view the ruins of the ancient city, enjoy some lunch outside, and now see how rugs are made."

"No," he said, "I mean, what brings you all together?"

"Oh. We're all followers of Jesus."

"Who?" he asked.

As I told the man about Jesus, it became very clear that he knew absolutely nothing about Him. In fact, this very intelligent, reasonably well-educated man thought that "Christ" was Jesus' last name. He came from somewhere east of Kuşadasi, Turkey, where we chatted that day. The man in his fifties had never heard of Jesus, to say nothing of the gospel.

Any historian worth his or her degree can tell you that Jesus lived in Galilee two millennia ago, became a famous rabbi with radical views, gathered a sizable following for a time, was crucified outside of Jerusalem, and had followers who later turned His teaching into a major world religion. Historians may not agree about whether He performed miracles or rose from the dead, and they often disagree about what He taught. Aside from spouting barely enough facts to fill a three-by-five card, few can actually answer the question put to the people at the mall: "Who is Jesus?"

As we approach the midpoint of Mark's narrative, we find that nearly everyone Jesus knew struggled with His identity. In fact, up to this point, even the Twelve—men who spent night and day observing virtually every word and deed of their Master—couldn't connect the dots. Only recently had they begun to see. But like the blind man in the previous segment, their spiritual eyesight came to them slowly. They had made progress, but the future leaders of the movement known as the church still needed a breakthrough.

— 8:27 —

An unknown period of time had passed since Jesus had restored the blind man's sight in Bethsaida (8:22-26). They probably returned to Capernaum—their headquarters, as it were—before traveling north to Caesarea Philippi.

This city should not be confused with Caesarea Maritima, the port city Herod the Great had built on the coast of the Mediterranean. Caesarea Philippi lay nearly 26 miles north of Capernaum at the base of the mountain range leading up to Mt. Hermon. Caesar Augustus had given the city to Herod the Great as a reward for his loyalty. To show his gratitude, Herod constructed a magnificent temple of white stone in Caesar Augustus's honor. When Herod the Great died, his son Philip the Tetrarch made the city even more beautiful and claimed it as his main residence.

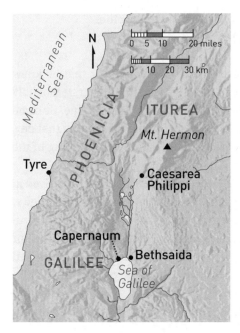

After healing a blind man in Bethsaida, Jesus and his disciples traveled from the region of Galilee to Caesarea Philippi.

In addition to the temple honoring Caesar Augustus, the city also boasted another temple. An underground spring bubbled up from a nearby cave and fed the Jordan River. In Old Testament times, pagans gathered on this site to worship Baal-gad, who was also known as Baal-hermon (cf. Josh. 11:17; Judg. 3:3; 1 Chr. 5:23). Later, the Greeks made the temple a shrine to Pan and the nymphs.[28]

Both Mark and Matthew name this location, probably because it was the site of both great power and concentrated myth, two significant challenges to the coming church. With Caesarea Philippi looming eleven hundred feet above the valley where they stood, Jesus asked, "Who do people say that I am?"

— 8:28-29 —

Jesus didn't ask the disciples' opinion; that would come later. He wanted them to reflect on the general consensus of Israel's population. Many Jews called Him a prophet (cf. Deut. 18:15-18). Others accepted Him as the Messiah—albeit a messiah conforming to their own wishful thinking—and wanted to make Him king (John 6:14-15). Was He John the Baptizer returning from the grave (Luke 9:7)? Was He an Old Testament prophet come as a herald of the new Israel (Mal. 4:5-6)? Clearly, Galileans still clung to their ignorance and superstition instead of embracing the gospel.

Jesus then turned the question to His inner circle of students: "But who do *you* say that I am?" (Mark 8:29, emphasis mine). Even though the "you" is plural, Peter leaped forward with a response. (No surprise.) On this occasion, his answer could not have been more on point. Matthew's account preserves the full statement: "You are the Christ, the

Son of the living God" (Matt. 16:16). Mark, however, condenses Peter's answer to, "You are the Christ," most likely to give greater emphasis to Jesus' discourse on discipleship and suffering.

The title "Christ" comes from the Greek term *christos* [5547], the translation of the Hebrew word *mashiach* [H4899], which is a cognate word in English: "Messiah." All of these words mean "anointed one." In some ancient Near Eastern cultures, a person receiving special recognition would become the center of a ceremony in which a priest or prophet applied a small amount of olive oil to the head. The honor came as a reward for valor on the battlefield or victory over a powerful enemy. The Hebrews eventually reserved it for commissioning their national leader. In Israel, "the Lord's anointed" was none other than the reigning king (e.g., 1 Sam. 2:10). Devout Jews, however, looked forward to the appearance of *the* Messiah, a king worthy of David's throne and one righteous enough to please God.

Peter unequivocally affirmed Jesus as this ultimate King of Israel.

— 8:30-31 —

Jesus ordered His men to keep this information to themselves (see comments on 1:43-44). He had to manage His public perception carefully to keep His message and mission on track. John 6:15 tells us that a crowd of Israelites enthused by the Lord's miraculous power tried to take Him by force and make Him king. That's because the religious teachers of Israel had prepared the Jews for a very different kind of messiah than the Old Testament promised. After more than a hundred years of Roman occupation, Israelites wanted the kind of Christ who would gather a great following, overtake corrupt Jerusalem, overthrow cruel Rome, and usher Israel into an unprecedented period of agricultural, economic, and military superabundance. After all, the Old Testament prophets did predict that the Messiah would receive the power and authority to rule the whole world (Pss. 2:7-9; 72:11; Dan. 7:13-14; Zech. 9:9-10).

Unfortunately, the Israelites overlooked the Old Testament passages predicting the Messiah's suffering on behalf of His people (Isa. 42:1-9; 49:1-13; 50:1-11; 52:13–53:12). Whereas the people expected the Messiah to raise an army and mount a military and political campaign to take Jerusalem by any means necessary, Jesus predicted a completely different path to glory. He would not be carried to power in the upward momentum of a populist movement; His path led Him downward, through suffering and into death.

"SON OF MAN"

MARK 8:31

Jesus frequently referred to Himself as the "Son of Man," which was a particularly meaningful title with roots deep in the soil of Israel's Scriptures. First, Jesus used it to call attention to His own humanity, which was vulnerable (Job 25:6; Pss. 8:4; 144:3; 146:3; Isa. 51:12; Ezek. 2:1; cf. Matt. 26:41; Mark 14:38). Being human, He suffered the pains of humanity, most especially in the ordeal of the cross.

More significantly, "Son of Man" is the title given by Daniel to the messianic figure in one of his visions. He was "one like a Son of Man," (Dan. 7:13) who received from the Ancient of Days everlasting dominion over all the earth to rule as its king.

Jews of Jesus' time struggled to understand the dual image of the Messiah presented in the various prophecies. Many theologians then, as now, suggested that perhaps the Messiah would really be two individuals, one who would die as the "Suffering Servant" (Isa. 52:13–53:12) and the other who would resurrect the first and then reign as supreme king.

The title "Son of Man" appears in Mark's Gospel fourteen times (Mark 2:10, 28; 8:31, 38; 9:9, 12, 31; 10:33, 45; 13:26; 14:21 [two times], 41, 62). Jesus undoubtedly referred to Himself as the "Son of Man" as a reference to His identity as the sole Messiah, who is in fact God.

— 8:32-33 —

Peter, acting as the Lord's unofficial campaign advisor, pulled the future King of Israel aside to "rebuke" His negative talk (8:32). The verb translated "rebuke" (*epitimaō* [2008]) is the same term Jesus used to silence a demonized man (1:25), to calm a raging storm (4:39), and to warn His disciples not to tell anyone His identity (8:30). It describes a severe censure or an authoritative order. Ray Stedman, on this passage, said, "The language here suggests that Peter did this with an air of protective superiority."[29] And in purely human terms, the brash disciple was absolutely correct. Of course, that was also his error. Jesus didn't come to conform His plan to the corrupt paradigm of a fallen world.

Before Peter could finish his rebuke, Jesus brought His student back into line with His heavenly agenda. In saying to Peter, "Get behind Me, Satan" (8:33), Jesus established a clear precedent, saying, in effect, "If you don't follow My plan, you have adopted Satan's; there's no compromise or middle ground." He could make the correlation between "man's interests" and Satan's plan because He understood the full implications of the Fall. When humanity chose sin over obedience in the Garden of Eden, we all became co-conspirators with Satan against God's world order.

— 8:34-37 —

Having shocked Peter back into line, Jesus called the crowd to Himself—disciples, followers, seekers, critics, and skeptics—to clarify His disposition toward the current world order. According to the current paradigm, the axioms of success are as follows:

- Would-be kings serve others as long as "public service" ultimately satisfies their need for greater power.
- One becomes a great military leader by sending other people into battle.
- The way to the top of the sociopolitical ladder is to use others like rungs.
- Because money is the most potent kind of power, you should collect of lot of it and give away only what will make you appear charitable.
- You only live once, so give out of your abundance and sacrifice nothing that might keep you comfortable.

Jesus turned the world's paradigm upside down. To receive glory, Christ's followers would need to follow His downward path toward rejection, ridicule, persecution, self-sacrifice, and even martyrdom. Jesus referred to this manner of life as "taking up one's cross" (see 8:34). Executioners forced a condemned person to carry the implement of his own death to the place of execution. Therefore, to take up one's cross was to die to one's own agenda. Jesus calls His followers to do this daily.

The Greek term rendered "follow" means "to move behind someone in the same direction" or "to come after."[30] The command calls us to do as He did, to follow in His footsteps. He gave all for the sake of the kingdom of God, holding all earthly things loosely. Not surprisingly, He made this a necessary condition of discipleship. To establish this "deny, take up, and follow" model as mandatory, Jesus offered a penetrating paradox:

"Whoever wishes to save his life will lose it, but whoever loses his life for My sake and the gospel's will save it." (8:35)

The Greek word translated "life" is *psychē* [5590], which can mean either "life" or "soul." Therefore, we can paraphrase the paradox two ways. It could be read like this:

> Whoever wishes to save his physical life will lose his spiritual life, but whoever turns over his physical life for My sake and the gospel's will save his spiritual life.

Or the verse could just as easily be paraphrased this way:

> Whoever wishes to save his soul will lose his soul, but whoever turns over his soul for My agenda, he is the one who will get to keep his soul.

The first rejects selfishness. The second rejects self-righteousness. The aristocratic Sadducees and Herodians believed in no afterlife, so the idea of sacrificing personal happiness made no sense. The Pharisees believed in an afterlife, but they believed heaven could be earned by meticulously practicing the religion of good deeds. Therefore, either interpretation works well.

Jesus also compared the relative worth of earthly riches to the eternal abundance of heaven. He asked the audience to do a mental cost-benefit analysis and then judge the soundness of that kind of investment. The conclusion is obvious: Why forfeit eternal joy in the next life by clinging to fleeting happiness in this one?

— 8:38 —

The idea of being "ashamed" is raised in this verse because of the Roman method of execution known as crucifixion. The ancient ordeal of crucifixion not only maximized suffering, but it also heaped shame upon agony. The process was designed to shame the victims, beginning with scourging. The entire garrison of Roman soldiers typically attended the precursor to crucifixion and entertained themselves by taunting the people being scourged, spitting or urinating on them, and devising humiliating games to demean them. They stripped the condemned naked, hung around their neck a sign detailing their crimes, laid the instrument of their demise on their shoulders, and forced them to walk from the garrison to the place of crucifixion outside the city.

In another paradox, Jesus declared that to be ashamed of Him and His words will put people on the wrong side of the war when He returns in power to destroy evil. In truth, we are certain to bear shame, one way or another. We will either bear the shame of discipleship now or we will bear the shame of divine rejection at the final judgment.

This discourse undoubtedly clarified several issues for any followers who might be on the fence between discipleship and rejecting Christ. Jesus left no middle ground. There is no room for fair-weather disciples in the kingdom of God. Those following Jesus merely for free meals and quick access to healing need not waste their time or His. People expecting Jesus to lead them into a life of comfort and prosperity would soon be disappointed. The Christ whom God sent planned to lead the people of God into suffering. Such an exacting message had a way of thinning the crowds.

With the halfhearted disciples turning away and heading home, Jesus began the process of cultivating followers, developing in them a deep, loyal resilience that would see them through the dark days of the future without His physical presence. Having shown the disciples the difficult path they must follow, Jesus determined to reveal their destination. His program for cultivating His disciples began with a glimpse of the glory to come.

APPLICATION: MARK 8:27-38
Setting Our Minds on the Things of God

Peter's two contrasting responses to Jesus in Mark 8:27-33 couldn't be starker. At first, he boldly proclaimed that Jesus is the long-expected Messiah (8:29)—contrary to numerous differing opinions about the prophet from Nazareth. The next moment, Peter rebuked Jesus for revealing God's plan that the Messiah must suffer (8:32). In doing so, Peter revealed maturity in his confession of faith in Jesus Christ but immaturity in his unwillingness to put God's plans, purposes, and priorities above everything else.

This leads me to two practical principles that I think catch the substance of this passage, both of them related to Peter's contrasting responses to Jesus' teachings. The first relates to the right-minded confession. The second relates to the wrongheaded priorities. Both of them are relevant for us today.

The first principle is this: *Be careful about the words you listen to.* We live in a world in which we're constantly bombarded with widely differing opinions on everything from morality to entertainment, from religion to politics. Not surprisingly, there's no shortage of perspectives on who Jesus was, what His life means, how His teaching relates to us, or what kinds of beliefs and practices He would approve of.

Like Peter, we need to have a clear understanding of the one true faith in order to avoid the countless counterfeits vying for control of our minds. So be careful about whom you listen to. Be sure their views on God, Jesus, truth, and goodness are guided by the Scriptures. Verify the counsel from the Word of God. Don't let a personal relationship or personal preferences nullify the print on the page of Scripture. If the claims of pastors, professors, or even parents contradict what God has written, reject their claims. Like Peter, confess the truth even in the midst of a world of error.

This is the second principle: *Release the worldly things you're clinging to.* Peter had a clear picture of what it was supposed to mean to be the Christ, and God's plan for the suffering Messiah didn't measure up. No doubt, Peter anticipated a great deliverer who would vanquish the enemies of Israel and set up a kingdom within weeks, if not days. And he would be right there to rule with his king. The truth didn't live up to Peter's tightly held, worldly opinion.

Unlike Peter, we need to let go of our worldly ideas, release the things we're holding closely, and surrender possessions or positions that don't measure up to God's plans and priorities. All of us have our own lists of worldly things that tend to crowd out the things of God. They're the things we spend our time and money on, talk and worry about, or make space and excuses for—they could be people, ideas, attitudes, actions, or material possessions. Whatever they are, let them go.

Let this prayer by A. W. Tozer be your guide as you release these things and set your mind on the things of God:

Father, I want to know Thee, but my coward heart fears to give up its toys. . . . Please root from my heart all those things which I have cherished so long and which have become a very part of my living self, so that Thou mayest enter and dwell there without a rival. . . . Then shall my heart have no need of the sun to shine in it, for Thyself wilt be the light of it, and there shall be no night there.[31]

DISCIPLES CULTIVATED
(MARK 9:1-13:37)

This may seem obvious, but it needs to be said: *Effective leaders know their destinations.* They know where to lead their followers, and they understand how to get them there safely.

You might be surprised to find out how many leaders of companies and ministries haven't taken the time to define their destinations. They haven't described success, so they cannot measure progress. They haven't determined their objectives, so they cannot set intermediate goals. They haven't developed a vision, so they cannot communicate one. Yet they presume to lead others. Where? Who knows? Ask them about leadership, and many will tell you whom they lead and what they do from day to day. However, when you ask them the simple question "To what are you leading your followers?" the honest answer would be, "I don't know where we're going, but we're making great time!"

Jesus knew exactly where He was leading the disciples. He understood clearly the goal of His mission on earth. Satan had led humanity into rebellion and replaced God's world order with a corrupt order given over to sin, selfishness, greed, destruction, disease, death, and decay. Jesus came to begin His campaign to retake creation from the dominion of evil and to inaugurate the kingdom of God on earth.

From the very beginning of His earthly ministry, Jesus poured wisdom into His disciples. Sure, He educated them in the Scriptures and taught them theology. Education is unquestionably a crucial part of preparation for ministry. But a witness for Christ can be effective without schooling; none, however, can be useful without wisdom. That's why He spent so much time immersing the Twelve in real-life difficulties. He sent them to minister without physical provisions. He challenged them to feed multitudes with too little food. Soon, He would leave several of them to "mind the store," as it were, while He trekked to the summit of Mount Hermon. Each lesson became an opportunity to transform His students at a core level. These were, after all, the men He would leave to guide the church and to carry forward His redemptive plan for the world.

In the time Jesus had left with His disciples, His role would change; He would become an iron file to their rough edges as He honed them to razor-sharp readiness for ministry.

KEY TERMS IN MARK 9:1-13:37

basileia (βασιλεία) [932] "kingdom," "dominion," "royal power"
This term denotes the dominion of a lawful king, which the Greeks saw as something derived from Zeus. In the Old Testament, Israel was originally a theocracy, a nation whose King was God. Therefore, Israel was the kingdom of God. Even when a human sat on the throne of Israel, that ruler's power was derived from God. The Gospels depict the earth as the dominion of evil, or Satan, a usurper of the rightful throne of God. Jesus came to reestablish divine rule—the kingdom of God.

euangelion (εὐαγγέλιον) [2098] "gospel," "joyous news"
This Greek term describes the favorable report of a messenger from the battlefield or the official proclamation that an heir to the king had been born. In the New Testament, this word refers to the news that Jesus' death and resurrection forgives sins and gives eternal life. The English term "gospel" comes from the Old English compound "good-spell," where "spell" means "tale." The gospel is the "good story" about Christ's person and work.

thaumazō (θαυμάζω) [2296] "to be amazed," "to marvel," "to be in awe"
This word means to be extraordinarily impressed, awed, or even disturbed by something, especially when confronted with some form of divine revelation. In the Septuagint it indicates worship, honor, and admiration, generally referring to "religious experience [that brings the subject] face to face with what transcends human possibilities."[1]

kairos (καιρός) [2540] "era," "season," "period of time"
In nonbiblical literature, this term refers to a decisive point in time or circumstance. In the New Testament, *kairos* usually has some connection to the kingdom of God. "This era" or "this age" is characterized by the dominion of evil that began after the Fall (Gen. 3) and will end with the return of Christ and the establishment of His kingdom. "The era to come" is always synonymous with God's kingdom, which will last forever. When the idea of a "season" appears in the text, look for metaphorical connections to "this era" or "the era to come."

phobeō (**φοβέω**) [5399] "to fear," "to respect," "to show reverence"

The fully developed meaning of this word arises from its ancient definition, which is "to flee." The emotion described by *phobeō* develops from the action of being startled and then running away for the sake of self-preservation. The idea of "the fear of God" emerges from the concept of trembling before Him because of His awesome power. In this case, fear manifests as a healthy respect for Him as the ultimate Judge, whose anger burns against sin. Throughout this section of Mark, the religious authorities are shown to fear people rather than God, a sure sign of their apostasy.

A Glimpse of the Glory to Come
MARK 9:1-13

NASB

1 And Jesus was saying to them, "Truly I say to you, there are some of those who are standing here who will not taste death until they see the kingdom of God after it has come with power."

2 Six days later, Jesus took with Him Peter and ᵃJames and John, and brought them up on a high mountain by themselves. And He was transfigured before them; 3 and His garments became radiant and exceedingly white, as no launderer on earth can whiten them. 4 Elijah appeared to them along with Moses; and they were talking with Jesus. 5 Peter said to Jesus, "Rabbi, it is good for us to be here; let us make three ᵃtabernacles, one for You, and one for Moses, and one for Elijah." 6 For he did not know what to answer; for they became terrified. 7 Then a cloud ᵃformed, overshadowing them, and a voice ᵃcame out of the cloud, "This is My beloved Son, ᵇlisten to Him!" 8 All at once they looked around and saw no one with them anymore, except Jesus alone.

9 As they were coming down from the mountain, He gave them orders

NLT

1 Jesus went on to say, "I tell you the truth, some standing here right now will not die before they see the Kingdom of God arrive in great power!"

2 Six days later Jesus took Peter, James, and John, and led them up a high mountain to be alone. As the men watched, Jesus' appearance was transformed, 3 and his clothes became dazzling white, far whiter than any earthly bleach could ever make them. 4 Then Elijah and Moses appeared and began talking with Jesus.

5 Peter exclaimed, "Rabbi, it's wonderful for us to be here! Let's make three shelters as memorials*— one for you, one for Moses, and one for Elijah." 6 He said this because he didn't really know what else to say, for they were all terrified.

7 Then a cloud overshadowed them, and a voice from the cloud said, "This is my dearly loved Son. Listen to him." 8 Suddenly, when they looked around, Moses and Elijah were gone, and they saw only Jesus with them.

9 As they went back down the mountain, he told them not to tell

not to relate to anyone what they had seen, ªuntil the Son of Man rose from the dead. ¹⁰They ªseized upon ᵇthat statement, discussing with one another ᶜwhat rising from the dead meant. ¹¹They asked Him, saying, "*Why is it* that the scribes say that Elijah must come first?" ¹²And He said to them, "Elijah does first come and restore all things. And *yet* how is it written of the Son of Man that He will suffer many things and be treated with contempt? ¹³But I say to you that Elijah has ªindeed come, and they did to him whatever they wished, just as it is written of him."

9:2 ªOr *Jacob* 9:5 ªOr *sacred tents* 9:7 ªOr *occurred* ᵇOr *give constant heed* 9:9 ªLit *except when* 9:10 ªOr *kept to themselves* ᵇLit *the statement* ᶜLit *what was the rising from the dead* 9:13 ªLit *also*

anyone what they had seen until the Son of Man* had risen from the dead. ¹⁰So they kept it to themselves, but they often asked each other what he meant by "rising from the dead." ¹¹Then they asked him, "Why do the teachers of religious law insist that Elijah must return before the Messiah comes?*" ¹²Jesus responded, "Elijah is indeed coming first to get everything ready. Yet why do the Scriptures say that the Son of Man must suffer greatly and be treated with utter contempt? ¹³But I tell you, Elijah has already come, and they chose to abuse him, just as the Scriptures predicted."

9:5 Greek *three tabernacles*. 9:9 "Son of Man" is a title Jesus used for himself. 9:11 Greek *that Elijah must come first?*

Like any great leader, Jesus not only knew His objective, but He also communicated the vision to His followers. Throughout His ministry, He described the kingdom of God through illustrations, parables, demonstrations, and even by personal example. All the same, He faced an impossible challenge: how to describe something no words can describe. Like trying to explain the color blue to a man born blind, Jesus found that nothing in human experience could help His followers imagine something beyond human imagining.

Fortunately, all things are possible with God. While completely human, Jesus is more than a mere man. What is humanly impossible becomes possible with the Son of God. Jesus cast a vision of His mission objective by giving His followers a glimpse of the glory to come, all the while realizing that they would not fully understand what He was saying. But in times of silence in the years to come, the disciples would reflect on this glimpse of glory, and the Holy Spirit would help them understand its richness and the meaning of its truth.

— 9:1 —

This verse is what scholars call a "hinge verse." It links the previous segment with the next and turns the reader in a new direction. Mark 9:1 could serve as a conclusion to 8:34-38, in which Jesus summoned the crowd and warned that genuine disciples would abandon the corrupt world system in favor of a new, altogether unique, kingdom-of-God mentality. True followers would trace the suffering, selfless, humble footsteps of their leader, Jesus Christ, even if the world punished them for their decision. (Don't forget the circumstances Mark's audience faced.) Jesus also warned that failure to adopt this new, kingdom-of-God manner of living was proof that an individual had not become a true follower. To drive the point home, Jesus raised the image of His ultimate return, His consummate conquest of earth, and His final judgment.

In Mark 9:1, Jesus let the crowd know that some standing among them would not die until they saw "the kingdom of God arrive in great power" (NLT). Interpreters have scratched their heads for centuries trying to decide exactly what Jesus meant by these words. Part of the difficulty stems from the fact that the Bible presents the kingdom of God not as one simple thing but as a complex concept. Most generally it refers to God's eternal, sovereign rule over all (Ps. 145:12-13; Dan. 4:3) or His spiritual presence in righteousness and power (Rom. 14:17; 1 Cor. 4:20). In the New Testament, the arrival of the promised Messiah—God in the flesh—indicated the coming of the kingdom of God in a new phase, though His heavenly power and glory were mostly veiled to those who saw Him (John 1:10). Later, after the ascension, the coming of the Spirit to empower the church would hail the coming of a mysterious form of the kingdom during the church age (Acts 2), during which Christ would reign in the hearts of believers through the Spirit (John 3:3; 18:36). Ultimately, though, all of these forms of the kingdom of God were anticipations of the eternal reign of Christ that will begin at His second coming, expand throughout the Millennium (Luke 13:29; Rev. 20), and continue on into eternity (Dan. 2:44; Rev. 21).

It's no wonder commentators have offered numerous interpretations of what Jesus meant when He said that some standing among the crowd would not die before they saw the kingdom of God arrive in great power. Did He refer to those who would witness His resurrection, ascension, and enthronement in heaven (cf. Rev. 3:21) or to the coming of the Holy Spirit at Pentecost (Acts 1:6-8)? Was He talking about the advancement of the spiritual kingdom through the preaching of the gospel around the world (Matt. 13:31-32)? Maybe He was referring to John's vision of the apocalypse, when he would witness the coming of Christ in the form of prophetic visions (Rev. 1).

You can thumb through commentaries on the Gospels and find these and other explanations for the meaning of Jesus' words in Mark 9:1. But I think the answer to our questions is actually right in front of us. I think

Jesus was referring to what is about to take place in Scripture. A few of those standing there—three, to be precise—would witness an unveiling of Christ's heavenly power and glory and catch a brilliant glimpse of the power of the kingdom. A veil would be briefly pulled back on the fabric of this world, allowing Peter, James, and John to see the kingdom of heaven poised just beyond our physical realm, centered on the person of Jesus Christ, and ready at any moment to break into time and space.

This event is called the Transfiguration. Though Mark wasn't himself present at this astonishing glimpse of the kingdom of God, he likely got his information directly from Peter (cf. 1 Pet. 5:13). Peter himself mentions the Transfiguration in his second letter, using language reminiscent of Mark 9:1:

> For we did not follow cleverly devised tales when we made known to you the power and coming of our Lord Jesus Christ, but we were eyewitnesses of His majesty. For when He received honor and glory from God the Father, such an utterance as this was made to Him by the Majestic Glory, "This is My beloved Son with whom I am well-pleased"—and we ourselves heard this utterance made from heaven when we were with Him on the holy mountain. (2 Pet. 1:16-18)

In the above passage Peter acknowledges that his experience "on the holy mountain" revealed "the power and coming of our Lord Jesus Christ." While the ultimate fulfillment of the kingdom will not occur until Christ "comes in the glory of His Father with the holy angels" (Mark 8:38), a few of His closest followers were "eyewitnesses of His majesty" on the Mount of Transfiguration before they tasted death.

— 9:2-3 —

Mark and Matthew both state that the time between Jesus' prediction and his glorious transfiguration was six days.[2] Earlier, Mark placed Jesus and His disciples in the region around Caesarea Philippi, a city on the southwestern face of Mount Hermon near the base. With an elevation of 9,232 feet, Mount Hermon is the highest mountain of its range and would have been the perfect place for Jesus to find almost complete solitude. Before hiking up more than nine thousand feet, Jesus selected only three of His disciples to accompany Him: Peter (Mark's source), James, and John.

Both Mark and Matthew chose the Greek term *metamorphoō* [3339], a cognate of the English "metamorphosis," to describe what Jesus experienced (cf. Matt. 17:2). Many translations render this verb "transfigure." The body of Jesus was altered in its appearance. His garments became as bright as lightning, according to Luke (see NASB note at Luke 9:29), who was not present but apparently heard eyewitness accounts (see Luke 1:2). Peter, who saw the event firsthand, most likely described Jesus' garments to Mark as radiating like the sun. The Greek term he uses here, *stilbō* [4744], means "to cast rays of light," "to shine," or "to gleam." And His clothes became (imagine it!) whiter than white. For a few moments the earthly veil concealing Christ's true incarnate divinity was pulled aside, and the brilliance of His divine glory was revealed to His three disciples.

— 9:4 —

If the disciples didn't know they were witnessing something supernatural—very unlikely—then the appearance of Elijah and Moses would have removed all doubt. These two great figures were to Hebrew history what George Washington and Abraham Lincoln are to American history. Moses served as God's human instrument in establishing the nation of Israel in the land promised to Abraham in Genesis 12:1-3. He gave them the Law from God and he facilitated the "land covenant" that dictated the terms of their occupation of Canaan (Deut. 28). Elijah, like Abraham Lincoln during the Civil War, guided Israel during a tumultuous and violent time of self-affliction.

All three men appeared together and conversed as normally as people meeting at a coffee shop. It would be too much to suggest specific symbolism, but this glimpse of humanity's glorious future helps us understand that God and all His people throughout the history of the earth will share easy company. God's people will have bodies, but they will be luminous, incorruptible, otherworldly. *Imagine that!*

— 9:5-6 —

Like many people, Peter decided to fill the moment with words when respectful silence would have been a better choice. His nerves got the better of him, and he blurted out an absurd suggestion. Heavenly, glorified, transfigured people don't need tents (cf. 1 Cor. 15:35-51; Phil. 3:21; 1 Jn. 3:2-3). Jesus didn't climb Mount Hermon for a camping trip with two of Israel's most revered prophets.

Mark explains that Peter and the other men were beyond fearful. The Greek word translated "terrified," *ekphobos* [1630], is a rare and intense form of *phobos* [5401], from which we get our word "phobia."

— 9:7-8 —

After Peter blurted out his absurd suggestion, a cloud formed around Jesus, Elijah, and Moses and cast a dark shadow. The image is reminiscent of Exodus 19:9: "The LORD said to Moses, 'Behold, I will come to you in a thick cloud, so that the people may hear when I speak with you and may also believe in you forever.'" God's words to the men recall the Lord's baptism (Mark 1:11). God the Father again affirmed Jesus as His Son and confirmed Jesus' words as His own. The implication of this statement was, "He has much to tell you. You have nothing to tell Him. You are in the presence of deity on earth. Stay silent. *Listen!*"

The Father called Jesus "My beloved Son." The disciples probably needed to hear this affirmation of the Father's love for the Son so they would not misunderstand His suffering to come. Jesus did not suffer because the Father was displeased with Him; He suffered because the world hates Jesus.

This would have been profoundly comforting to persecuted Christians in Rome for obvious reasons. The message was, "You suffer because you are following in Christ's footsteps," and its hearers knew that God was immensely pleased with His Son.

Within moments, the event concluded. The cloud disappeared, the two venerated prophets vanished, and Jesus' appearance returned to normal.

— 9:9-10 —

As Jesus and the three disciples descended the mountain, He ordered them to keep what they had witnessed to themselves until "the Son of Man rose from the dead" (9:9). Naturally, that provoked a discussion! This was not new information (cf. 8:31). Still, Jesus said it as casually as if He had said the sun would rise in the morning. The three others immediately began to speculate. They had seen Jesus raise a girl from the dead (5:41-42). According to Luke, they also had seen Jesus bring a man back from the dead (Luke 7:14). Perhaps they wondered who would raise Jesus. Or maybe they questioned the necessity of Jesus dying; maybe they could prevent the tragedy in the first place.

— 9:11-13 —

The question put to Jesus appears, at first, out of place. It would seem more natural for the three to probe Jesus about His death and resurrection. Their question, however, is very astute. They were continuing to wrestle with the theology they had been taught all their lives. The scribes—experts in reading and interpreting the Scriptures—taught that

Elijah would reappear and turn the hearts of the Jews back to God just before the appearance of the Messiah (cf. Mal. 4:5). Jesus declared that John the Baptizer had fulfilled this prophecy (Matt. 11:14). Now, the literal return of Elijah had just occurred. Yet Israel had not yet repented. And Jesus had predicted His own death, not a rise to political and military power as the king of Israel.

Jesus challenged the men to reconcile two Old Testament images of the Messiah that appeared to be in conflict. The prophets described the Messiah as both a conquering king and a sacrificial martyr—a man who would die to save the people of Israel (Isa. 42:1-9; 49:1-13; 50:1-11; 52:13–53:12), yet one who would reign forever as their king (Isa. 9:1-7; 11; 35; Dan. 7:14; Zech. 9:9-10). How could both be true?

The resurrection, of course, explains everything. The Messiah would die on behalf of His covenant people, subsequently rise from the grave, and then rule as their King forever.

Jesus then affirmed that an Elijah did come to Israel, and he did turn many hearts toward God. Yet Israel remained in rebellion. Israel, as represented by its officials, killed this Elijah figure, whom Jesus had identified as John the Baptizer (Matt. 11:14). This, in turn, left the fate of Israel unresolved. They had not yet "restored the hearts of the fathers to their children and the hearts of the children to their fathers" (see Mal. 4:6). Another important event needed to occur to make that possible.

APPLICATION: MARK 9:1-13

The Golden Discipline

A folksy American proverb advises, "Never pass up an opportunity to keep your mouth shut."

That may not be the application you were expecting from this passage, but in light of the disciples' misunderstandings in this passage and the weight of the revelation they received, I think it's warranted. Choosing to exercise the discipline of silence can help us avoid some embarrassing social blunders. As I look back, I remember very few times I have regretted remaining silent. But the times I wish I had shut my mouth are too many to count. More importantly, however, the discipline of silence has many other benefits, including spiritual growth. Let me offer a few of them.

When you have protracted times of silence, you gain greater wisdom. In fact, these times make you learn lessons you will never forget. Lessons learned in silence stay with you. But this takes protracted time in solitude. Usually the longer it's been since the last time and the busier you are, the more time it will take for your mind to calm down enough to reflect on the things you have studied, the sermons you have heard, the Scriptures you have memorized, the prayers you have prayed. As you allow silence to become your companion, you give opportunity for the Holy Spirit to bring chaos into clarity. He will teach you deep and wonderful things when you shut out the world and give Him your ears.

Silence in the presence of others allows you to observe them with greater discernment. When you're talking, you're not observing. You're interested in what you're saying. You're often preoccupied with what they might be thinking about you. When you're quiet, you're watching. Silent listening and observation are characteristics of a great counselor; they listen to what their clients are saying—and, just as importantly, what they are *not* saying—in order to gain insight. Then they speak with greater discernment.

Silence encourages greater self-awareness. When you give time to silent reflection, you develop a more accurate view of yourself. Without silence, you live your life in ignorance. You don't know who you are. You remain unaware of how you impact others through your behavior.

Henri Nouwen, a priest harried by the busyness of life, decided to give himself six months in a monastery to be silent. He writes,

> I realized I was caught in a web of strange paradoxes. While complaining about too many demands, I now felt uneasy when none were made. While speaking about the burden of letter writing, I now found an empty mailbox made me sad. While fretting about tiring lecture tours, I felt disappointed when there were no such invitations. While speaking nostalgically about an empty desk, I found myself fearing the day on which that would become true. In short: while desiring to be alone, I was frightened of being left alone. The more I became aware of these paradoxes, the more I started to see how much I had fallen in love with my own compulsions and illusions, and how much I needed to step back and wonder, "Is there a quiet stream underneath the fluctuating affirmations and rejections of my little world?"[3]

When we begin to see ourselves as God sees us, we discover how selfish we are—how thoughtless, how superficial, how shallow. We develop an increased self-awareness (and the Lord knows how greatly we need that). When we see ourselves for who we really are, we give God greater opportunity to heal us, transform us, and conform us to the image of His Son.

In silence, you glean greater meaning from life experiences. Your daughter runs away from home. That's the time to be quiet and consider the reasons. Your wife says, "I no longer love you." That's the time to find some solitude and think. Your boss says, "We've decided to let you go." Be quiet. Let God instruct you as you resist the temptation to react or to justify yourself or to explain away the event.

These are life experiences you never wanted to experience, but maybe this time God's sovereignty has allowed the difficulty to be yours. The question to ask in silence is, *How will God use this for my good and for His glory?*

Silence allows you to cultivate genuine contentment. Through protracted periods of quietness you learn to be more content with what you have and where you are in life. You don't always need to buy something else. You don't need "more." You don't need "another." You don't need a "bigger." You need to push the pause button. In quietness you find out that contentment takes the place of that hunger for more and more.

Silence invites you to become intimately acquainted with God. The purpose of silence is not to receive extrabiblical instructions or secret messages from on high. Yet somehow in the crucible of silence, the Holy Spirit boils the truth we receive from Scripture down to its essence, reveals specific insights that are pertinent, and then applies them to our most perplexing problems and our most stubborn misconceptions. As He transforms our hearts to beat more truly for Him, we reflect His character as our decisions accomplish His will.

Confronting an Unclean Spirit
MARK 9:14-29

NASB

14 When they came *back* to the disciples, they saw a large crowd around them, and *some* scribes arguing with them. 15 Immediately, when the entire crowd saw Him, they were amazed and *began* running up to greet Him.

NLT

14 When they returned to the other disciples, they saw a large crowd surrounding them, and some teachers of religious law were arguing with them. 15 When the crowd saw Jesus, they were overwhelmed with awe, and they ran to greet him.

NASB

¹⁶And He asked them, "What are you discussing with them?" ¹⁷And one of the crowd answered Him, "Teacher, I brought You my son, possessed with a spirit which makes him mute; ¹⁸and ᵃwhenever it seizes him, it ᵇslams him *to the ground* and he foams *at the mouth,* and grinds his teeth and ᶜstiffens out. I told Your disciples to cast it out, and they could not *do it.*" ¹⁹And He answered them and said, "O unbelieving generation, how long shall I be with you? How long shall I put up with you? Bring him to Me!" ²⁰They brought ᵃthe boy to Him. When he saw Him, immediately the spirit threw him into a convulsion, and falling to the ground, he *began* rolling around and foaming *at the mouth.* ²¹And He asked his father, "How long has this been happening to him?" And he said, "From childhood. ²²It has often thrown him both into the fire and into the water to destroy him. But if You can do anything, take pity on us and help us!" ²³And Jesus said to him, " 'If You can?' All things are possible to him who believes." ²⁴Immediately the boy's father cried out and said, "I do believe; help my unbelief." ²⁵When Jesus saw that a crowd was ᵃrapidly gathering, He rebuked the unclean spirit, saying to it, "You deaf and mute spirit, I ᵇcommand you, come out of him and do not enter him ᶜagain." ²⁶After crying out and throwing him into terrible convulsions, it came out; and *the boy* became so much like a corpse that most *of them* said, "He is dead!" ²⁷But Jesus took him by the hand and raised him; and he got up.

NLT

¹⁶"What is all this arguing about?" Jesus asked.

¹⁷One of the men in the crowd spoke up and said, "Teacher, I brought my son so you could heal him. He is possessed by an evil spirit that won't let him talk. ¹⁸And whenever this spirit seizes him, it throws him violently to the ground. Then he foams at the mouth and grinds his teeth and becomes rigid.* So I asked your disciples to cast out the evil spirit, but they couldn't do it."

¹⁹Jesus said to them,* "You faithless people! How long must I be with you? How long must I put up with you? Bring the boy to me."

²⁰So they brought the boy. But when the evil spirit saw Jesus, it threw the child into a violent convulsion, and he fell to the ground, writhing and foaming at the mouth.

²¹"How long has this been happening?" Jesus asked the boy's father.

He replied, "Since he was a little boy. ²²The spirit often throws him into the fire or into water, trying to kill him. Have mercy on us and help us, if you can."

²³"What do you mean, 'If I can'?" Jesus asked. "Anything is possible if a person believes."

²⁴The father instantly cried out, "I do believe, but help me overcome my unbelief!"

²⁵When Jesus saw that the crowd of onlookers was growing, he rebuked the evil* spirit. "Listen, you spirit that makes this boy unable to hear and speak," he said. "I command you to come out of this child and never enter him again!"

²⁶Then the spirit screamed and threw the boy into another violent convulsion and left him. The boy appeared to be dead. A murmur ran through the crowd as people said, "He's dead." ²⁷But Jesus took him by the hand and helped him to his feet, and he stood up.

²⁸When He came into *the* house, His disciples *began* questioning Him privately, "Why could we not drive it out?" ²⁹And He said to them, "This kind cannot come out by anything but prayer."

9:18 ªOr *wherever* ᵇOr *tears him* ᶜOr *withers away*
9:20 ªLit *him* 9:25 ªOr *running together* ᵇOr *I Myself command* ᶜOr *from now on*

²⁸Afterward, when Jesus was alone in the house with his disciples, they asked him, "Why couldn't we cast out that evil spirit?"
²⁹Jesus replied, "This kind can be cast out only by prayer.*"

9:18 Or *becomes weak.* 9:19 Or *said to his disciples.* 9:25 Greek *unclean.* 9:29 Some manuscripts read *by prayer and fasting.*

Reality—that's where we live. And it can be so irritating at times.

No one loves Thanksgiving more than I. But after the delight of a great meal with family and loved ones gathered around a grand dinner table, there's always a stack of dishes to scrape, wash, dry, and stack after the meal. That's reality.

Now take graduating from school. How marvelous is that! After many months or years of classes, reading assignments, papers, late-night studying, and tuition payments, you receive your diploma or degree. A cap slung into the air, a gown, a ceremony, a celebration . . . and then you have to find a job. That's reality.

Return from vacation and guess what's waiting for you? A stack of bills and a backlog of email messages. After the honeymoon, there's marriage and a lifetime of adjustments. After the birth of a child, there's responsibility. After the purchase of a home, there's maintenance. Reality. Reality. Reality. That's where we live.

After the disciples experienced the exhilaration and wonder of the Transfiguration (9:1-13), they came down from the mountain to face reality.

Reality eventually forces us to our knees before God, the only One with the power and compassion to act in a truly decisive manner. As the disciples failed to cast out an unclean spirit, they would return to this fundamental lesson of discipleship: Like our Master, we can do nothing apart from God the Father. Disciples must continually turn to God in prayer.

— 9:14-15 —

A few days earlier, Jesus, Peter, James, and John had left the crowds and the other disciples to hike up the 9,232-foot Mount Hermon, where they experienced a foretaste of God's kingdom, also known as the kingdom of heaven. Having observed the transfiguration of Jesus, having witnessed the appearance of Elijah and Moses, and having heard the voice of God, the three disciples descended from their "mountaintop experience" to face the world again. In a poignant and palpable way, the three men learned how Jesus felt coming down from heaven to enter the strife and chaos of our fallen world. After glimpsing glory, they walked into an argument between the scribes and some of Jesus' followers.

As the ugly scene unfolds, we see the scribes bullying the Lord's followers, undoubtedly using their education like a club to beat them down and criticize them after a failed attempt at exorcism (9:18). And we see nine disciples tentatively standing their ground. And between them stands the distraught father of a boy tormented by demons. The chaos subsided just long enough for the crowd to part and the principal players to greet Jesus.

— 9:16-18 —

Jesus didn't have to be omniscient to see that the nine disciples He left behind had involved themselves in a controversy and had gotten in over their heads. Jesus asked, in effect, "What is the nature of this argument?" The Greek verb rendered "discussing" (9:16) in this context means "contend with persistence for a point of view," "dispute," "debate," or "argue."[4] But before one of the disciples could reply, a voice from the crowd replied. The father of the afflicted boy dismissed both sides of the theological debate to focus on his son's need.

The man described a horrific scene. Read 9:17-18 closely. Then try to imagine this happening to your child or grandchild or the child of someone close to you. The disciples stood there, caught somewhere between bewilderment and confusion, maybe wondering if they were seeing things. They cared for the boy and empathized with this father. The evil thing inside the child would seize him, take control of his body, and slam him to the ground. The Greek term translated "slam" also means "tear." The demon would tear at him, cause him to foam at the mouth, and grind his teeth so that he would stiffen in convulsions like someone suffering from a grand mal seizure. To help readers appreciate the severity of the boy's affliction and the desperation of the father, Mark recounts the symptoms several times in this short space (9:18, 20, 22, 26).

Earlier, we read of the "man from the tombs" in the region of the Gerasenes (5:1-20), who could be heard shrieking at all hours; this boy, however, had been rendered mute. The father described what could be mistaken for epilepsy, a condition often misunderstood during medieval times in Europe. But both Mark and Matthew recorded the underlying cause as demonic, not psychological or physiological (cf. Matt. 17:15, 18-19). In this case, modern medicine could not have helped.

The father came to Jesus for help, but he found only His students. These disciples should have been able to help the boy; they had been given authority to cast out demons (Mark 3:15) and had successfully cast out demons in the past without Jesus present (6:13). Yet, in this case, they failed.

— 9:19 —

Jesus asked two rhetorical questions, lamenting the brokenness of the world and expressing His exasperation with people's faithlessness. Matthew and Luke record the Lord's phrasing as "unbelieving and perverted generation" (Matt. 17:17; Luke 9:41). He directed His rebuke not at the disciples specifically, but at all of humanity. He indicted the father of the boy, His own disciples, the watching crowd, and all people throughout history. Our initial estrangement from God in the Garden "perverted" His pristine world order—that is, it distorted, twisted, and corrupted all of creation—and rendered us helpless against the power of evil. Without the power of God intervening on our behalf, we remain powerless against Satan's most effective weapon: deception. The devil wants us to doubt the power of God and to question His goodness.

His lament also expressed exasperation at the spiritual myopia of His followers, including the men He would leave to carry on the kingdom movement He began (cf. Mark 4:40; 6:50-52; 8:17-21).

Unlike sinful, selfish leaders, He didn't stalk off to sulk, leaving the crowd in their unbelieving ignorance. He immediately ordered the boy brought over.

— 9:20-22 —

Apparently, the man's son had not been present during the conflict or Jesus' dialogue with the people. When the boy came before Jesus, the demon reacted by throwing him into a "convulsion" (9:20). The verb *sysparassō* [4952] means "to agitate violently" or "pull about." The demon threw the boy to the ground in a writhing, foaming fit because evil cannot stand the presence of righteousness.

Jesus responded calmly, asking a question like a discerning physician at a patient's bedside would. Mark's account alone includes this detail. While Luke highlighted Christ's power and the amazed response of the crowd and Matthew uses this as an illustration of the potential of faith, Mark stresses the compassion of Jesus for people.

Take note of the father's appeal: "If You can . . . take pity . . ." His request reveals a level of doubt concerning Jesus' power and kindness.

— 9:23-24 —

Jesus responded first to the issue of power. As God in human flesh, Jesus affirmed His omnipotence to accomplish anything He determined to do. The only limitation is the person in need of God's aid. The Lord has determined to make His activity contingent upon belief in Him (see comments on 6:4-5.) The Greek verb *pisteuō* [4100] means "to consider something to be true and therefore worthy of one's trust," "trust," or "be confident about."[5] God's ability is never in question.

Jesus' promise in 9:23 is often misquoted by false teachers of the "Word of Faith" movement. This heretical system of teaching declares that God has given the power to believers to "name and claim" virtually anything, including health and prosperity, and that people only need to exercise enough belief in order for their wish to come to pass. But this is not what Jesus taught. Here, the *object* of faith is crucial. He calls us to believe in God's power and goodness. Regardless of what we desire to have, we surrender our will to His, trusting that God knows what we need better than we do. Trust in His power and goodness means we trust that God will do everything *He desires* to do in us and through us.

Very few of us doubt God's ability to do anything He pleases to do; we more often struggle with His willingness to be kind or merciful because, in our selfishness, we think that getting what we want is a sign of God's kindness and that being denied our desires indicates God's displeasure. Personally, I have lived long enough to thank God for unfulfilled requests! Gaining the benefit of twenty-twenty hindsight has often revealed that what I thought I wanted would have been disastrous for me.

The boy's father understood immediately. The only barrier to seeing his son cleansed of the demon was his own disbelief in God's power or goodness. Therefore, he pleaded for mercy, not for his son's condition, but for his own underdeveloped confidence in God. His plea is a paradox that almost every Christian can appreciate: "I do believe; help my unbelief." It is also a request God delights to hear and will always honor.

— 9:25-27 —

Jesus acted quickly when He saw the crowd growing. He didn't want to make a spectacle of the boy. He didn't want any kind of sensationalism to distract from His message or mission. So He issued two commands to the demon: "come out of him" and "do not enter him again" (9:25). The first is a command of deliverance; the other is a command of protection.

It is noteworthy that following the exorcism, the source of extreme exhaustion finally departed, and the boy found rest for the first time in many years. The relief he felt must have been overwhelming. In fact, he experienced relief so peaceful that the crowd thought he was dead. For the benefit of the witnesses, however, Jesus stood the boy up and had him walk on his own rather than have him carried off. He wanted everyone to receive the benefit of this lesson on faith and God's character.

— 9:28-29 —

After the incident, Jesus took time to debrief with His students. The disciples were perplexed. Earlier, Jesus had delegated His authority to cast out demons (3:15), and they had experienced remarkable success during their two-by-two canvassing of villages in Galilee, Judea, and the surrounding areas (6:13). They wondered why this demon didn't respond to their commands (9:18). Note how they framed the question, however: "Why could we not drive it out?" (9:28).

Jesus' response brings together three interrelated issues: divine authority, trust in God's power and goodness, and prayer. If I might use an unsophisticated mental picture, think of a reservoir, a pipeline, and a faucet. The reservoir of God's omnipotence always exists and cannot be depleted, but it does people no good if they do not have a means to receive what God wants them to have. Faith—believing in the Lord's power and mercy—is the pipeline from the reservoir of heaven to the life of the believer. Prayer is the faucet.

This demonized boy didn't have a special kind of demon or even an especially stubborn one. "This kind" (9:29) refers to demonic spirits in general. And prayer isn't the magic ingredient of an exorcist's ritual. Jesus didn't pray before, during, or after commanding the spirit to leave. His statement about prayer reminded the disciples that their authority over demons was derivative. In the words of one expositor,

> The disciples' problem . . . has been a loss of the sense of dependence on Jesus' unique [power over demons] which had undergirded their earlier exorcistic success. They have become blasé and thought of themselves as now the natural experts in such a case, and they must learn that in spiritual conflict there is no such automatic power. Their public humiliation has been a necessary part of their re-education to the principles of the kingdom of God.[6]

The authority of God lay in reserve. As believers, the pipeline had been established between heaven and the disciples. They failed, however, to recognize their complete and permanent dependence upon Him. Jesus had given them a faucet, not a reservoir. He gave them authority dependent upon His own, not omnipotence to use independently. "Prayer," writes another expositor, "is the focusing and directing of faith in specific requests to God. Both faith and prayer testify that spiritual power is not in oneself but in God alone, and both wait in trust upon his promise to save."[7]

APPLICATION: MARK 9:14-29

The Privilege of Prayer

As believers, we are creatures endowed with divine authority, but we possess no divine power.

Beware anyone who tells you that God has given you His power. He has not. He has given His people something much better. He has given us unhindered, unrestricted, unlimited direct access to Him personally. He did not give us a measure of omnipotence to go off on our own to use as we desire. He has made divine power an organic part of our relationship with Him.

This passage in the Gospel of Mark teaches us that God continually asks, "Do you believe *I* can do anything?" When a patient needs healing, when a debt needs canceling, when a relationship needs reconciliation, when an impossible situation needs a miracle, our starting place is trust in the power and goodness of God. The Lord's "anything" might not align with our agenda, so this trust in God's nature and character must remain strong in the face of confusion or uncertainty. Therefore, I have four questions for you to answer, okay? Be absolutely, painfully, and unequivocally honest as you answer each question for yourself.

Question #1: *Do you believe God can do anything?* This question isn't as easy as it might seem. Some people believe they are too bad to save, that their sins are too numerous or too shameful to forgive. Many of us declare with our mouths that we believe in God's ability, but we say otherwise with our actions when we presume to solve a problem on our own that only He can solve. We also contradict ourselves when we continue to fret and worry about a situation we have given over to God.

Question #2: *Are you willing to leave the "anything" up to Him?* You may believe He can do anything, but are you willing to let Him do what

He determines is best? Are you willing to let God be God, and accomplish His will in His way, and do everything according to His schedule? After all, His benefit of omniscience gives Him a perspective that may see your desires as harmful or even destructive. Often, what we think is good or honorable might not be in the best interests of everyone involved.

Question #3: *Will you stop worrying, quit interrupting, cease striving, and simply pray?* I confess to you that there are times in my life when I'm fully convinced my agenda is the right one, and I feel the need to help God along. In my prayers, I sometimes spell out what I need from Him and how He should carry out my plan. And when He doesn't do what I ask, or when I don't see progress, my emotions take over. When I feel that inner turmoil begin to rise, that's my signal to pray again, release the issue into the hands of God, trust in His sovereign mercy, and find worry-free inner rest.

Question #4: *Will you accept the answer He chooses to give?* Will you set aside your disappointment to receive what God wants to give you instead of what you want for yourself? Will you trust Him to give you what you need rather than expect Him to grant what you wish? The issues here are submission and surrender. Submission is setting aside your own agenda to respond in obedience to God's authority. Surrender is admitting that His way is best.

If you can respond in the affirmative for each of these four questions, you have moved into a whole new category of people who now understand what to do when faced with something that's completely beyond human control. You will then be prepared to see God work in wondrous and amazing ways.

A Cross, a Crown, and a Child
MARK 9:30-50

NASB

30 From there they went out and *began* to go through Galilee, and He did not want anyone to know *about it.* 31 For He was teaching His disciples and telling them, "The Son of Man is to be ªdelivered into the hands of men, and they will kill Him; and when He has been killed, He will

NLT

30 Leaving that region, they traveled through Galilee. Jesus didn't want anyone to know he was there, 31 for he wanted to spend more time with his disciples and teach them. He said to them, "The Son of Man is going to be betrayed into the hands of his enemies. He will be killed, but three

NASB

rise three days later." ³²But they ªdid not understand *this* statement, and they were afraid to ask Him.

³³They came to Capernaum; and when He ªwas in the house, He *began* to question them, "What were you discussing on the way?" ³⁴But they kept silent, for on the way they had discussed with one another which *of them was* the greatest. ³⁵Sitting down, He called the twelve and said to them, "If anyone wants to be first, ªhe shall be last of all and servant of all." ³⁶Taking a child, He set him ªbefore them, and taking him in His arms, He said to them, ³⁷"Whoever receives ªone child like this in My name receives Me; and whoever receives Me does not receive Me, but Him who sent Me."

³⁸John said to Him, "Teacher, we saw someone casting out demons in Your name, and we tried to prevent him because he was not following us." ³⁹But Jesus said, "Do not hinder him, for there is no one who will perform a miracle in My name, and be able soon afterward to speak evil of Me. ⁴⁰For he who is not against us is ªfor us. ⁴¹For whoever gives you a cup of water to drink ªbecause of your name as *followers* of Christ, truly I say to you, he will not lose his reward.

⁴²"Whoever causes one of these ªlittle ones who believe to stumble, it ᵇwould be better for him if, with a heavy millstone hung around his neck, he ᶜhad been cast into the sea. ⁴³If your hand causes you to stumble, cut it off; it is better for you to enter life crippled, than, having your two hands, to go into ªhell, into the unquenchable fire, ⁴⁴[ªwhere THEIR WORM DOES NOT DIE, AND THE FIRE IS NOT QUENCHED.] ⁴⁵If your foot causes you to stumble, cut it off; it is better for you to enter life lame, than, having your two feet, to be cast into ªhell, ⁴⁶[ªwhere THEIR WORM DOES NOT DIE, AND THE FIRE IS NOT

NLT

days later he will rise from the dead." ³²They didn't understand what he was saying, however, and they were afraid to ask him what he meant.

³³After they arrived at Capernaum and settled in a house, Jesus asked his disciples, "What were you discussing out on the road?" ³⁴But they didn't answer, because they had been arguing about which of them was the greatest. ³⁵He sat down, called the twelve disciples over to him, and said, "Whoever wants to be first must take last place and be the servant of everyone else."

³⁶Then he put a little child among them. Taking the child in his arms, he said to them, ³⁷"Anyone who welcomes a little child like this on my behalf* welcomes me, and anyone who welcomes me welcomes not only me but also my Father who sent me."

³⁸John said to Jesus, "Teacher, we saw someone using your name to cast out demons, but we told him to stop because he wasn't in our group."

³⁹"Don't stop him!" Jesus said. "No one who performs a miracle in my name will soon be able to speak evil of me. ⁴⁰Anyone who is not against us is for us. ⁴¹If anyone gives you even a cup of water because you belong to the Messiah, I tell you the truth, that person will surely be rewarded.

⁴²"But if you cause one of these little ones who trusts in me to fall into sin, it would be better for you to be thrown into the sea with a large millstone hung around your neck. ⁴³If your hand causes you to sin, cut it off. It's better to enter eternal life with only one hand than to go into the unquenchable fires of hell* with two hands.* ⁴⁵If your foot causes you to sin, cut it off. It's better to enter eternal life with only one foot than to be thrown into hell with two feet.*

QUENCHED.] ⁴⁷If your eye causes you to stumble, throw it out; it is better for you to enter the kingdom of God with one eye, than, having two eyes, to be cast into ªhell, ⁴⁸where THEIR WORM DOES NOT DIE, AND THE FIRE IS NOT QUENCHED.
⁴⁹"For everyone will be salted with fire. ⁵⁰Salt is good; but if the salt becomes unsalty, with what will you ªmake it salty *again?* Have salt in yourselves, and be at peace with one another."

9:31 ªOr *betrayed*   9:32 ªLit *were not knowing*
9:33 ªLit *had come*   9:35 ªOr *let him be*   9:36 ªLit *in their midst*   9:37 ªLit *one of such children*
9:40 ªOr *on our side*   9:41 ªLit *in a name that you are Christ's*   9:42 ªI.e. humble   ᵇLit *is better for him if a millstone turned by a donkey is hung*   ᶜLit *has been thrown*   9:43 ªGr *Gehenna*   9:44 ªVv 44 and 46, which are identical to v 48, are not found in the early mss   9:45 ªGr *Gehenna*   9:46 ªSee v 44, note   9:47 ªGr *Gehenna*   9:50 ªLit *season it*

⁴⁷And if your eye causes you to sin, gouge it out. It's better to enter the Kingdom of God with only one eye than to have two eyes and be thrown into hell, ⁴⁸'where the maggots never die and the fire never goes out.'*
⁴⁹"For everyone will be tested with fire.* ⁵⁰Salt is good for seasoning. But if it loses its flavor, how do you make it salty again? You must have the qualities of salt among yourselves and live in peace with each other."

9:37 Greek *in my name.*   9:43a Greek *Gehenna;* also in 9:45, 47.   9:43b Some manuscripts add verse 44, 'where the maggots never die and the fire never goes out.' See 9:48.   9:45 Some manuscripts add verse 46, 'where the maggots never die and the fire never goes out.' See 9:48.   9:48 Isa 66:24.   9:49 Greek *salted with fire;* other manuscripts add *and every sacrifice will be salted with salt.*

God has much to teach us, but we often miss precious truths because we are preoccupied, or we live in denial, or we're simply not open to receiving what He has to show us. I'm not referring to knowledge, however. There's a difference between being educated—having knowledge—and being wise. I have known some well-educated fools. They're smart, but they're not wise. Conversely, many godly people have little or no academic training, but they're brimming with wisdom. The difference between these two types has almost nothing to do with coursework or degrees; the difference is their relationship with God. He is full of wisdom, and His plan is marked by wisdom. His desire is to help us rise above mere intelligence to appreciate a realm that is deeper and more profound than we're able to comprehend on our own.

Up to this point, Jesus' lessons for the disciples had been largely practical in nature: how to minister, how to utilize His delegated authority, how to carry out their roles as instruments of Christ's agenda. The time had now come to prepare them for leadership. Unfortunately, the disciples had poor examples to follow. They had seen the politics of the Herodians and how they gained, wielded, and retained power, all with brutal cunning. They had seen the religious authority of the aristocratic Sadducees, who led Israel by a policy of compromise, carefully balancing their Jewish identity with Roman culture. The disciples had seen the Pharisees lord their religiosity over their peers to maintain control over them. They understood the nature of leadership according to the fallen and corrupt world system. They understood what greatness was in the world's eyes.

In cultivating the disciples, Jesus had to begin an educational process that taught Leadership 101—leadership as it operates in the kingdom of God. He had dropped clues into His earlier lessons with the disciples. He had predicted that for the Messiah to become king of Israel, He must first be rejected, suffer, die, and rise again. The time had come, however, to dispense with preliminaries and get down to serious training. It was time to cultivate some wisdom in the area of leadership.

— 9:30-32 —

After His encounter with the demonized boy near Caesarea Philippi, Jesus had taken His disciples south to travel around Galilee. On other occasions, He traveled from Capernaum to some location to conduct ministry only to find that rumors had arrived in advance and drew crowds large enough to keep Him from moving freely. This time, He appears to have bypassed Capernaum to get ahead of any rumors.

As the men moved from town to town, Jesus piqued the disciples' curiosity with repeated predictions of His own arrest, execution, and resurrection. He had mentioned this at least twice before in Mark's narrative (8:31; 9:12). It was now a central theme of His discussions with the Twelve. They didn't respond in wisdom to this teaching.

Not only did the disciples fail to understand His predictions, but they were afraid to ask questions about them. They had undoubtedly heard the Lord's sharp rebuke in response to Peter—"Get behind Me, Satan" still rang in their ears (see 8:33). They may have also lived in denial; they simply didn't want to hear of it. The thought of losing Jesus by execution was unthinkable. They had left their former lives to help Jesus establish the new kingdom. David McKenna offers a helpful perspective: "We must go easy on the disciples here. They're in the middle of reworking every concept of the Messiah by which they have been taught. We who live on the other side of the resurrection do not have the same excuse."[8]

— 9:33-34 —

Eventually, Jesus and the disciples returned home to Capernaum, where He began to press them on their ongoing discussion. He already knew the answer to His question; He merely wanted to use their conversations as an opportunity to impart wisdom. They didn't want to admit that they had debated the merits of each man to hold certain offices when Jesus set up the new kingdom. Who would be prime minister? Who would become secretary of state? Peter, James, and John probably claimed chief roles because they were most often entrusted with sensitive information and had witnessed events the others had not.

The kingdom of God, however, operates on a completely foreign paradigm from that of the world. The qualifications for a leader cannot be more different. The expectations for leadership in the kingdom turn the relationship of servant and master upside down. Furthermore, fear becomes a completely different matter in the kingdom. In the world system, subjects live in mortal terror of offending leaders, whose wrath may be as capricious and unpredictable as storms on the Sea of Galilee. In the kingdom of God, the highest-ranking leaders have the most to fear of anyone.

Jesus took this opportunity to explain what civics and government would be like in the coming kingdom.

— 9:35-37 —

Jesus sat down. His posture set the tone for His lesson and put the disciples at ease. People who wanted to preach or rebuke would stand; teachers sat. This would be a gentle lesson, not a withering condemnation.

He used what expert teachers would call a deductive lesson outline. An inductive lesson begins with what the class already accepts as truth and then leads the students to discover a new insight or a fresh concept. A deductive outline begins with a proposition. After stating a truth the audience does not yet accept, the teacher then supports the proposition with illustrations, evidence, facts, and irrefutable logic. If the teacher is successful, students accept the proposition as truth.

Jesus opened His lesson with a paradox that stated the new truth He wanted the disciples to accept. He didn't expect them to understand the proposition at first. Acceptance would come by the end of His lesson.

I would paraphrase the Lord's opening statement this way: *The kingdom of God inverts everything you understand about leadership in this world system.*

The Lord's first illustration utilized a child—someone too small, too weak, and too helpless to be considered great by the world's standards. Christianity has taught Western civilization to cherish children as a gift from God. Christians learned this from the Jewish Scriptures, which gave children intrinsic worth because they bear the image of God. Before the

253

influence of Christianity, pagan cultures valued people based on their usefulness to the family and to the state. Healthy, newborn sons were prized because they extended the family's wealth and power and gave stability to kingdoms. Newborn daughters and unhealthy baby boys were frequently abandoned to the elements in a practice called exposure. They were considered a drain on valuable resources and didn't produce a suitable ROI ("return on investment").

In ancient Near Eastern culture, the act of "receiving" someone (9:37) meant you treated that person like a member of the family. This can be seen in the rules of hospitality, for example, which demanded that a traveling stranger be given shelter and provision. Jesus declared that giving kindness to a child, the lowest-ranking member of the social order according to the world's system, was the equivalent of giving kindness to the top-ranking member of society in the new kingdom.

In this world, we don't show kindness to emotionally disturbed vagrants. Imagine, however, the lavish reward of kindness a president or a king who needs help would receive. In the present world order, everyone serves the monarch, who receives the best of everything. In the kingdom of God, the least powerful receive the kindness of the most powerful.

— 9:38 —

John reported that the disciples had seen someone casting out demons and having some success at it. John didn't say that the individual had *tried* to cast out demons; he actually did cast out demons in the name of Jesus. John and the others had tried to shut him down because he didn't fit into the organizational structure as the disciples had defined it. In terms of warfare, unknown people were shooting at the enemy, but they weren't wearing military uniforms, they didn't obey a command structure, and they couldn't be controlled by the established hierarchy. James Edwards comments on John's report: "It is not a little presumptuous at this stage of discipleship for John to think himself and the other disciples worthy of being followed. This is yet another echo of their inflated self-importance."[9] Jesus didn't pounce on John's presumption. Instead, He took the disciple's complaint as an opportunity to explain how allegiance works in the kingdom of God.

— 9:39-41 —

Jesus redefined the concept of allegiance and citizenship. One could become a Roman citizen in several ways. All of them depended upon merit or money. People acquired citizenship by serving in the military, colonizing a new territory, or accomplishing something noteworthy. During corrupt times, many were able to bribe an official to give them the privilege. The kingdom of God rejects the idea of citizenship based on merit.

To become a citizen of God's kingdom, one simply exercises faith—something clearly necessary for performing a miracle in Christ's name. Anyone who carries out the King's agenda gives reasonable evidence of faith, the sole criteria for citizenship. Jesus also said, in effect, "If someone is shooting at the enemy, by all means—let him! If someone gives aid or comfort to us on the field of battle, consider him an ally."

— **9:42** —

With a frightening image, Jesus explained the sobering responsibility of leadership in God's kingdom. Having made the point that someone carrying out God's agenda in Christ's name offers reasonable evidence of genuine saving faith, He warned that accepting this visible role of leadership carries with it immense responsibility—great reward for faithful teaching, and grave penalties for leading others astray. If anyone should tremble, it's the people who lead others.

Jesus warned that leaders must not cause the people they serve to "stumble." The Greek term for this is *skandalizō* [4624], which means, literally, "to spring forward and back," "to slam shut," or "to close on something." The word *skandalon* [4625] brings to mind the image of a baited trap with a spring-loaded door. Anything unfortunate enough to enter was doomed. Later writers used the term figuratively to describe any means by which a person is brought to his or her end. Jesus warned that false teaching or insincere leadership has the potential to harm innocent believers and bring them to their spiritual end.

Michael Svigel

Replica of an **ancient millstone** used for crushing olives

Jesus used a chilling image to describe the penalty for causing this kind of harm. A millstone was a large, heavy stone used to grind grain into flour. In ancient literature and folklore, a body lost to the sea could not be resurrected on the last day and was therefore doomed to eternity in the abyss. The Lord put those two horrific images together to warn of spiritual destruction.

— 9:43-48 —

Jesus also contrasted the systems of values maintained in each kingdom. Under the present world order, self-preservation is king. We value nothing more than our own bodies. We sacrifice to keep our bodies warm, fed, covered, protected, adorned, comfortable, and healthy. And, whenever possible, we give our bodies any pleasure wealth can afford. I'm not suggesting that we should instead abuse or neglect our bodies; they are, after all, gifts from God that we have a responsibility to steward with wisdom. Be that as it may, physical comfort is not our first priority in God's kingdom. Jesus declared righteousness to be the preeminent concern of the King and His kingdom (Matt. 6:33; cf. Rom. 14:17).

Before capitalism and democracy became common, nations were subject to the absolute sovereign rule of a king. His desires became the law of the land. The standards of morality and legality reflected the king's own system of values. In God's kingdom, where Christ is the king, one cannot become a genuine citizen without submitting to His righteousness. What is more, no middle ground exists between God's kingdom and the corrupt world system.

To drive this point home, Jesus employed a rhetorical device called a "hyperbole," which uses extreme exaggeration to underscore a statement and to make an emotional impact. To redouble the severity of His warning, Jesus used repetition, applying the same illustration three times. Each warning follows a specific pattern:

> If your _____ causes you to stumble, _____;
> it is better for you to enter life _____, than, having your two
> _____, to be cast into hell.

Of course, Jesus didn't intend for anyone to practice self-mutilation; that would violate God's law against harming oneself (Deut. 14:1). Anything that causes one to "stumble" (compromise one's faith or lead to deeper sinfulness) should be removed. And we should be ruthless about protecting our righteousness from temptation.

The word rendered "hell" is sometimes transliterated as *Gehenna* in English, from the Greek *geenna* [1067], which is itself a transliteration of the Hebrew name for the valley of Hinnom (e.g., Josh. 15:8). This refers to the steep ravine just outside the southwestern wall of Jerusalem where two Old Testament kings practiced human sacrifice (2 Kgs. 16:3; 21:6). Later, King Josiah abolished the practice and made a symbolic statement by turning the ravine into a garbage dump (2 Kgs. 23:10), where fire burned the rubbish day and night. Subsequent generations of Jews referred to the place as a metaphor for eternal torment.

The Jews also thought of intestinal worms as a picture of the inner corruption that warranted divine punishment. So when Jesus characterized hell as "unquenchable fire" and a place "where their worm does not die," He was drawing upon imagery very familiar to the disciples (cf. Isa. 66:24).

— 9:49-50 —

Mark alone records the enigmatic statement "For everyone will be salted with fire." It seems like a strange mix of metaphors until you study the Hebrew sacrifices. God required the Hebrews to bring unblemished animals for their sin offerings, which were to be consumed entirely upon the altar. Salt, a symbol of the covenant (Num. 18:19), was a necessary ingredient in sacrifices (Lev. 2:13). Jesus used these Old Testament symbols to illustrate the cost of discipleship, which would involve suffering and sacrifice.

Discipleship—citizenship in the kingdom of God—demands complete, unreserved commitment, even to the point of sacrificing one's body before succumbing to sin (Rom. 12:1). Fortunately, a relatively brief period of suffering here on earth will have been nothing compared to the "glory that is to be revealed to us" (Rom. 8:18).

APPLICATION: MARK 9:30-50

Leadership: How to Achieve Greatness

At no point does the way of Jesus differ more sharply from the way of the world than on the subject of personal greatness. I appreciate the words of one man who has been honest enough to put this into language that anyone can understand:

The Church is in great need of deliverance from these very attitudes. There is a mindset that defines ministry as a kind of lordship: sitting in the honored seat, being the feted guest at luncheons, speaking to vast throngs, building monuments and collecting honorary titles. This type of attitude values being served. For those caught up in such thinking, Christianity exists to give *me* eternal life, to increase *my* physical health, to coddle *my* body, to enlarge *my* power, to elevate *my* prestige.

Some of us in ministry have attended ministerial conventions which were given wholly to personality promotion, and which ended with a well-defined (though unspoken) pecking order. The "important people" were easy to identify; busy, busy, busy, going from one "important" meeting to another, playing up to the media. True, there were no popes in sedan chairs, but there were executive limos with smoked glass, and fawning, patronizing followers.[10]

Jesus has a message for all who serve in ministry: *It isn't about you!*

Jesus said to His disciples, though not in so many words, "You're going to carry on when I'm gone. If you throw your weight around, the message is completely nullified. You aren't destined for a life of privilege and comfort. You're going to be abused; you're going to be maligned. You're going to be misunderstood. You're going to be criticized until the end of your life. Most of you will die a martyr's death. It's the kind of life and death that will do honor to My message and will turn the world upside down. Otherwise, you'll blend right into the world in which you have been raised, and there will be no difference between you and the next selfish person who comes along."

So what must we learn from the Lord's warning to these future leaders? Two truths.

First, *serving others is essential.* If you are growing up in Christ, your desire to help and serve others will become increasingly more important. It's not that you have no ambition; it's just that your ambition is kept in check—that your passion for serving others directs your ambitions in education, career, and, yes, even ministry. But the purpose of your ambition should be to serve others. It's not to buy a bigger mansion. It's not to "strut your stuff." It's not to run with the big dogs. It's not to build your own little kingdom. It's to help build the kingdom of God.

Second, *personal greatness should be incidental.* That's a hard lesson for many to learn. I have a feeling you weren't raised like that, and the models you've chosen as your heroes may not fit that mold. Because that's true, I can assure you that there's nothing that disarms an individual more quickly than seeing someone who *could be* great in his or her own eyes yet remains absolutely humble in service to others. That's what Jesus wanted for the Twelve, and that's what He wants for all of His followers.

What about Divorce?
MARK 10:1-12

NASB

¹Getting up, He went from there to the region of Judea and beyond the Jordan; crowds gathered around Him again, and, according to His custom, He once more *began* to teach them. ²*Some* Pharisees came up to Jesus, testing Him, and *began* to question Him whether it was lawful for a man to ªdivorce a wife. ³And He answered and said to them, "What did Moses command you?" ⁴They said, "Moses permitted *a man* TO WRITE A CERTIFICATE OF DIVORCE AND ªSEND *her* AWAY." ⁵But Jesus said to them, "ªBecause of your hardness of heart he wrote you this commandment. ⁶But from the beginning of creation, *God* MADE THEM MALE AND FEMALE. ⁷FOR THIS REASON A MAN SHALL LEAVE HIS FATHER AND MOTHERª, ⁸AND THE TWO SHALL BECOME ONE FLESH; so they are no longer two, but one flesh. ⁹What therefore God has joined together, let no man separate."

¹⁰In the house the disciples *began* questioning Him about this again. ¹¹And He said to them, "Whoever ªdivorces his wife and marries another woman commits adultery against

NLT

¹Then Jesus left Capernaum and went down to the region of Judea and into the area east of the Jordan River. Once again crowds gathered around him, and as usual he was teaching them.

²Some Pharisees came and tried to trap him with this question: "Should a man be allowed to divorce his wife?"

³Jesus answered them with a question: "What did Moses say in the law about divorce?"

⁴"Well, he permitted it," they replied. "He said a man can give his wife a written notice of divorce and send her away."*

⁵But Jesus responded, "He wrote this commandment only as a concession to your hard hearts. ⁶But 'God made them male and female'* from the beginning of creation. ⁷'This explains why a man leaves his father and mother and is joined to his wife,* ⁸and the two are united into one.'* Since they are no longer two but one, ⁹let no one split apart what God has joined together."

¹⁰Later, when he was alone with his disciples in the house, they brought up the subject again. ¹¹He told them, "Whoever divorces his wife and marries someone else

NASB

her; [12]and if she herself ªdivorces her husband and marries another man, she is committing adultery."

10:2 ªOr *send away*   10:4 ªOr *divorce* her
10:5 ªOr *With reference to*   10:7 ªMany late mss
add *and shall cling to his wife*   10:11 ªOr *sends*
away   10:12 ªOr *sends away*

NLT

commits adultery against her. [12]And if a woman divorces her husband and marries someone else, she commits adultery."

10:4 See Deut 24:1.   10:6 Gen 1:27; 5:2.
10:7 Some manuscripts do not include *and is joined to his wife.*   10:7-8 Gen 2:24.

When it comes to theological and moral issues, everyone has an opinion. Almost without exception, our opinions have been formed in one of three ways (or at least a combination of the three). First, we base our opinions on what we have been taught. We respect what our elders have believed and usually adopt their opinions as our own. Second, we glean information and insight from what we have read. Intelligent authorities have written on the subject, we respect their credentials, and their arguments appear sound, so we allow our opinions to be shaped by books and articles. Third, we form opinions based on what we have experienced. The pain of a particular circumstance can shape our thinking on the issue involved, and we can speak with the authority of firsthand knowledge. Rarely, however, do I see people base their opinions on a serious, in-depth, careful examination of the sacred Scriptures.

While the religious authorities of Jesus' day revered the Word of God and devoted themselves to hours of studying it, they did not actually *obey* it. In fact, their theological traditions frequently violated the face-value reading of Scripture, leading them to feel justified in doing the opposite of what God had commanded. Their ability to feel morally superior to others while disobeying the very Scriptures they revered was something that irritated Jesus as much as anything on earth!

As Jesus began His last journey to Jerusalem—a defining march toward His destiny—He encountered several individuals with opinions that violated Scripture. Mark uses these encounters to show how far afield devoutly religious Jews had drifted and how faulty their views of God's original teaching had become. Because the priests and rabbis had long since abandoned the Scriptures for man-made customs, God's covenant people had become ignorant of the Law and misinformed about what God expected of them.

The first issue involves the ancient and sacred institution of marriage.

— 10:1 —

All three of the synoptic Gospels (Matthew, Mark, and Luke) describe a moment in Jesus' ministry when He decided to take the war against evil to Jerusalem, and this is the moment in Mark's narrative (cf. Matt. 19:1; Luke 9:51). Jesus got up from His seated position as a teacher (see Mark 9:35-50) and left from Capernaum (cf. 9:33). Mark downplays the drama of this pivotal moment, however, stating that "crowds gathered around Him again, and, according to His custom, He once more began to teach them." But don't let Mark's "business as usual" language lull you into thinking nothing different was occurring. Having the benefit of twenty-twenty hindsight, we know that this trip to Jerusalem would be very different from all the rest. Mark's style reflects life as we live it; we rarely recognize pivotal moments when they occur.

While the disciples suspected nothing, Jesus understood His mission and knew the implications of this particular trip up to the temple. As had happened in many other places and countless times before, crowds gathered around Jesus, and He responded by teaching them. It also came as no surprise that Pharisees came out of the woodwork to provoke Him. In this encounter, however, Jesus would challenge the theological intellect of Israel's two great rabbinical schools, each named for a legendary teacher of the Law.

Shammai, a Pharisee, had been a crusty, rigid teacher of theology, advocating a very disciplined interpretation of Scripture. He allowed the face-value meaning of words and phrases to guide his interpretation and application, which made him unpopular with more liberal Pharisees, who interpreted the Scriptures very loosely and augmented the Law with innumerable traditions and customs. They became theologically innovative, at least in part, in order to give divine authority to customs that served their political and social purposes.

Jews remembered Hillel, another Pharisee, as a winsome, engaging teacher whose legendary kindness made him a political success. The school of Hillel became extremely creative in its interpretation of Scripture, finding ways to have the text say almost anything they needed. In time, its students came to dominate the religious culture of the temple and hold the highest offices in the Sanhedrin.

By the end of this conversation about marriage and divorce, Jesus would declare both schools incorrect. To appreciate the significance of this, imagine a self-taught country lawyer presuming to tell the law schools of Harvard and Yale that they had been misinterpreting constitutional law for more than a hundred years. Conversely, imagine that this upstart lawyer was, in fact, James Madison in disguise. The Author of sacred Scripture had come to confront the men who had corrupted His message.

— 10:2-4 —

The Pharisees asked Jesus what appears to be a straightforward question. On the surface, they asked His opinion on whether it was lawful—that is, morally permissible—for a man to divorce his wife. The literal meaning of the word translated "divorce" (*apolyō* [630]) is "send away," although the process was more formal than this makes it sound. In Judea and Galilee, Jews getting married were typically joined by legal agreement, and their divorce required a legal document to address the terms of their original contract. Regardless, the Pharisees didn't really care what Jesus thought about divorce; they chose this topic to determine which method of Scripture interpretation He would employ. They approached Jesus with Deuteronomy 24:1-4 on their minds:

> When a man takes a wife and marries her, and it happens that she finds no favor in his eyes because he has found some indecency in her, and he writes her a certificate of divorce and puts it in her hand and sends her out from his house, and she leaves his house and goes and becomes another man's wife, and if the latter husband turns against her and writes her a certificate of divorce and puts *it* in her hand and sends her out of his house, or if the latter husband dies who took her to be his wife, then her former husband who sent her away is not allowed to take her again to be his wife, since she has been defiled; for that is an abomination before the LORD, and you shall not bring sin on the land which the LORD your God gives you as an inheritance.

How Jesus answered the divorce question would reveal which school He favored. The Mishnah preserves the oral tradition of the rabbis Shammai and Hillel. Here is a short section of their deliberations:

> The House of Shammai say, "A man should divorce his wife only because he has found grounds for it in unchastity, since it is said, *Because he has found in her indecency in anything* (Deut. 24:1). And the House of Hillel say, "Even if she spoiled his dish, since it is said, *Because he has found in her indecency in anything.*" R. Aqiba says, "Even if he found someone else prettier than she, since it is said, *And it shall be if she find no favor in his eyes* (Deut. 24:1)."[11]

Pharisees of the Hillel school concluded that marriages could be created and dissolved on a whim. They arrived at their conclusion by focusing on the Hebrew phrase translated "some indecency," which is literally "a matter of nakedness." The Jews used this expression to describe any act that brought shame on the individual—that is, "a shameful matter." In fact, Deuteronomy 23:12-14 uses this same phrase with reference to the indecency of having a latrine inside the camp. In the context of Deuteronomy 24, however, Shammai insisted that this phrase must refer to sexual sin, such as adultery. Hillel, however, noted a curiosity in Moses' choice of words and elaborated with a creative interpretation. One writer notes,

> Hillel asked, why did Moses use the phrase "cause of sexual immorality" when he could simply have said "sexual immorality"? Hillel reasoned that the seemingly superfluous word *cause* must refer to another, different ground for divorce, and since this other ground is simply called a "cause," he concluded that it meant *any* cause. . . .
>
> Hillel therefore thought that two types of divorce were taught in Deuteronomy 24:1: one for "sexual immorality" (adultery) and one they named "Any Cause."[12]

When Jesus responded to the Pharisees, He sent them to the Scriptures. They responded with their flawed "any cause" understanding of the passage in Deuteronomy 24.

— 10:5-9 —

Brilliantly and wisely, Jesus certainly didn't side with Hillel, but neither did he entirely side with the more conservative Shammai. In fact, He objected to both of their presuppositions. He considered their debate entirely irrelevant because Deuteronomy 24:1-4 didn't sanction divorce so much as it acknowledged the practice among the Jews and then established limits to keep divorce and remarriage from becoming an elaborate wife-swapping scheme. According to this law, a man couldn't divorce his wife and then remarry his first wife again later, after she had married and divorced a second man. Once the woman became the wife of another man, she could not return to her first husband because "she has been defiled" (Deut. 24:4).

God permitted divorce as a concession because His people were hardhearted. This had nothing to do with being unkind or cruel; to have a "hard heart" in that culture meant to be spiritually underdeveloped and resistant to wisdom. Because the Law didn't ban divorce altogether, both schools, that of Shammai and that of Hillel, took this as a sign of God's approval. Jesus refuted this by appealing to Genesis 1, in which God ordained the institution of marriage and established its parameters. God determined that one man and one woman should leave their families of origin to become joined as "one flesh" (Gen. 2:22-24). Figuratively speaking, the two were to become indivisible.

With the command "What therefore God has joined together, let no man separate" (Mark 10:9), Jesus declared marriage an act of God, not a declaration of the courts, the church, or any human agency. Whereas other people may have arranged for a couple to meet and to marry, set the terms of the marriage contract, and even superintended the ceremony, "God has joined together" a husband and wife. Therefore, judges and theologians can write all the legal documents they want, but their court rulings change nothing in heaven if God considers the couple married.

Matthew records the sole reason a person may pursue a divorce without violating God's moral standard—namely, "for the reason of *porneia* [4202]" (Matt. 5:32). This Greek word described a broad range of sexual sin, not just adultery. The text does not read, "except for the reason of *moicheia* [3430]," which would limit the sexual sin to adultery. Jesus elected to use a term that came to encompass a range of illicit sexual activities, including adultery, homosexuality, incest, bestiality, and child molestation. In the eyes of God, a couple may choose to divorce if *porneia* severs their bond.[13]

— 10:10-12 —

Behind closed doors, the disciples pressed Jesus to help them get a better understanding. This was a revelation for them as well. The Lord reiterated the nature of marriage, which He had ordained to be a permanent union between a man and a woman. Moreover, it is a union entered by the choice of two people but sealed in heaven. Earthly institutions such as churches or courts merely assent to what God has accomplished, but no human agency has the power to dissolve the union. Unless God recognizes a union as dissolved, the man or woman who obtains a divorce and marries another commits adultery, regardless of what a court, a judge, or any earthly institution says.

APPLICATION: MARK 10:1-12

Timely Advice for Troubling Times

Having seen how Jesus interacted with a misguided religious opinion about marriage, I'll offer three suggestions that will help us avoid their errors.

First, *don't form your opinions based on the climate of our culture.* Insulate yourself from the shifting winds of popular culture—also known as popular opinion—or stability will forever elude you. For those who do not do this, relationships cannot last, to say nothing of marriages.

People often ask how I have been able to stay married to the same woman for so long. I tell them that it's because Cynthia hasn't left me. Of course, that goes both ways. There have been many times I have wanted to run away and start over in some strange city under an assumed name. Cynthia readily admits that there were times when she thought we wouldn't make it. We're together because, at various times, each of us have chosen to ignore the opinions of our culture and remain committed.

Second, *avoid self-righteous judgmentalism and legalism.* Be grateful if your marriage survives and your family remains intact. You can sustain your gratitude by avoiding any semblance of judgment for those whose marriages have ended. You don't know enough to judge the reason. You don't know the details. You don't know what they've endured. And you certainly don't know what God thinks about their particular circumstances. Let God be the judge; you concentrate on loving them without reservation.

Finally, *leave room for God's grace to rescue those who are victimized.* Having served as a pastor for five decades, I could tell you stories of marriages gone bad that would keep you up at night. Marital violence can be worse than a megacity mugging. Emotional and psychological scars last for years among abused spouses and for a lifetime among children. Disease, substance abuse, felony activity, multiple affairs— the circumstances sometimes require a less-than-ideal life change. Sometimes that includes divorce. Suspend any and all words of condemnation. Leave room for God's grace to rescue the lives of people who would otherwise go under.

Let's Get These Things Straight
MARK 10:13-31

13 And they were bringing children to Him so that He might touch them; but the disciples rebuked them. 14 But when Jesus saw this, He was indignant and said to them, "Permit the children to come to Me; do not hinder them; for the kingdom of God belongs to such as these. 15 Truly I say to you, whoever does not receive the kingdom of God like a child will not enter it *at all*." 16 And He took them in His arms and *began* blessing them, laying His hands on them.

17 As He was setting out on a journey, a man ran up to Him and knelt before Him, and asked Him, "Good Teacher, what shall I do to inherit eternal life?" 18 And Jesus said to him, "Why do you call Me good? No one is good except God alone. 19 You know the commandments, 'DO NOT MURDER, DO NOT COMMIT ADULTERY, DO NOT STEAL, DO NOT BEAR FALSE WITNESS, Do not defraud, HONOR YOUR FATHER AND MOTHER.'" 20 And he said to Him, "Teacher, I have kept all these things from my youth up." 21 Looking at him, Jesus felt a love for him and said to him, "One thing you lack: go and sell all you possess and give to the poor, and you will have treasure in heaven; and come, follow Me." 22 But at these words ᵃhe was saddened, and he went away grieving, for he was one who owned much property.

23 And Jesus, looking around, said to His disciples, "How hard it will be

13 One day some parents brought their children to Jesus so he could touch and bless them. But the disciples scolded the parents for bothering him.

14 When Jesus saw what was happening, he was angry with his disciples. He said to them, "Let the children come to me. Don't stop them! For the Kingdom of God belongs to those who are like these children. 15 I tell you the truth, anyone who doesn't receive the Kingdom of God like a child will never enter it." 16 Then he took the children in his arms and placed his hands on their heads and blessed them.

17 As Jesus was starting out on his way to Jerusalem, a man came running up to him, knelt down, and asked, "Good Teacher, what must I do to inherit eternal life?"

18 "Why do you call me good?" Jesus asked. "Only God is truly good. 19 But to answer your question, you know the commandments: 'You must not murder. You must not commit adultery. You must not steal. You must not testify falsely. You must not cheat anyone. Honor your father and mother.'*"

20 "Teacher," the man replied, "I've obeyed all these commandments since I was young."

21 Looking at the man, Jesus felt genuine love for him. "There is still one thing you haven't done," he told him. "Go and sell all your possessions and give the money to the poor, and you will have treasure in heaven. Then come, follow me."

22 At this the man's face fell, and he went away sad, for he had many possessions.

23 Jesus looked around and said to his disciples, "How hard it is for the

for those who are wealthy to enter the kingdom of God!" 24 The disciples were amazed at His words. But Jesus answered again and said to them, "Children, how hard it is to enter the kingdom of God! 25 It is easier for a camel to go through the eye of a needle than for a rich man to enter the kingdom of God." 26 They were even more astonished and said to Him, "ªThen who can be saved?" 27 Looking at them, Jesus said, "With people it is impossible, but not with God; for all things are possible with God."

28 Peter began to say to Him, "Behold, we have left everything and followed You." 29 Jesus said, "Truly I say to you, there is no one who has left house or brothers or sisters or mother or father or children or farms, for My sake and for the gospel's sake, 30 ªbut that he will receive a hundred times as much now in ᵇthe present age, houses and brothers and sisters and mothers and children and farms, along with persecutions; and in the age to come, eternal life. 31 But many *who are* first will be last, and the last, first."

10:22 ªOr *he became gloomy*   10:26 ªLit *And*
10:30 ªLit *if not*   ᵇLit *this time*

rich to enter the Kingdom of God!" 24 This amazed them. But Jesus said again, "Dear children, it is very hard* to enter the Kingdom of God. 25 In fact, it is easier for a camel to go through the eye of a needle than for a rich person to enter the Kingdom of God!"

26 The disciples were astounded. "Then who in the world can be saved?" they asked.

27 Jesus looked at them intently and said, "Humanly speaking, it is impossible. But not with God. Everything is possible with God."

28 Then Peter began to speak up. "We've given up everything to follow you," he said.

29 "Yes," Jesus replied, "and I assure you that everyone who has given up house or brothers or sisters or mother or father or children or property, for my sake and for the Good News, 30 will receive now in return a hundred times as many houses, brothers, sisters, mothers, children, and property—along with persecution. And in the world to come that person will have eternal life. 31 But many who are the greatest now will be least important then, and those who seem least important now will be the greatest then.*"

10:19 Exod 20:12-16; Deut 5:16-20.   10:24 Some manuscripts read *very hard for those who trust in riches.*   10:31 Greek *But many who are first will be last; and the last, first.*

A wise person once noted that Christian maturity often occurs in three stages: conversion of the heart, conversion of the mind, and then conversion of the purse. I think we would have to admit that the most difficult conversion involves our finances. Admittedly, for many, the love of money is a deal breaker. Their relationship with money and possessions prevents them from trusting God for their daily provision in this life as well as their eternal provision in the next. Those who don't have much often crave more. Those who have more live in fear of losing it.

Currency itself is not evil. It is, after all, nothing more than metal or paper. Still, we cannot ignore the incredible power it has to distort our thinking. In this sense, money commands the same deluding power that idols held over ancient people. It is a false god, promising to provide for our needs today and tomorrow. It promises to give us power over others and, therefore, protection from the harm they might do. Money promises to make us happy by giving us all the things we were once denied. And, like any idol, it promises all these things in exchange for first priority in all things. Money will tolerate the worship of other gods—it is remarkably inclusive—as long as we worship at the altar of greed first.

To make matters worse, false teachers calling themselves Christian have twisted our thinking by telling two lies:

1. Prosperity is a sign of God's approval.
2. Poverty is a sign of God's displeasure.

This false teaching—the great heresy of our times—can be stated simply in five words: "Love Jesus and get rich." Many churches and ministries flourish by pandering to the greed of their constituency, and they exploit the deep pain felt by the have-nots of the world. They're saturated with all manner of gimmicks and manipulative techniques to convince people that they can bargain with God. "Demonstrate your faith by sending money to me," they say, "and God will send you His blessings many times over."

These false teachers compound their sin by living extravagantly on the donations of people who can ill afford to part with the few dollars they have. I once saw with my own eyes a televangelist brag about having the heels on his shoes plated with gold, and the audience applauded as if this were proof of God's approval.

The heresy that calls people to "love Jesus and get rich" corrupts authentic Christianity in two insidious ways. First, it tells the followers of Christ that they can obey two masters; Jesus said we cannot (Matt. 6:24; Luke 16:13). Second, it tells people who would follow Jesus that God's favor can be earned: "Prove your faith by your good deeds in order to release blessings from heaven." When Jesus encountered these lies in the first century, He set the record straight. This segment of Mark's narrative will set forth two foundational principles.

1. The kingdom of heaven is for the weak and helpless, not the entitled and self-righteous.
2. The kingdom of heaven is a gift of grace, not a reward to be earned.

— 10:13 —

Mark relies heavily on the themes of childhood and youth to set the record straight concerning faith, grace, and the kingdom of God. The Gospel writer got his information from Peter, who witnessed the Lord in action. Jesus frequently turned to children to illustrate our relationship with God.

Children today are viewed in a completely different way than they were in the first century. A significant reason is the influence of Christianity on Western culture. For example, the practice of exposure, leaving an unwanted child to the elements, wasn't outlawed by Rome until AD 375, after Christianity had become the dominant religion. During the first century, Jews led the rest of the ancient world in the treatment of women and children; still, Jewish men didn't consider women as their equals. Children were cherished as gifts from God, but they were not considered the most valuable members of society. On the contrary, they contributed little in terms of protection or provision, so they ranked low in terms of power, privilege, and influence.

These socially insignificant people commanded too much of the Messiah's attention in the view of the disciples. One does not become king by associating with poor and powerless people; would-be kings curry the favor of the rich and powerful. So the disciples—who thought of themselves as Jesus' handlers—began to discourage parents from bringing children to the future king of Israel. The Greek word for "children," *paidion* [3813] refers to offspring ranging from infants to preteens. In the custom of the day, parents wanted Jesus to "touch them"—that is, place His hand on their heads or shoulders and pronounce God's blessing on them for the future. While Jesus blessed, however, the disciples "rebuked" (*epitimaō* [2008]). It's the same term Jesus used to admonish Peter (8:33) and to cast out demons (1:25; 9:25). It's the same word Mark used to describe a stern warning Jesus issued from time to time (3:12; 8:30).

— 10:14-15 —

This caused Jesus to become righteously angry. He ordered His disciples to let the children come to Him because they were ideal illustrations of genuine discipleship. Not because they're innocent: Children have twisted, fallen natures like all people. Not because they're pleasant: Anybody who has experience rearing children can tell you that they can occasionally be absolutely horrid. Jesus praised children because they are incapable of pretense: They come just as they are. No affectation.

No hesitation. No inhibition. And they trust completely. They haven't yet learned to be suspicious or proud.

Most importantly of all, children come to God empty-handed. They have nothing to offer. They can do nothing for anyone. Helpless, defenseless, messy, unsophisticated, disobedient, unable to keep themselves clean or dress themselves—they're completely needy. They know only how to reach out and receive help.

— 10:16 —

Having put the disciples in their place, Jesus scooped up a child and then gathered another into His arms, and another, laying hands on them and blessing them. The way He welcomed and blessed children illustrates the first great principle of salvation: Divine favor—deliverance from hell and entrance to heaven—is God's gift to people who cannot earn His goodwill (cf. Rom. 6:23; Eph. 2:8-9).

— 10:17-19 —

As Jesus traveled toward Jerusalem, He encountered a man eager to please God and to receive eternal life in the coming kingdom. His first words offer a clue as to how he imagined his relationship with God. He called Jesus "Good Teacher" (10:17), a very uncommon way for someone to address a rabbi. He either hoped to flatter Jesus or he knew Jesus to be more than a mere theology teacher and spiritual guide.

Jesus didn't deny being good; He merely challenged the man's superficial notion of goodness. Humans like to measure their relative worth against one another; it's easier to feel superior that way. Jesus reset the bar where it belongs. God's perfect, unblemished righteousness is the true standard of goodness. By that benchmark, all of humanity falls pathetically short (Rom. 3:23).

Even if Jesus hadn't had the benefit of supernatural knowledge, two factors would have prompted Him to anticipate the man's view of salvation. First, the prevailing theology in Israel taught that natural-born Jews would inherit the kingdom of God unless they forfeited their birthright through sin. In other words, salvation was theirs to lose, but only if they failed to be good. They drew this from Deuteronomy 30:15-20. But this particular promise dealt with what we know as God's "land covenant" with Israel. He required obedience to the Law as a condition of remaining in Canaan and receiving His protection from invasion. He never intended this to be the standard of salvation. He never expected moral perfection from anyone. In fact, He gave the Israelites a temple and a system of sacrifices as the means by which they could, by faith, receive God's grace.

Jesus also saw from the man's clothing and demeanor that he came from a lifestyle of wealth and privilege, which first-century Jews regarded as proof of God's favor. The man was a natural-born Jew and bore the signs of God's stamp of approval on his moral character. So it's surprising to see him asking Jesus how he might "inherit eternal life." Regardless, his question appears sincere.

Jesus affirmed the notion that one can earn salvation *in theory*. All one must do is maintain a perfect moral record. He then referenced five of the Ten Commandments that prescribe moral goodness toward one's neighbors (Mark 10:19; cf. Exod. 20:12-16; Deut. 5:16-20). The phrase "do not defraud" (Mark 10:19) is not one of the Ten Commandments per se. It may be a personally directed application of the tenth commandment, "You shall not covet" (Exod. 20:17). The rich and powerful would be especially tempted to covet and then commit fraud to obtain what they desired.

— 10:20-22 —

Without hesitation, the man affirmed his own righteousness from childhood to the present day. And from a first-century Jewish perspective, he *was* righteous, much like a lifelong church-attendee who can say, "I never miss a church service. I tithe faithfully. I volunteer for everything. I'm faithful to my spouse. I never cheat on my taxes. I follow the Golden Rule. I never knowingly hurt anyone . . . I'm a good person." And we could readily agree; that person is indeed a wonderful example of righteousness. We want to hire people like that to guard our money and protect our children. The man kneeling before Jesus was a good person . . . *compared to other people.*

The phrase "looking at him" (10:21) is a translation of an emphatic form of the verb *emblepō* [1689], which in this context could be paraphrased "fixing his gaze earnestly on him" or "looking intently into his soul." Jesus perceived the essence of this man the way only the Creator of humanity could, and He loved him (*agapaō* [25]). The only other time this verb appears in Mark's narrative is in reference to the two greatest commandments (12:29-33), which perhaps hints at the contrast of heart of the rich young man when he cites the same commands.

That Jesus saw the man truly and loved him deeply is essential to understanding the Lord's instructions. He didn't challenge the young man's faulty standard of goodness, and He graciously gave him a pass on his self-righteousness. Jesus could address those issues in the course of time (as He does with us!). He instead exposed the core issue in the man's life: the idol of wealth. The young man had made an unholy religion by combining obedience to the Law with the expectation of prosperity: "Love God and get rich." Or, in his case, "love God and stay rich." Jesus invited him to leave one master to follow another, to exchange the treasure of the corrupt world system for the incorruptible treasure of God's eternal kingdom.

Take note of the command "Follow Me." It's the invitation to become a disciple (cf. 1:17; 2:14), to bear the burden of discipleship (cf. 8:34), and then to join Jesus in the privilege of sharing one's personal wealth.

The man did not follow Jesus. The word rendered "saddened" (10:22) means "having a dark or gloomy appearance; being or becoming gloomy or dark."[14] It can also describe being in a "state of intense dismay" or being "shocked" or "appalled."[15] The scene calls to mind the response of Cain when God expressed displeasure with his substandard sacrifice. "Cain became very angry and his countenance fell" (Gen. 4:5). The Hebrew expression translated "his countenance fell" describes depression, the root of which is often anger. The young man left "grieving." This is the same word used of Jesus in the garden of Gethsemane, where He was overcome with severe mental anguish and emotional distress (Matt. 26:37).

The man wanted Jesus to suggest righteous deeds he could add to his growing list of self-validating "good." He wanted to pad his moral résumé to have assurance of God's eternal favor beyond his temporal blessings. But Jesus asked of him the one deed that, *for him*, would indicate genuine saving faith. This didn't only represent exchanging wealth for complete dependence upon God: Giving away all he owned required a complete overhaul of his theology. To give away all his possessions and become a pauper would require that he admit the worthlessness of his supposed "goodness." That was something he absolutely *would not* do.

— 10:23-25 —

To us, the Lord's remark doesn't seem extraordinary because we've had two thousand years to adjust. Much of Western culture is built upon Christendom as a foundation, so we can't appreciate how revolutionary Jesus' comment appeared to first-century Jews. Hebrews in His day had all but forgotten that salvation had always been by grace alone through faith alone (cf. Gen. 15:6; Rom. 4:3, 20-22; Gal. 3:6; Jas. 2:23). Jesus' statement—"How hard it will be for those who are wealthy to enter the

Exciting Faith

MARK 10:28-30

My older brother, Orville, was a missionary for more than thirty years in Buenos Aires. Before that, he had done some short-term mission work, and he stopped off for a quick visit with our parents before heading off again.

Now, you have to appreciate the kind of man our father was. Look up the word "responsible" in the dictionary, and his picture is there! To him, risks were for those who failed to plan. Responsible people left nothing to chance. As far as he was concerned, faith was something you'd exercise when your three backup plans fell through and you'd run out of all other options. My father was a believer, but he never understood the life of faith. Not really.

My brother, on the other hand, was stimulated by faith. He has lived his entire adult life on the raw edge of faith. To him, life doesn't get exciting until only God can get us through some specific challenge. That drove our dad nuts!

After a great supper of good ole collard greens, corn bread, onions, and red beans, my mother and sister went into the kitchen, leaving my father at one end of the table and Orville at the other. I was sitting on one side between them. Then it started.

"Son, how much money do you have for your long trip?"

"Oh, Dad, don't worry about it. We're gonna be fine."

Before he could change the subject, my father pressed the issue. "Son, how much money do you have in your wallet?"

Orville smiled as he said, "I don't have any money in my wallet."

I sat silent, watching this verbal tennis match.

"How much money do you have? You're gettin' ready to go down to South America! How much money you got?"

With that, my brother dug into his pocket, pulled out a quarter, set it on its edge on his end of the table, then gave it a careful thump. It

(continued on next page)

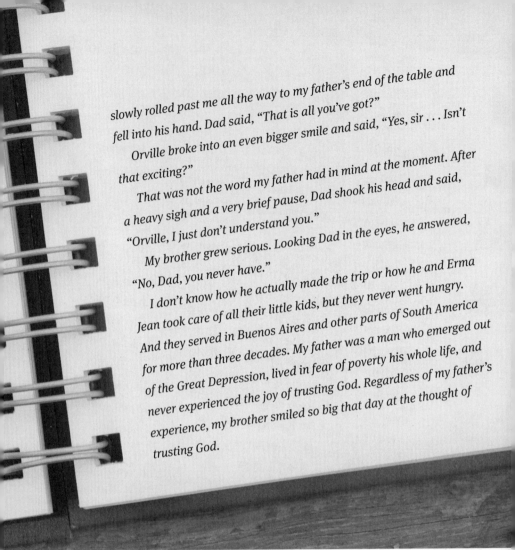

slowly rolled past me all the way to my father's end of the table and fell into his hand. Dad said, "That is all you've got?"

Orville broke into an even bigger smile and said, "Yes, sir . . . Isn't that exciting?"

That was not the word my father had in mind at the moment. After a heavy sigh and a very brief pause, Dad shook his head and said, "Orville, I just don't understand you."

My brother grew serious. Looking Dad in the eyes, he answered, "No, Dad, you never have."

I don't know how he actually made the trip or how he and Erma Jean took care of all their little kids, but they never went hungry. And they served in Buenos Aires and other parts of South America for more than three decades. My father was a man who emerged out of the Great Depression, lived in fear of poverty his whole life, and never experienced the joy of trusting God. Regardless of my father's experience, my brother smiled so big that day at the thought of trusting God.

kingdom of God!" (Mark 10:23)—turned contemporary theology upside down. According to the religious experts of His day, the rich were virtually guaranteed a place in God's kingdom because their wealth gave evidence of God's blessing.

When the disciples expressed amazement at the Lord's inversion of the Jews' theology, He emphasized how difficult it is for *anyone* to enter the kingdom. His metaphor confirms how difficult it is for rich people to receive the grace that God extends to all of humanity.

— 10:26-27 —

The disciples asked a logical question, given their presuppositions. Compared to God, no one is righteous. Compared to others, everyone could be considered wealthy by someone else. Therefore, no one can enter the kingdom of God!

Jesus eased their worries by reminding them of an old truth: All things are possible with God (see Gen. 18:14; Job 42:2; Jer. 32:17; Zech. 8:6; and especially Luke 1:37). Of course, this suggests another truth the disciples would ponder later. If it is impossible for people to choose Christ over wealth, and all things are possible with God, then He must do the choosing for those who are saved. (But that is a topic I'll leave for you to ponder as well.)

— 10:28-31 —

Peter watched the rich young man sulk off and disappear over the horizon. He then considered his own path to this point, having left his nets and all those in his family immediately to follow Jesus as a disciple. Would *he* enter the kingdom? Would his sacrifice be rewarded? Had he presumed too much?

Jesus affirmed Peter and reassured him that he had indeed made the right choice. The Lord explained that God will never ask us to sacrifice anything without giving us a staggering return on our investment . . . eventually. But this isn't the simple math used by false teachers of the so-called prosperity gospel. They say, "Give God a dollar (using my bank account), and He will give you one hundred in return." But faith isn't a get-rich scheme. The economy in God's kingdom is far better.

Jesus said we will receive a hundredfold return "in the present age" as well as "in the age to come" (10:30). To understand this, we have to set aside the idea that God is a mutual fund. The Lord doesn't pay us to sacrifice our worldly assets; He does something far more wonderful. He grants us complete access to everything that is His. When we release our hold on everything here on earth, He makes us fully vested owners of His kingdom along with Him. All of His resources are placed at our disposal, and everything He owns becomes ours to use as long as we act in the best interests of the kingdom (see John 14:13-15; 15:7-8, 14-17; 16:23-27).

Jesus concluded by returning to a familiar theme: reversal (cf. Mark 9:35). By this time, the disciples had become accustomed to the line. It became a reminder that a kingdom mentality completely rearranges all of our cherished priorities. The kingdom of God inverts the earthly scheme. This became the disciples' cue to set aside their old way of viewing the world and to see things through new, spiritually sensitive eyes.

APPLICATION: MARK 10:13-31

Setting Life Straight

You may have heard the expression "It's my way or the highway." When someone we know says that to us, it doesn't go over well. We don't take kindly to other people declaring such an autocratic, authoritarian stance. But that was essentially the Lord's message to the rich young man. Jesus, however, is no ordinary human. Despite having the body and the nature of a man, He is also entirely God. Therefore, Jesus has the right, as our Creator, to dictate terms.

Jesus said, seemingly on more than one occasion, "No servant can serve two masters; for either he will hate the one and love the other, or else he will be devoted to one and despise the other. You cannot serve God and wealth" (Luke 16:13). That's His way of saying, "It's My way or the highway. You can pursue wealth or you can pursue the kingdom of God—one or the other, not both. You must sacrifice one to obtain the other."

He doesn't say that to be selfish or merely to have His own way. Jesus says that because He is our Creator, He knows what is best for us, and He knows that any passionate pursuit of wealth leads to heartache, loneliness, depression, futility, and emptiness in this life—and in the life to come, eternal separation from Him.

In practical terms, it boils down to these two alternatives:

On the one hand, *if your highest priority is to be rich, prepare yourself for dreadful consequences.* Let me be clear. Wealth is not bad. It can be hazardous to your spiritual health, but material wealth isn't evil. The *pursuit* of wealth and the *priority* of wealth, however, can destroy your soul. This can ruin your family. It can tear your home apart. If you chase after wealth, your life will eventually become empty and lie in tatters at your feet. By serving a rival god—an idol of your own making—you forfeit the provision, protection, and guidance that God longs to give you. And if you die apart from Him, estranged from your Maker, you will spend eternity separated from Him.

But *if you sacrifice the pursuit of wealth for the kingdom, prepare yourself for numerous rewards.* When you set aside the obsessive pursuit of wealth and determine to become a part of God's kingdom, you allow God to be God. Yes, God may bless you with wealth, but your priority will continue to be His kingdom and His goodness (Matt. 6:33).

On the other hand, He might have you live as meagerly as Jesus and His disciples. If so, you will experience a contentment that rich people often spend fortunes trying to find. When you keep God in God's place, you allow Him to give you what you need. And He knows you better than you know yourself.

If you haven't met the Master, let me encourage you to meet Him now—not by doing good works or by being a good person, but by coming to Him just as you are and accepting His justification and redemption by faith.

> For by grace you have been saved through faith; and that not of yourselves, it is the gift of God; not as a result of works, so that no one may boast. (Eph. 2:8-9)

We accept God's gift of salvation simply by placing our faith in Christ alone for the forgiveness of our sins. You can meet Jesus and begin a relationship with Him by trusting in Him alone as your Savior. Here's a simple prayer you can use to express your faith:

> *Dear God,*
> *I know that my sin has put a chasm between You and me. Thank You for sending Your Son, Jesus, to bridge that chasm by dying in my place. I trust in Jesus alone to forgive my sins. I willingly accept His gift of eternal life. I ask Jesus to be my personal Savior and the Lord of my life. Thank You. In Jesus' name, amen.*

Prediction, Ambition, Submission
MARK 10:32-45

NASB

32They were on the road going up to Jerusalem, and Jesus was walking on ahead of them; and they were amazed, and those who followed were fearful. And again He took the twelve aside and began to tell them what was going to happen to Him, 33saying, "Behold, we are going up to Jerusalem, and the Son of Man will be ªdelivered to the chief priests and the scribes; and they will condemn Him to death and will ᵇhand

NLT

32They were now on the way up to Jerusalem, and Jesus was walking ahead of them. The disciples were filled with awe, and the people following behind were overwhelmed with fear. Taking the twelve disciples aside, Jesus once more began to describe everything that was about to happen to him. 33"Listen," he said, "we're going up to Jerusalem, where the Son of Man* will be betrayed to the leading priests and the teachers

NASB

Him over to the Gentiles. ³⁴They will mock Him and spit on Him, and scourge Him and kill *Him*, and three days later He will rise again."

³⁵ªJames and John, the two sons of Zebedee, came up to Jesus, saying, "Teacher, we want You to do for us whatever we ask of You." ³⁶And He said to them, "What do you want Me to do for you?" ³⁷They said to Him, "ªGrant that we may sit, one on Your right and one on *Your* left, in Your glory." ³⁸But Jesus said to them, "You do not know what you are asking. Are you able to drink the cup that I drink, or to be baptized with the baptism with which I am baptized?" ³⁹They said to Him, "We are able." And Jesus said to them, "The cup that I drink you shall drink; and you shall be baptized with the baptism with which I am baptized. ⁴⁰But to sit on My right or on *My* left, this is not Mine to give; but it is for those for whom it has been prepared."

⁴¹Hearing *this*, the ten began to feel indignant with ªJames and John. ⁴²Calling them to Himself, Jesus said to them, "You know that those who are recognized as rulers of the Gentiles lord it over them; and their great men exercise authority over them. ⁴³But it is not this way among you, but whoever wishes to become great among you shall be your servant; ⁴⁴and whoever wishes to be first among you shall be slave of all. ⁴⁵For even the Son of Man did not come to be served, but to serve, and to give His ªlife a ransom for many."

10:33 ªOr *betrayed* ᵇOr *betray* 10:35 ªOr *Jacob*
10:37 ªLit *Give to us* 10:41 ªOr *Jacob* 10:45 ªOr *soul*

NLT

of religious law. They will sentence him to die and hand him over to the Romans.* ³⁴They will mock him, spit on him, flog him with a whip, and kill him, but after three days he will rise again."

³⁵Then James and John, the sons of Zebedee, came over and spoke to him. "Teacher," they said, "we want you to do us a favor."

³⁶"What is your request?" he asked.

³⁷They replied, "When you sit on your glorious throne, we want to sit in places of honor next to you, one on your right and the other on your left."

³⁸But Jesus said to them, "You don't know what you are asking! Are you able to drink from the bitter cup of suffering I am about to drink? Are you able to be baptized with the baptism of suffering I must be baptized with?"

³⁹"Oh yes," they replied, "we are able!"

Then Jesus told them, "You will indeed drink from my bitter cup and be baptized with my baptism of suffering. ⁴⁰But I have no right to say who will sit on my right or my left. God has prepared those places for the ones he has chosen."

⁴¹When the ten other disciples heard what James and John had asked, they were indignant. ⁴²So Jesus called them together and said, "You know that the rulers in this world lord it over their people, and officials flaunt their authority over those under them. ⁴³But among you it will be different. Whoever wants to be a leader among you must be your servant, ⁴⁴and whoever wants to be first among you must be the slave of everyone else. ⁴⁵For even the Son of Man came not to be served but to serve others and to give his life as a ransom for many."

10:33a "Son of Man" is a title Jesus used for himself. 10:33b Greek *the Gentiles.*

This would be Jesus' final journey to Jerusalem. He had made the trip many times during His earthly lifetime. Like all good Jewish men, He had attended the three required festivals each year since at least His twelfth birthday (Deut. 16:16; Luke 2:42). He had also attended many of the non-mandatory feasts and had ministered in the region around the sacred city quite often. This journey would be different, however. This time He would walk into Jerusalem only to walk out bearing a cross on His back. Death waited for Him there, and He knew it.

The Twelve, however, continued to be reluctant to receive Jesus' message about His suffering and death. In fact, their heads seem to be in the clouds altogether—in this passage, it is striking to see James and John focused on ruling from glorious thrones next to Jesus even as Jesus speaks of his humiliating execution. As we read, Jesus guides us to reflect on the true servanthood that is essential to discipleship and to spiritual leadership.

— 10:32-34 —

In keeping with rabbinic custom, Jesus led His students on the trek. Mark highlights this in the phrase, "walking on ahead of them" (10:32). For the Gospel writer, this is a reality of the disciples' life with Jesus as their teacher, but also functions as the greatest example of the life Christians are called to live. Jesus walked the path of suffering ahead of His disciples, who followed wherever He led them. The example would not have been lost on Mark's persecuted believers in Rome, who might soon face the outrageous tortures of Nero.

The journey had been joyful in years past. Not this time. Jesus had predicted His suffering, death, and resurrection many times before, but it always seemed a remote potential many horizons ahead of them. No more. The Master marched toward His ordeal with somber resolve, while His disciples watched Him in amazement. In time, they grew fearful of what lie ahead.

It's difficult to tell which would be worse—knowing the details of the horror that awaited them in Jerusalem or not knowing anything. At times, the imagination can project far worse things than are possible in real life. Not so in this case. Jesus thought it best to prepare His men rather than allow fear to distract them. So He pulled them aside and described everything that would happen.

In Jerusalem, Jesus would be "delivered" (10:33), or "handed over," a verb that carries strong implications of betrayal. He would be taken before the chief priests of the temple and the scribes—experts in Old

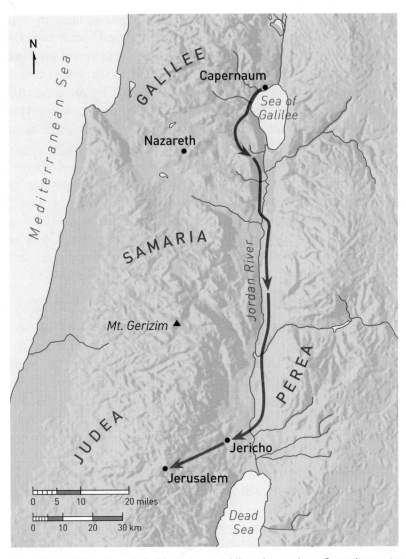

Jews from Galilee traveled this route—avoiding the unclean Samaritans—to Jerusalem to celebrate the Passover at the temple.

Testament Law—who served them. The chief priests were typically appointed as part of an intricate political system in which the secular ruler appointed the high priest,[16] who then used his power to surround himself with cronies. These figureheads were the technical rulers of the temple, but day-to-day operations continued to be run by the order of Levites.

Shortly after the Maccabean Revolt, the Jews began to dress the high priest in the purple and gold of royalty and look to the person in the office of high priest for kingly leadership (1 Macc. 14:35-49). The understanding since that time had been that the high priest would merely keep the Messiah's seat warm and then vacate the throne when He arrived (1 Macc. 14:41). In truth, few can relinquish great power once they have tasted it.

Jesus predicted that the temple officials would "hand Him over" to the Gentiles, an egregious betrayal against any Jew, to say nothing of the Messiah. The Gentiles would, in turn, hand him over to death after bringing immense shame upon Him. Then, on the third day after His death, He would rise again.

The Lord used a narrative style called "polysyndeton," a word that literally means "many things bound together." It uses a long, rapid string of connectives to link events in close succession. A novelist might express a lover's devotion this way: "Neither worry nor gloom nor fear nor pain nor threats against his mortal flesh would keep him from the one he loves." The style has a way of building and compounding something to achieve a strong emotional impact. Jesus wanted His men to appreciate what lie ahead so they would be prepared. Terrible events would start suddenly and unfold quickly.

— 10:35-37 —

Unfortunately, the Lord's warnings failed to find an attentive ear among the Twelve. In fact, the disciples appear tragically obtuse. The Lord had barely inhaled after explaining the horror to come when James and John sidled up to Him with a request. They said, in effect, "We're going to ask You for something; promise You'll grant our request." They then pulled a political maneuver that's as old as politics itself: office seeking. It is the political equivalent of line jumping. Don't wait to be recognized for your abilities—ingratiate yourself with the decision-maker and boldly request the position you want. They didn't hold back.

To sit on the Lord's "right" and "left" (10:37) referred to the respective ranks of second and third in command of the coming kingdom. While Jesus prepared Himself for rejection, humiliation, suffering, torture, and death, His closest companions jockeyed for positions of power in His imminent administration as king of Israel. The "glory" they imagined had Jesus being feted with a ticker-tape parade and wearing purple and gold. The disciples hadn't heard anything He said, so they didn't have a clue about the future they faced.

— 10:38-40 —

Mark uses the literary irony of this moment to great effect. The reader knows full well the fate that awaited Jesus. The Lord and His disciples saw the issues of power, position, leadership, and responsibility from completely different points of view. According to the corrupt world system, positions of power become the means by which people serve themselves. They govern well merely to safeguard their office. In the kingdom of God, power is something you give away, and the highest positions go to the lowest servants. The way to the "top" is paved with self-sacrifice and suffering. In the coming days, Jesus would become the absolute sovereign of this new kingdom order by suffering what no other human could bear.

When Jesus asked if they could suffer as He would, James and John said, "We are able" (10:39). In time, they would be. James would become the first disciple to be killed for the sake of the gospel. John would live to see all of his friends be baptized in persecution and then drink the bitter cup of martyrdom. John himself would be tortured, then later exiled to the barren isle of Patmos for years. Still, the two men had no idea of the destiny they had committed themselves to fulfill.

Imagine the impact this would have had on Mark's original audience, Christians facing uncertain days in Rome. The disciples were not ready for the "baptism" or the "cup" awaiting them. Not at that moment. When their moments of truth arrived, however, they would be "able" because God made them able.

— 10:41-45 —

When the other ten disciples heard this conversation, they became "indignant" (10:41). It's the same Greek term used to describe Jesus' reaction when He discovered the disciples keeping children away from Him. This is righteous anger in response to a moral misstep. They were right to be angry. Of course, they might also have been upset because James and John got to Jesus first. They, too, longed to occupy "box seats" in the future kingdom.

Before their flaring emotions turned ugly, Jesus called the disciples in to review an earlier lesson (cf. 9:35; 10:31). Jesus used the term "Gentiles" (10:42) to illustrate the world's style of leadership. Jewish leaders were indeed guilty of the same abuses of authority, but only because they had departed from the Hebrew paradigm established by God. The temple authorities, the Sadducees, and the Herodians had adopted the Gentile model of leadership and power, which uses authority as a means of controlling others for selfish gain.

Jesus said, "It is not this way among you" (10:43). Power is for service. In the corrupt world system, slaves bow the knee to their masters,

Reverend Doctor Jerk

MARK 10:42-45

I was doing a favor for a friend. He had asked me to participate in a little television panel discussion. My friend, who was producing the show, said, "Would you meet one of the panelists at the airport? We have too many guys to meet and not enough time. Maybe you and a friend could meet so-and-so, the president of a little Bible school."

I was in blue jeans, a T-shirt, and a jacket. A friend and I stood at the gate (pre-9/11) waiting for the plane to unload, and unfortunately, missed the man we were waiting for. So I said to my buddy, "Well, we'd better go down to the baggage claim and see if we can meet him there." On the way down we saw a guy with his hat pulled down tight, his tie cinched up tight, and his shirt starched stiff as a board, all decked out in a dark, three-piece suit. I nudged my friend and said, "That's gotta be him."

So I walked up and I called him by his name. "Are you so-and-so?"

He replied, "DOCTOR so-and-so," and dropped his bags for us to carry them.

My buddy and I picked up his bags and I said, "We thought you looked like the man we were looking for."

He said, "Oh, really? Tell me, what does a president look like?"

I wanted to say, "A JERK—a first-class jerk!" But I exercised some restraint.

Everyone stayed at the same motel that night and somebody—I'm not sure who—ordered him a couple of Bud Lights and some pretzels delivered to his door at two o'clock in the morning. Hmmmm.

If you find yourself craving the limelight and listening for public applause, do us all a big favor: Don't do it in the name of religion. Find another vocation. You'll hurt the cause.

and citizens bow to the king. In the kingdom of God, the King bows in service to His subjects and commands us to do the same (John 13:5-15). In fact, He calls those who hold the greatest authority in His kingdom to be "slave of all" (see Mark 10:44).

Because we live in a Christianized culture—and one that is democratic and capitalistic—we cannot fully appreciate how radical Jesus' teaching was in the first century. Free Romans and Greeks considered slavery a shameful existence; they would sooner end their own lives than become enslaved to others. Moreover, they measured personal greatness in terms of authority. In fact, they thought of the Roman emperor—the chief sovereign of the most powerful nation—as godlike because he possessed the power to command much of the known world.

Jesus contrasted the kingdom command structure with that of the world by declaring Himself the CSO—that is, the "Chief Serving Officer." The eternal Son of God described His task as serving. Mark chose to use the Greek term *diakoneō* [1247], which originally meant "to wait tables." In the broad sense, it means to "function as an intermediary," "act as go-between/agent," or "be at one's service."[17] This came from the lips of one who could heal with a touch, compel the weather to change immediately, provide food for thousands, and cause demons to tremble before Him. As one expositor writes, "At no place do the ethics of the kingdom of God clash more vigorously with the ethics of the world than in the matters of power and service."[18]

APPLICATION: MARK 10:32-45

Get Real with Real Serving

Over the years, I have acquired a particular distaste for terms that make ugly things sound pretty or try to conceal the truth of a matter. A good example is when senators or prime ministers call themselves "public servants" as though these offices were thrust upon them and they reluctantly accepted the reins of political power. More often than not, these politicians gained their position through a long, grueling, and sometimes ruthless climb up the ladder.

I also find the term "church growth" troublesome. "Growth" in this case doesn't refer to maturity or godliness. It means number of people.

Many ministers want large numbers of people because increasing attendance strokes the ego. Another expositor describes this well:

> Our world "(and even the church) is full of Jameses and Johns, go-getters and status-seekers, hungry for honour and prestige, measuring life by achievements, and everlastingly dreaming of success."[19] One need not look far to see preachers who do not preach to reach people but preach to reach the top, to become ecclesiastical superstars. They see discipleship to Jesus in terms of rank and privilege. They assume that Jesus is someone who will achieve things for them and give them the status of lords. . . .
>
> Despite all the warnings in Scripture, pagan values continue to seep into the church and govern its actions. Many ministers still dream of the big church, of the presidency of an institution or of a denomination, or of being acclaimed in national magazines as a mover and a shaker. All too frequently these people achieve their dreams because of their single-minded purpose to attain them at all costs, regardless of how much suffering they cause others along the way and how much they cause the work of Christ to suffer. The church has had to endure power struggles that make it look no different from the pagan corporate world.
>
> But the church cannot thrive if its leaders are competing with one another for positions of power. That pattern can only lead to anger and hatred.[20]

I've seen so much of this I could scream. Virtually every pastors' conference bulges with bloated egos who can't wait to talk about how big their churches have become or how many people they baptized last month. I find no passage in the Bible that says, "Talk about how big your ministry has grown and how many have started to attend."

Instead of seeking more power and greater celebrity, let us follow Christ's lead and seek greater opportunities to serve. I don't mean for you to seek high-profile positions in the church and then *call* it service; I mean go where few people see you, get your hands dirty doing what no one else wants to do, and tell no one what you did. When we can do this on a regular basis, and give no thought to recognition, then we can call ourselves servants in the truest sense of the term.

What's a King Doing on a Donkey?
MARK 10:46–11:11

NASB

46 Then they came to Jericho. And as He was leaving Jericho with His disciples and a large crowd, a blind beggar *named* Bartimaeus, the son of Timaeus, was sitting by the road. 47 When he heard that it was Jesus the Nazarene, he began to cry out and say, "Jesus, Son of David, have mercy on me!" 48 Many were sternly telling him to be quiet, but he kept crying out all the more, "Son of David, have mercy on me!" 49 And Jesus stopped and said, "Call him *here*." So they called the blind man, saying to him, "Take courage, stand up! He is calling for you." 50 Throwing aside his cloak, he jumped up and came to Jesus. 51 And answering him, Jesus said, "What do you want Me to do for you?" And the blind man said to Him, "ᵃRabboni, *I want* to regain my sight!" 52 And Jesus said to him, "Go; your faith has ᵃmade you well." Immediately he regained his sight and *began* following Him on the road.

11:1 As they approached Jerusalem, at Bethphage and Bethany, near the Mount of Olives, He sent two of His disciples, 2 and said to them, "Go into the village opposite you, and immediately as you enter it, you will find a colt tied *there*, on which no one yet has ever sat; untie it and bring it *here*. 3 If anyone says to you, 'Why are you doing this?' you say, 'The Lord has need of it'; and immediately he ᵃwill send it back here." 4 They went away and found a colt tied at the door, outside in the street; and they untied it. 5 Some of the bystanders were saying to them, "What are

NLT

46 Then they reached Jericho, and as Jesus and his disciples left town, a large crowd followed him. A blind beggar named Bartimaeus (son of Timaeus) was sitting beside the road. 47 When Bartimaeus heard that Jesus of Nazareth was nearby, he began to shout, "Jesus, Son of David, have mercy on me!"

48 "Be quiet!" many of the people yelled at him.

But he only shouted louder, "Son of David, have mercy on me!"

49 When Jesus heard him, he stopped and said, "Tell him to come here."

So they called the blind man. "Cheer up," they said. "Come on, he's calling you!" 50 Bartimaeus threw aside his coat, jumped up, and came to Jesus.

51 "What do you want me to do for you?" Jesus asked.

"My Rabbi,*" the blind man said, "I want to see!"

52 And Jesus said to him, "Go, for your faith has healed you." Instantly the man could see, and he followed Jesus down the road.*

11:1 As Jesus and his disciples approached Jerusalem, they came to the towns of Bethphage and Bethany on the Mount of Olives. Jesus sent two of them on ahead. 2 "Go into that village over there," he told them. "As soon as you enter it, you will see a young donkey tied there that no one has ever ridden. Untie it and bring it here. 3 If anyone asks, 'What are you doing?' just say, 'The Lord needs it and will return it soon.'"

4 The two disciples left and found the colt standing in the street, tied outside the front door. 5 As they were untying it, some bystanders

you doing, untying the colt?" ⁶They spoke to them just as Jesus had told *them,* and they gave them permission. ⁷They brought the colt to Jesus and put their coats on it; and He sat on it. ⁸And many spread their coats in the road, and others *spread* leafy branches which they had cut from the fields. ⁹Those who went in front and those who followed were shouting:

"Hosanna!
Blessed is He who comes in the name of the Lord;
¹⁰ Blessed *is* the coming kingdom of our father David;
Hosanna in the highest!"

¹¹Jesus entered Jerusalem *and came* into the temple; and after looking around at everything, He left for Bethany with the twelve, since it was already late.

10:51 ªI.e. My Master   10:52 ªLit *saved you*
11:3 ªLit *sends*

demanded, "What are you doing, untying that colt?" ⁶They said what Jesus had told them to say, and they were permitted to take it. ⁷Then they brought the colt to Jesus and threw their garments over it, and he sat on it.

⁸Many in the crowd spread their garments on the road ahead of him, and others spread leafy branches they had cut in the fields. ⁹Jesus was in the center of the procession, and the people all around him were shouting,

"Praise God!*
Blessings on the one who comes in the name of the Lord!
¹⁰ Blessings on the coming Kingdom of our ancestor David!
Praise God in highest heaven!"*

¹¹So Jesus came to Jerusalem and went into the Temple. After looking around carefully at everything, he left because it was late in the afternoon. Then he returned to Bethany with the twelve disciples.

10:51 Greek uses the Hebrew term *Rabboni.*
10:52 Or *on the way.*   11:9 Greek *Hosanna,* an exclamation of praise that literally means "save now"; also in 11:10.   11:9-10 Pss 118:25-26; 148:1.

Jesus is *fascinating.* I mean that in the formal sense of the word. He's alluring, spellbinding, irresistibly attractive. People found Him fascinating at least in part because He defied expectations. He said the unexpected and did the unpredictable. We have examples of both of these things in the next two stories in Mark's narrative.

While Jesus' life defied people's expectations, it had been predicted many years earlier in the writings of several Old Testament prophets. These next two stories play upon those early predictions to show that Jesus was, without any doubt, the Messiah Israel had been expecting. These episodes in Jesus' ministry occurred during the last leg of His final journey to Jerusalem, where He would fulfill many of the promises made in the Old Testament.

— 10:46-47 —

The traditional route from Galilee to Jerusalem took Jews on the east side of the Jordan River, which allowed them to circumvent Samaria, a land they considered contaminated with half-breed Jews and spiritual compromisers (see map of their travel route on page 280). Jesus, of course, traveled in and around Samaria often during His ministry; He came to seek and to save the lost, regardless of their heritage. He followed the traditional route to stay with the caravan. Hundreds of Jews would have lined this path in the days leading up to the Passover feast.

JERICHO

MARK 10:46

Sitting in the Jordan River Valley just north of the Dead Sea, at 846 feet below sea level, Jericho is one of the lowest cities on earth. That sounds like a terrible place to live, but the aptly called "City of Palms" happens to be one of the loveliest places to visit in all of the Middle East. In fact, the first-century Jewish historian Josephus described Jericho as "the most fruitful country of Judea, which bears a vast number of palm trees, besides the balsam tree, whose sprouts they cut with sharp stones, and at the incisions they gather the juice, which drops down like tears."[21] Josephus continues, "This country withal produces honey from bees: it also bears that balsam which is the most precious of all the fruits in that place, cypress trees also, and those that bear myrobalanum; so that he who should pronounce this place to be divine would not be mistaken, wherein is such plenty of trees produced as are very rare, and of the most excellent sort."[22]

Jericho's temperate climate made it an ideal retreat for royals, who built enormous palaces, complete with swimming pools, gardens, and bathhouses, as well as a hippodrome and a theater. The city also sat on one of the busiest trade routes in the ancient world, which had formalized connections to important coastal cities in northern Israel as well as to Egypt to the south.

This fertile, luxurious city became a favorite resting place for Jews headed for Jerusalem. They needed to gather their strength—pilgrims faced a 2,950-foot climb in less than 20 miles along a craggy, serpentine road lined with bandits.

Jericho lay along the caravan route to Jerusalem as the last stop before the difficult climb to the sacred city. While near Jericho, Jesus encountered a blind beggar, who had positioned himself alongside the road to receive the monetary mercy of pilgrims. Of course, he wasn't the only beggar; the road would have been lined with them during the Passover pilgrimage season.

This particular group of travelers had joined Jesus, perhaps expecting Him to march into Jerusalem and begin His political and religious campaign to claim the throne. This was, for them, a messianic procession. If the beggar overheard their chatter, he would have discerned that Jesus claimed to be the Messiah and that the group with Him believed His claim. When he heard the name "Jesus of Nazareth," he immediately called Him by His messianic title, "Son of David" (10:47; cf. 2 Sam. 7:8-16; Isa. 11:1-5; Jer. 23:5-6; Ezek. 34:23-24).

Mark's Gospel identifies the beggar as Bartimaeus, the son of Timaeus (Mark 10:46). This level of detail strongly suggests that Mark's audience knew the formerly blind man as a follower of Jesus. He may have become a prominent leader in the early days of the Christian movement. In any case, the man addressed Jesus by His messianic title and asked for mercy.

— 10:48-49 —

The Greek term rendered "cry out" in 10:47 is *krazō* [2896], which one lexicon defines as "to make a vehement outcry," "cry out," "scream," "shriek," or "when one utters loud cries, without words capable of being understood," and is used "of mentally disturbed persons, epileptics, or the evil spirits living in them."[23] This was not the routine calling of a longtime beggar like "alms for the blind." The man set aside all dignity and restraint to make himself unavoidable by shrieking at the top of his lungs. Despite attempts by others to shut him up, Jesus took note of the man's desperate crying and engaged him directly.

It worked. Jesus paused, causing the crowd around Him to stop. He then instructed His disciples to "call him" (10:49 [*phōneō* (5455)]). This stands in contrast to the man's impassioned "crying out," a word that Mark often uses to describe pleas for mercy (3:11; 5:7; 9:24). In this case, a cry for mercy is answered by a call to come.

— 10:50-52 —

Bartimaeus wasted no time responding to Jesus' call. The Lord then asked him a surprising question. To us the answer would appear obvious, but only because we have come to terms with Jesus' identity as the miracle-working Son of God and the mercy-giving Savior from sin. The question was a test of faith. "What do you want Me to do for you?" (10:51) could have been answered with, "A couple of spare shekels for a poor blind man, Sir." His asking of Jesus what he asked of every other traveler would have revealed the substance of his faith and the priority of his life. Far too many ask far too little of Jesus; they seek an extra margin of comfort in their miserable slavery to sin when they could ask for—and receive—a full measure of God's forgiveness, mercy, and saving grace!

As I stated in my comments on the parallel passage in *Insights on Luke* (Luke 18:39-42), "there's more than meets the eye for those who have eyes to see! The man's physical blindness reflected his spiritual condition."[24] Fortunately, he didn't settle for a few extra shekels; he asked for his sight, a request only God could grant. The word rendered "regain sight" is *anablepō* [308], which can mean "to gain sight" or, as New Testament writers often use the term, "to look up" (Mark 6:41; 7:34; 8:24; 16:4). Jesus accepted the man's request as a double entendre and a clear indication of his faith. The Lord responded with a double entendre of His own: "Your faith has made you well" (10:52). "Made well" is translated from the Greek word *sōzō* [4982], which means "I save." The context determines the meaning. In one sense, Bartimaeus was saved from his blindness; in another, from sin.

Mark indicates that Bartimaeus responded to the miracle by following Jesus. The imperfect tense of "following" is what grammar experts call an "ingressive imperfect," meaning that the subject started something and then continued on. Bartimaeus began following that very day and continued for the rest of his life.

— 11:1-6 —

Jesus and his disciples traveled from Jericho to Jerusalem. In the Gospel of John, they stay with Martha, Mary, and Lazarus in Bethany.

Having made the arduous climb from Jericho to the outskirts of Jerusalem, Jesus prepared to enter the city. He paused to secure lodging near Jerusalem in a location kept secret from His enemies. The Gospel of John states that Jesus stayed with His friend Lazarus and Lazarus's two sisters, Martha and Mary, who shared a home in Bethany (John 12:1-2). This small town lay on the eastern slope of the Mount of Olives (Zech. 14:4) about 2 miles outside the walls of Jerusalem.

For no fewer than twenty Passover celebrations, Jesus had come to Jerusalem to celebrate the deliverance of Israel from bondage in Egypt. He had entered the city many, many times before, but this time was different. The time had come for Him to assert His messianic claims. Long before Jesus entered the world as a baby, Israel had sold its birthright to Gentiles and ceased to be "the kingdom of God." On this day, Jesus came to fulfill the promises Israel had broken, to become the obedient Son Israel had failed to be, to take His rightful place on the throne of Israel as its King, to take control of the temple as its High Priest, and to reestablish Israel as a theocracy under the rule of God.

Usurpers held Israel for ransom; Jesus came to redeem His covenant nation.

— 11:7 —

Jesus chose to ride a colt because this trip down the Mount of Olives, across the Kidron Valley, and into Jerusalem would mark a change in His relationship with the religious and political authorities ruling Judea. He planned to enter Jerusalem as their King. He would assert His authority over both the throne and the temple. But He would not ride into the city in a show of force like a warrior king. Instead of riding a warhorse, Jesus sat atop a symbol of peace, a donkey. This "Triumphal Entry" looked nothing like the Roman *triumphus*, the lavish parade celebrating a victorious general returning home. In the early days of the empire, the conquering hero rode a white warhorse and wore the battle dress of a Roman general, a red cloak.[25] In contrast, Jesus fulfilled a specific prophecy:

> Rejoice greatly, O daughter of Zion!
> Shout in triumph, O daughter of Jerusalem!
> Behold, your king is coming to you;
> He is just and endowed with salvation,
> Humble, and mounted on a donkey,
> Even on a colt, the foal of a donkey. (Zech. 9:9)

— 11:8-10 —

The King's subjects—thousands of kingdom citizens—had followed Him from Galilee and joined many others living in Judea. As Jesus rode into the city, they lined the road with cloaks and leafy branches (cf. 2 Kgs. 9:12-13). They shouted "Hosanna!" (Mark 11:9), which is a transliteration from a Hebrew expression meaning "Oh, save us now!" They also quoted from Psalm 118:26, a familiar messianic psalm and one of the six "ascent" psalms sung in thanksgiving to God during Passover.

Throughout the ages, prophets had begged the rulers of Jerusalem to trust in the Lord for the city's protection, not in treaties or alliances or compromises or submission to pagan rulers (Deut. 23:6; Ezra 9:12; Isa. 30:1-3; 31:1; Jer. 43:7; Amos 5:4-7). Because these Jewish authorities ignored the prophets, Israel had become a Roman province ruled by a Roman procurator (see the feature on Pontius Pilate on page 376). Jesus came in peace, offering these wayward leaders an opportunity to humble themselves, repent of their sins, receive His grace, accept Him as their Messiah, embrace Him as their king, and experience genuine liberty. How they responded to His arrival would determine their fates as individuals and decide the future of the nation for centuries to come.

— 11:11 —

After Jesus rode into Jerusalem with throngs of followers cheering His arrival, He entered the temple. He had arrived late in the day, so the lights were dim and the grand courts empty, except for perhaps the echoes of a few shuffling feet and distant conversations. There's a subtle pathos in Mark's description of the scene. He records no conversation, so for once, the disciples appear to have allowed the Lord a moment or two of silence.

The Messiah looked around at everything, probably in deep contemplation over what might have been if only God's people had remained faithful. The magnificent temple could have been a visible symbol of Israel's divine purpose as God's light on a hill (see Ps. 43:3; Isa. 9:2; 42:6-9; 49:6; 60:1-3). Now the temple was doomed—a tragic end Jesus could see with the clarity of omniscient divinity. In AD 70, Titus would lay siege to the city and utterly destroy the great house of God.[26]

Eventually, the Master and His disciples returned to Bethany, where He would prepare Himself and His followers for the ordeal to come.

APPLICATION: MARK 10:46-11:11

Lessons from the Journey to Jerusalem

As I review the last leg of Jesus' journey to Jerusalem, I find three lessons worth contemplating. I will present them in reverse chronological order, starting with the Lord's silent reflection in the temple and ending with His encounter with Bartimaeus.

The first lesson is gleaned from the Lord's poignant visit to God's house: *In moving moments when we're tempted to talk, silence is far more appropriate.*

There's something about the sound of silence when you stand in front of a memorial and you read the etchings in stone. Or when you're at a cemetery and you read an epitaph. Some moments are ruined by words. When you're with someone who's grieving a loss, resist the urge to fill the silence with chatter. Just be there with them. Let your presence and silence do the talking, and let God use that moment for His purposes.

I love the words of one man who said, "I rarely regret the things I did not say."

I draw the second lesson from the Lord's triumphal entry: *In significant settings when we're prompted to be proud, genuine humility is far more impressive.*

Almost everybody has had a time in their lives when they've been honored for something. Attention turns to you, the spotlight falls on you, and the tendency of your flesh is to bask in your pride because now people are noticing and applauding you.

I remember Marian Anderson, the magnificent vocalist, who had risen from the ghetto to a packed-out performance at Carnegie Hall. She went on to sing at the Lincoln Memorial before thousands. After one performance at the Metropolitan, acclaimed conductor Arturo Toscanini declared that she had the greatest voice he'd ever heard. She even performed for the queen of England. When she reached the pinnacle of her career, she was asked what she thought was the most significant moment in her life. She answered that the greatest moment of her life came when she realized her mother wouldn't have to take in wash anymore.

A little humility would go a long way in all of our lives. Ask God to bring you to the place where you can see beyond the crowds, beyond the applause, and beyond the public approbation. Those things never turned Jesus' head. He threw His leg over that little donkey and rode into Jerusalem with His feet barely clearing the ground. He embraced His moment of triumph with humility, exactly as the prophets had foretold.

The third lesson takes us to the blind beggar: *In terrifying times when we're blinded by bitterness, vulnerable confession is far more helpful.*

If you will allow me to highlight the spiritual dimension of this story, I see a man who realized how dark he was deep within. He didn't shriek because he was tired of being blind; he screamed for divine mercy because he needed to be rescued from sin. Tragically, there are many who live their lives never realizing how dark the darkness is within them.

My mind goes back to a scene that was made famous on the television show *60 Minutes*. Journalist Mike Wallace focused on a story about Adolf Eichmann, the Nazi architect of the Jewish Holocaust. In that report, Wallace posed an intriguing question. He asked, "How is it possible for a man to act as Eichmann acted? Was he a monster? A madman? Or was he perhaps something even more terrifying: Was he normal?"[27]

Yehiel Dinur, a Jewish concentration camp survivor who testified against Eichmann at the Nuremburg trials, admitted that when he first laid eyes on the man, he was overcome with a terrible thought. It was not a godlike army officer who had sent so many to their deaths. Eichmann was an ordinary man. Dinur said, "I was afraid about myself. In that moment I saw that I am capable to do this. I am exactly like he." [28]

Wallace concluded his report with this penetrating summation: Eichmann is in all of us.

Our only hope is honest confession, humble repentance, sincere faith, and complete submission. When we confront the terrifying truth about ourselves, we'll find that God is greater than all of our monsters.

Seeing Another Side of Jesus
MARK 11:12-33

NASB	NLT
12On the next day, when they had left Bethany, He became hungry. 13Seeing at a distance a fig tree in leaf, He went *to see* if perhaps He would find anything on it; and when He came to	12The next morning as they were leaving Bethany, Jesus was hungry. 13He noticed a fig tree in full leaf a little way off, so he went over to see if he could find any figs. But there were

it, He found nothing but leaves, for it was not the season for figs. [14]He said to it, "May no one ever eat fruit from you again!" And His disciples were listening.

[15]Then they came to Jerusalem. And He entered the temple and began to drive out those who were buying and selling in the temple, and overturned the tables of the money changers and the seats of those who were selling [a]doves; [16]and He would not permit anyone to carry [a]merchandise through the temple. [17]And He *began* to teach and say to them, "Is it not written, 'MY HOUSE SHALL BE CALLED A HOUSE OF PRAYER FOR ALL THE NATIONS'? But you have made it a ROBBERS' [a]DEN." [18]The chief priests and the scribes heard *this,* and *began* seeking how to destroy Him; for they were afraid of Him, for the whole crowd was astonished at His teaching.

[19]When evening came, [a]they would go out of the city.

[20]As they were passing by in the morning, they saw the fig tree withered from the roots *up.* [21]Being reminded, Peter said to Him, "Rabbi, look, the fig tree which You cursed has withered." [22]And Jesus answered saying to them, "Have faith in God. [23]Truly I say to you, whoever says to this mountain, 'Be taken up and cast into the sea,' and does not doubt in his heart, but believes that what he says is going to happen, it will be *granted* him. [24]Therefore I say to you, all things for which you pray and ask, believe that you have received them, and they will be *granted* you. [25]Whenever you stand praying, forgive, if you have anything against anyone, so that your Father who is in heaven will also forgive you your transgressions. [26][[a]But if you do not forgive, neither will your Father who is in heaven forgive your transgressions."]

only leaves because it was too early in the season for fruit. [14]Then Jesus said to the tree, "May no one ever eat your fruit again!" And the disciples heard him say it.

[15]When they arrived back in Jerusalem, Jesus entered the Temple and began to drive out the people buying and selling animals for sacrifices. He knocked over the tables of the money changers and the chairs of those selling doves, [16]and he stopped everyone from using the Temple as a marketplace.* [17]He said to them, "The Scriptures declare, 'My Temple will be called a house of prayer for all nations,' but you have turned it into a den of thieves."*

[18]When the leading priests and teachers of religious law heard what Jesus had done, they began planning how to kill him. But they were afraid of him because the people were so amazed at his teaching.

[19]That evening Jesus and the disciples left* the city.

[20]The next morning as they passed by the fig tree he had cursed, the disciples noticed it had withered from the roots up. [21]Peter remembered what Jesus had said to the tree on the previous day and exclaimed, "Look, Rabbi! The fig tree you cursed has withered and died!"

[22]Then Jesus said to the disciples, "Have faith in God. [23]I tell you the truth, you can say to this mountain, 'May you be lifted up and thrown into the sea,' and it will happen. But you must really believe it will happen and have no doubt in your heart. [24]I tell you, you can pray for anything, and if you believe that you've received it, it will be yours. [25]But when you are praying, first forgive anyone you are holding a grudge against, so that your Father in heaven will forgive your sins, too.*"

NASB

27 They came again to Jerusalem. And as He was walking in the temple, the chief priests and the scribes and the elders came to Him, 28 and *began* saying to Him, "By what authority are You doing these things, or who gave You this authority to do these things?" 29 And Jesus said to them, "I will ask you one question, and you answer Me, and *then* I will tell you by what authority I do these things. 30 Was the baptism of John from heaven, or from men? Answer Me." 31 They *began* reasoning among themselves, saying, "If we say, 'From heaven,' He will say, 'Then why did you not believe him?' 32 But ªshall we say, 'From men'?"—they were afraid of the people, for everyone considered John to have been a real prophet. 33 Answering Jesus, they said, "We do not know." And Jesus said to them, "Nor ªwill I tell you by what authority I do these things."

11:15 ªLit *the doves* 11:16 ªLit *a vessel;* i.e. a receptacle or implement of any kind 11:17 ªLit *cave* 11:19 ªI.e. Jesus and His disciples 11:26 ªEarly mss do not contain this v 11:32 ªOr *if we say* 11:33 ªLit *do I tell*

NLT

27 Again they entered Jerusalem. As Jesus was walking through the Temple area, the leading priests, the teachers of religious law, and the elders came up to him. 28 They demanded, "By what authority are you doing all these things? Who gave you the right to do them?"

29 "I'll tell you by what authority I do these things if you answer one question," Jesus replied. 30 "Did John's authority to baptize come from heaven, or was it merely human? Answer me!"

31 They talked it over among themselves. "If we say it was from heaven, he will ask why we didn't believe John. 32 But do we dare say it was merely human?" For they were afraid of what the people would do, because everyone believed that John was a prophet. 33 So they finally replied, "We don't know."

And Jesus responded, "Then I won't tell you by what authority I do these things."

11:16 Or *from carrying merchandise through the Temple.* 11:17 Isa 56:7; Jer 7:11. 11:19 Greek *they left;* other manuscripts read *he left.* 11:25 Some manuscripts add verse 26, *But if you refuse to forgive, your Father in heaven will not forgive your sins.* Compare Matt 6:15.

When people think of Jesus Christ, they often imagine a man with stringy hair, a pale complexion, and a wispy build, moving about with faraway eyes and a passive, feeble demeanor. Or they think of Him as a combination of Mister Rogers, Clark Kent, and Santa Claus dressed in a robe and sandals. These notions usually come from a faulty understanding of the term "meek." Jesus described His temperament as "gentle and humble in heart" (Matt. 11:29). The King James Version of the Bible renders it "meek and lowly in heart."

While He was meek, that in no way means that He was weak. Jesus was commenting on his behavior and attitude, not his capability. Comparatively, a prize stallion could have a gentle spirit, making him a hospitable ride for inexperienced riders. The quality of meekness might be thought of as strength under control. Jesus was always fair and just; He was not always nice and soft-spoken.

A scene from C. S. Lewis's allegory *The Lion, the Witch and the Wardrobe* offers a wonderful illustration of Jesus' character. When the children enter the magical world of Narnia, a family of beavers gives them shelter from the cold along with a hot meal. During their visit, Mr. Beaver mentions Aslan, the King.

"Is—is he a man?" asked Lucy.
"Aslan a man!" said Mr. Beaver sternly. "Certainly not. I tell you he is the King of the wood and the son of the great Emperor-beyond-the-Sea. Don't you know who is the King of Beasts? Aslan is a lion—*the* Lion, the great Lion."
"Ooh!" said Susan. "I'd thought he was a man. Is he—quite safe? I shall feel rather nervous about meeting a lion."
"That you will, dearie, and no mistake," said Mrs. Beaver; "if there's anyone who can appear before Aslan without their knees knocking, they're either braver than most or else just silly."
"Then he isn't safe?" said Lucy.
"Safe?" said Mr. Beaver; "don't you hear what Mrs. Beaver tells you? Who said anything about safe? 'Course he isn't safe. But he's good. He's the King, I tell you."[29]

That distinction is crucial to understanding the full character of Jesus. It's also key to understanding His purpose for coming to earth the first time (called by scholars "the First Advent") and how it differs from His future return (known as "the Second Coming" or "the Second Advent"). The same gracious, merciful, forgiving, serving, sacrificial Savior of the First Advent will one day return in power as a warrior king to crush evil and to sit in judgment over all who align themselves with Satan by refusing His salvation. The Jesus of the two advents is the same God-man in both cases. Jesus is good, but all who oppose His goodness will find Him anything but "safe."

In this account from Mark's Gospel, we see a glimpse of Jesus as He will present Himself at the end of days. The disciples were about to see a side of Jesus they had not considered. Perhaps like us, they weren't prepared for the prospect of His terrifying wrath.

— 11:12-14 —

This segment of Mark's narrative is an example of the "sandwich structure" (see comments on 3:20-21; 5:25-27; 6:7-32). Note the progression:

11:12-14 Jesus curses the fruitless fig tree.

11:15-18 Jesus rebukes the faithless chief priests and scribes.

11:19-21 The disciples notice the withered fig tree.

Jesus allows this object lesson to serve as a backdrop to His discussion on faith and prayer.

The first scene follows the Triumphal Entry, in which Jesus rode into Jerusalem on a donkey in fulfillment of messianic prophecy. The chief priests and scribes—who represented the political and religious authority of the temple—had seen His symbolic ride, had heard the shouting of thousands calling Jesus their Messiah, and they understood His purpose in coming to Jerusalem. On that Sunday—celebrated today as Palm Sunday—Jesus merely visited the temple to take it in. On this day, however, Jesus intended to take command of the temple as His first official act as the recognized Messiah. This, too, would be a fulfillment of prophecy:

> "Behold, I am going to send My messenger, and he will clear the way before Me. And the Lord, whom you seek, will suddenly come to His temple; and the messenger of the covenant, in whom you delight, behold, He is coming," says the LORD of hosts. "But who can endure the day of His coming? And who can stand when He appears? For He is like a refiner's fire and like fullers' soap. He will sit as a smelter and purifier of silver, and He will purify the sons of Levi and refine them like gold and silver, so that they may present to the LORD offerings in righteousness." (Mal. 3:1-3)

So Jesus and His disciples left Bethany to walk down the Mount of Olives, across the Kidron Valley, and up the ravine to enter the temple complex. On the way, the group passed a fig tree "in leaf" (Mark 11:13), a phrase describing what people in the ancient Near East would have understood to be the time when fig trees produce small, edible buds. These buds eventually fall off and figs grow in their place. If no buds appear, however, then the plant is barren; it will produce no fruit.

Every farmer knows that a fruit tree that bears no fruit is completely worthless. It takes up valuable land and resources for no good purpose, which means it's better used for firewood. Therefore, Jesus pronounced judgment on the tree, saying, "May no one ever eat fruit from you again!" (11:14).

Bear in mind that the walk from Bethany to Jerusalem took less than forty-five minutes and the men had just left the breakfast table. The

Lord didn't curse the tree out of anger because He desperately needed a meal. He made this a visual aid for a lesson He would soon teach the disciples.

— 11:15-17 —

Soon after the fig tree incident, Jesus entered the temple. In former days, the temple had been the holiest place on earth. Inside a special chamber, behind a thick tapestry veil, a glowing, otherworldly light hovered over the ark of the covenant. This was a symbol of God's presence among the Hebrew people. One dared not desecrate this place, or one would face the very real possibility of immediate death.

When Jesus entered the temple, He challenged a long-standing practice sanctioned by the chief priests. Years earlier, a corrupt high priest by the name of Annas had been deposed by the Roman governor of Syria, but he continued to pull the strings of power from behind the scenes. This included a moneymaking scheme that raked in fortunes each festival season. The chief priests refused to accept any currency except shekels minted in Israel. Money changers within the temple precincts gladly exchanged any currency for Jewish shekels at an inflated rate and then pocketed the difference.

Jesus angrily confronted the corrupt merchants and money changers, overturned their tables, and refused to allow anyone to conduct any further business within the temple precincts. To accomplish this, Jesus had to become a physically imposing figure, someone perceived as dangerous and therefore not to be defied. While taking command, Jesus quoted from Isaiah and Jeremiah:

> "My house will be called a house of prayer for all the peoples." The Lord GOD, who gathers the dispersed of Israel, declares, "Yet others I will gather to them, to those already gathered." (Isa. 56:7-8)

> "Has this house, which is called by My name, become a den of robbers in your sight? Behold, I, even I, have seen it," declares the LORD. (Jer. 7:11)

— 11:18 —

None of this was lost on the corrupt chief priests. They understood who Jesus claimed to be, and they recognized His message from Old Testament Scripture. They weren't merely offended; they became sufficiently enraged to seek His destruction. They feared His influence because of the adoring multitudes, they feared the penetrating truth of His message, and they feared His ability to expose their sins. So they thought of ways to kill Him. The Greek word translated "destroy" is particularly violent. It was used in reference to the eternal torment of hell, to murder, and to the devastation caused by a storm.

— 11:19-21 —

According to Matthew, Mark, and Luke, Jesus didn't cleanse the temple and then leave; He healed and taught the people throughout the day (cf. Matt. 21:12-17; Luke 19:45-48). As dusk fell upon the temple that Monday evening, Jesus and His men made their way back to Bethany. As they passed the fig tree, they found it "withered" (Mark 11:20). The Greek term used here means "to stop a flow (such as sap or other liquid) in something and so cause dryness," "to become dry to the point of being immobilized," or "to be paralyzed."[30] This is a fitting description for the religious life of Israel, which had become chronically works-based and arrogantly xenophobic. Put bluntly, the temple, like the fig tree, had become good for nothing.

— 11:22-25 —

When the disciples noted the withered fig tree, Jesus responded with a lesson on faith and prayer (cf. Matt. 21:21-22). The fig tree represents Israel as God's covenant people; they gave the appearance of life and health yet failed to bear fruit. The nation became good for nothing because its spiritual and political leaders had long since placed their faith in something other than God. They relied upon treaties with stronger nations and political intrigue against their enemies. Consequently, they became like all their godless peers.

In just a few days, the nation would reject its Messiah, committing the ultimate act of faithlessness. In response, they would be cursed, never to bear fruit again.

The topic of faith naturally led to a discussion about prayer. Jesus placed three conditions on effective petitions before God, all having to do with trust. First, pray without doubting God's power or goodness to accomplish what you ask. Second, pray with an acceptance that God's power and goodness has accomplished what you ask. Third, pray with all grudges against others removed through forgiveness. The New Testament affirms throughout that disharmony with others will hinder our prayers and that forgiveness gives prayer wings (e.g., Matt. 18:15-20; 1 Pet. 3:7).

— 11:26 —

Almost all early manuscripts omit this verse, which suggests that it may have been inserted by later scribes as a parallel reference to Matthew 6:15 (see section on postscripts, page 402). While it was not part of Mark's original manuscript, it is nevertheless Scripture because it is original to Matthew's Gospel. The fact is, our refusal to extend the grace of forgiveness to others proves that we have not truly received the grace of forgiveness from God. If, however, we have received God's forgiveness, which comes with the transforming gift of His Holy Spirit, it is not possible for us to withhold forgiveness from others.

This becomes a warning to any in the church who nurture grudges: You might not be the Christian you think you are; so, Christian, forgive those who have sinned against you.

— 11:27-28 —

"The chief priests and the scribes" (11:27) represented the ruling authorities of the temple in Jerusalem. They also happened to be the same men who "began seeking how to destroy Him; for they were afraid of Him" (11:18). They challenged His authority to evict the money changers and merchants, as well as His authority to teach in the temple. He had not gone to their schools or come up through their ranks. He had not been sanctioned by a recognized cleric or appointed by a Roman official. They understood His face-value claim to be the Messiah, but they had refused to affirm Him. Moreover, they followed the paradigm of the world, in which clerics install kings, and no king can rule without the assent of the priestly class.

Their challenge also baited Jesus. To answer their question would be a de facto admission that He owed them answers. If He had offered any justification or explained Himself in any way, He would have played into their ploy to assert their own authority over Him.

— 11:29-32 —

Jesus didn't fall into their trap. Instead, He turned the tables, demanding they answer His question first. His question reveals a crucial difference in how He and the religious leaders viewed authority. They saw authority as something stemming from power. According to the world, "Might makes right." The one with the biggest army sets the agenda and makes the rules based on what that person decides is right. For the chief priests, authority came down to them from the Roman emperor, who appointed the high priest, who, in turn, appointed them.

For Jesus, authority stems from truth. God is truth. He is the Author of truth, so a person is authoritative only to the extent of being aligned with God. What is more, God is omnipotent—the ultimate power—with whom no one compares, not even the emperor.

Jesus asked the rulers of the temple to answer a simple question: Was the baptism of John by God's order, or was it the invention of a mere man? The question goes to the issue of truth. If they acknowledged John's ministry as genuinely God-ordained, they would have to explain why they opposed him, and why they assented to his execution by Herod Antipas. Moreover, they would have to agree with John that Jesus is the Messiah. John the Baptizer was the one who said, "Behold, the Lamb of God who takes away the sin of the world" (John 1:29). He was the one who said, "After me One is coming who is mightier than I, and I am not fit to stoop down and untie the thong of His sandals. I baptized you with water; but He will baptize you with the Holy Spirit" (Mark 1:7-8). On the other hand, if the religious leaders denounced John's baptism as merely a grassroots movement of human origin, they would stand in opposition to popular opinion, which affirmed John as a genuine prophet.

The question was simple to answer if one merely needed to state an opinion. But because the religious leaders thought only in terms of power, and because they had little regard for truth, they searched for a response that would give them the political advantage. Consequently, they faced a no-win scenario. They either had to affirm Jesus as Messiah or alienate the majority of rank-and-file Jews, who would almost certainly flee to Jesus, whom John had affirmed.

— 11:33 —

If the confrontation between Jesus and the religious authorities were a game of chess, this would have been checkmate. The chief priests and scribes refused to commit to a response, pretending not to know whether John was an authentic prophet of God. Because they would not fulfill their end of the bargain by answering Jesus' question, He declined to answer theirs.

While Jesus didn't play politics—He's God; He has no need of human approval—He nevertheless came out the political victor. He didn't appear pugnacious or disrespectful by flatly refusing to play His enemies' game; He made a reasonable request, which the priests and scribes ultimately refused to honor.

Mark concludes this encounter, but we will see that Jesus' confrontation with the illegitimate rulers of God's house was far from over. He would soon become the aggressor in their conflict—He would press the truth while they would resort to power.

APPLICATION: MARK 11:12-33
Strength and Truth

As I reflect on the principles emerging from this passage, my mind is drawn to these specific areas: the strength of Jesus, the corruption of the temple, and the resistance of the leaders.

Being strong is not the same thing as being arrogant.
Merriam-Webster's Collegiate Dictionary defines "arrogance" as "an attitude of superiority manifested in an overbearing manner or in presumptuous claims or assumptions."[31] Jesus stood His ground, asserted Himself boldly, refused to sugarcoat His words, and defended truth on the strength of His convictions, but He never treated anyone cruelly. He never modeled an overbearing manner. Although the chief priests and scribes deserved no respect, Jesus nevertheless treated them with respect.

Be careful about tolerance in the day in which we live. You'll be pushed to become tolerant to the point of compromising your own convictions for the sake of peace. By the time Jesus arrived in Jerusalem, the leaders of Israel looked and behaved more Roman than Hebrew. They had compromised their historic faith for the sake of treaties, and the temple had become a commercial enterprise—a secular institution with religious trappings, a fig tree with luscious green leaves and no fruit.

Operating within the realm of God's authority is not incompatible with true humility. Jesus asserted divine authority with humility and dignity. We mustn't become timid about asserting what we know to be truth for fear of appearing immodest. As G.K. Chesterton lamented, "We are on the road to producing a race of [people] too mentally modest to believe in the multiplication table."[32] I urge you, therefore, to stand up for what you believe. Stand firm. Stand strong. When you know the truth, stand for the truth. Don't give in. Don't let it go. However, in the process, guard against arrogance.

*Confronting religious corruption is no less dangerous
than confronting political corruption.*

I would even go so far as to say that religious corruption is the more dangerous of the two. I need only point out the jihad of Muslim extremists, who savagely commit murder and genocide in the name of Allah. Jesus confronted corrupt, power-hungry sociopaths masquerading as clerics.

A powerful extrabiblical example of this can be seen in the Reformation stand of Martin Luther, a Roman Catholic monk who confronted the corruption of the Vatican. He published his indictment of church abuses to begin a dialogue; he never planned to start a movement. When the Church responded with threats, he eventually wrote a letter to the pope stating, "The Roman church, once the holiest of all, has become the most licentious den of thieves, the most shameless of all brothels, the kingdom of sin, death, and hell. It is so bad that even Antichrist himself, if he should come, could think of nothing to add to its wickedness."[33] He didn't intend this to insult; these were his honest convictions.

I urge you to keep your thinking straight about the church. Watch for corruption. Guard it against merchandising and marketing. That's never the purpose of the place of worship. It is to be a house of prayer, a place of preaching, a place of great music, and a place of meaningful meditation, dialogue, and fellowship with other believers. Corruption has no place in a setting like that.

*Refusing to face the truth will not shield
you from the impact of the truth.*

The religious leaders wouldn't answer Jesus' question about John the Baptizer (11:30), but their "we do not know" (11:33) revealed their guilt. From a human perspective, they had the advantage of power over Jesus, and they eventually used it to kill Him. They won a clear victory over truth—in the short term. Their blissful, self-imposed ignorance ended with the siege of Jerusalem in AD 70 and its utter destruction in AD 135. Of course, by that time, these men had already entered eternity to face God, who forcefully reintroduced them to the truth they had tried to ignore.

My urgent exhortation here is this: Face the truth. Whenever you perceive God's Word speaking to you, embrace the message, even if it hurts. You will face the truth at one time or another. That much is guaranteed.

A Violent and Bloody Parable
MARK 12:1-12

NASB

¹And He began to speak to them in parables: "A man PLANTED A VINEYARD AND PUT A ᵃWALL AROUND IT, AND DUG A VAT UNDER THE WINE PRESS AND BUILT A TOWER, and rented it out to ᵇvine-growers and went on a journey. ²At the *harvest* time he sent a slave to the vine-growers, in order to receive *some* of the produce of the vineyard from the vine-growers. ³They took him, and beat him and sent him away empty-handed. ⁴Again he sent them another slave, and they wounded him in the head, and treated him shamefully. ⁵And he sent another, and that one they killed; and *so with* many others, beating some and killing others. ⁶He had one more *to send,* a beloved son; he sent him last *of all* to them, saying, 'They will respect my son.' ⁷But those vine-growers said to one another, 'This is the heir; come, let us kill him, and the inheritance will be ours!' ⁸They took him, and killed him and threw him out of the vineyard. ⁹What will the ᵃowner of the vineyard do? He will come and destroy the vine-growers, and will give the vineyard to others. ¹⁰Have you not even read this Scripture:

'THE STONE WHICH THE BUILDERS REJECTED,
THIS BECAME THE CHIEF CORNER *stone;*
¹¹ THIS CAME ABOUT FROM THE LORD,
AND IT IS MARVELOUS IN OUR EYES'?"

¹²And they were seeking to seize Him, and *yet* they feared the ᵃpeople, for they understood that He spoke the parable against them. And *so* they left Him and went away.

12:1 ᵃOr *fence* ᵇOr *tenant farmers,* also vv 2, 7, 9
12:9 ᵃLit *lord*   12:12 ᵃLit *crowd*

NLT

¹Then Jesus began teaching them with stories: "A man planted a vineyard. He built a wall around it, dug a pit for pressing out the grape juice, and built a lookout tower. Then he leased the vineyard to tenant farmers and moved to another country. ²At the time of the grape harvest, he sent one of his servants to collect his share of the crop. ³But the farmers grabbed the servant, beat him up, and sent him back empty-handed. ⁴The owner then sent another servant, but they insulted him and beat him over the head. ⁵The next servant he sent was killed. Others he sent were either beaten or killed, ⁶until there was only one left—his son whom he loved dearly. The owner finally sent him, thinking, 'Surely they will respect my son.'

⁷"But the tenant farmers said to one another, 'Here comes the heir to this estate. Let's kill him and get the estate for ourselves!' ⁸So they grabbed him and murdered him and threw his body out of the vineyard.

⁹"What do you suppose the owner of the vineyard will do?" Jesus asked. "I'll tell you—he will come and kill those farmers and lease the vineyard to others. ¹⁰Didn't you ever read this in the Scriptures?

'The stone that the builders rejected
has now become the cornerstone.
¹¹ This is the LORD's doing,
and it is wonderful to see.'*"

¹²The religious leaders* wanted to arrest Jesus because they realized he was telling the story against them—they were the wicked farmers. But they were afraid of the crowd, so they left him and went away.

12:10-11 Ps 118:22-23.   12:12 Greek *They.*

Every public speaker desires to speak clearly and well. This is especially critical for preachers, who must show that abstract principles of theology have practical application for real life. It's hard work. Clear communication doesn't happen automatically. It's a result of thinking through the message with some imagination and often making use of stories. After all, just dumping a pile of information into people's heads isn't clear communication. Handing them an outline won't help matters much either; an outline is no more a message than a menu is a meal. Information goes in one ear and out the other unless we give the listener's brain a reason to retain our message.

As I observe how Jesus communicated His message, I find Him using stories often to make difficult truths accessible and to make His messages stick. There's something about stories that disarms us. They make us want to listen. And they can convey complex truths clearly. The most common kind of story in the New Testament is the parable (see the feature on parables, page 110).

Warren Wiersbe describes the power of the parable this way:

A parable starts off as a *picture* that is familiar to the listeners. But as you carefully consider the picture, it becomes a *mirror* in which you see yourself, and many people do not like to see themselves. This explains why some of our Lord's listeners became angry when they heard His parables, and even tried to kill Him. But if we see ourselves as needy sinners and ask for help, then the mirror becomes a *window* through which we see God and His grace.[34]

Simply put, a parable is an illustration that paints a picture in the imagination using the listener's own experiences. As Jesus continued to teach in the temple, He would have to make His lessons especially clear and impactful because He spoke to a mixed audience. In addition to His devoted followers, there gathered a large number of people who had little exposure to the rabbi from upper Galilee. They came to hear Him with heads full of facts mixed with fiction and folklore. He also had to contend with a sizable number of enemies—chief priests and scribes—who wanted to discredit Him if possible, or kill Him if necessary.

The time had come for Him to explain His mission as the Messiah and to declare Himself the Son of God. In so doing, He would also be issuing a warning to the temple leadership that God's patience with their lack of repentance and refusal of the Messiah would not last forever. To get His message across clearly before His enemies could cut Him off,

Jesus used an emotionally charged parable using images and themes no Jew could misinterpret.

— 12:1 —

Jesus often drew upon familiar images to teach His largely agrarian audience: shepherd and sheep, sower and seed, wine and wineskins, master and servants. Of all His metaphors, none resonated in the Hebrew heart more profoundly than the relationship of the vinedresser to his vineyard. For centuries, Israel's prophets had drawn upon this image to describe God's special care for His covenant nation, Israel (Ps. 80:8-16; Isa. 5:1-7).

Drawing upon this rich cultural imagery, Jesus told the story of a vineyard (Israel), its owner (God), and tenant farmers (the religious leaders). The owner planted the vineyard with care, took pains to protect it from intruders, and even constructed a place to crush the grapes and collect the juice so that the farmers would have no excuse for not harvesting the fruit of the vines.

By now, every Jew within earshot was leaning forward.

— 12:2-3 —

The NASB inserts the word "harvest" (12:2; note the italic font) because the Greek phrase is simply "at the time," using the term *kairos* [2540], which means "a point of time," "a defined moment for an event," or "a special time." In this case, the owner waited three full years as required by Mosaic Law:

> "When you enter the land and plant all kinds of trees for food, then you shall count their fruit as forbidden. Three years it shall be forbidden to you; it shall not be eaten. But in the fourth year all its fruit shall be holy, an offering of praise to the LORD. In the fifth year you are to eat of its fruit, that its yield may increase for you; I am the LORD your God." (Lev. 19:23-25)

At the right time, the owner sent a slave to receive the produce, all of which would be offered to God as a sacrifice of thanksgiving. As the story unfolded, the Lord's audience would recognize the "slave" as one of God's Old Testament prophets. The tenant farmers beat the slave and ran him off, presumably to keep the produce for themselves.

— 12:4-5 —

Jesus' story shows remarkable patience on the part of the vineyard owner. Most anyone in the audience would have gathered a posse and paid a visit to the tenant farmers . . . Mafia-style. Instead, he sent one slave after another to collect his due. Some were beaten, others killed.

By now the audience could see clearly the parallel to the prophets of old, who had come to Israel's political and religious leaders with divine warnings only to face brutal persecution or merciless martyrdom (not unlike what the Christians faced in Rome).

— 12:6-8 —

Finally, the vineyard owner sent his own son, thinking the tenant farmers would show him respect and turn over the produce. The son is "beloved" (12:6), which raises the stakes for the owner and adds powerful drama to the story. The term also draws our attention back to earlier events. This Greek word, *agapētos* [27], appears in Mark's narrative only two other times: at Jesus' baptism and His transfiguration.

> Immediately coming up out of the water, He saw the heavens opening, and the Spirit like a dove descending upon Him; and a voice came out of the heavens: "You are My beloved Son, in You I am well-pleased." (1:10-11)

> Then a cloud formed, overshadowing them, and a voice came out of the cloud, "This is My beloved Son, listen to Him!" (9:7)

The verb rendered "respect" (*entrepō* [1788]; 12:6) means "to cause to turn (in shame)" or "to show deference to a person in recognition of special status."[35] But the tenant farmers showed outrageous hubris. They plotted to destroy the owner's son in order to inherit the vineyard in his place! This was a logical and legal impossibility. Murderers do not inherit the estates of the people they kill. Murderers inherit only the penalty of murder: execution by stoning. Their over-the-top ambition made them criminally insane.

They seized the son, killed him, and threw his body out of the vineyard.

— 12:9-11 —

Jesus undoubtedly saw the outrage intensifying in His audience. At the climax of the drama, He asked what they thought the owner would do. Everyone who had a son would have stood on tiptoe and called for the most painful death imaginable for the despicable tenant farmers.

There's irony in Jesus' choice of terms for the farmers' fate. "Kill" (12:7-8) would be appropriate. "Punish" would be legally accurate. But "destroy" recalls the plans of the Pharisees (3:6) and the temple authorities (11:18). In this case, "destroy" has the sense of condemnation to eternal torment (cf. 1:24). The Greek term (*apollymi* [622]) carries the sense of "loss" or being forever "lost."

After the faithless tenant farmers were destroyed, the owner would give the vineyard to others, a cryptic reference to the church. Jews would have shuddered at the prospect of God giving their inheritance to others; they correctly understood God's covenant with Abraham to be unconditional and irrevocable. They couldn't foresee, however, an intervening period in which "others" would become stewards of God's Word and redemptive plan for the world. Moreover, they could not have anticipated how the Messiah and His church would position Israel to receive all the covenant promises . . . eventually.

Just in case anyone in the audience wasn't paying attention, Jesus quoted a messianic psalm predicting the Messiah's rejection, God's saving grace, and His eventual position of supreme authority:

> The stone which the builders rejected
> Has become the chief corner stone.
> This is the LORD's doing;
> It is marvelous in our eyes.
> This is the day which the LORD has made;
> Let us rejoice and be glad in it. (Ps. 118:22-24)

The psalm predicts the rejected Messiah's vindication. More specifically, the word "rejected" here means "to deem worthless or inauthentic by means of testing." The rejected stone ultimately becomes the most important stone in the whole structure. When laying a stone foundation, the cornerstone becomes the reference by which every other stone is measured and set.

— 12:12 —

The temple rulers knew which part they played in the Lord's violent and bloody parable. They failed to discredit Jesus in public, so they determined to "seize" Him privately and make Him simply disappear—despite the clear warning of the parable. Like the criminally insane tenant farmers, the temple rulers really believed that killing Jesus would allow them to inherit for themselves what God had merely given them to steward on His behalf. Only the fear of losing the support of the people prevented them from seizing the Son, killing Him, and throwing His body out of the temple (cf. 12:8).

APPLICATION: MARK 12:1-12

The End of Grace

Many don't realize that the grace of God has limits. He is "merciful and gracious, slow to anger and abundant in lovingkindness and truth" (Ps. 86:15), but His grace is not endless. With this parable, Jesus not only identified Himself as the Messiah for the sake of seekers and predicted His future for the sake of posterity, but He also served notice to the rebels holding the temple that God's patience had reached its end. Israel had beaten and killed many prophets, and now the son of the vineyard owner stood in their midst. This was the last of God's gracious gestures.

Perhaps your heart doesn't resonate with this parable; you wouldn't beat God's messengers and you wouldn't kill His Son. So, let me use another parable to illustrate the limits of grace.

Jesus told the story of a wealthy man with a golden touch, a man who prospered at every turn (Luke 12:16-21). A French painter, inspired by this story, took up his brushes and palette and painted the rich man sitting at his desk surrounded by little bags of money packed with shekels. Outside the figure's window, a bumper crop grows lush and green. The corn is popping. The grain has come to large, golden heads. And he wears a contented smile that says, "This is all mine!" You can sense his plans for building another barn, moving into a larger house, and buying more land.

The painter decided the painting needed more. He turned it over and, on the underside of the canvas, he painted the picture again. Same desk, same man, same bags of money, same window, same crops. But the long, bony fingers of the death angel reach for him, and the angel's lips are pursed, saying, "Fool. Fool. This night your soul will be required of you" (see Luke 12:20).

One day—perhaps sooner than you expect—death will transport you from this realm to the courtroom of heaven, where you must give an account of your life. By then, it will be too late for repentance. The time for receiving forgiveness will have passed. Grace will have already reached its end. If you refused the gift of eternal life throughout your lifetime, judgment awaits you in eternity.

Jesus warned, "The time is fulfilled, and the kingdom of God is at hand; repent and believe in the gospel" (Mark 1:15). Heed His call now. Today could be nearer to the end of grace for you than you ever imagined.

Questions, Questions, Questions
MARK 12:13-44

NASB

¹³Then they sent some of the Pharisees and Herodians to Him in order to trap Him in a statement. ¹⁴They came and said to Him, "Teacher, we know that You are truthful and ᵃdefer to no one; for You are not partial to any, but teach the way of God in truth. Is it ᵇlawful to pay a poll-tax to Caesar, or not? ¹⁵Shall we pay or shall we not pay?" But He, knowing their hypocrisy, said to them, "Why are you testing Me? Bring Me a ᵃdenarius to look at." ¹⁶They brought *one*. And He said to them, "Whose likeness and inscription is this?" And they said to Him, "Caesar's." ¹⁷And Jesus said to them, "Render to Caesar the things that are Caesar's, and to God the things that are God's." And they ᵃwere amazed at Him.

¹⁸*Some* Sadducees (who say that there is no resurrection) came to Jesus, and *began* questioning Him, saying, ¹⁹"Teacher, Moses wrote for us that IF A MAN'S BROTHER DIES and leaves behind a wife AND LEAVES NO CHILD, HIS BROTHER SHOULD ᵃMARRY THE WIFE AND RAISE UP CHILDREN TO HIS BROTHER. ²⁰There were seven brothers; and the first took a wife, and died leaving no children. ²¹The second one ᵃmarried her, and died leaving behind no children; and the third likewise; ²²and *so* ᵃall seven left no children. Last of all the woman died also. ²³In the resurrection, ᵃwhen they rise again, which one's wife will she be? For ᵇall seven had married her." ²⁴Jesus said to them, "Is this not the reason you are mistaken, that you do not ᵃunderstand the Scriptures or the power

NLT

¹³Later the leaders sent some Pharisees and supporters of Herod to trap Jesus into saying something for which he could be arrested. ¹⁴"Teacher," they said, "we know how honest you are. You are impartial and don't play favorites. You teach the way of God truthfully. Now tell us—is it right to pay taxes to Caesar or not? ¹⁵Should we pay them, or shouldn't we?"

Jesus saw through their hypocrisy and said, "Why are you trying to trap me? Show me a Roman coin,* and I'll tell you." ¹⁶When they handed it to him, he asked, "Whose picture and title are stamped on it?"

"Caesar's," they replied.

¹⁷"Well, then," Jesus said, "give to Caesar what belongs to Caesar, and give to God what belongs to God."

His reply completely amazed them.

¹⁸Then Jesus was approached by some Sadducees—religious leaders who say there is no resurrection from the dead. They posed this question: ¹⁹"Teacher, Moses gave us a law that if a man dies, leaving a wife without children, his brother should marry the widow and have a child who will carry on the brother's name.* ²⁰Well, suppose there were seven brothers. The oldest one married and then died without children. ²¹So the second brother married the widow, but he also died without children. Then the third brother married her. ²²This continued with all seven of them, and still there were no children. Last of all, the woman also died. ²³So tell us, whose wife will she be in the resurrection? For all seven were married to her."

²⁴Jesus replied, "Your mistake is that you don't know the Scriptures, and you don't know the power of

of God? 25 For when they rise from the dead, they neither marry nor are given in marriage, but are like angels in heaven. 26 But ªregarding the fact that the dead rise again, have you not read in the book of Moses, in the *passage* about *the burning* bush, how God spoke to him, saying, 'I AM THE GOD OF ABRAHAM, AND THE GOD OF ISAAC, AND THE GOD OF JACOB'? 27 He is not the God ªof the dead, but of the living; you are greatly mistaken."

28 One of the scribes came and heard them arguing, and recognizing that He had answered them well, asked Him, "What commandment is the ªforemost of all?" 29 Jesus answered, "The foremost is, 'HEAR, O ISRAEL! THE LORD OUR GOD IS ONE LORD; 30 AND YOU SHALL LOVE THE LORD YOUR GOD WITH ALL YOUR HEART, AND WITH ALL YOUR SOUL, AND WITH ALL YOUR MIND, AND WITH ALL YOUR STRENGTH.' 31 The second is this, 'YOU SHALL LOVE YOUR NEIGHBOR AS YOURSELF.' There is no other commandment greater than these." 32 The scribe said to Him, "Right, Teacher; You have truly stated that HE IS ONE, AND THERE IS NO ONE ELSE BESIDES HIM; 33 AND TO LOVE HIM WITH ALL THE HEART AND WITH ALL THE UNDERSTANDING AND WITH ALL THE STRENGTH, AND TO LOVE ONE'S NEIGHBOR AS HIMSELF, is much more than all burnt offerings and sacrifices." 34 When Jesus saw that he had answered intelligently, He said to him, "You are not far from the kingdom of God." After that, no one would venture to ask Him any more questions.

35 And Jesus *began* to say, as He taught in the temple, "How *is it that* the scribes say that ªthe Christ is the

God. 25 For when the dead rise, they will neither marry nor be given in marriage. In this respect they will be like the angels in heaven.

26 "But now, as to whether the dead will be raised—haven't you ever read about this in the writings of Moses, in the story of the burning bush? Long after Abraham, Isaac, and Jacob had died, God said to Moses,* 'I am the God of Abraham, the God of Isaac, and the God of Jacob.'* 27 So he is the God of the living, not the dead. You have made a serious error."

28 One of the teachers of religious law was standing there listening to the debate. He realized that Jesus had answered well, so he asked, "Of all the commandments, which is the most important?"

29 Jesus replied, "The most important commandment is this: 'Listen, O Israel! The LORD our God is the one and only LORD. 30 And you must love the LORD your God with all your heart, all your soul, all your mind, and all your strength.'* 31 The second is equally important: 'Love your neighbor as yourself.'* No other commandment is greater than these."

32 The teacher of religious law replied, "Well said, Teacher. You have spoken the truth by saying that there is only one God and no other. 33 And I know it is important to love him with all my heart and all my understanding and all my strength, and to love my neighbor as myself. This is more important than to offer all of the burnt offerings and sacrifices required in the law."

34 Realizing how much the man understood, Jesus said to him, "You are not far from the Kingdom of God." And after that, no one dared to ask him any more questions.

35 Later, as Jesus was teaching the people in the Temple, he asked, "Why do the teachers of religious law claim that the Messiah is the son

son of David? ³⁶David himself said ªin the Holy Spirit,

'THE LORD SAID TO MY LORD,
"SIT AT MY RIGHT HAND,
UNTIL I PUT YOUR ENEMIES
BENEATH YOUR FEET."'

³⁷David himself calls Him 'Lord'; so in what sense is He his son?" And the large crowd ªenjoyed listening to Him.

³⁸In His teaching He was saying: "Beware of the scribes who like to walk around in long robes, and *like* respectful greetings in the market places, ³⁹and chief seats in the synagogues and places of honor at banquets, ⁴⁰who devour widows' houses, and for appearance's sake offer long prayers; these will receive greater condemnation."

⁴¹And He sat down opposite the treasury, and *began* observing how the people were putting ªmoney into the treasury; and many rich people were putting in large sums. ⁴²A poor widow came and put in two ªsmall copper coins, which amount to a ᵇcent. ⁴³Calling His disciples to Him, He said to them, "Truly I say to you, this poor widow put in more than all ªthe contributors to the treasury; ⁴⁴for they all put in out of their ªsurplus, but she, out of her poverty, put in all she owned, ᵇall she had to live on."

12:14 ªLit *it is not a concern to You about anyone;* i.e. You do not seek anyone's favor ᵇOr *permissible* 12:15 ªThe denarius was a day's wages 12:17 ªOr *were greatly marveling* 12:19 ªLit *take* 12:21 ªLit *took* 12:22 ªLit *the seven* 12:23 ªEarly mss do not contain *when they rise again* ᵇLit *the seven* 12:24 ªOr *know* 12:26 ªLit *concerning the dead, that they rise* 12:27 ªOr *of corpses* 12:28 ªOr *first* 12:35 ªI.e. the Messiah 12:36 ªOr *by* 12:37 ªLit *was gladly hearing Him* 12:41 ªI.e. copper coins 12:42 ªGr *lepta* ᵇGr *quadrans;* i.e. 1/64 of a denarius 12:43 ªLit *those who were putting in* 12:44 ªOr *abundance* ᵇLit *her whole livelihood*

of David? ³⁶For David himself, speaking under the inspiration of the Holy Spirit, said,

'The LORD said to my Lord,
Sit in the place of honor at my right hand
until I humble your enemies beneath your feet.'*

³⁷Since David himself called the Messiah 'my Lord,' how can the Messiah be his son?" The large crowd listened to him with great delight.

³⁸Jesus also taught: "Beware of these teachers of religious law! For they like to parade around in flowing robes and receive respectful greetings as they walk in the market-places. ³⁹And how they love the seats of honor in the synagogues and the head table at banquets. ⁴⁰Yet they shamelessly cheat widows out of their property and then pretend to be pious by making long prayers in public. Because of this, they will be more severely punished."

⁴¹Jesus sat down near the collection box in the Temple and watched as the crowds dropped in their money. Many rich people put in large amounts. ⁴²Then a poor widow came and dropped in two small coins.*

⁴³Jesus called his disciples to him and said, "I tell you the truth, this poor widow has given more than all the others who are making contributions. ⁴⁴For they gave a tiny part of their surplus, but she, poor as she is, has given everything she had to live on."

12:15 Greek *a denarius.* 12:19 See Deut 25:5-6. 12:26a Greek *in the story of the bush? God said to him.* 12:26b Exod 3:6. 12:29-30 Deut 6:4-5. 12:31 Lev 19:18. 12:36 Ps 110:1. 12:42 Greek *two lepta, which is a kodrantes* [i.e., a quadrans].

Questions are an indispensable part of the teaching-and-learning process. I often hear from professors that they can assess students better by the questions they ask than by the answers they give. Questions from students allow teachers to fill in gaps in their learning, so confident teachers always open the floor for questions. And wise teachers know how to use questions as a means of helping students think for themselves.

Not all classroom queries advance learning, however. I have been in classes where some wise guy decided he wanted to stump the teacher with pointless questions or waste everybody's time with a fruitless debate. This might have been Jesus' experience while teaching in the temple were He not the source of divine wisdom.

The chief priests and scribes needed to discredit the man claiming to be the Messiah or else lose their hold on power. So they sent people to mingle with the crowds, pretend to be seekers, and attempt to catch Jesus in a theological or political trap. Most of their questions were carefully designed to drive a wedge between Jesus and the multitudes hanging on His every word. But in each case, Jesus answered with wisdom that won the trust of sincere hearts and reinforced His identity as the Messiah. In turn, He began to ask penetrating questions that left the Pharisees, Sadducees, and scribes with reason to reconsider their respective identities before God.

— 12:13 —

According to this brief verse, no fewer than five Jewish factions conspired to undermine Jesus' claim to be the Messiah of Israel. "They" refers to the chief priests, scribes, and elders mentioned in 11:27. These men sent Pharisees and Herodians to trap Jesus. This collection of splintered groups comprised the Sanhedrin, a governing body of seventy Jewish statesmen. The Sanhedrin was, for Israel, the equivalent of a combined parliament and supreme court. And, like in modern political bodies, power in the Sanhedrin was shared by two sharply opposing parties: the aristocratic Sadducees and the popular Pharisees.

Normally these groups were at each other's throats, but now they shared a common threat to their power, so they banded together as partners in crime to eliminate Jesus.

— 12:14-15 —

"They" now refers to the Pharisees and Herodians. Because the Pharisees held themselves to the highest standards of Jewish Law and advocated complete separation from all Gentile influence, they enjoyed the respect and admiration of the Jewish masses. The Herodians were either descendants of Herod the Great or served the royal family in some capacity. They derived their power from participation in the

Roman royal court, much like the barons, dukes, and earls of medieval England. For example, Herod Agrippa I was a playmate of Emperor Claudius while attending school in Rome. This association gave the Herodians immense power at the expense of Israel's self-respect.

So the superreligious Pharisees and the ultra-Romanized Herodians approached Jesus with a carefully contrived flattery. They pretended to honor Him as a truthful and impartial teacher so the watching multitude would not suspect their bad intentions. Furthermore, by calling Him impartial, they isolated Him politically so the people wouldn't know how to categorize Him. They asked, "Is it lawful to pay a poll-tax to Caesar, or not?" (12:14).

"Lawful" in this context means an action that is appropriate or morally permissible within Jewish Law. The "poll-tax" refers to the census demanded of Jews, which had begun a few years after the death of Herod the Great. This tax, based on a head count of the entire Roman Empire, was extremely divisive in Israel because participating was tantamount to declaring oneself a subject of Rome instead of God (cf. Acts 5:37). Both factions saw the question as a no-win for Jesus. A yes put Him on the side of the Herodians, who derived wealth and power from their royal connections in Rome. A no would have affirmed the position of the Pharisees, who advocated complete separation from all Gentiles, especially Romans.

Jesus didn't see the world from their limited, horizontal, secular perspective. Therefore, He objected to how they framed the issue. Both factions saw the poll-tax issue as a question of loyalty to Rome or to the kingdom of God. Rather than play into their ploy, Jesus called them on their "test"—hypocrisy fools humanity, but never the Lord Jesus. He asked for a Roman coin called a denarius.

— 12:16-17 —

This coin, minted by the Romans, bore the image of Emperor Tiberius, along with the inscription "TI CAESAR DIVI-AVG F AVGVSTVS," or "Tiberius Caesar, Augustus, son of Divine Augustus."

Jesus' response accepts as a sad fact that we live in a difficult tension between the realities of existing in a fallen world and the upward call of God's kingdom. Earthly governments exist within the sovereign plan of God, and He expects us to submit to their authority when their laws do not require us to violate His moral standard. God does not ask us to choose between our earthly government and His kingdom; He calls us to choose which will rule our hearts—wealth or righteousness.

Classical Numismatic Group, Inc./cngcoins.com

When Jesus is questioned about taxes in Mark 12:13-17, He is handed a Roman coin. It was likely a coin that looked like this one that bears an image of Tiberius Caesar, who was the emperor of Rome during Jesus' ministry.

Until Christ returns, we need money, but we must not serve it. We obey governing authorities, but we do not serve them when their law conflicts with God's.

At this, the enemies of Jesus left the scene feeling "amazed" (12:17). They undoubtedly marveled at His ability to confound their most ingenious strategies, but more than that, they were amazed by His ability to reframe their perspectives in spite of their resistance.

— 12:18-23 —

At the time of Jesus, Jews had vague notions of an afterlife (Job 14:14; Ps. 17:15) and even a resurrection (Job 19:26), but for the most part, they referred to all experiences beyond death as Sheol, an existence as mysterious as the ocean depths. The Pharisees had developed a rich doctrine of rewards and punishments in the hereafter, but their political rivals, the Sadducees, believed the soul perished with the body. According to them, God punished the wicked and rewarded the righteous in this life . . . and then sent them to the grave. Naturally, rich people would want to see divine justice this way!

The question devised by the Sadducees assumed for the sake of argument that an afterlife exists. They then proposed a ridiculous yet plausible circumstance they hoped would demonstrate the absurdity of Jesus' teaching on the kingdom of God as eternal and otherworldly. Their hypothetical circumstance involved the Jewish custom of levirate marriage. According to this custom, if a man died and his widow had been left without children, an eligible relative—usually a brother of the dead husband—was to marry her, father children, and then rear them as heirs of the dead man's estate (Deut. 25:5-6). They accepted

Civil Disobedience

MARK 12:17

I hang around with conservative Christians, so I sometimes need to clarify some things related to government rule. Some ultraconservative elements come dangerously close to sedition; due to their disdain for certain presidents and officials, some would love to see the government overthrown. The fact is, they will never like any human government because it's always going to be corrupt in some way or another.

So, when is insurrection or outright defiance against a government appropriate? After all, no Christian should ever support anarchy. We're not to be engaged in burning buildings, or taking justice into our own hands, or harming people we oppose politically or socially. However, there are three times when it is right to resist:

1. When a law commands us to violate a command of God. When told to keep silent about the resurrection of Jesus, the apostles said to their government officials, "Whether it is right in the sight of God to give heed to you rather than to God, you be the judge; for we cannot stop speaking about what we have seen and heard" (Acts 4:19-20). And they were beaten for their disobedience.

2. When an authority commits immoral or unethical acts. It is not enough to refuse participation when a government harms innocent people. We must actively intervene on behalf of victims of institutionalized abuse.

3. When an authority compels us to compromise our Christian convictions. This can become awfully subjective, but we must not participate in or tolerate any act that violates our Spirit-guided conscience.

Jesus acknowledged the sovereignty of God and His authority over us when He tells us to render to God the things that are God's. He did not, however, advocate the overthrow of the government merely because it was not God's kingdom. The Lord ordains government authority to keep humanity from tearing itself apart.

THE SADDUCEES

MARK 12:18-27

The Sadducees were a peculiar faction of Jews. Conservative by Jewish standards—some would say conveniently so—they accepted no teaching or tradition beyond what could be found in the Pentateuch, the first five books of the Old Testament and the only Scripture to have come from the hand of Moses.[36] Based on their reading of these Scriptures, they did not believe in life after death or resurrection or angels or spirits.

Sadducees resembled the deists of the eighteenth century—vehemently skeptical of anything supernatural and fatalistic to the core. They believed God to be ineffably remote, leaving each person free to craft his or her own fate with no prospect of eternal reward or punishment. Therefore, the Sadducees believed that punishment for sin was the duty of the people and that such punishment should be both merciless and severe.[37] They believed each person had free will; therefore, each was responsible for the events of his or her life, including sickness, poverty, misfortune, and even manner of death. The Jewish historian Josephus described the Sadducees as contentious with everyone, including one another, even thinking it "an instance of virtue to dispute with those teachers of philosophy whom they frequent."[38]

this custom as divinely ordained because of its appearance in the Pentateuch (the first five books of the Old Testament).

In the scenario, one brother after another dies, leaving the poor widow grief stricken seven times over and still childless. When the righteous are raised from the dead to live in God's kingdom, with whom will she live as wife? In their minds, the absurdity of the question proves the absurdity of resurrection.

— 12:24-27 —

Jesus answered their question in two stages. First, He explained that life in the kingdom of God will not be the same kind of existence we know on this side of the grave (12:24-25). He then demonstrated that Moses did, in the Pentateuch, affirm the doctrine of life after death (12:26-27).

The Sadducees assumed that an afterlife would simply replicate the kind of life we know now. Jesus clarified that everything will be changed. People get married as part of God's plan to fill the earth, but in heaven, they will be like the angels: nonsexual, immortal, and completely devoted to God. Of course, this comparison to angels affirmed another doctrine the Sadducees rejected.

Jesus went on to demonstrate from the Pentateuch that Moses assumed a resurrection in his writings. He quoted Exodus 3:6, in which God tells Moses, "I am the God of your father, the God of Abraham, the God of Isaac, and the God of Jacob." God used the present tense, not the past tense, indicating that He is now, and forever will be, the God of these Hebrew patriarchs.

The Lord summed up His assessment of the Sadducees' theology by calling them "mistaken" (Mark 12:27), which is a translation of the Greek word *planaō* [4105]. Our word for "planet" is related to this term, which means "to proceed without a sense of proper direction," "go astray," "be misled," or "wander about aimlessly."[39] This was a stinging indictment of the men who supposedly led Israel in spiritual matters. The Sadducees occupied the top positions in the temple.

— 12:28-31 —

Not far away from all of this, a man listened to the dialogue with great interest. He was a scribe, a man who devoted himself to copying the Scriptures by hand with meticulous care. He spent many hours each day reading and writing the Word of God, which gave him ample time to memorize passages and think about them. Consequently, scribes like him were widely regarded as experts on the Law and its interpretation. Of all the clerics in the temple, scribes should have been the most biblical in their theology. Unfortunately, they were as guilty of twisting the sacred text to suit their purposes as the Sadducees and Herodians—sometimes even more so.

This particular scribe approached Jesus with an open mind and an astute question. He wanted Jesus' opinion on which of the Old Testament commandments was *prōtos* [4413], "first" (12:28-29). This could mean "greatest," but it's unlikely. The NASB wisely renders it "foremost" for reasons the Lord explains. Jesus quoted the Shema. *Shema* is the Hebrew term for "hear," the first word in the great Hebrew confession of faith: "Hear, O Israel! The LORD is our God, the LORD is one! You shall love the LORD your God with all your heart and with all your soul and with all your might" (Deut. 6:4-5).

He then quoted from Leviticus 19:18, the last part of which reads, "You shall love your neighbor as yourself; I am the LORD." Jesus saw these two commandments like teeth in gears, meshing to drive Israel toward the blessings God had promised to Abraham's descendants. He saw the vertical and horizontal components of divine grace, of which God's people are to be stewards.

— **12:32-34** —

For the first and only time in any of the Gospels, a religious leader of Israel calls Jesus "right" or "correct." In affirming Jesus, the scribe had found a kindred spirit, and he quoted Scripture right back at Him (cf. Deut. 4:35; 6:5; Lev. 19:18). These commandments are "foremost" (not merely "greatest") because—in a manner of speaking—they give birth to all the others. Perhaps looking over his shoulder at the smoke rising from the altar, the scribe declared that sacrifices and worship mean nothing apart from obedience to God (1 Sam. 15:22; Hos. 6:6; Mic. 6:6-8).

Jesus heard in the man's reply evidence of a potential follower. He was not yet a believer, not yet a disciple. Unlike his peers, however, this scribe was facing the right direction. At this rate, he would become a believer in Jesus the Messiah soon enough.

After the last round of failed attempts to discredit Jesus, His enemies withdrew to consider a different strategy. He had revealed them to be the fools they were.

— **12:35-37** —

Having set His opponents back on their heels, Jesus could have left well enough alone, but He didn't. He pressed the attack. He came to earth not merely to survive, not to save His own skin, but to defeat evil and to save those who would believe in Him. His enemies had exhausted their questions; now Jesus would ask a question of them. He pointed out that the scribes acknowledged the Messiah as a descendant of King David. Yet in Psalm 110:1, David called his descendant "my Lord." How could this be if the Messiah was not God?

The logic of Jesus' question is called "transitive relation," which follows this familiar pattern:

A = C
B = C
Therefore, A = B.

So here's the Lord's question broken down into simple logic:

David called his descendant, the Messiah, "my Lord." (A = C)
David called God "the LORD." (B = C)
Therefore, David saw the Messiah as equal with God. (A = B)

Mark comments that the crowd took delight in listening to Jesus, inferring that they not only enjoyed learning from Him, but that they also liked seeing the temple leaders silenced and humbled by His flawless logic.

— 12:38-40 —

The scribes were respected and feared as Israel's premier experts on the Law—no less so than certain Ivy League lawyers today. Having shamed them into the shadows of the temple, Jesus warned rank-and-file Jews to beware of their pride. "Long robes" (12:38) refers to the Greek *stolē* [4749], the first-century version of expensive, hand-tailored suits (see Num. 15:38-40). "Respectful greetings" refers to the deference the scribes expected in recognition of their exalted status. "Chief seats in the synagogues" (Mark 12:39) were the chairs reserved for honored leaders. "Places of honor at banquets" typically went to people holding the highest social rank in the community.

Jesus warned that pride is the mask worn by hypocrites. While they present themselves as respectable and honorable, they "devour widows' houses" (12:40). This is hyperbole for taking advantage of helpless people. As men of Scripture, they should have known that God cares for the helpless and expected them to do the same. As men involved in hearing legal cases and rendering judgment, they should have been applying the Law fairly without respect for the social status of the people involved. Jesus openly declared them guilty of fraud and cruelty. He further warned that, because of their advanced knowledge, they bore a greater responsibility than others to live, teach, and apply the truth, so their condemnation would be more severe than for others.

— 12:41-42 —

Mark contrasts the righteousness of the scribes with the character of a poor widow. According to the Sadducees, God rewards the righteous in this life, after which one goes into nothingness. Therefore, they reasoned, rich people are shown to be righteous by their riches, while poor people are proven wicked by their poverty. While the Pharisees did believe in rewards and punishments in the afterlife, they also believed wealth to be a sign of God's favor and misfortune to be the result of God's judgment for sin. This short episode set the record straight for the poor, persecuted Christians facing hardship under the Roman emperor.

Jesus sat in the Court of Women opposite thirteen horn-shaped receptacles, which collected the freewill offerings of worshipers (see Deut. 16:10-11). The scribes made a grand show of their supposed generosity, dropping large sums of money into the temple coffers. Meanwhile, a poor widow—someone ancient societies would have regarded as cursed with double judgment—entered with her offering: two lepta [3016]. The word "lepta" originally meant "peeling." Each sliver of copper was worth one one-hundredth of a denarius. If a denarius equaled one day's wage, she offered one-fiftieth of a day laborer's income.

— 12:43-44 —

The Lord didn't disparage large donors with His lesson; He merely honored generous people with little material wealth. The widow gave next to nothing of real value to the temple, but she gave out of her need, not her surplus. She modeled genuine devotion—unreserved commitment—to the Lord. Sacrifice requires trust in God's power and goodness, and this kind of faith can come only from a grateful heart. God doesn't measure the value of one's gift by its monetary value, but by the relative sacrifice experienced by the giver.

APPLICATION: MARK 12:13-44

Recovering from Religiosity

I have a good friend named Buddy Greene who plays a harmonica very well, plays banjo (I love banjo), and plays guitar. Not all at once—but he probably could! He's the only guy I know who can play "The Flight of the Bumblebee" on harmonica. Wow! Anyway, Buddy Greene is an elder in his Presbyterian church, and he says, "My problem is that I'm a recovering Pharisee." There's an honest man.

It occurs to me that each of the religious factions Jesus faced can be found in most any church in the world. Look around and you'll see them. Pharisees. Sadducees. Scribes. In fact, look in the mirror and you'll probably find one of the three staring back at you. The question is, are you *recovering*?

The *Pharisee* is the earnest religious worker. This person is driven by duty and delights in doing good deeds and getting things done for God. Pharisees busy themselves in church activities: They never miss a meeting; they wear their piety on their sleeves; they're vocal and active about Christianity in their communities; and they live out their righteousness openly.

None of that sounds bad. In fact, it's quite good. The church could use more active, working, "out-there" believers. The problem is, these genuine believers in Jesus Christ derive *too much* satisfaction from their do-good lifestyle. Their spirituality can become so outwardly focused that they risk becoming self-righteous, judgmental of others, offensive—even obnoxious—in their communication of the gospel, and personally estranged from the God they love and serve so diligently.

Pharisees need more humility. If you're a recovering Pharisee, take your spiritual life to a deeper level by taking it underground. What I mean by that is *do more good things anonymously.* Serve behind the scenes more often, and let your good works become something you share with God and no one else. Resist the urge to tell others how they can live better or solve problems or improve their spiritual lives. Spend more time praying and less time talking. When preaching the gospel, use fewer words and more acts of kindness.

The *Sadducee* is the casual Christian—a good and moral person, well-liked and respected among peers. Christian Sadducees are sophisticated, savvy, and shrewd. They know the talk *and* the walk. They often give large sums to their churches and to charities that tug at their heartstrings. They attend church fairly regularly and can be counted on to head up a committee. In fact, many can be found leading elders' or deacons' meetings.

In truth, however, an authentic and growing relationship with Jesus Christ doesn't rank high on the Sadducee's list of priorities. This is ironic for Sadducees serving as elders or deacons, but for Sadducees, church is merely a social cause or an outlet for their business acumen. That's because the Sadducee is a businessperson first, family person next—and then Jesus appears somewhere lower down the list of tasks. Spirituality is an accessory for the Sadducee. Church is less about fellowship and more about civic duty. Church attendance serves a Sadducee's other interests.

If you're a Sadducee, step down from leadership in the church. If you're a "church boss," your pastor is praying for your repentance. If you're the respectable church benefactor, your pastor is thanking God for your generosity but longing for your spiritual maturity. Find a deeply spiritual, mature Christian to whom you can become accountable and ask that person to become your mentor.

The *scribe* is the most perplexing and concerning of all. This theologically astute individual has likely engaged in a lifelong study of Scripture. Scribes have all the head knowledge of a scholar but the practical heart skills of a novice. Scribes can stand before classrooms to teach, but they find practical application of spiritual truths difficult. They excel in abstract thinking and struggle with commonsense Christianity. They can analyze the parable of the Good Samaritan while walking past people in need with no thought of connecting the two.

If you're a scribe, put down your pen, close your Bible (yes, I said that!), get out of your study, go find someone in need, roll up your sleeves, and get to work! The local hospital needs chaplains. The homeless and hungry need someone who can help them get through this day, and then long-term assistance to help them climb out of perpetual poverty. Battered women and children need advocates. The lost need to hear the gospel. Returning veterans need compassion as well as spiritual guidance.

Scribes, your hothouse religion needs a fresh breath of realism.

A Prophet We Can Trust
MARK 13:1-37

NASB

[1] As He was going out of the temple, one of His disciples said to Him, "Teacher, behold [a]what wonderful stones and [a]what wonderful buildings!" [2] And Jesus said to him, "Do you see these great buildings? Not one stone will be left upon another which will not be torn down."

[3] As He was sitting on the Mount of Olives opposite the temple, Peter and [a]James and John and Andrew were questioning Him privately, [4] "Tell us, when will these things be, and what *will be* the [a]sign when all these things are going to be fulfilled?" [5] And Jesus began to say to them, "See to it that no one misleads you. [6] Many will come in My name, saying, 'I am *He!*' and will mislead many. [7] When you hear of wars and rumors of wars, do not be frightened; *those things* must take place; but *that is* not yet the

NLT

[1] As Jesus was leaving the Temple that day, one of his disciples said, "Teacher, look at these magnificent buildings! Look at the impressive stones in the walls."

[2] Jesus replied, "Yes, look at these great buildings. But they will be completely demolished. Not one stone will be left on top of another!"

[3] Later, Jesus sat on the Mount of Olives across the valley from the Temple. Peter, James, John, and Andrew came to him privately and asked him, [4] "Tell us, when will all this happen? What sign will show us that these things are about to be fulfilled?"

[5] Jesus replied, "Don't let anyone mislead you, [6] for many will come in my name, claiming, 'I am the Messiah.'* They will deceive many. [7] And you will hear of wars and threats of wars, but don't panic. Yes, these

end. [8] For nation will rise up against nation, and kingdom against kingdom; there will be earthquakes in various places; there will *also* be famines. These things are *merely* the beginning of birth pangs.

[9] "But [a] be on your guard; for they will deliver you to *the* [b] courts, and you will be flogged in *the* synagogues, and you will stand before governors and kings for My sake, as a testimony to them. [10] The gospel must first be preached to all the nations. [11] When they [a] arrest you and hand you over, do not worry beforehand about what you are to say, but say whatever is given you in that hour; for it is not you who speak, but *it is* the Holy Spirit. [12] Brother will betray brother to death, and a father *his* child; and children will rise up against parents and [a] have them put to death. [13] You will be hated by all because of My name, but the one who endures to the end, he will be saved.

[14] "But when you see the ABOMINATION OF DESOLATION standing where it should not be (let the reader understand), then those who are in Judea must flee to the mountains. [15] The one who is on the housetop must not go down, or go in to get anything out of his house; [16] and the one who is in the field must not turn back to get his coat. [17] But woe to those who are pregnant and to those who are nursing babies in those days! [18] But pray that it may not happen in the winter. [19] For those days will be a *time of* tribulation such as has not occurred since the beginning of the creation which God created until now, and never will. [20] Unless the Lord had shortened *those* days,

things must take place, but the end won't follow immediately. [8] Nation will go to war against nation, and kingdom against kingdom. There will be earthquakes in many parts of the world, as well as famines. But this is only the first of the birth pains, with more to come.

[9] "When these things begin to happen, watch out! You will be handed over to the local councils and beaten in the synagogues. You will stand trial before governors and kings because you are my followers. But this will be your opportunity to tell them about me.* [10] For the Good News must first be preached to all nations.* [11] But when you are arrested and stand trial, don't worry in advance about what to say. Just say what God tells you at that time, for it is not you who will be speaking, but the Holy Spirit.

[12] "A brother will betray his brother to death, a father will betray his own child, and children will rebel against their parents and cause them to be killed. [13] And everyone will hate you because you are my followers.* But the one who endures to the end will be saved.

[14] "The day is coming when you will see the sacrilegious object that causes desecration* standing where he* should not be." (Reader, pay attention!) "Then those in Judea must flee to the hills. [15] A person out on the deck of a roof must not go down into the house to pack. [16] A person out in the field must not return even to get a coat. [17] How terrible it will be for pregnant women and for nursing mothers in those days. [18] And pray that your flight will not be in winter. [19] For there will be greater anguish in those days than at any time since God created the world. And it will never be so great again. [20] In fact, unless the Lord shortens that time of calamity, not a single

NASB

no ᵃlife would have been saved; but for the sake of the ᵇelect, whom He chose, He shortened the days. ²¹And then if anyone says to you, 'Behold, here is ᵃthe Christ'; or, 'Behold, *He is* there'; do not believe *him;* ²²for false Christs and false prophets will arise, and will show ᵃsigns and wonders, in order to lead astray, if possible, the elect. ²³But take heed; behold, I have told you everything in advance.

²⁴"But in those days, after that tribulation, THE SUN WILL BE DARKENED AND THE MOON WILL NOT GIVE ITS LIGHT, ²⁵AND THE STARS WILL BE FALLING from heaven, and the powers that are in ᵃthe heavens will be shaken. ²⁶Then they will see THE SON OF MAN COMING IN CLOUDS with great power and glory. ²⁷And then He will send forth the angels, and will gather together His ᵃelect from the four winds, from the farthest end of the earth to the farthest end of heaven.

²⁸"Now learn the parable from the fig tree: when its branch has already become tender and puts forth its leaves, you know that summer is near. ²⁹Even so, you too, when you see these things happening, ᵃrecognize that ᵇHe is near, *right* at the ᶜdoor. ³⁰Truly I say to you, this ᵃgeneration will not pass away until all these things take place. ³¹Heaven and earth will pass away, but My words will not pass away. ³²But of that day or hour no one knows, not even the angels in heaven, nor the Son, but the Father *alone.*

³³"Take heed, keep on the alert; for you do not know when the *appointed* time ᵃwill come. ³⁴*It is* like a man away on a journey, *who* upon leaving his house and ᵃputting his slaves in charge, *assigning* to each

NLT

person will survive. But for the sake of his chosen ones he has shortened those days.

²¹"Then if anyone tells you, 'Look, here is the Messiah,' or 'There he is,' don't believe it. ²²For false messiahs and false prophets will rise up and perform signs and wonders so as to deceive, if possible, even God's chosen ones. ²³Watch out! I have warned you about this ahead of time!

²⁴"At that time, after the anguish of those days,

the sun will be darkened,
    the moon will give no light,
²⁵ the stars will fall from the sky,
    and the powers in the heavens
      will be shaken.*

²⁶Then everyone will see the Son of Man* coming on the clouds with great power and glory.* ²⁷And he will send out his angels to gather his chosen ones from all over the world*— from the farthest ends of the earth and heaven.

²⁸"Now learn a lesson from the fig tree. When its branches bud and its leaves begin to sprout, you know that summer is near. ²⁹In the same way, when you see all these things taking place, you can know that his return is very near, right at the door. ³⁰I tell you the truth, this generation* will not pass from the scene before all these things take place. ³¹Heaven and earth will disappear, but my words will never disappear.

³²"However, no one knows the day or hour when these things will happen, not even the angels in heaven or the Son himself. Only the Father knows. ³³And since you don't know when that time will come, be on guard! Stay alert*!

³⁴"The coming of the Son of Man can be illustrated by the story of a man going on a long trip. When he left home, he gave each of his slaves instructions about the work

one his task, also commanded the doorkeeper to stay on the alert. ³⁵ Therefore, be on the alert—for you do not know when the ªmaster of the house is coming, whether in the evening, at midnight, or when the rooster crows, or in the morning— ³⁶ in case he should come suddenly and find you asleep. ³⁷ What I say to you I say to all, 'Be on the alert!'"

13:1 ªLit *how great* 13:3 ªOr *Jacob* 13:4 ªOr *attesting miracle* 13:9 ªLit *look to yourselves* ᵇOr *Sanhedrin* or *Council* 13:11 ªLit *lead* 13:12 ªLit *put them to death* 13:20 ªLit *flesh* ᵇOr *chosen ones* 13:21 ªI.e. the Messiah 13:22 ªOr *attesting miracles* 13:25 ªOr *heaven* 13:27 ªOr *chosen ones* 13:29 ªOr *know* ᵇOr *it* ᶜLit *doors* 13:30 ªOr *race* 13:33 ªLit *is* 13:34 ªLit *giving the authority to* 13:35 ªLit *lord*

they were to do, and he told the gatekeeper to watch for his return. ³⁵ You, too, must keep watch! For you don't know when the master of the household will return—in the evening, at midnight, before dawn, or at daybreak. ³⁶ Don't let him find you sleeping when he arrives without warning. ³⁷ I say to you what I say to everyone: Watch for him!"

13:6 Greek *claiming, 'I am.'* 13:9 Or *But this will be your testimony against them.* 13:10 Or *all peoples.* 13:13 Greek *on account of my name.* 13:14a Greek *the abomination of desolation.* See Dan 9:27; 11:31; 12:11. 13:14b Or *it.* 13:24-25 See Isa 13:10; 34:4; Joel 2:10. 13:26a "Son of Man" is a title Jesus used for himself. 13:26b See Dan 7:13. 13:27 Greek *from the four winds.* 13:30 Or *this age,* or *this nation.* 13:33 Some manuscripts add *and pray.*

Some people go absolutely crazy over prophecy. Even rational people can lose all sense of reason and discernment when it comes to future events. Every generation since the Resurrection has produced extremists who cast aside the Bible and common sense in order to follow the siren call of false prophets. These crackpots pretend to have knowledge the Bible doesn't have, or that they have a unique code that unlocks the Bible's "secrets," as they rake in large amounts of money from conferences, books, videos . . . and donations. Some lead their minions to establish secure compounds, collect provisions and arms, and then begin setting dates for the Lord's return. Inevitably, when reality fails to meet their expectations, these cult leaders sound like my GPS: "Recalculating . . ."

In my observation, there appear to be two extremes in response to prophetic matters. The first is *gullibility*. Some people want to believe any and every so-called prophet of God. Their readiness to believe in something—anything—prepares them to receive teaching so absurd it would be comical if not so tragic. One notable radio preacher predicted the return of Christ several times, only to issue "adjustments" to his calculations when his predictions were faulty. Finally, after his last two failed predictions, including the publication of a tract called "God Gives Another Infallible Proof That Assures the Rapture Will Occur May 21, 2011," he issued an apology and admitted to asking God's forgiveness for predicting Judgment Day. "Recalculating . . ."

I remember the widely circulated booklet *88 Reasons Why The Rapture Will Be In 1988*. The author followed this with *The Final Shout:*

Rapture Report 1989. Then *23 Reasons Why a Pre-Tribulation Rapture Looks Like It Will Occur on Rosh-Hashanah 1993* (I detected a softening of his assurance with this one). Millions of copies were sold. Thousands prepared for the Rapture of the church. "Recalculating . . ."

These and other end-times prophets should be relieved they lived in this generation, not in ancient days, when false prophets were dragged to the edge of the city and stoned for speaking error in the name of God. These days, those who are not gullible simply laugh, roll their eyes, and write these people off as insane.

If gullibility is one extreme response to prophecy, you will find at the other end of the spectrum *cynicism.* While the gullible person believes everything, the cynic believes nothing. Cynics are cowardly. They maintain the illusion of intelligence because they can impressively argue *against* almost anything; but they proceed to throw the baby out with the bathwater, refusing to grapple with the Bible's prophecies and saying we can know nothing at all. Prophecy involves bizarre images and metaphors and predicts extraordinary and cataclysmic events, so cynics find it an easy target for their ridicule. Press the debate on its meaning, however, and they'll run for cover. Cynics lack the courage to believe in anything.

I grew up in the real world. I was reared in a godly household with parents who witnessed two world wars separated by the Great Depression yet never doubted the goodness or sovereignty of God. They taught me and my siblings to pray with earnest belief while working hard to live the Christian life with authenticity in our little part of the world. Thanks to my upbringing as a child and my education in preparation for ministry, I remain committed to what might be termed "a healthy balance." We—that is, all authentic disciples of Jesus—have an interest in whatever God's Word teaches, and we want to handle that accurately, carefully, and practically. We should explain it as clearly as we can while guarding against foolish extremes. We must refuse all teaching that sets dates and dogmatically declares hard-and-fast predictions of future events.

With all of that in mind, we now turn to a lengthy discourse of Jesus, which pulls the veil back from the future to allow a glimpse of things to come. This revelation of the future begins with a backward glance.

— 13:1-2 —

As dusk began to fall upon the temple, Jesus and His twelve students made their way through the eastern gate, down the ravine called

Kidron, and up the Mount of Olives toward their quarters in Bethany. In previous days, He stood toe-to-toe with five of Israel's most powerful political groups—Pharisees, Sadducees, scribes, chief priests, and Herodians. Usually, these factions battled one another for supremacy, their mutual struggle maintaining a fragile balance that barely kept Rome out of Judea. For once, however, they united to rid themselves of a threat to their power, and it didn't matter that their rival happened to be their long-anticipated Messiah, the Son of God.

Just moments earlier, Jesus had witnessed a poignant illustration of Israel's spiritual failing. Wealthy Jews gave large sums of money to the temple treasury and received great fanfare from the temple leaders. Nevertheless, their large donations represented only a small fraction of their giving capacity. Meanwhile, a poor widow gave next to nothing in terms of currency. Jesus noted that her giving was all she had to live on. Whereas Israel's privileged caste gave out of their surplus, the widow gave sacrificially. This, for Jesus, illustrated the spiritual poverty of the temple and His covenant people.

As the disciples glanced back at the magnificent structure erected by Herod the Great, they commented on its beauty. Today the temple is gone, but the foundation stones remain. Even those are impressive to see. One can only imagine how breathtaking the original temple must have been, with its massive white stones bathed in the evening sunlight. His voice colored in mourning, Jesus acknowledged the grandeur of the building and then, without hesitation, warned that it would be completely destroyed.

He, of course, meant this literally. The temple would not survive another forty years. As we look back with the benefit of Christian theology, we see that He also spoke figuratively. According to many, the temple occupied the very place where Abraham, by faith, offered his promised son, Isaac, as a sacrifice to God. As you will remember, the Lord spared Isaac and supplied a ram to take his place on the altar. Soon the Lamb of God would be sacrificed "once for all," and become "the mediator of a new covenant" in which animal sacrifices would be obsolete (see Heb. 9:11-15). After the Lamb of God died for the sins of the world, blood would never again have to be shed in the temple.

— 13:3-4 —

The Lord's words probably silenced the Twelve until they stopped for a rest somewhere on the western face of the Mount of Olives. As day gave way to evening, four of His disciples wanted to know more about the fate of the temple. They wanted to know the details of the future so they could be prepared to meet it. They asked, in effect, "When will these things occur?" and "What precipitating events should we look for?"

— 13:5-8 —

This begins what serious Bible students call "the Olivet discourse." Recorded here and in the other two synoptic Gospels (see Matt. 24 and Luke 21:5-36), Jesus predicted the future of Jerusalem, Israel, and the world in broad brushstrokes. Some of the events have come to pass; some still remain in our future; some have a dual fulfillment, meaning the predictions came to pass but a more complete fulfillment awaits. How we determine which events are which has been the subject of debate for centuries, and we will not solve the riddle in this short space. So, rather than speculate, we will keep our eyes on the big picture.

The first section of His discourse warns that evil will continue to rule the earth for some time. Bad things will happen, but they will not necessarily serve as "signs when all these things are going to be fulfilled" (see Mark 13:4). The earth is fallen, so false messiahs and brutal wars will plague the world as they always have. While wars, disasters, and famines are terrible, these will be insignificant compared to end-time tragedies.

— 13:9-13 —

Turning from a description of the general affliction of evil, Jesus warned that believers would endure persecution at the hands of an evil world and that the apostles would be the first to suffer. Jesus detailed the kind of persecutions true disciples would encounter. Jesus used whipping in the synagogue as a picture of official censure and rejection by the apostles' Jewish brothers and sisters. More generally, this image includes the loss of acceptance among one's own people.

Christians would be turned over to government officials to face formal charges "as a testimony" for the spiritual benefit of these leaders (13:9). This would be one means by which the gospel would be "preached to all the nations" (13:10). The Greek term *ethnos* [1484] refers to all people who are not Hebrew. Christians would suffer this betrayal at the hands of their Jewish kinsmen and even their own blood relatives and household members.

Naturally, Mark's audience in Rome saw themselves in this prediction.

— 13:14-23 —

Mark 13:5-13 describes the reign of evil in our fallen world, an unknown span of time in which the ebb and flow of fortune continues. A specific event will interrupt the status quo to signal the beginning of what might be termed a transitional period. The present dominion of evil will give way to the kingdom of God. The time between these two eras has been called by Bible scholars "the Great Tribulation" based on the term in 13:19. Jesus called the event that would signal this transitional period the "abomination of desolation," a phrase He derived from the writings of Daniel, the Old Testament prophet (13:14; cf. Dan. 9:27; 11:31; 12:11).

The two Greek terms in this phrase are *bdelygma* [946] and *erēmōsis* [2050]. The first term describes anything that's loathsome, disgusting, and personally repugnant. The Old Testament frequently uses the Hebrew equivalent to describe sinful activities that God finds especially revolting. While any sin—regardless of how small—violates God's character, some acts He considers to be a personally directed affront.

The second term, *erēmōsis*, means "devastation," "destruction," or "depopulation." This describes the aftermath of a plague or a genocidal army invasion. The Greek Old Testament (called the Septuagint) uses this word to translate a similar Hebrew word. God spoke of this "desolation" when describing the penalties of disobedience (Lev. 26:34-35).

Both Daniel and Jesus used this expression to describe the unmistakable sign that the transition had begun. We must speculate; however, actual observers of the "abomination of desolation" will recognize it without question. This may be an event not unlike when Antiochus IV Epiphanes entered the Jerusalem temple and shamelessly offered a pig on the altar (circa 167 BC). Some people think it describes a person. The Lord described the "abomination of desolation" standing or rising where it should not, as though this harbinger would have a will and legs on which to stand.

What follows this signal of the last days will be upheaval, pestilence, conflict, persecution, and disaster like nothing the world has ever seen. In both quantity and quality, the evil events will be unprecedented. As always, false messiahs will arise to lead the gullible and foolhardy astray. During this time, however, the false christs will be given supernatural power from Satan to accomplish his purposes.

— 13:24-27 —

After this transitional period of tribulation, the end of the world as we know it will occur. After this ending, a new beginning for creation will occur on what the Old Testament refers to as "the Day of the Lord" (cf. Isa. 13:6-10; Joel 2:1-31; 3:9-17), an event in which God will bring human history to a culminating end and then summon all of humanity to stand trial before Him. Jesus identified this "Day" as His return.

Against the dark backdrop of false messiahs, Jesus, the true Messiah, will come. Like the dimming of the houselights in a theater and the pause before the overture, the sky will go dark—no sun, no moon, no stars—and the Son of Man will break into time and space like the dawn. The Lord used the title "Son of Man" many times, but Jews who knew their Scriptures would have immediately thought of Daniel's oracle:

> "I kept looking in the night visions,
> And behold, with the clouds of heaven
> One like a Son of Man was coming,
> And He came up to the Ancient of Days
> And was presented before Him.
> And to Him was given dominion,
> Glory and a kingdom,
> That all the peoples, nations and men of every language
> Might serve Him.
> His dominion is an everlasting dominion
> Which will not pass away;
> And His kingdom is one
> Which will not be destroyed." (Dan. 7:13-14)

Upon His return, the Messiah will gather His people to be with Him. It will also be the ultimate fulfillment of God's promise to recall Israel from exile (cf. Deut. 30:3-5; Zech. 2:6-7). God will bring prosperity, peace, restoration, and blessing to Israel in fulfillment of all His earlier promises (Joel 3:18-21).

— 13:28-29 —

Jesus cautioned the disciples that God's people should not be taken unaware by these events (cf. 13:23). To illustrate, He pointed to the familiar cycles of the fig tree, which John Grassmick describes well:

> In Palestine fig trees produced crops of small edible buds in March followed by the appearance of large green leaves in early April. This early green "fruit" (buds) was common food for local peasants. (An absence of these buds despite the tree's green foliage promising their presence indicated it would bear no fruit

that year.) Eventually these buds dropped off when the normal crop of figs formed and ripened in late May and June, the fig season.[40]

Any reasonable person with average skills in observation should be able to recognize end-time events unfold. They are described in sufficient detail so those living on earth at that time will know what they're looking for. And when these events take place, people will not have any question about what comes next.

— 13:30-31 —

Jesus promised that "this generation" would not pass away until these end-time events took place (13:30). This has caused a fair amount of confusion because, obviously, the disciples died before His return. In fact, *we* have not seen these events come to pass after two millennia of history.

The term "this generation," though, need not refer to Jesus' contemporaries. It could also refer to the generation alive at the time of the events Jesus described in His prophecy. In that case, "this generation" refers to the Jews who will witness the Great Tribulation of the future. These will see the return of Christ and His ruling as King.

— 13:32-37 —

Jesus could not have been clearer on two points. First, no one can set a date on when these events will take place. Second, believers must remain alert. No individual can predict when the Day of the Lord will come. Jesus urges all to live in a state of perpetual readiness—continuing to live, making plans, fulfilling our obligations, and planning for the future, yet prepared for the return of Christ and the visible, literal establishment of God's kingdom on earth.

While Jesus gave us a glimpse into the future, His "Olivet discourse" is neither a complete script nor a detailed playbook. Jesus gave us sufficient information, but it's by no means exhaustive. He left many questions unanswered. We want details because knowledge of the future is power, and we like to control our own destinies. Instead, we have received enough information to assure us that, despite the apparent success of evil, God remains in control. We see enough of the future to know that God's plan will be completed, justice will eventually prevail, the faithful will be vindicated, the unfaithful will be held accountable, and that obedience to God is still our best prospect of entering a peaceful, prosperous future.

APPLICATION: MARK 13:1-37

Stay Away, Stay Awake, Stay Alert

Many preachers and teachers have a hard time trying to make the end-times practical. Over the years I've heard prophecy enthusiasts go on and on about the details of the Tribulation and the Second Coming, but when it comes time to ask the "So what?" question, they've had very little to say. At least not to all of us living now.

But "all Scripture is . . . profitable for teaching, for reproof, for correction, for training in righteousness," not so we can simply have more accurate end-times charts, but "so that the man of God may be adequate, equipped for every good work" (2 Tim. 3:16-17). So let's take a moment to answer the "So what?" regarding Jesus' lengthy, detailed discourse on the Mount of Olives. Like all Scripture, those words were given for our edification. So I have three simple, two-word applications drawn from Jesus' words—practical principles each of us needs to take to heart.

First, *stay away*. Stay away from anybody who makes specific predictions. Too many want to foolishly point at current events and announce, "This is it! This is the event predicted in the Bible. This is the Antichrist! These are the last days!" Stay away from that. Others want to get out their calculators and start counting down to the date of Christ's return. It's hard to imagine a more direct contradiction to Jesus' clear words in Mark 13, but over the course of my ministry I've seen it dozens of times—sometimes by educated, respected Bible teachers I thought should know better. So stay away.

Second, *stay awake*. Jesus warned about being "asleep" when He comes (Mark 13:35-37). And in one of his great end-times passages, the apostle Paul warned, "But you, brethren, are not in darkness, that the day would overtake you like a thief; for you are all sons of light and sons of day. We are not of night nor of darkness; so then let us not sleep as others do" (1 Thes. 5:4-6). I think of a guard who falls asleep and lets his prisoners escape. Or a babysitter who falls asleep and lets the toddler she's caring for make a mess . . . or worse. Or a driver who dozes off at the wheel and causes a wreck. In this age of darkness, we can't afford to doze off spiritually. We need to stay awake. We need to keep our eyes open and our Bibles open, avoiding dangerous deception.

Third, *stay alert*. People who are "on the alert" (Mark 13:33) aren't simply awake and aware—they have a sense of urgency, not complacency. They stay informed, not ignorant. They are proactive, not passive. Because we don't know when the Lord will return, we're always "on the alert." We keep our hearts and lives pure, our priorities straight, our minds and words holy. Why? Because we believe in the imminent return of Christ—not that He will come immediately but that He could come at any moment. So we stay alert.

Let's learn a lesson from the past—from all the false prophets and teachers who weren't just bad at math, but bad at reading the Bible. When you hear them date setting and sign seeking, walk out. Turn them off. Stop listening to them. Instead, follow Jesus' lesson: Stay away, stay awake, and stay alert.

DISCIPLES CHALLENGED
(MARK 14:1–16:20)

There are certain Scriptures that should be observed with additional reverence and handled delicately in terms of analysis. Prayers in the Bible certainly call for a light touch; these intimate expressions of the heart were never intended to be analyzed. Narrative accounts of death need to be handled carefully, or we risk becoming like diagnostic equipment in a lab and lose all sense of the humanity involved. This portion of Mark's narrative calls for special treatment. As we enter a discussion of the final days of the Lord's life and ministry on earth, a strong sense of reverence slows my pace and makes my spirit grow quiet.

We will carefully observe the historical and cultural details surrounding these events and diligently study Mark's choice of words and phrases, but I hope not at the expense of entering into the humanity of the Lord's experience. While He was—and is—God, we must not forget that Jesus was—and is—a man. A human with flesh that felt pain. A person whose emotions could become overburdened. A man with the same weaknesses and frailty and temptations and feelings we bear. As we study the profound theology surrounding the God-man and His atoning sacrifice for sin, let us not forget that—resurrection notwithstanding—this was a horrible, tragic death. The agony and injustice we feel when a good man dies is warranted here. In fact, more so.

As we walk this Via Dolorosa, this "Way of Suffering," with Jesus and His followers, let's avoid the common blunders that tourists make. Let us walk softly over this hallowed ground, observe with sensitivity the anguishing events, and speak in hushed, reverential tones. If we do, Mark's carefully crafted narrative will have its intended effect. We will become sensitive followers of Jesus, ready to follow in His steps and prepared to bear the joys and responsibilities of discipleship.

In this final phase of His earthly ministry, Jesus would claim the kingdom's victory over Satan's dominion. No longer would sin and death unremittingly hold men captive—life and freedom would be available to all in Jesus' name. But at the same time, the disciples would face their most brutal and instructive challenges. They would see their Master suffer overwhelming agony in Gethsemane, and after conquering there, He would be betrayed to unjust execution. The disciples would be overcome by fear and confusion to the point of collapse, but they would see their Master faithfully turn to God the Father in the face of it all. They would fall away, but they would be restored.

Such scenes must have struck a deep chord with Mark's audience—persecuted Christians in Rome, frightened by the prospect of death and saddened at the loss of friends. They knew well the temptation to fall away. They knew the doubt and fear we all face in some measure. They would be reminded of God's faithfulness and Jesus' victory. They needed to be reminded that it was God's grace—the same grace available to them—that had brought the disciples back from despair in such dark hours.

KEY TERMS IN MARK 14:1–16:20

paradidōmi (παραδίδωμι) [3860] "to hand over," "to surrender," "to transfer possession"
Built on the verb *didōmi* [1325] meaning "to give," this term carries the idea of surrendering possession of something to the control of another. Based on the context, some translators will render the term "betray," but the Greek word does not suggest whether the motivation is good or evil. We see it used extensively in the Passion narratives, in which Jesus is given over to the Sanhedrin by Judas (14:10), to Pilate by the Sanhedrin (15:1), to the soldiers by Pilate (15:15), and finally, when Jesus gives over His spirit to death (John 19:30).

pheugō (φεύγω) [5343] "to flee," "to escape," "to avoid"
This verb describes moving away from something hastily because of fear. This is a natural response to danger. In the Gospel of Mark, Jesus moves deliberately toward danger (i.e., the cross) as part of His mission, while everyone flees from Jesus because of the danger associated with Him. For Mark, fear and fleeing serve as indications of apostasy (5:14; 13:14; 14:50, 52; 16:8). Rather than fearing men and fleeing danger, the unspoken expectation is that Christ followers should fear God and accept danger as a natural consequence.

---

christos (Χριστός) [5547] "Messiah," "Anointed One"
This term itself derives from *chriō* [5548], which means "to rub," "to smear on," or "to anoint [with oil]." Prior to the New Testament, it was never used of a person except in Hebrew literature. The Septuagint used *christos* to translate the Hebrew word *mashiach* [H4899] (transliterated "messiah" in English), a term reserved for the king and referring to the custom of anointing a man's head with olive oil to designate him as Israel's ruler. While Israel had many "christs" (i.e., kings), the nation anticipated an ultimate "Christ," *the* Messiah, a larger-than-life consummate king.

Love and Loyalty
MARK 14:1-21

NASB

¹ Now the Passover and Unleavened Bread were two days away; and the chief priests and the scribes were seeking how to seize Him by stealth and kill *Him;* ² for they were saying, "Not during the festival, otherwise there might be a riot of the people."

³ While He was in Bethany at the home of Simon the leper, and reclining *at the table,* there came a woman with an alabaster vial of very costly perfume of pure ᵃnard; *and* she broke the vial and poured it over His head. ⁴ But some were indignantly *remarking* to one another, "Why has this perfume been wasted? ⁵ For this perfume might have been sold for over three hundred ᵃdenarii, and *the money* given to the poor." And they were scolding her. ⁶ But Jesus said, "Let her alone; why do you bother her? She has done a good deed to Me. ⁷ For you always have the poor with you, and whenever you wish you can do good to them; but you do not always have Me. ⁸ She has done what she could; she has anointed My body beforehand for the burial. ⁹ Truly I say to you, wherever the gospel is

NLT

¹ It was now two days before Passover and the Festival of Unleavened Bread. The leading priests and the teachers of religious law were still looking for an opportunity to capture Jesus secretly and kill him. ² "But not during the Passover celebration," they agreed, "or the people may riot."

³ Meanwhile, Jesus was in Bethany at the home of Simon, a man who had previously had leprosy. While he was eating,* a woman came in with a beautiful alabaster jar of expensive perfume made from essence of nard. She broke open the jar and poured the perfume over his head.

⁴ Some of those at the table were indignant. "Why waste such expensive perfume?" they asked. ⁵ "It could have been sold for a year's wages* and the money given to the poor!" So they scolded her harshly.

⁶ But Jesus replied, "Leave her alone. Why criticize her for doing such a good thing to me? ⁷ You will always have the poor among you, and you can help them whenever you want to. But you will not always have me. ⁸ She has done what she could and has anointed my body for burial ahead of time. ⁹ I tell you the truth, wherever the Good News is

preached in the whole world, what this woman has done will also be spoken of in memory of her."

¹⁰ Then Judas Iscariot, who was one of the twelve, went off to the chief priests in order to ᵃbetray Him to them. ¹¹ They were glad when they heard *this*, and promised to give him money. And he *began* seeking how to betray Him at an opportune time.

¹² On the first day of Unleavened Bread, when ᵃthe Passover *lamb* was being sacrificed, His disciples said to Him, "Where do You want us to go and prepare for You to eat the Passover?" ¹³ And He sent two of His disciples and said to them, "Go into the city, and a man will meet you carrying a pitcher of water; follow him; ¹⁴ and wherever he enters, say to the owner of the house, 'The Teacher says, "Where is My guest room in which I may eat the Passover with My disciples?"' ¹⁵ And he himself will show you a large upper room furnished *and* ready; prepare for us there." ¹⁶ The disciples went out and came to the city, and found *it* just as He had told them; and they prepared the Passover.

¹⁷ When it was evening He came with the twelve. ¹⁸ As they were reclining *at the table* and eating, Jesus said, "Truly I say to you that one of you will ᵃbetray Me—ᵇone who is eating with Me." ¹⁹ They began to be grieved and to say to Him one by one, "Surely not I?" ²⁰ And He said to them, "*It is* one of the twelve, ᵃone who dips with Me in the bowl. ²¹ For the Son of Man *is to* go just as it is written of Him; but woe to that man ᵃby whom the Son of Man is betrayed! *It would have been* good ᵇfor that man if he had not been born."

14:3 ᵃAn aromatic oil extracted from an East Indian plant   14:5 ᵃThe denarius was equivalent to a day's wages   14:10 ᵃOr *hand Him over*
14:12 ᵃLit *they were sacrificing*   14:18 ᵃOr *deliver Me over* ᵇOr *the one*   14:20 ᵃOr *the one*
14:21 ᵃOr *through* ᵇLit *for him if that man had not been born*

preached throughout the world, this woman's deed will be remembered and discussed."

¹⁰ Then Judas Iscariot, one of the twelve disciples, went to the leading priests to arrange to betray Jesus to them. ¹¹ They were delighted when they heard why he had come, and they promised to give him money. So he began looking for an opportunity to betray Jesus.

¹² On the first day of the Festival of Unleavened Bread, when the Passover lamb is sacrificed, Jesus' disciples asked him, "Where do you want us to go to prepare the Passover meal for you?"

¹³ So Jesus sent two of them into Jerusalem with these instructions: "As you go into the city, a man carrying a pitcher of water will meet you. Follow him. ¹⁴ At the house he enters, say to the owner, 'The Teacher asks: Where is the guest room where I can eat the Passover meal with my disciples?' ¹⁵ He will take you upstairs to a large room that is already set up. That is where you should prepare our meal." ¹⁶ So the two disciples went into the city and found everything just as Jesus had said, and they prepared the Passover meal there.

¹⁷ In the evening Jesus arrived with the Twelve. ¹⁸ As they were at the table* eating, Jesus said, "I tell you the truth, one of you eating with me here will betray me."

¹⁹ Greatly distressed, each one asked in turn, "Am I the one?"

²⁰ He replied, "It is one of you twelve who is eating from this bowl with me. ²¹ For the Son of Man* must die, as the Scriptures declared long ago. But how terrible it will be for the one who betrays him. It would be far better for that man if he had never been born!"

14:3 Or *reclining.*   14:5 Greek *for 300 denarii.* A denarius was equivalent to a laborer's full day's wage.   14:18 Or *As they reclined.*   14:21 "Son of Man" is a title Jesus used for himself.

If calendars had hung in Jewish homes in the first century, there would always be at least one date circled in red and marked in Hebrew: "Passover." This one-day celebration was followed by the seven-day Feast of Unleavened Bread, so called because God had instructed all Jewish families to sweep their houses clean of all dust and to be certain that not a speck of yeast remained. During this time, the population in Jerusalem would swell to ten times its normal size as Jews traveled there, arriving from all over the world.

Passover was a celebration of Israel's release from bondage in Egypt and their official beginning as a nation. This year, however, some Jews had something in mind other than a celebration of freedom. The enemies of Jesus—members of Israel's ruling council, the Sanhedrin—were busy planning Jesus' downfall. Their attempts to discredit Him had failed, so they abandoned politics in favor of intrigue. If they couldn't defame and defeat Jesus, they would murder Him. What remained was to find the right opportunity to arrest Him—timing and inside information would be important in order to avoid a scene.

None of this was a surprise to Jesus, who continued to prepare His disciples for His approaching death. He knew that each one would face difficult choices in the trying days to come, but He also knew the plans He had for them.

— 14:1-2 —

This section of Mark's story begins two days before Passover, which always occurred on the evening of the fourteenth day of the first month in the Jewish lunar calendar. The chief priests and scribes wanted to abduct Jesus and kill Him privately to avoid inciting the people to riot. They had stood idly by while Herod Antipas killed another popular prophet (Mark 6:21-29), so they could ill afford to anger the masses with another unjust murder of a well-respected leader. If they could make Jesus simply disappear, they could pretend to mourn with the nation.

— 14:3 —

While Jesus didn't fear death, He didn't harbor a death wish. He came to die on behalf of His people as Scripture had predicted, but He wasn't suicidal. He knew His divinely ordained path led to the cross, but He would not make killing Him convenient. In the days leading up to the Passover celebration, Jesus was either appearing before thousands of witnesses or maintaining a low profile. When not ministering in the temple, Jesus lived a short distance away in Bethany with His friends.

The Jewish Calendar and Festival Cycle

One evening, a man hosted a banquet—perhaps at the request of Lazarus, Martha, and Mary (cf. John 12:2)—that Jesus attended with His disciples. According to Luke, the host was a Pharisee in terms of his theology and politics (Luke 7:36-39). Mark (along with Matthew) identifies the man as "Simon the leper" (cf. Matt. 26:6-13). He most likely did not have the disease any longer, or no one would have come to his place for dinner! He may have been healed by Jesus but, more likely, he simply had a skin disorder associated with what we now know as Hansen's disease and had been declared clean by the temple (cf. Lev. 14:1-32). But as often happens, the least flattering nickname stuck.

In the traditional manner of the ancient Near East, the guests reclined at the table. They didn't sit in chairs at a high table; they lay around a low table, propped on the left elbow with a cushion for support. They ate facing the table with their feet angled away from the food. Sometime during the meal, a woman approached Jesus from behind with an alabaster vase in her hands. She broke it open and anointed His head with pure nard. According to Luke, she also anointed His feet. By the time she finished her extravagant act of worship, she had used it all.

The woman's worship bears many of the qualities God desires of His

341

people. Her worship was unreserved. She broke the vial that John tells us amounted to a *litra* [3046], about 12 ounces by weight (John 12:3)—a significant amount of perfumed oil! Her worship was costly. Mark goes out of his way to explain how expensive the perfume was. This concentrated oil could have been diluted to make many other perfumed products, but it was pure. This extract from a plant native to the Himalayas would have been imported. And her worship was uninhibited. Imagine dowsing yourself with 12 ounces of "1000" by Jean Patou, which used to sell for $110 per quarter ounce. The aroma overtook the room and drew criticism from onlookers. The woman didn't care; she thought of nothing but the object of her worship: her Savior.

— 14:4-5 —

Others in the room—Simon, his Pharisee friends, even the disciples—began "scolding" the woman (14:5). Greek writers sometimes used this term to describe the snorting and braying of horses. John indicates that Judas Iscariot, the money keeper, led the vicious verbal assault (John 12:4-5). Those who didn't snort their disapproval condemned her silently with glares and frowns. As they watched nearly a year's wages oozing onto the floor, they thought only of the wasted expense. Judas pretended to care for the poor.

— 14:6-9 —

We cannot know for certain what was in Mary's mind as she worshiped the Lord with her aromatic treasure, but the Lord gave it profound theological purpose. In coming to her defense, Jesus praised her devotion as a good deed and used the occasion to signal the coming of His own death. The first step in preparing a body for burial was to rinse it with water and anoint it with perfumed oil. Phillip Keller offers a perspective I hadn't considered before. He describes the effect of her worship this way:

> The delicious fragrance ran down over His shining hair and thick beard. It enfolded His body with its delightful aroma. Even His tunic and flowing undergarment were drenched with its enduring pungency. Wherever He moved during the ensuing forty-eight hours the perfume would go with Him: into the Passover, into the Garden of Gethsemane, into the high priest's home, into Herod's hall, into Pilate's praetorium, into the crude hands of those who cast lots for His clothing at the foot of the cross.[1]

Jesus would go into His ordeal already prepared for the grave.

— 14:10-11 —

The Gospel of John gives particular attention to Judas during this episode. Something about the evening brought the false disciple to his end. It may have been the public rebuke he received. The Lord's attitude toward the woman's "waste" may have triggered his betrayal. Most likely, however, he had heard his Messiah predict His own demise one too many times. Like most Jews, he longed for a military-political king who would stand against Rome's authority and restore Israel's fortunes. But Jesus didn't speak of conquest; He kept talking about dying.

Judas began colluding with Jesus' enemies to "betray" Him. The term used for this means, literally, to "hand over." While in public, thousands of witnesses protected Jesus from harm. The religious leaders wouldn't risk inciting their anger. To make Jesus disappear quietly, they needed an insider to help them carry out a quiet abduction, preferably at a time and place with no witnesses.

— 14:12-16 —

Mark indicates the day as "the first day of Unleavened Bread, when the Passover lamb was being sacrificed" (14:12). His description of the day fits the Gentile view of the Jewish festival. Technically, "Unleavened Bread" doesn't start until the fifteenth of Nisan, which begins at sundown the day the lambs are sacrificed. But by Gentile reckoning, which begins a new day at midnight, this was Thursday, the fourteenth day of Nisan.

Like most out-of-town guests, Jesus and His disciples would have had to rent or borrow banquet space somewhere inside the city walls. It seems like—to maintain security—Jesus had two of His men follow a plan that would keep the location and the hosts a secret. They were to look for a signal: the unusual sight of a man carrying a water jar. Usually women carried water from the community well to the home. This would have been like looking for a man in our day carrying a purse. Without engaging him publicly, they were to follow the man to the right house. The owner would know from the designation "the Teacher" that the disciples were in fact His representatives and should be given access to the upper room (14:14).

In those days, houses were simple structures with a second story added for the sake of hospitality or to generate extra income. Guests could use an external stairway to access the upper room without disturbing anyone below. This room would have already been swept clean of leaven in anticipation of the feast and would have contained all the necessary furnishings. The disciples were to prepare the lamb they had already secured by the tenth day of Nisan (Exod. 12:3). In addition to the lamb, which would be killed in the temple later that day, they needed bitter herbs, unleavened bread, and wine.

By midday on the fourteenth, all work came to an end as a representative of each family carried their lamb to the temple. At about three o'clock in the afternoon, a Levite blew the ram's horn, worshipers filled the temple court, and the massive gates closed behind them. Each representative then killed his lamb, skinned it, and drained its blood into a basin.

While this mass killing of lambs is hard for the twenty-first-century reader to imagine, killing a lamb and preparing it for supper was as ordinary a task as driving to the supermarket to shop for groceries. For Passover, however, the lamb was killed in the temple to be consecrated as a substitute. Worshipers drained the animal's blood into a basin held by a priest, who then splashed it against the base of the altar to signify atonement for sin. The fat and kidneys were burnt on the altar as a part of the peace offering, reaffirming good relations between God and the worshiper's family.

After the sacrifice, each household representative took the lamb home before sunset and roasted the meat. In keeping with God's instructions to Moses, the disciples smeared some of the blood on the doorposts and lintel of the main entrance of their dwelling.

— 14:17-21 —

Within a short space of days, we find Jesus and His disciples again reclining at a banquet. Earlier, a woman had used such an occasion to express her worship and devotion for her Savior, lavishing upon Him what would have been nearly a year's income for a laborer. This banquet would be different. Jesus would announce that one of their number—one of the Twelve—would hand Him over (14:18). The other men knew exactly what this meant. A trusted disciple would betray his Master.

Matthew and John, writing many years later, both singled out Judas at this point (Matt. 26:25; John 13:26-27), but Mark chose to leave the betrayer standing quietly among the Twelve. He had already been identified for us in Mark 14:10-11, but in this scene Judas stood among his peers, saying along with them, "Surely not I?" (14:19; cf. Matt. 26:22). The image of betrayers among the faithful must have resonated deeply among the persecuted believers in Rome. All four Gospels indicate that Jesus knew the identity of the mole but didn't expose Judas to his peers. He would later reveal the betrayer to Peter and John (John 13:24-26), but at this time, Jesus merely affirmed that it was one of their number, a kinsman, a man sharing the bitter herb dip representing the bitterness of their bondage in Egypt. With Judas blinking in disbelief like his innocent companions, Jesus issued a chilling warning, using the classic Hebrew "woe" (Mark 14:21). This Old Testament interjection was a mourning sound—a deep moan—uttered in response to personal anguish or prompted by pity for the suffering of another. It could also convey a warning, as if to say, "I deeply pity you if this is true." Nonexistence would be a better option than betraying the Son of God or His people.

APPLICATION: MARK 14:1-21
Choose Grace

As we review the stories of these two banquets, three truths emerge that may help you to discern where you are in your relationship with God and to determine how you will respond to Him.

First, *Christ has a prearranged plan for each of our lives.* The disciples may have wondered where they were to spend Passover. Rooms were undoubtedly in short supply with so many people crowding the city. And the room had to be cleared of all leaven no less than two days in advance. As the day approached, they received no instructions until the last possible moment. Then they discovered that Jesus had planned every meticulous detail for their celebration. He had prearranged the meal, the people involved, the man with the water jar, and the owner of the home waiting for the disciples. He'd had the room prepared in keeping with the Law and furnished with everything they needed.

Frequently when you go through really difficult times and later look back, you realize how everything ended up being put together as only God could have done it. At the time it may have seemed so unplanned—even chaotic. But looking back, you can see a plan unfolding.

God formulates plans to accomplish one objective: to deepen your relationship with Him. As you mature in faith, you will learn to discern the Father's will and flow with it instead of striving to do things your own way. When you first begin your spiritual journey, you think you know better than He does, so you resist things that are uncomfortable or distasteful.

Take note of something interesting in this passage, however. In God's prearranged plan, the disciples had to prepare the meal. They were involved. So we're not like robots moving through a prearranged plan. God gives us a critical role to fill, but it's all for a purpose known only to Him, and ultimately, to bring us into closer intimacy with Him.

Second, *Christ continues to express His love and extend His grace even to the worst among us.* Jesus knew far more about Judas than we'll ever know. We know about his despicable deed, his betrayal of the Lord into the hands of His enemies. But Jesus could see deeply into the darkness of Judas's heart, and He knew the depths of the man's sinfulness as only God can. Yet He allowed Judas to stand among the faithful and invited him to attend His last meal. And, to the very end, He gave His betrayer an opportunity to turn from sin, to repent, and to receive forgiveness.

We can vilify Judas as a monster, but our depravity is just as deep and dark as his. We made ourselves enemies of God through the rebellion of sin, yet He graciously extended grace to save us from our own depravity. How gracious He has been to us, even though we continue to engage in selfishness, impure motives, unfaithfulness, and acts that reveal a lack of devotion. He has every right to write us off and wipe us out, but His love overflows and His grace comes to our rescue. We cannot do anything so wicked that it will turn away His love. He extends His grace to us day after day.

When Jesus shared a final meal with Judas, He said, in effect, "Judas, think about this. Consider what you're doing. This is your moment to turn from sin and to accept me as your Messiah, your Savior."

Third, *anyone is free to reject Christ's offer and retreat into darkness.* Yes, any one of us. Judas didn't have to do what he did; he *chose* to betray his Master. God prearranged His plan, but He didn't compel Judas to sin. Judas chose evil, and God used it to accomplish His will.

Where do you stand today? You're no Judas, but you face a choice much like his. You can serve evil, or you can submit to Christ. Are you faithful in your marriage, or are you betraying it? Do you honor your calling, or do you undermine it? Are you honest at your workplace, or do you take shortcuts? Are you a Judas in these ways? God's grace will let you continue for a time; meanwhile, He extends grace and invites you to repent and receive His forgiveness. There will come a day, however, when God will say, "That's enough."

Today is the day to turn. The word is "repent." It means to change your mind, to turn around, to retreat from the darkness of your own transgressions and move toward the light of Christ's truth. Confess your sin and let the grace of God restore you.

Special Meal, Shocking Temptation
MARK 14:22-42

NASB

²²While they were eating, He took *some* bread, and ªafter a blessing He broke *it,* and gave *it* to them, and said, "Take *it;* this is My body." ²³And when He had taken a cup *and* given thanks, He gave *it* to them, and they all drank from it. ²⁴And He said to them, "This is My blood of the covenant, which is poured out for many. ²⁵Truly I say to you, I will never again drink of the fruit of the vine until that day when I drink it new in the kingdom of God."

²⁶After singing a hymn, they went out to the Mount of Olives.

²⁷And Jesus said to them, "You will all ªfall away, because it is written, 'I WILL STRIKE DOWN THE SHEPHERD, AND THE SHEEP SHALL BE SCATTERED.' ²⁸But after I have been raised, I will go ahead of you to Galilee." ²⁹But Peter said to Him, "*Even* though all may ªfall away, yet I will not." ³⁰And Jesus said to him, "Truly I say to you, that ªthis very night, before a rooster crows twice, you yourself will deny Me three times." ³¹But *Peter* kept saying insistently, "*Even* if I have to die with You, I will not deny You!" And they all were saying the same thing also.

³²They came to a place named Gethsemane; and He said to His disciples, "Sit here until I have prayed." ³³And He took with Him Peter and ªJames and John, and began to be very distressed and troubled. ³⁴And He said to them, "My soul is deeply grieved to the point of death; remain

NLT

²²As they were eating, Jesus took some bread and blessed it. Then he broke it in pieces and gave it to the disciples, saying, "Take it, for this is my body."

²³And he took a cup of wine and gave thanks to God for it. He gave it to them, and they all drank from it. ²⁴And he said to them, "This is my blood, which confirms the covenant* between God and his people. It is poured out as a sacrifice for many. ²⁵I tell you the truth, I will not drink wine again until the day I drink it new in the Kingdom of God."

²⁶Then they sang a hymn and went out to the Mount of Olives.

²⁷On the way, Jesus told them, "All of you will desert me. For the Scriptures say,

'God will strike* the Shepherd,
    and the sheep will be
        scattered.'

²⁸But after I am raised from the dead, I will go ahead of you to Galilee and meet you there."

²⁹Peter said to him, "Even if everyone else deserts you, I never will."

³⁰Jesus replied, "I tell you the truth, Peter—this very night, before the rooster crows twice, you will deny three times that you even know me."

³¹"No!" Peter declared emphatically. "Even if I have to die with you, I will never deny you!" And all the others vowed the same.

³²They went to the olive grove called Gethsemane, and Jesus said, "Sit here while I go and pray." ³³He took Peter, James, and John with him, and he became deeply troubled and distressed. ³⁴He told them, "My soul is crushed with grief to the point of death. Stay here and keep watch with me."

here and keep watch." ³⁵ And He went a little beyond *them,* and fell to the ground and *began* to pray that if it were possible, the hour might ªpass Him by. ³⁶ And He was saying, "Abba! Father! All things are possible for You; remove this cup from Me; yet not what I will, but what You will." ³⁷ And He came and found them sleeping, and said to Peter, "Simon, are you asleep? Could you not keep watch for one hour? ³⁸ Keep watching and praying that you may not come into temptation; the spirit is willing, but the flesh is weak." ³⁹ Again He went away and prayed, saying the same ªwords. ⁴⁰ And again He came and found them sleeping, for their eyes were very heavy; and they did not know what to answer Him. ⁴¹ And He came the third time, and said to them, "ªAre you still sleeping and resting? It is enough; the hour has come; behold, the Son of Man is being ᵇbetrayed into the hands of sinners. ⁴² Get up, let us be going; behold, the one who betrays Me is at hand!"

14:22 ªLit *having blessed* **14:27** ªOr *stumble* **14:29** ªOr *stumble* **14:30** ªLit *today, on this night* **14:33** ªOr *Jacob* **14:35** ªLit *pass from Him* **14:39** ªLit *word* **14:41** ªOr *Keep on sleeping therefore* ᵇOr *delivered*

³⁵ He went on a little farther and fell to the ground. He prayed that, if it were possible, the awful hour awaiting him might pass him by. ³⁶ "Abba, Father,"* he cried out, "everything is possible for you. Please take this cup of suffering away from me. Yet I want your will to be done, not mine." ³⁷ Then he returned and found the disciples asleep. He said to Peter, "Simon, are you asleep? Couldn't you watch with me even one hour? ³⁸ Keep watch and pray, so that you will not give in to temptation. For the spirit is willing, but the body is weak." ³⁹ Then Jesus left them again and prayed the same prayer as before. ⁴⁰ When he returned to them again, he found them sleeping, for they couldn't keep their eyes open. And they didn't know what to say. ⁴¹ When he returned to them the third time, he said, "Go ahead and sleep. Have your rest. But no—the time has come. The Son of Man is betrayed into the hands of sinners. ⁴² Up, let's be going. Look, my betrayer is here!"

14:24 Some manuscripts read *the new covenant.* **14:27** Greek *I will strike.* Zech 13:7. **14:36** *Abba* is an Aramaic term for "father."

What do you do when someone strong in your life suddenly becomes weak? For as long as you can remember, you've been able to lean on that individual. You've found that person stable, strong, faithful, and reliable, and now all of that has changed.

Children face this challenge when a parent suddenly becomes ill or can no longer live independently. They've always had that mother or father there for support, advice, guidance, and perspective. This also occurs in divorce. The children have always known that mom and dad were standing together, pulling together, working together—but then their once solid home fractures. An empty seat at the dinner table reminds everyone that a parent is missing.

Athletes know the stabilizing influence of a coach, who always has a plan for winning, who challenges, encourages, and inspires. As the season runs on and the competition becomes intense, the coach drags the team out of confusion, unites the players, and gives the group a common goal on which to focus. But what if, suddenly and unexpectedly, their coach is gone for whatever reason? When that coach is taken away from the game, the team falters. The coach is the tenth man on the baseball diamond, the twelfth man on the football field—as important as any player in the game, if not more so.

Jesus understood His role as the leader to His disciples. He had prepared them from the beginning to take the reins of leadership one day, but He knew how difficult the transition would be. For three years— probably more—He had been their shepherd, coach, friend, confidant, teacher, and guiding force. Everything the group faced He handled. If it was a storm, He could calm it. If it was a disease, He could heal it. If it was a physical abnormality, He could correct it. He cast out demons, fed multitudes, silenced critics, and freed sinners. Now, the time approached for Him to walk the Way of Suffering alone. The disciples would have to carry on without His physical presence.

He had one final evening with His companions, and He wanted to make the most of the time. Following their celebration of the Passover meal together, the shock would begin to set in as His disciples saw Him tempted as never before and found themselves afraid and confused in the face of the events He had told them about throughout His ministry.

— 14:22 —

We have no literature that describes the rituals observed during the Passover meal in the first century. What we know today as the seder developed over the centuries after the destruction of Jerusalem. The seder traditions most likely grew out of common elements observed during Jesus' time. If the Lord observed the customs preserved by the Mishnah, He recast some of the symbols to assign them new significance. For example, the head of the household would hold up a portion of the unleavened bread and would call it "the bread of affliction." Jesus broke this bread and declared, "This is My body," which the disciples would soon see beaten and bruised by His enemies.

This, of course, became the first of two elements we observe today in Communion.

— 14:23-25 —

The first ceremonial cup called for the head of the household to recite a blessing called the *kiddush* (literally, "sanctification"). This prayer blesses God for His faithfulness to Israel in the Exodus, for giving them the Law, for granting a day of rest, and for calling them to celebrate feast days. Instead of sipping the wine, Jesus passed it to His disciples saying, "This is My blood of the covenant, which is poured out for many" (14:24). Throughout Israel's history, God had sealed covenants with the blood of a sacrifice (cf. Exod. 24:8; Lev. 17:11-14). Jeremiah prophesied that there would be another covenant made by God where he would write His Law on their hearts; this covenant was known to faithful Jews as the new covenant (Jer. 31:31-34). Within hours, the disciples would see the Messiah's blood flow freely from the cross.

This wine, representing Christ's blood, would be the second of two elements observed by Christians in Communion.

Jesus also announced that He would no longer drink wine until His mission was complete. This may have been a reference to a Jewish custom known as the Nazirite vow, a promise to abstain from all grape products and to refrain from cutting one's hair until a consecrated task had been completed.

— 14:26 —

According to John and Luke, Jesus spent considerable time teaching final lessons to the disciples, preparing them for the difficult hours to come and the confusing days that would follow. Mark moves the action along. After the meal, Jesus led the group—now minus Judas—across the Kidron Valley to a customary spot on the western slope of the Mount of Olives. This may be the same place where Jesus had given the Olivet discourse a few days earlier.

— 14:27-28 —

To prepare His disciples, Jesus peered into their future and declared to them that they would all "fall away" (14:27). The verb Mark uses is *skandalizō* [4624]. In the passive voice, it means "to fall into a trap" or "to come to one's end." Jesus substantiated His prediction by appealing to the prophecy of Zechariah:

> "Awake, O sword, against My Shepherd,
> And against the man, My Associate,"
> Declares the LORD of hosts.
> "Strike the Shepherd that the sheep may be scattered;
> And I will turn My hand against the little ones." (Zech. 13:7)

He reassured them, however, that this would not spell the end of

A Table for Common Union

MARK 14:22-25

An Old English proverb says, "Spread the table and contention will cease." A shared meal has the power to bring people together. Enemies often find common ground when breaking bread together. Friends grow closer while lingering over a good meal seasoned with great conversation. Busy families discover that the dinner table becomes the hub around which household life revolves; it's where each person finds connection. We gather to eat when we conduct business, make peace, build teams, find romance, celebrate achievements, congratulate winners, console losers, and of course, observe holidays.

The Lord knows the power of the shared meal to bring people together, so it should be no surprise that He ordered Israel to observe several commemorative "feasts" each year, three of which were mandatory. The Feast of the Passover continues to be one of the most important feasts in the national life of Israel because it calls for families to share a special, symbolic meal that rehearses their origin.

When God freed Israel from bondage in Egypt, Moses received instructions to prepare a lamb a certain way and to honor the Lord's presence by spreading the lamb's blood on the lintel and doorposts of every Israelite's house (Exod. 12). When the death angel moved through Egypt to take the life of the firstborn male in each household, he "pass[ed] over" every home bearing the blood of a sacrificial lamb (see Exod. 12:23). In keeping with the instructions given for the first Passover in Egypt, families smeared some of the blood on the doorposts and lintel of the main entrance. For the meal, they prepared meat from the sacrificial lamb along with bitter herbs, unleavened bread, and wine.

Normally, Jews gathered around the table with their families, so it's significant that Jesus and the Twelve observed the Passover feast together. The Lord's students had no idea how momentous this particular meal would be. As Jews—sons of the old covenant—they observed a tradition nearly fifteen hundred years old. As apostles of the new covenant, they would help institute a new tradition that would last two thousand years . . . and counting. It is a meal Christians continue to celebrate as Communion, a word derived from the Latin term communio—"sharing in common."

their relationship. Even though His followers would fall away due to weakness and fear, God would remain faithful. The new covenant, once entered by faith, cannot be broken by unfaithfulness. The elect will persevere to the end. After His resurrection—which He had predicted at least three times (Mark 8:31; 9:31; 10:34)—Jesus promised to meet them in Galilee, where He would put the mission back on track.

— 14:29-31 —

Peter boldly protested, "Even though all may fall away, yet I will not" (14:29), implying that he loved Jesus more than the other disciples. Jesus saw the impulsive disciple's inevitable failure, and He gave him the precise details of his future rejection of Jesus. He would use this later to reassure Peter that his faithlessness, a direct result of his weakness, did not change his divine calling. Jesus had foreseen his failure. If God intended to reject Peter for his weakness, He would have simply left him on his fishing boat more than three years earlier.

The others joined Peter, insisting they would stand by Jesus, even if it cost them their lives. They undoubtedly had a battle of swords in mind, and they probably would have died with Jesus if the battle was the kind that involved armed conflict with flesh-and-blood enemies. But the remaining eleven disciples had no idea what they would soon face. Their first great challenge would take place within the hour. In a beautiful garden setting, the unwary disciples would encounter the ugly face of evil and suffer the first of several failures.

— 14:32-34 —

Luke states that Gethsemane was located on the Mount of Olives (Luke 22:39), while John describes the place as a garden "over the ravine of the Kidron" (John 18:1). Both Gospels indicate that Jesus and His disciples often went there for solitude and prayer (Luke 22:39; John 18:2). The name Gethsemane means "oil press," probably because the owner cultivated olives and had installed a press on the grounds (but the meaning becomes especially meaningful in this narrative). At night the garden would have been particularly foreboding with its ancient, gnarled olive trees and narrow paths barely lit by the moon. Blanketed by thick darkness in the place of crushing, Jesus endured the assault of Satan.

Jesus could have left the disciples in the upper room or sent them ahead to Bethany, but He brought them with Him and asked them to remain nearby. Jesus bore the nature of a man, and people need

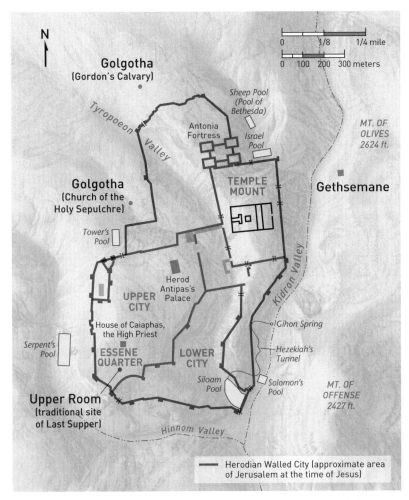

N

| 0 | 1/8 | 1/4 mile |
| 0 | 100 | 200 | 300 meters |

Golgotha
(Gordon's Calvary)

Tyropoeon Valley

Sheep Pool
(Pool of
Bethesda)

Antonia
Fortress

Israel
Pool

MT. OF
OLIVES
2624 ft.

Golgotha
(Church of the
Holy Sepulchre)

TEMPLE
MOUNT

Gethsemane

Tower's
Pool

Kidron Valley

UPPER
CITY

Herod
Antipas's
Palace

Gihon Spring

House of Caiaphas,
the High Priest

Serpent's
Pool

ESSENE
QUARTER

LOWER
CITY

Hezekiah's
Tunnel

Siloam
Pool

Solomon's
Pool

MT. OF
OFFENSE
2427 ft.

Upper Room
(traditional site
of Last Supper)

Hinnom Valley

— Herodian Walled City (approximate area
of Jerusalem at the time of Jesus)

After supper, Jesus and his disciples walked across town, past the Temple Mount, to Gethsemane on the Mount of Olives.

companionship. God created us for relationships, not only with Himself, but with other people. As Jesus faced that long, torturous night, He invited His closest friends to join Him in prayer. He stationed most of the men by the entrance to the enclosed garden and asked Peter, James, and John to stay near and remain within sight.

Mark describes Jesus as "distressed" and "troubled" (Mark 14:33). One lexicon describes the Greek term for "distressed" (*ekthambeō* [1568]) as an intensified form of a verb meaning "to be moved to a relatively intense emotional state because of something causing great surprise or perplexity."[2] The word could also be rendered "terrified." Something in the garden came upon Jesus suddenly with great emotional intensity,

The name **Gethsemane** means "olive press." This olive grove is the traditional site of Jesus' last anguished night before His arrest. Because many such gardens occupied the Mount of Olives, no can be certain of the exact location. Regardless, Gethsemane looked very similar to this picture.

leaving Him feeling anxious "to the point of death" (14:34). He immediately expressed His distress and called upon the men to "keep watch," in Mark 13:34-37 ("be on the alert"), a word that has a distinct end-time nuance. The idea is "Be ready for the inevitable."

— 14:35-36 —

This is the only instance recorded in Scripture where the Son's will struggled with the will of His Father. Here the humanity of Jesus is on full display. Those who have trouble seeing Jesus as human should make a serious study of this passage. We tend to highlight the divinity of Jesus while downplaying His humanity. A surprisingly powerful desire to avoid the suffering of the cross overtook Jesus, and He begged the Father to let Him avoid "this cup" (14:36). He struggled with the temptation to avoid the personal injustice of bearing God's wrath for the world's sin. After all, why should He have to suffer on behalf of sinful humanity? No moral imperative required God to sacrifice His Son. He would be no less holy or righteous if He allowed all people to suffer the just consequences of their own rebellion. Nothing required Jesus to suffer on the cross . . . except His unconditional love for people and unreserved obedience to His Father.

In other words, Satan offered Jesus an alternative to obedience; he made self-service and self-preservation appear more attractive. So we see a man in a garden with two options before Him: obedience to God or loyalty to self. Unlike Adam, however, Jesus cried out to the Father, acknowledging the depth of His temptation and His desperate need for the Father's strength. While Mark gives us the gist of the Son's petition in one sentence, his description reveals a long, agonizing prayer. Jesus called upon God for an hour (14:37). The phrase "fell to the ground" (14:35) uses the imperfect tense—"was falling"—suggesting that Jesus walked a short distance and fell, walked a little further, and fell again. For an hour, Jesus walked and fell in anguish, pleading for relief from His mission.

— 14:37-39 —

Jesus returned to where He had left Peter, James, and John to find them sleeping instead of praying and watching as He had requested. He pleaded with Peter to remain faithful in his "keeping watch and praying" (14:38). Jesus understood from personal experience the vulnerability and weakness of being human. While He did not have a sin-sick nature enslaved to selfishness, He felt the powerful lure of self-preservation. He understood firsthand the dangers mere humans face when they neglect to seek God's strength when their own strength falters.

Jesus felt the continual, unrelenting onslaught of temptation, so He retreated again into the shadows of the olive trees to pray, and He prayed "the same words" (14:39). He again asked for permission to abandon His mission, to avoid the agony of bearing God's punishment for all of humanity's collective sin. For another hour, He looked for a way out, but again He arrived at a place of submission to God's will.

— 14:40-42 —

Jesus prayed to overcome His temptation for three hours, repeating and rehearsing His desire to escape His destiny, each time yielding to the will of His Father.

It is important to remember that *this* is where Jesus struggled, not on the cross. The cross became the place of victory. There He dealt the ultimate deathblow to death, winning the victory over sin, the grave, and the devil. His struggle took place in Gethsemane, where temptation told Him to slip away into the night and disappear like a vapor. This is where evil pitched its last, desperate battle to derail the redemptive plan of God. Evil lost the fight.

Jesus emerged the victor over temptation. Adam had succumbed and dragged all of humanity into slavery to sin. Jesus triumphed, and through His obedience made a way for humanity to approach God, to find release from bondage to sin, and to be lifted up from depravity. Jesus finally felt the relief and the release that come from submitting to the Father. The struggle ended when He emerged from the twisted shadows of the garden, fully resolute to complete His mission.

He ordered His men to rise from sleep so they might witness first-hand His betrayal, mistreatment, injustice, death, burial, and resurrection. With the struggle over and with temptation behind Him, He stepped forward to greet His alleged friend who had betrayed Him.

APPLICATION: MARK 14:22-42
Your Gethsemane

Mark, under the direction of the Holy Spirit, didn't include this part of Jesus' biography merely for historical purposes. Just as Jesus entered His Gethsemane, you and I will inevitably enter ours. For many of us, there will be more than one Gethsemane—a time when we are tempted to avoid doing what we should because we know that doing right will cost us dearly and hurt us deeply. Such times may well be accompanied by fear and confusion, and by friends who seem distracted and un-available. Based on my own journey and from my years as a spiritual guide, I know of at least four types of Gethsemane experiences. We must face these with unrestrained trust in God alone.

First, you might experience *relational struggles*. By this I mean challenges in your relationships with other people. Some of the most difficult relational struggles can happen in the context of maintaining a healthy relationship with one's spouse. In a marriage, there are a lot of struggles that come with living so closely with another individual, adjusting one's life, and adapting to a person so different. Marriages often enjoy a fairy-tale beginning and then give way to a mundane daily grind, punctuated by moments of pure joy and heartbreaking sorrow. This is real life. There will be moments when walking away looks infinitely more attractive than embracing the "for worse" part of marriage.

Family relationships can be overwhelming, especially when the people with whom you share a name happen to be borderline insane!

People at work apparently have as their job descriptions a directive to make your job impossible. Friends grow close and then pierce your heart. Leaders disappoint, followers rebel, and peers betray. We're surrounded by difficult individuals, each one creating for us moments in which we have a choice to either love unselfishly or sin to serve ourselves.

Usually, these relational struggles are relatively minor and resolve quickly. Sometimes, however, a relationship creates for us a Gethsemane moment, and what we decide has the power to affect many other lives at a significant level. The choices come down to two: obedience or selfishness.

Second, you might experience *vocational struggles.* This has to do with your work, your calling, your vocation. If your job involves a calling, there was a point when you said, as it were, "Lord, I commit to serve in this vocation." That decision may have been made in a dimly lit garden like Jesus in Gethsemane. You may have struggled with the plusses and minuses of following this vocational path instead of another. Then, having made this commitment, you will inevitably face a crisis in which you will doubt your calling or regret your commitment. Walking away will appear more reasonable than sticking to it.

I'm not suggesting that no one should change jobs. It's not uncommon for people to have multiple careers. Changing vocational tracks is not necessarily sinful. The question is a matter of motivation for quitting. All too often people leave their vocational commitments because the struggle to continue becomes too intense. They don't necessarily sense a calling to another occupation; they simply feel hopeless to continue, so they quit.

The Gethsemane garden is not the place to change the plan. The question asked in the garden is, "Will you obey, or will you quit?"

My advice: Obey first; reconsider your vocation when the struggle has been resolved.

Third, you might experience *personal struggles.* These are struggles within ourselves, not related so much to work or to marriage or to friendships. These are internal difficulties such as addiction, depression, resentment, racism, narcissism, or mental health disorders. Many of these struggles cannot be overcome without the help of others, so the decision must be to take the first step toward recovery. Usually, that first step requires a sacrifice of pride. Admit to others that you struggle. (They already know.) Admit to yourself that you need help. (You know this already.) And then do what you have been putting off too long.

This Gethsemane calls you to follow through on what you know is right and to set aside selfish pride.

Finally, you might experience *spiritual struggles*. This has to do with Christ's active role in your life. What place does He occupy in your day-to-day existence? I'm not talking about churchgoing and hymn singing, although I love both. I mean His place in your life twenty-four hours a day, seven days a week. Is He truly number one? Is He the preeminent force of your life . . . your Lord . . . your Master? Do you *long* to honor Him more than anything or anyone else, or do you fight against His will? How important is "stuff"—money, possessions, power, position—and how difficult is it to sacrifice all this for the kingdom of God?

Do you sense a strong tug at your conscience to do something difficult or sacrificial that would help others, or advance the gospel, or otherwise please God? Never doubt it: Gethsemane calls for sacrifice over comfort. Gethsemane is God's invitation to set aside what you love today in exchange for unseen, unimaginable grace.

An Enemy's Deceitful Kiss
MARK 14:43-52

NASB

43 Immediately while He was still speaking, Judas, one of the twelve, came up ªaccompanied by a crowd with swords and clubs, *who were* from the chief priests and the scribes and the elders. 44 Now he who was betraying Him had given them a signal, saying, "Whomever I kiss, He is the one; seize Him and lead Him away ªunder guard." 45 After coming, Judas immediately went to Him, saying, "Rabbi!" and kissed Him. 46 They laid hands on Him and seized Him. 47 But one of those who stood by drew his sword, and struck the slave of the high priest and ªcut off his ear. 48 And Jesus said to them, "Have you come out with swords and clubs to arrest Me, as *you would* against a robber?

NLT

43 And immediately, even as Jesus said this, Judas, one of the twelve disciples, arrived with a crowd of men armed with swords and clubs. They had been sent by the leading priests, the teachers of religious law, and the elders. 44 The traitor, Judas, had given them a prearranged signal: "You will know which one to arrest when I greet him with a kiss. Then you can take him away under guard." 45 As soon as they arrived, Judas walked up to Jesus. "Rabbi!" he exclaimed, and gave him the kiss.

46 Then the others grabbed Jesus and arrested him. 47 But one of the men with Jesus pulled out his sword and struck the high priest's slave, slashing off his ear.

48 Jesus asked them, "Am I some dangerous revolutionary, that you come with swords and clubs to arrest

49 Every day I was with you in the temple teaching, and you did not seize Me; but *this has taken place* to fulfill the Scriptures." 50 And they all left Him and fled.

51 A young man was following Him, wearing *nothing but* a linen sheet over *his* naked *body;* and they seized him. 52 But he ᵃpulled free of the linen sheet and escaped naked.

14:43 ᵃLit *and with him*   14:44 ᵃLit *safely*
14:47 ᵃLit *took off*   14:52 ᵃLit *left behind*

me? 49 Why didn't you arrest me in the Temple? I was there among you teaching every day. But these things are happening to fulfill what the Scriptures say about me."

50 Then all his disciples deserted him and ran away. 51 One young man following behind was clothed only in a long linen shirt. When the mob tried to grab him, 52 he slipped out of his shirt and ran away naked.

It is a sad fact that loyalty is extremely rare. Unfailing faithfulness is exceedingly difficult to find. Because that is true, it's the number one quality I seek when hiring someone. I can teach knowledge. I can train skills. Give me a teachable man or woman with loyal character, and my organization will take wings and fly. But I can't make a loyal employee out of an untrustworthy candidate.

All four Gospels indicate that Jesus knew that Judas would sell his loyalty and betray his Master. Nevertheless, He washed the feet of the duplicitous disciple (John 13:2-5), gave him an honored place next to Him at the Last Supper, and offered him a tender gesture of friendship (John 13:26), *knowing* what Judas planned to do. What grace! Rather than reject and remove Judas—as I most certainly would have done without hesitation—Jesus drew him closer. To the end, Jesus loved His enemy.

Judas set off to complete his evil errand during or shortly after the Passover meal with Jesus and the disciples, which was held somewhere inside the city walls. He undoubtedly knew Jesus would head for His customary location to pray (cf. Luke 21:37; John 18:2) and arranged to have Him arrested there. Meanwhile Jesus prepared Himself and urged the other eleven disciples to pray and keep watch. When Judas finally stepped into the walled garden, the Lord was waiting for him.

— 14:43-44 —

As Judas approached Jesus, a small army assembled by the Sanhedrin took up positions around the garden perimeter. There were temple guards supported by Roman troops, all of them armed with swords and ready for battle. The Greek term for "clubs" (14:43) describes any object crafted from wood for a specific purpose. This could be a pole, a club, a cross, or—as would be reasonable in this context—stocks, "a device for confining the extremities of a prisoner."[3] They came ready to take Jesus into custody.

Judas had arranged to give the arresting force a signal to help them identify Jesus in the dark and avoid arresting the wrong man by mistake. It is important to note that Judas could have simply pointed to Jesus and shouted, "This is the man you seek!" He instead arranged a clandestine signal so that he might remain anonymous after the Lord's arrest. He planned to kiss Jesus in the custom of the ancient Near East to signal to the band of armed priests and teachers whom they should arrest.

Interestingly, Judas appears to have anticipated a kind of protective custody. The term rendered "under guard" (14:44) means, literally, "securely" or "reliably." It carries the idea of safeguarding something. Judas had apparently rationalized his betrayal so completely that he really thought he was doing a good deed, perhaps even thinking he acted in the Lord's best interests. It's not uncommon for unfaithful spouses to convince themselves that their adultery and abandonment is somehow good for everyone involved; they often feel noble as they carry out their treachery.

— 14:45-47 —

Judas greeted Jesus with what should have been a customary kiss on each cheek, much like we see today in the Middle East. A kiss was a customary greeting exchanged between a disciple and his master. This greeting was primarily a sign of respect, but Judas's kiss would have a sinister return.

Judas used his affection as a means of handing Jesus over to His enemies, and the treacherous disciple hoped to do so without losing the Lord's confidence or abdicating his high standing among his peers. His kiss was followed by the shouts and chaos of an invading army. They seized Jesus by force and put Him in stocks. During the melee, one of the disciples (Peter) drew his sword—really a long dagger intended for close-range fighting—and severed the ear of a temple servant.

— 14:48-49 —

Jesus' question was rhetorical. He meant to shame them by pointing out the absurdity of their actions. They could have arrested Him in public, but they clearly didn't want to answer publicly for their actions. Moreover, they treated Him like a "robber" (14:48), that is, a guerrilla

The Antithesis of Love

MARK 14:43-46

Having helped a number of people recover from betrayal has me convinced that a single act of treachery can scar someone so deeply that he or she may never completely recover. Trust can forever become a challenge. The bruise is deep. Betrayal is wounding to the soul. In fact, this is such a despicable act that the Bible includes this penetrating proverb: Faithful are the wounds of a friend, but deceitful are the kisses of an enemy (Prov. 27:6).

This is what Bible students call an antithetical proverb, an aphorism with two lines that stand in stark contrast. The verse creates a deep impact because both statements are counterintuitive. We don't make friends of people who wound us, and we don't let enemies come close enough to kiss us. We usually don't think of friendly wounds and malicious kisses.

According to this proverb, wounds inflicted by a friend are trustworthy. The Hebrew verb from which "faithful" is derived means "to confirm," "to support," or "to make sure and lasting." It's the act of a parent giving provision and protection to a child, or a nurse carrying an infant. The wounds of a friend cause short-term bruising to help us avoid a far worse pain in the future. This is your friend saying, "You have spinach in your teeth" or "You treat people poorly when you're hungry" or "You frequently talk over people and they feel demeaned by you" or "Your habit is turning into an addiction." A loyal friend will say things like that. They always do this in private, not to embarrass you, but to help you avoid future sorrow. Those are "faithful wounds."

On the other side, "the kisses of an enemy" have no good intentions. When an enemy kisses, betrayal always follows. "Kisses" can refer to a literal greeting, common in the ancient Near East, but it can also represent any gesture of kindness, affirmation, or encouragement. In other words, a treacherous person maintains a loving façade while harboring ill will or evil intentions. This deceitful kiss, whether literal or figurative, is the lowest, most cowardly form of betrayal. It is the absolute antithesis of love.

bandit who robbed as a means of funding his political insurrection. Jesus had earlier used this language against the temple authorities as He chased out the money changers (11:17).

But people without conscience cannot be shamed. Nothing Jesus said would turn them from their sin. He accepted the injustice as an indication that this, too, fulfilled prophecy and merely validated His identity as the Messiah (14:49; cf. Zech. 13:7).

— 14:50-52 —

By the time the soldiers led Jesus toward the garden entrance, the Twelve had disappeared into the night. Some ran without looking back, Judas among them. A handful cowered in the shadows watching Jesus from a distance. Just as Jesus had predicted, they all fell away (14:27).

Mark includes a curious note about a young man on the scene. The Greek indicates that he was a boy between twelve and seventeen. Curiously, he appears to have no other connection with the narrative, and the detail serves no obvious purpose. Among the chaos of torches, swords, stocks, scattering disciples, a deceptive kiss, and a lopped-off ear, the boy, dressed only in a linen undergarment, followed Jesus and the guard detachment down the slope. Obviously, he wasn't part of the raiding party, or he would have known to get dressed. He stood in the ancient equivalent of boxer shorts.

Some suggest—and I find this reasonable—that the young man was John Mark, the human author of this Gospel. John Mark was the son of a woman named Mary, probably one of Jesus' female benefactors (cf. Matt. 27:55; Mark 15:40-41; Luke 23:49; John 19:25; Acts 12:12). He may have been sleeping under the stars in the garden not far from the disciples. If this was the young man's identity, what we perceive as a cryptic detail was recognized by first-century Christians as a cameo appearance of the writer. Mark may have inserted this detail to admit to his own weak faithlessness that night in the garden.

When the guards saw the boy following them, they tried to grab him, but they failed to seize anything but his undershirt. It tore away and the young man ran into the darkness wearing nothing. Like a painter who signs the corner of a masterpiece, it's possible Mark signed this work to say that he became an eyewitness to some of the events.

Mark never again mentions Judas. After his betrayal, the traitor scurried into the darkness along with the "faithful" eleven, never to be seen again in this narrative. We know from Matthew's Gospel that he felt great remorse and shortly thereafter hanged himself (Matt. 27:5). Do not be fooled, however. Remorse is a far cry from repentance. Judas died in his sin, refusing to humble himself, confess his sin openly, seek Jesus' forgiveness, and then live humbly and contritely in that merciful acceptance. He served evil and was eventually consumed by evil.

APPLICATION: MARK 14:43-52

Lessons for the Judas in All of Us

Judas will forever be remembered as the most heinous traitor of all time. However, we are foolish to think that his story cannot become ours. Despite all the advantages he enjoyed as a close associate of Jesus, the promising young disciple became a Satan-possessed monster. And if we think we could never become something so despicable, we have failed to heed the warning of Scripture. Judas's act of betrayal originated as a sinful plan in his heart. Though he walked among the Twelve, his secret sin could not remain hidden forever. So also with sinful intentions in our lives. Secret sin is an indiscriminate killer, and those who think they are immune are the most vulnerable of all.

Four timely principles worth our consideration emerge from the tragic example of Judas.

First, *association with godliness is no guarantee that we will become godly.* Joining a healthy church and cultivating relationships with spiritually mature people should be a priority. We need healthy influences. However, associating with mature believers will not nourish the soul any more than merely sitting at a table in a restaurant will nourish the body. To grow wise and to develop spiritually, we must personally take in what Jesus has offered. For that to occur, we must submit to the truth we receive through His Word. Otherwise, we deceive ourselves and become our own worst enemy. A quaint, old English couplet says it all:

Still, as of old,
Man by himself is priced;
For thirty pieces Judas sold
Himself, not Christ.[4]

Second, *moral corruption in secret is deadlier than visible moral corruption.* There is no cancer deadlier than one that goes undetected. The same is true of sin. Keeping our sinful nature carefully concealed keeps us from applying the remedy Jesus provided through the gift of salvation. One of His disciples later wrote, "If we confess our sins, He is faithful and righteous to forgive us our sins and to cleanse us from all unrighteousness" (1 Jn. 1:9). Failure to confess our sins and receive forgiveness forces us to cope with the deadly effects of sin in ways that are sure to cause more damage later. In the case of Judas, it consumed him and resulted in suicide.

Third, *Satan and his demons are looking for any opportunity to work against the Lord.* Scripture teaches that the person who bears unresolved sin is an ideal vessel by which the devil can attack the people and plans of God (Eph. 4:25-27; cf. Gen. 4:6-7). At first, this person appears to be immune, but when Satan has done all the damage he can do, he leaves the vessel to be consumed by the sin it has carried.

Fourth, *no sorrow can compare to the remorse of those who discover too late that they have misunderstood Jesus and spurned His love.* Satan's primary tool is deception, which he uses to twist unresolved sin and selfish motivation to serve his purposes. Once he's finished using someone, he cruelly unmasks the truth to reveal the consequences of the person's foolish choices. The flood of shame, humiliation, regret, self-condemnation, and hopelessness can be overwhelming. Jesus, on the other hand, said (and continues to say), "If you continue in My word, then you are truly disciples of Mine; and you will know the truth, and the truth will make you free" (John 8:31-32). There is always hope for repentance and restoration through Jesus Christ, who has conquered the devil and offers victory to those who take shelter in Him.[5]

A Rush to Judgment
MARK 14:53-72

NASB

53 They led Jesus away to the high priest; and all the chief priests and the elders and the scribes gathered together. 54 Peter had followed Him at a distance, right into the courtyard of the high priest; and he was sitting with the aofficers and warming himself at the bfire. 55 Now the chief priests and the whole aCouncil kept trying to obtain testimony

NLT

53 They took Jesus to the high priest's home where the leading priests, the elders, and the teachers of religious law had gathered. 54 Meanwhile, Peter followed him at a distance and went right into the high priest's courtyard. There he sat with the guards, warming himself by the fire.

55 Inside, the leading priests and the entire high council* were trying

against Jesus to put Him to death, and they were not finding any. ⁵⁶For many were giving false testimony against Him, but their testimony was not consistent. ⁵⁷Some stood up and *began* to give false testimony against Him, saying, ⁵⁸"We heard Him say, 'I will destroy this ªtemple made with hands, and in three days I will build another made without hands.'" ⁵⁹Not even in this respect was their testimony consistent. ⁶⁰The high priest stood up *and came* forward and questioned Jesus, saying, "Do You not answer? ªWhat is it that these men are testifying against You?" ⁶¹But He kept silent and did not answer. Again the high priest was questioning Him, and ªsaying to Him, "Are You ᵇthe Christ, the Son of the Blessed *One?*" ⁶²And Jesus said, "I am; and you shall see THE SON OF MAN SITTING AT THE RIGHT HAND OF POWER, and COMING WITH THE CLOUDS OF HEAVEN." ⁶³Tearing his clothes, the high priest said, "What further need do we have of witnesses? ⁶⁴You have heard the blasphemy; how does it seem to you?" And they all condemned Him to be deserving of death. ⁶⁵Some began to spit at Him, and ªto blindfold Him, and to beat Him with their fists, and to say to Him, "Prophesy!" And the officers ᵇreceived Him with ᶜslaps *in the face.*

⁶⁶As Peter was below in the courtyard, one of the servant-girls of the high priest came, ⁶⁷and seeing Peter warming himself, she looked at him and said, "You also were with Jesus the Nazarene." ⁶⁸But he denied *it,* saying, "I neither know nor understand what you are talking about." And he went out onto the ªporch.ᵇ

to find evidence against Jesus, so they could put him to death. But they couldn't find any. ⁵⁶Many false witnesses spoke against him, but they contradicted each other. ⁵⁷Finally, some men stood up and gave this false testimony: ⁵⁸"We heard him say, 'I will destroy this Temple made with human hands, and in three days I will build another, made without human hands.'" ⁵⁹But even then they didn't get their stories straight!

⁶⁰Then the high priest stood up before the others and asked Jesus, "Well, aren't you going to answer these charges? What do you have to say for yourself?" ⁶¹But Jesus was silent and made no reply. Then the high priest asked him, "Are you the Messiah, the Son of the Blessed One?"

⁶²Jesus said, "I AM.* And you will see the Son of Man seated in the place of power at God's right hand* and coming on the clouds of heaven.*"

⁶³Then the high priest tore his clothing to show his horror and said, "Why do we need other witnesses? ⁶⁴You have all heard his blasphemy. What is your verdict?"

"Guilty!" they all cried. "He deserves to die!"

⁶⁵Then some of them began to spit at him, and they blindfolded him and beat him with their fists. "Prophesy to us," they jeered. And the guards slapped him as they took him away.

⁶⁶Meanwhile, Peter was in the courtyard below. One of the servant girls who worked for the high priest came by ⁶⁷and noticed Peter warming himself at the fire. She looked at him closely and said, "You were one of those with Jesus of Nazareth.*"

⁶⁸But Peter denied it. "I don't know what you're talking about," he said, and he went out into the entryway. Just then, a rooster crowed.*

NASB

⁶⁹ The servant-girl saw him, and began once more to say to the bystanders, "This is *one* of them!" ⁷⁰But again he denied it. And after a little while the bystanders were again saying to Peter, "Surely you are *one* of them, for you are a Galilean too." ⁷¹But he began to ᵃcurse and swear, "I do not know this man you are talking about!" ⁷²Immediately a rooster crowed a second time. And Peter remembered how Jesus had made the remark to him, "Before a rooster crows twice, you will deny Me three times." ᵃAnd he began to weep.

14:54 ᵃOr *servants* ᵇLit *light* 14:55 ᵃOr *Sanhedrin* 14:58 ᵃOr *sanctuary* 14:60 ᵃOr *what do these testify?* 14:61 ᵃLit *says* ᵇI.e. the Messiah 14:65 ᵃOr *cover over His face* ᵇOr *treated* ᶜOr *blows with rods* 14:68 ᵃOr *forecourt, gateway* ᵇLater mss add *and a rooster crowed* 14:71 ᵃOr *put himself under a curse* 14:72 ᵃOr *Thinking of this, he began weeping* or *Rushing out, he began weeping*

NLT

⁶⁹When the servant girl saw him standing there, she began telling the others, "This man is definitely one of them!" ⁷⁰But Peter denied it again.

A little later some of the other bystanders confronted Peter and said, "You must be one of them, because you are a Galilean."

⁷¹Peter swore, "A curse on me if I'm lying—I don't know this man you're talking about!" ⁷² And immediately the rooster crowed the second time.

Suddenly, Jesus' words flashed through Peter's mind: "Before the rooster crows twice, you will deny three times that you even know me." And he broke down and wept.

14:55 Greek *the Sanhedrin.* 14:62a Or *The 'I AM' is here;* or *I am the LORD.* See Exod 3:14. 14:62b Greek *seated at the right hand of the power.* See Ps 110:1. 14:62c See Dan 7:13. 14:67 Or *Jesus the Nazarene.* 14:68 Some manuscripts do not include *Just then, a rooster crowed.*

Few Christians today have a complete understanding of what transpired between the garden of Gethsemane and Golgotha. We understand what Jesus went through in the garden, and hopefully we understand what He went through at the cross. Few people, unfortunately, can recount the journey from His prayer of "Father! . . . remove this cup from Me" (14:36) to His final declaration, "It is finished" (John 19:30).

Most people think that there was one trial when there were, in fact, several. Many know that Jesus stood before Pilate; few know that He stood before other authority figures and a political body. Many would say He was found guilty of a crime, but this isn't the case. He was *declared* guilty, but never *found* guilty. As we'll see, Israel's official authorities committed crimes in order to condemn an innocent man. The trials that put Jesus of Nazareth on a criminal's cross were a classic example of a rush to judgment. They represent the darkest day in the history of jurisprudence.

Believe it or not, there is a bright side in all of this darkness. When you look at the circumstances through a theological lens, this miscarriage of justice is not a meaningless tragedy. What the enemies of Jesus intended for evil, God used for the good of all humanity. This would become the culmination of a divine plan that had been in the works since the day Adam and Eve fell . . . and before. Jesus opened for us a way out of the past, with its repeated sins and failures, and into a future of fellowship with the Father. While you and I hope to live a full, comfortable, and satisfying life, Jesus came to give His life as an atoning sacrifice for sin. He knew from the Scriptures that His life would lead to suffering on behalf of His people. By the time He approached Jerusalem, He knew His life would end on a Roman cross.

— 14:53-54 —

The first trial of Jesus took place immediately after His arrest in Gethsemane (see "The Trials of Jesus" on page 368). The arresting party took Him straight to the home of Annas, who was not the official high priest but was very much the power behind the supreme office in Israel's politics. Afterward, Jesus was sent to the son-in-law of Annas, a man named Caiaphas, the actual high priest. Mark and Luke both compress the events of the first and second trials.

Peter followed Jesus but kept his distance. While John gained entrance to the trial itself (John 18:15), Peter stood in the courtyard, hiding his identity and warming himself by a fire with a group of servants and soldiers.

— 14:55-59 —

Mark gained much of his information from his mentor, Peter, who stood outside the courtroom, but he depended upon the eyewitness account of John for details of the trial itself.

Jesus stood before Caiaphas and members of the Sanhedrin, who unsuccessfully sought evidence to convict Jesus of something—anything—to justify putting Him to death. The trial itself was illegal. According to their own rules, trials could not be held in secret, or at night, or in a venue other than the council's meeting hall in the temple. Additionally, no advocate for the accused had been provided. And, worst of all, capital cases were supposed to begin with an accusation and then move immediately to arguments for *acquittal*.[6] In this trial, the council summoned evidence in hopes of finding a credible accusation.

The best they could find was a half-truth that twisted the context of a lesson Jesus had given in the temple. After one of many temple cleansings, the Sadducees had challenged Jesus, asking, "What sign do You show us as your authority for doing these things?" (John 2:18). Jesus had replied with a grave prophecy in which He claimed both authority and superiority over the temple:

THE TRIALS OF JESUS

Trial	Officiating Authority	Scripture	Accusations	Legality	Type	Result
1	Annas, former high priest from AD 6–15	John 18:12-23	No specific charges brought.	Illegal: • No jurisdiction • Held at night • No charges • No witnesses • Abused during trial	Jewish and Religious	Found "guilty" of irreverence and sent to Caiaphas
2	Caiaphas, high priest from AD 18–36, and the Sanhedrin	Matthew 26:57-68 Mark 14:53-65 John 18:24	Claimed to be the Messiah, the Son of God, which they deemed blasphemy.	Illegal: • Held at night • False witnesses • No formal charge • Abused during trial	Jewish and Religious	Declared "guilty" of blasphemy and held for sentencing until morning.
3	Sanhedrin	Mark 15:1 Luke 22:66-71	As a continuation of the earlier trial before the Sanhedrin, the charges remained the same.	Illegal: • Accusation changed • No witnesses • Improper vote	Jewish and Religious	Sentenced to be turned over to Romans for execution.
4	Pilate, governor of Judea from AD 26–36	Matthew 27:11-14 Mark 15:2-5 Luke 23:1-7 John 18:28-38	Charged with treason and sedition against Rome.	Illegal: • Found "not guilty," yet kept in custody • No defense representation • Abused during trial	Roman and Civil	Declared "not guilty" and pawned off on Herod Antipas to find a loophole.
5	Herod Antipas, governor of Galilee from 4 BC–AD 39	Luke 23:8-12	No specific charges brought. Questioned at length by Herod.	Illegal: • No jurisdiction • No specific charges • Abused during trial	Roman and Civil	Mistreated, mocked, falsely accused, and returned to Pilate without a decision made.
6	Pilate	Matthew 27:15-26 Mark 15:6-15 Luke 23:13-25 John 18:39–19:16	As a continuation of the earlier trial before Pilate, the charges remained the same.	Illegal: • Declared "not guilty," yet condemned.	Roman and Civil	Declared "not guilty" but sentenced to be crucified to mollify the angry mob. Simultaneously, a man guilty of murder, treason, and sedition was released.

Jesus answered them, "Destroy this temple, and in three days I will raise it up." The Jews then said, "It took forty-six years to build this temple, and will You raise it up in three days?" But He was speaking of the temple of His body. (John 2:19-21)

The witnesses immediately twisted the words of Jesus to make Him appear guilty of blaspheming the temple. The Hebrew phrase translated "made with hands" (Mark 14:58) referred to anything constructed for the purpose of worshiping false gods. Jesus hadn't used the phrase in His lesson, but the accusation was enough to agitate the council.

— 14:60-62 —

While the council did find two witnesses willing to tell the same lie—thereby giving the appearance of corroboration—the charge of blaspheming the temple was not a capital offense. They needed more. At this point in the mock trial, the high priest broke several more of the Sanhedrin's rules. According to Mishnah *Sanhedrin* 3:3-4, the accused may not be compelled to present evidence against themselves, and the presiding judge may not examine a witness or the accused. Caiaphas pressed Jesus on His claim to be the Messiah and the Son of God.

While Jesus was literally the Son of God, the Jews used this title to describe their king. If Jesus used this title for Himself, they thought they might have a case of sedition against Him. Jesus affirmed His position, quoting from Psalm 110:1 and Daniel 7:13 to emphasize His messianic claim and to convict the corrupt religious leaders. If anyone was guilty of treason in this trial, it was the Sanhedrin, the people condemning their King.

— 14:63-65 —

At first glance, Caiaphas appeared zealous for the righteousness of God when he tears his robes and accuses Jesus of blaspheming God. But in truth, he and his father-in-law wanted Jesus dead for two reasons: (1) Jesus defied the high priest's claim to rule the temple, and (2) He had threatened to shut down their money machine.

By the end of this second trial, the council had found the charges they needed to discredit Jesus in the eyes of the public and to convince the government that His death served Roman interests. Now they needed to stage a trial for the benefit of the public. Their rules stated that the members were to meet in pairs, share a sparse meal, and discuss the case exhaustively before issuing a final ruling the following day. None of that occurred. They used the time to vent their hatred for

Jesus, taking turns spitting, punching, ridiculing, and taunting Him. This took place despite their rule that brutality against the accused was not permitted.

— 14:66-68 —

Earlier, Peter had followed the Lord's procession from Gethsemane to the homes of Annas and then Caiaphas. As the second trial came to a close, Peter stood at a charcoal fire across from a servant girl who recognized him as a disciple. That undoubtedly put a chill up Peter's back. He flatly denied being a disciple or even knowing Jesus personally. To avoid any further discussion, he slipped further into the shadows, moving closer to the gate.

— 14:69-71 —

The servant girl wasn't fooled. She openly discussed his identity with others in the courtyard, trying to convince them she was right. When the crowd put the question to him, he denied being a disciple and denied knowing Jesus personally.

Time passed, and one of the bystanders brought up the subject yet again. "Surely you are one of them, for you are a Galilean too" (14:70). They could hear Peter's accent as clearly as a New Yorker can spot a Texan. His manner of speaking and his rural demeanor gave him away. To make his denial convincing, he "began to curse" (14:71), which means he called down divine curses upon himself if he were lying. A curse would be something like, "May God burn me alive if I'm not telling the truth." He also began to "swear," meaning that he swore oaths. "I don't know Him, and if I'm lying, I'll become a Nazirite for seven years."

— 14:72 —

About that time, the rooster crowed and the Lord's prediction flooded Peter's memory. Just hours earlier, Jesus had told him that he would deny Him three times before the rooster's morning call (14:30). The dawn brought with it the realization that he had not only "fallen away" from his friend (see 14:27), but he had also sought the approval of people who hated Jesus and served His enemies. He also recalled his confident boast, "Even though all may fall away, yet I will not" (14:29). Humiliated by shame and overwhelmed with guilt, Peter fled once more and wept bitterly.

APPLICATION: MARK 14:53-72

Getting Out of the Past

Jesus had warned Peter and the other disciples shortly after supper, and no fewer than three times in Gethsemane, urging the men to keep watch and to pray. He reminded them that while the spirit is willing, the flesh is weak (see 14:38). Even the Son of God looked to the Father for strength when temptation bore down on Him. In spite of these calls for readiness, the disciples ran and Peter denied Jesus with oaths and curses.

Thousands of miles and thousands of years removed from Peter's denial of Christ, we might be tempted to feel smug about our willingness to stand strong for Jesus. Before we look down on this weak, impulsive disciple, let's be cautious. He meant what he said when he pledged to stand with Jesus and go down fighting. In the nighttime assault on Gethsemane, Peter drew his weapon, intending to fend off the Lord's attackers (14:47; cf. John 18:10). But the Lord didn't want that kind of loyalty. He had called disciples, not soldiers. Peter simply had a lot to learn about discipleship on God's terms and not his own.

We're not much different today. The miles and the years haven't changed human nature. How many times have you fallen on your face? How many warnings have you ignored only to suffer the consequences? How often have you promised you wouldn't commit *that* sin again—the one that continues to haunt your conscience and tempt your flesh? While you may not deny Christ openly, you deny Him by your repeated sin.

How easy it would be to leave Peter drowning in sorrow, bitterly weeping, filled with shame. But Jesus didn't. Within a few days, Jesus would call Peter to His side, saying, "Do you love Me? . . . Tend My sheep" (John 21:17). Jesus said, though not in so many words, "Peter, get your past failure out of your mind and focus on the future I have for you." When Peter received his Master's forgiveness and learned to draw strength from the Father, the former firebrand would become a stabilizing presence in the early church.

Today I invite you to leave the memories of your past failures with the only One who can neutralize their poisonous effect. I challenge you to entrust your failings to the One who died so that you might really live. I encourage you to trust in His forgiveness and turn from your past to consider the future God has for you. Rise from your shame, guilt, and sorrow and ask, "How may I serve You, Lord, with the rest of my life?" He will hear and forgive. What grace!

The Condemnation of the Innocent
MARK 15:1-15

NASB

¹Early in the morning the chief priests with the elders and scribes and the whole ªCouncil, immediately held a consultation; and binding Jesus, they led Him away and delivered Him to Pilate. ²Pilate questioned Him, "Are You the King of the Jews?" And He answered him, "*It is as* you say." ³The chief priests *began* to accuse Him ªharshly. ⁴Then Pilate questioned Him again, saying, "Do You not answer? See how many charges they bring against You!" ⁵But Jesus made no further answer; so Pilate was amazed.

⁶Now at *the* feast he used to release for them *any* one prisoner whom they requested. ⁷The man named Barabbas had been imprisoned with the insurrectionists who had committed murder in the insurrection. ⁸The crowd went up and began asking him *to do* as he had been accustomed to do for them. ⁹Pilate answered them, saying, "Do you want me to release for you the King of the Jews?" ¹⁰For he was aware that the chief priests had handed Him over because of envy. ¹¹But the chief priests stirred up the crowd *to ask* him to release Barabbas for them instead. ¹²Answering again, Pilate said to them, "Then what shall I do with Him whom you call the King of the Jews?" ¹³They shouted ªback, "Crucify Him!"

NLT

¹Very early in the morning the leading priests, the elders, and the teachers of religious law—the entire high council*—met to discuss their next step. They bound Jesus, led him away, and took him to Pilate, the Roman governor.

²Pilate asked Jesus, "Are you the king of the Jews?"

Jesus replied, "You have said it."

³Then the leading priests kept accusing him of many crimes, ⁴and Pilate asked him, "Aren't you going to answer them? What about all these charges they are bringing against you?" ⁵But Jesus said nothing, much to Pilate's surprise.

⁶Now it was the governor's custom each year during the Passover celebration to release one prisoner—anyone the people requested. ⁷One of the prisoners at that time was Barabbas, a revolutionary who had committed murder in an uprising. ⁸The crowd went to Pilate and asked him to release a prisoner as usual.

⁹"Would you like me to release to you this 'King of the Jews'?" Pilate asked. ¹⁰(For he realized by now that the leading priests had arrested Jesus out of envy.) ¹¹But at this point the leading priests stirred up the crowd to demand the release of Barabbas instead of Jesus. ¹²Pilate asked them, "Then what should I do with this man you call the king of the Jews?"

¹³They shouted back, "Crucify him!"

14But Pilate said to them, "Why, what evil has He done?" But they shouted all the more, "Crucify Him!" 15Wishing to satisfy the crowd, Pilate released Barabbas for them, and after having Jesus scourged, he handed Him over to be crucified.

15:1 ªOr *Sanhedrin* 15:3 ªOr *of many things* 15:13 ªOr *again*

14"Why?" Pilate demanded. "What crime has he committed?"

But the mob roared even louder, "Crucify him!"

15So to pacify the crowd, Pilate released Barabbas to them. He ordered Jesus flogged with a lead-tipped whip, then turned him over to the Roman soldiers to be crucified.

15:1 Greek *the Sanhedrin;* also in 15:43.

Something within us craves justice. That's one of the ways we bear God's image. We carry within us His love of moral balance. We want unrighteousness, wickedness, and brutality to be judged swiftly, and we long to see righteousness rewarded. We love it when justice rolls down, and we feel outrage when the innocent or defenseless are mistreated. That's what makes living in a fallen world such a challenge.

This corrupt world system rewards evil and punishes good. Decent, kind people often suffer at the hands of violent, greedy people. Megalomaniacs too often rise to power and turn the lives of others into hell on earth. Adolf Hitler. Joseph Stalin. Mao Zedong. Nicolae Ceauşescu. Pol Pot. Idi Amin. Saddam Hussein. Kim Jong-il. (That's in just the last century, and those examples came to mind so readily I barely paused to think.) Often, the good die young and the wicked live long. The evil and greedy rich get richer while the godly and good poor slide deeper into poverty. For many people, crime *does* pay. There's no doubt—we live in a world in which justice frequently gets turned upside down to favor the wicked and harm the righteous.

Atheists often use this "problem of evil" to argue against the existence of God. Their reasoning goes like this:

If God is all powerful, He *can* eradicate evil.
If God is completely good, He *would* eradicate evil.
Therefore, because evil continues to exist, a completely good, all-powerful God does not exist.

Even those who don't accept this reasoning still cry out, "Where is God? Why doesn't He end this suffering? Why does He not intervene?" We read that Job—righteous, long-suffering Job—reached a point in his anguish when he wished he could meet God in court to hear the Creator explain Himself (Job 9:32-35).

The heartbreaking cries of suffering victims and the angry denials of radical atheists paint a picture of God either as nonexistent or as cruel, uncaring, and aloof. The New Testament, however, offers eyewitness evidence that God is very much in touch with our struggles. He's anything but aloof or distracted. The Gospels testify that God cares about justice and empathizes with our suffering so much that He became one of us and made the problem of evil His own. God the Son left heaven, a place of perfect peace and justice, to endure our struggle with us. He loves us so much that He voluntarily became the most innocent victim who ever lived and endured the greatest injustice ever perpetrated. Because He endured, entrusting all to the Father's care, we can too.

After the nighttime arrest at Gethsemane, Jesus was taken to the respective homes of Annas and Caiaphas, who conducted illegal trials in order to find a suitable charge against Jesus. To create a legal pretext for killing Jesus, they needed a capital offense that would discredit Him among the general population of Jews as well as convince the Roman governor that His death would serve the interests of the empire. While the Romans left most matters of jurisprudence involving Jews in the hands of the Sanhedrin, they reserved the power of execution for themselves.

As dawn approached, the chief priests and scribes found their charges: blasphemy, an affront to the Jews; and sedition, treason against Rome. In an outrageous inversion of justice, guilty men put on their robes of religion and then sat in judgment over the Son of God.

— 15:1 —

The word rendered "Council" is the Greek term *synedrion* [4892], which influenced the origins of "Sanhedrin" in English. The leading members of this Jewish parliament/supreme court had already met and examined Jesus (the first and second trials) when he appeared before Annas and then Caiaphas. When dawn broke, the high priest convened the entire body in the "Chamber of Hewn Stone," a semicircular hall at the east end of the Royal Portico of the temple. The earlier trials had not been official; the temple leaders needed to make their charges and Jesus' conviction a matter of public record. They "held a consultation" (third trial) to formalize their foregone conclusion. To the casual observer, the officials held a speedy trial and quickly exposed Jesus' guilt (cf. Luke 22:66-71). Mark gets to the bottom line without details. They consulted, bound Him, led Him away, and handed Him over to the Roman procurator, Pontius Pilate.

Model by Alec Garrard © Leen Ritmeyer

At the east end of the Royal Portico in the temple, seventy-one elders sat in semicircular rows around an area resembling a threshing floor. The Sanhedrin officially met here to set national and religious policy and to rule on civil and criminal cases. All of their deliberations and decisions were open to the public.

— 15:2-5 —

While Rome could be brutal in conquest and unrelenting in maintaining control of a region, they remained flexible on all but two issues: rebellion and taxes. They generally allowed each local government to administer their unique policies, honor cultural traditions, and even worship their own gods. They granted this latitude as long as local rulers quelled any hint of rebellion and kept tax money flowing into Rome. Failed rebellions

PONTIUS PILATE

MARK 15:1

By the time Jesus began His public ministry, Emperor Tiberius had retired to a lavish villa on the island of Capri, leaving the day-to-day administration of the empire in the hands of his trusted right-hand man, Lucius Sejanus. Sejanus had earned the emperor's trust by transforming a small regiment of the imperial bodyguard into the Praetorian Guard, a kind of secret police force that became an influential factor in Roman politics. Moreover, he had shrewdly eliminated all of his political rivals through slick maneuvering and violent intrigue. One of the rivals he had destroyed was none other than Drusus, the emperor's own son, whom he had slowly poisoned with the help of the unfortunate man's wife.

With Drusus dead of seemingly natural causes, Sejanus enjoyed ruling as the de facto leader of Rome and saw to it that his friend Pontius Pilate received one of the most prestigious appointments in the empire: procurator of Judea. While extremely challenging, the post offered unlimited potential for political greatness in the empire. Sejanus wanted a strong ruler to keep Judea peacefully subservient despite the Jews' mounting discontent.

The historian Philo of Alexandria described Pilate as "a man of a very inflexible disposition, and very merciless as well as very obstinate."[7] Pilate's inflexibility had served him well in the past, but it nearly became his undoing in Judea. Where he brought brute force, finesse was required. He failed to understand the delicate balance between autonomy and control needed to govern Judea. Soon after taking command from his headquarters in Caesarea Maritima, Pilate sent a clear message to Jerusalem, letting the people know he was in charge. Normally, the procurator's army wintered in Caesarea, but Pilate ordered the soldiers to spend the winter in Jerusalem. Moreover, he ordered them to bear Caesar's image on their shields and to display it in key locations throughout the city. He determined that Jerusalem should be treated like all other conquered nations. Of course, this violated the Jewish law prohibiting "graven images" (see Deut. 4:15-18).

Before long, a large delegation of temple leaders marched en masse to Caesarea in protest. The resulting standoff became a test of wills. For Pilate to remove the images would be a humiliating show of weakness, yet keeping the peace was his sole responsibility. The Jewish leaders refused to go home until the images were removed, and this caused Pilate to respond with force. The Jewish historian Josephus described the procurator's means of breaking the stalemate:

> On the sixth day [of the protest] he ordered his soldiers to have their weapons privately, while he came and sat upon his judgment-seat, which seat was so prepared in the open place of the city, that it concealed the army that lay ready to oppress them:

and when the Jews petitioned him again, he gave a signal to the soldiers to encompass them round, and threatened that their punishment should be no less than immediate death, unless they would leave off disturbing him, and go their ways home. But they threw themselves upon the ground, and laid their necks bare, and said they would take their death very willingly, rather than the wisdom of their laws should be transgressed; upon which Pilate was deeply affected with their firm resolution to keep their laws inviolable, and presently commanded the images to be carried back from Jerusalem to Cesarea.[8]

Due to constant conflict and discontent, Jewish leaders eventually petitioned Tiberius for Pilate's removal. By that time, Tiberius had discovered that Sejanus had poisoned his son, and ordered him executed. As the citizens of Rome dragged the mutilated body of Sejanus around the streets, Pilate suddenly found himself without a friend in the world.

usually resulted in mass deaths in battle, after which the survivors were crucified along the roads leading into and out of their cities.

The Jewish leaders knew the best way to convince Pilate to execute Jesus was to label Him a "Christ" or "Messiah." Every few years, a rebel would emerge, claim to be the Messiah, gather a sizable following, and lead an insurrection. Most of these false messiahs discredited themselves or fell in battle against local troops, so they never amounted to much. If, however, the Sanhedrin could make a case for Jesus' unusual popularity, the procurator might not risk His influence growing any further.

Pilate pursued a line of questioning that would determine whether Jesus claimed to be the Messiah as the council alleged. He first asked if Jesus considered Himself "the King of the Jews" (15:2). Pilate's question in Greek emphasizes the word "You." If Jesus answered in the affirmative, He could be convicted of sedition. Jesus gave a cryptic response, emphasizing "you" as Pilate had done. A paraphrase might be, "If *you* say so."

Some have wondered why Jesus didn't simply say, "Yes. I am the King of the Jews." He didn't for several reasons:

- To say yes would have put Him on the same level as the previous false messiahs who had stood before Pilate. The procurator would have disposed of the case without an opportunity to know Jesus as Savior.
- To say yes would have played into Pilate's preexisting notions and prejudices instead of leading him closer to the truth. Jesus is a King in every sense of the term, but His kingship doesn't

rule by the strength of armies; His kingship rests on the power of truth. This King doesn't rise to power through insurrection; this King washes the feet of His subjects.

• To say yes would have diverted attention away from the crucial question: "Who do *you* say that I am?" (cf. 8:29, emphasis mine). Salvation for each individual—Pilate included—depends upon the answer to that question.

When Jesus turned the question back to Pilate, His accusers sensed their opportunity slipping away and began piling on the accusations. Pilate appeared to have ignored the animated council to focus on the composed defendant. By this time, Jesus had determined to say nothing. Mark's double negative in the Greek (*ouketi oudeis* [3765 + 3762]) emphasizes the Lord's resolve. He understood that no amount of talking would change the mind of someone willfully resistant to the truth. He would endure His ordeal in silence (cf. Isa. 53:7).

— 15:6-11 —

The procurator now found himself in a difficult dilemma. He had emerged the loser in earlier political scrapes with the Jewish leaders. This, combined with unfavorable circumstances in Rome—his chief benefactor had been executed for treason—left him vulnerable. He couldn't afford another complaint against him, yet he could see clearly that Jesus was innocent. To find a way out of the jam, he decided to use a Passover tradition against the Sanhedrin.

Pilate's predecessors had typically released one man from prison during the Passover festival as a goodwill gesture. Normally, they chose someone accused of a relatively minor offense. Pilate thought he might dissuade the crowd from demanding the death of Jesus by offering to release a notorious criminal—quite likely a member of the so-called Sicarii. His was called Barabbas, which is a nonsensical name. It means "son of a father." He had probably adopted this "John Doe" name to remain anonymous and to protect his family.

Barabbas awaited the worst punishment Rome had to offer: crucifixion, a horrific kind of death reserved for the very worst criminals. The Greek term rendered "insurrectionist" (15:7) describes someone we would call a terrorist. Surely the Jewish leaders wouldn't anger Rome by releasing a genuine threat to the empire. Surely they wouldn't discredit themselves by withholding justice from a vicious murderer.

Either Pilate underestimated the council's hatred for Jesus, or they simply called his bluff.

— 15:12-14 —

When his plan backfired, Pilate found that his political situation had only gotten worse. Now he had to choose between two unattractive options. If he released Jesus, he risked a riot among the Jews, something it was his duty to avoid at all costs. What is more, another complaint would be lodged against him in Rome and his career would be ended. If, on the other hand, he released Barabbas, he would be guilty of releasing a man Rome very much wanted dead.

Pilate appealed to the crowd twice, each time emphasizing the title "King of the Jews" (15:9, 12). When he pressed the crowd to confirm the charge against Jesus, insinuating that it wasn't compelling enough to warrant crucifixion, they simply shouted him down: "Crucify Him!" (15:13-14). Against all reason—"Why, what evil has He done?"—the crowd became more frenzied in their bloodlust.

— 15:15 —

With emotions running dangerously high, Pilate satisfied the crowd by releasing Barabbas and laying the sentence of crucifixion on Jesus in his stead.

Pilate proceeded to have Jesus scourged. According to Luke's Gospel, Pilate did this in an attempt to punish Jesus and then release him,

Ariely/Wikimedia

A replica model of the **Fortress of Antonia** that stood at the northwest corner of the temple complex. The fortress looked over the temple courts so that the Roman authorities could monitor the Jews gathering in the courts.

hoping that this would satisfy the crowd (Luke 23:16). Some called this brutal form of torture "the halfway death." It served two purposes in the Roman system. First, it was a fearsome punishment that carried a significant risk of death, either by shock during the beating or from infection during recovery. Second, as a precursor to crucifixion, scourging shortened the victim's time on the cross depending upon which whip the *lictor* chose. This expert in the grim art of torture knew exactly how to beat a man within an inch of his life.

Jesus was led to a Roman garrison called the Fortress of Antonia, which was adjacent to the temple. A soldier tied Him to a low wooden post and stripped Him naked or nearly so. Because the whip caused so much physical damage so quickly, the victim often passed out or went into shock after only a few lashes. To draw it out and to increase the entertainment value, the soldiers taunted and humiliated the victim.

When Jesus could bear no more without risk of death, the *lictor* backed off and then prepared Him for crucifixion.

APPLICATION: MARK 15:1–15

How to Endure Personal Injustice

I can think of few circumstances more intolerable than suffering abuse without hope of justice. The internal anguish can be brutal as our wounds cry out for retribution, hopelessness searches heaven for help, and loneliness pleads for a sympathetic ear. Injustice often isolates its victim so that he or she feels cut off from everyone, including God.

This may describe your situation right now. Perhaps you're enduring a grave injustice and you're powerless to set things right. While you undoubtedly feel alone and misunderstood, you can be assured that the Lord knows what you're experiencing. After all, He has personally suffered as you do now. You have a High Priest who can sympathize with your weaknesses and the pain you feel (Heb. 4:15). He cares deeply for you, and He will one day balance the scales of justice. You may not see the kind of justice you want or see it done according to your desires, but He will use this circumstance to your advantage. He will make you spiritually mature so that you can receive His good gifts.

The apostle Peter saw Jesus endure the greatest injustice ever suffered. No one was ever more innocent than Jesus. Few were ever more hypocritical and corrupt than the Sanhedrin. This impacted Peter so deeply that, many years later, he encouraged persecuted Christians with these words: "What credit is there if, when you sin and are harshly treated, you endure it with patience? But if when you do what is right and suffer for it you patiently endure it, this finds favor with God" (1 Pet. 2:20).

So how shall we respond when justice lies beyond our reach?

First, *let go of any expectation of justice.* Jesus accepted that He would not receive justice under the present world system. In fact, that's why He came to establish the kingdom of God! So, He didn't seek the affirmation of people, and He didn't look to the courts for justice. He spoke the truth without fear, He avoided the distractions of anger and bitterness, He submitted to the will of the Father, and He entrusted Himself to the One who will judge every soul.

Second, *stop trying to be heard.* The more you try to make your side of the story known, the less credible you appear. Set aside any hope of vindication in this world. Let God decide when, where, and how He will set the record straight. In the meantime, speak the truth in love and without apology. Speak truthfully and honorably to anyone who cares enough to listen. Follow any reasonable lead to establish the truth. But avoid pushing your agenda. Wait upon God and submit to His sovereign will. Press on!

Third, *seek comfort in Christ.* While imprisoned in Rome, Paul wrote to his friends in Philippi (where he had once been imprisoned) to let them know that he had not lost hope. He considered his unjust imprisonment as resulting in "greater progress for the gospel" (Phil. 1:12) and embraced his circumstances as an opportunity to "know [Christ] and the power of His resurrection and the fellowship of His sufferings" (Phil. 3:10).

When you suffer unjustly, you share an experience with Jesus Christ. You walk in His sandals, so you have a deeper understanding of what He endured to free you from the injustice of this world. Take comfort in knowing that you worship a God who understands your pain and shares your suffering.

And They Crucified Him
MARK 15:16-41

NASB

16 The soldiers took Him away into the ªpalace (that is, the Praetorium), and they called together the whole *Roman* ᵇcohort. 17 They dressed Him up in purple, and after twisting a crown of thorns, they put it on Him; 18 and they began to acclaim Him, "Hail, King of the Jews!" 19 They kept beating His head with a ªreed, and spitting on Him, and kneeling and bowing before Him. 20 After they had mocked Him, they took the purple robe off Him and put His *own* garments on Him. And they led Him out to crucify Him.

21 They pressed into service a passer-by coming from the country, Simon of Cyrene (the father of Alexander and Rufus), to bear His cross.

22 Then they brought Him to the place Golgotha, which is translated, Place of a Skull. 23 They tried to give Him wine mixed with myrrh; but He did not take it. 24 And they crucified Him, and divided up His garments among themselves, casting ªlots for them *to decide* ᵇwhat each man should take. 25 It was the ªthird hour ᵇwhen they crucified Him. 26 The inscription of the charge against Him ªread, "THE KING OF THE JEWS."

27 They crucified two robbers with Him, one on His right and one on His left. 28 [ªAnd the Scripture was fulfilled which says, "And He was numbered with transgressors."] 29 Those passing by were ªhurling abuse at Him, wagging their heads, and saying, "Ha! You who *are going to* destroy the temple and rebuild it in three days, 30 save Yourself, and come down from the

NLT

16 The soldiers took Jesus into the courtyard of the governor's headquarters (called the Praetorium) and called out the entire regiment. 17 They dressed him in a purple robe, and they wove thorn branches into a crown and put it on his head. 18 Then they saluted him and taunted, "Hail! King of the Jews!" 19 And they struck him on the head with a reed stick, spit on him, and dropped to their knees in mock worship. 20 When they were finally tired of mocking him, they took off the purple robe and put his own clothes on him again. Then they led him away to be crucified.

21 A passerby named Simon, who was from Cyrene,* was coming in from the countryside just then, and the soldiers forced him to carry Jesus' cross. (Simon was the father of Alexander and Rufus.) 22 And they brought Jesus to a place called Golgotha (which means "Place of the Skull"). 23 They offered him wine drugged with myrrh, but he refused it.

24 Then the soldiers nailed him to the cross. They divided his clothes and threw dice* to decide who would get each piece. 25 It was nine o'clock in the morning when they crucified him. 26 A sign announced the charge against him. It read, "The King of the Jews." 27 Two revolutionaries* were crucified with him, one on his right and one on his left.*

29 The people passing by shouted abuse, shaking their heads in mockery. "Ha! Look at you now!" they yelled at him. "You said you were going to destroy the Temple and rebuild it in three days. 30 Well then, save yourself and come down from the cross!"

cross!" [31] In the same way the chief priests also, along with the scribes, were mocking *Him* among themselves and saying, "He saved others; [a]He cannot save Himself. [32] Let *this* Christ, the King of Israel, now come down from the cross, so that we may see and believe!" Those who were crucified with Him were also insulting Him.

[33] When the [a]sixth hour came, darkness [b]fell over the whole land until the [c]ninth hour. [34] At the ninth hour Jesus cried out with a loud voice, "ELOI, ELOI, LAMA SABACHTHANI?" which is translated, "MY GOD, MY GOD, WHY HAVE YOU FORSAKEN ME?" [35] When some of the bystanders heard it, they *began* saying, "Behold, He is calling for Elijah." [36] Someone ran and filled a sponge with sour wine, put it on a reed, and gave Him a drink, saying, "[a]Let us see whether Elijah will come to take Him down." [37] And Jesus uttered a loud cry, and breathed His last. [38] And the veil of the temple was torn in two from top to bottom. [39] When the centurion, who was standing [a]right in front of Him, saw [b]the way He breathed His last, he said, "Truly this man was [c]the Son of God!"

[40] There were also *some* women looking on from a distance, among whom *were* Mary Magdalene, and Mary the mother of [a]James the [b]Less and Joses, and Salome. [41] When He was in Galilee, they used to follow Him and [a]minister to Him; and *there were* many other women who came up with Him to Jerusalem.

15:16 [a]Or *court* [b]Or *battalion*   15:19 [a]Or *staff* (made of a reed)   15:24 [a]Lit *a lot upon* [b]Lit *who should take what*   15:25 [a]I.e. 9 a.m.   [b]Lit *and*   15:26 [a]Lit *had been inscribed*   15:28 [a]Early mss do not contain this v   15:29 [a]Or *blaspheming*   15:31 [a]Or *can He not save Himself?*   15:33 [a]I.e. noon   [b]Or *occurred* [c]I.e. 3 p.m.   15:36 [a]Lit *Permit that we see;* or *Hold off, let us see*   15:39 [a]Or *opposite Him* [b]Lit *that He thus* [c]Or *a son of God* or *son of a god*   15:40 [a]Or *Jacob* [b]Lit *little* (either in stature or age)   15:41 [a]Or *wait on*

[31] The leading priests and teachers of religious law also mocked Jesus. "He saved others," they scoffed, "but he can't save himself! [32] Let this Messiah, this King of Israel, come down from the cross so we can see it and believe him!" Even the men who were crucified with Jesus ridiculed him.

[33] At noon, darkness fell across the whole land until three o'clock. [34] Then at three o'clock Jesus called out with a loud voice, *"Eloi, Eloi, lema sabachthani?"* which means "My God, my God, why have you abandoned me?"*

[35] Some of the bystanders misunderstood and thought he was calling for the prophet Elijah. [36] One of them ran and filled a sponge with sour wine, holding it up to him on a reed stick so he could drink. "Wait!" he said. "Let's see whether Elijah comes to take him down!"

[37] Then Jesus uttered another loud cry and breathed his last. [38] And the curtain in the sanctuary of the Temple was torn in two, from top to bottom.

[39] When the Roman officer* who stood facing him* saw how he had died, he exclaimed, "This man truly was the Son of God!"

[40] Some women were there, watching from a distance, including Mary Magdalene, Mary (the mother of James the younger and of Joseph*), and Salome. [41] They had been followers of Jesus and had cared for him while he was in Galilee. Many other women who had come with him to Jerusalem were also there.

15:21 *Cyrene* was a city in northern Africa.   15:24 Greek *cast lots.* See Ps 22:18.   15:27a Or *Two criminals.*   15:27b Some manuscripts add verse 28, *And the Scripture was fulfilled that said, "He was counted among those who were rebels."* See Isa 53:12; also compare Luke 22:37.   15:34 Ps 22:1.   15:39a Greek *the centurion;* similarly in 15:44, 45.   15:39b Some manuscripts add *heard his cry and.*   15:40 Greek *Joses;* also in 15:47. See Matt 27:56.

Whenever I approach this portion of a Gospel, I feel the need to issue a word of warning. Our observation of what the Lord endured on our behalf will involve some graphic explanations of extreme brutality.

When I preach on these passages, I try to find a balance between realism and sensitivity, because a congregation consists of a broad range of ages and personalities, some of whom cannot tolerate graphic violence or gore without feeling queasy. Fortunately, this medium allows me to explain the Lord's ordeal as forthrightly as necessary without concern. I can step away from writing and you can pause as often as you need. While I will be respectful of the Lord's sacrifice and deliberately avoid sensationalism, I must do justice to the violence He endured.

This segment of Mark's narrative represents a long, dark valley toward the end of the story of Christ's ministry on earth. The agony our Savior endured is almost beyond our imagination. In fact, the word "excruciating" is derived from the ordeal of crucifixion, which is undoubtedly one of the worst forms of execution ever devised by man. While not unheard of today, first-century subjects of the Roman Empire knew the practice very well; the prospect of dying on a cross was meant to keep noncitizens in line. Crucifixion was common enough in Jerusalem that the army reserved a special place for it just outside the city walls. Early in His ministry, Jesus knew He would enter this valley and that it would lead to the hill everyone called Golgotha, the Aramaic word for "skull."

As we descend into this valley to retrace the Way of Suffering, keep in mind that this tragedy leads to hope. Gethsemane and Golgotha lead to glory. This agony was necessary for victory to be made available to us.

— 15:16 —

Mark summarized Pilate's ruling in the case *Sanhedrin v. Jesus of Nazareth* with a single terse sentence: "Pilate released Barabbas for them, and after having Jesus scourged, he handed Him over to be crucified" (15:15). We can interpret from the account of the apostle John that Pilate subjected Jesus to scourging in the hope that the so-called halfway death would satisfy the bloodlust of His enemies (John 19:1-6). But the Sanhedrin would accept nothing less than the maximum sentence, the brutal execution reserved for enemies of Rome.

As strange as this might sound, scourging an individual before sending him to crucifixion was an act of mercy. This is because it hastened death on the cross. A sadistic executioner would attempt to keep the victim alive as long as possible. In a modern study of the effects of crucifixion on the human body, volunteer test subjects tied to a cross experienced great discomfort within the first half hour, and the pain became unbearable before an hour. Their forearms went numb and they felt as if their shoulders were being pulled from their sockets. To relieve the pain and numbness in their arms, they instinctively pushed up with their legs. Then their legs would cramp, fatigue, and turn cold until the volunteers arched their backs. But this soon became too difficult to bear, so they returned to one of the other positions. They had to keep their bodies in constant motion to cope with the pain in their arms, chest, back, and legs.[9] Historical records indicate that people sent to the cross without a scourging often endured this for days before the nonstop writhing finally left them too exhausted, dehydrated, and malnourished to pull in the next breath. This led to suffocation.

Mark and Matthew report that Jesus was taken to the courtyard of the "Praetorium" (cf. Matt. 27:27). The word translated "palace" in the NASB (*aulē* [833]) is better rendered "courtyard" because the Greek term describes an area open to the sky surrounded by buildings. The Praetorium mentioned most likely refers to the Fortress of Antonia, which, according to Josephus, sat just outside the northwest corner of the temple wall and rose high enough for sentries to keep watch over the courtyard.[10] When Herod the Great built the massive temple, officials in Rome worried that it could be used as a stronghold. To ease tensions, he refurbished the nearby garrison and named it Antonia in honor of his patron Mark Antony. The Romans used this structure to house a cohort of the Tenth Legion—approximately six hundred fighting men plus support personnel.

— 15:17-19 —

Scourging involved the use of a whip with long, leather tails, called a *flagrum*. A trained specialist in this form of torture called a *lictor* could choose from a variety of whips. To inflict the most damage, he might select a whip with small weights or bits of sheep bone braided into the straps. "The iron balls would cause deep contusions, and the leather thongs and sheep bones would cut into the skin and subcutaneous tissues. Then as the flogging continued, the lacerations would tear into the underlying skeletal muscles and produce quivering ribbons of bleeding flesh."[11] This caused "rib fractures and severe lung bruises and lacerations with bleeding into the chest cavity and partial or complete [collapse of the lung]."[12]

As modern physicians have noted, just a few minutes of lashing could send the victim into shock and cause the victim to pass out. To

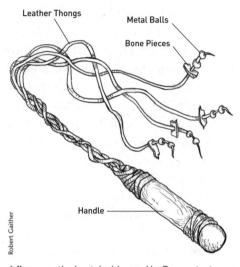

Leather Thongs

Metal Balls

Bone Pieces

Handle

Robert Gaither

A **flagrum**, the brutal whip used by Roman torturers (see note on 15:17-19)

extend the suffering and to entertain bored troops, the *lictor* would turn the scourging into a spectacle. The Roman cohort gathered around to watch, and they mocked Jesus with a cruel coronation. According to Mark, the soldiers dressed Him in purple in order to make a spectacle of the royal claims of Jesus. The soldiers added a crown of thorns and pressed it down on His head. A replica brought to me from Israel has numerous needle-sharp thorns that are 2–3 inches long, making it too dangerous to handle. The soldiers used a reed as a royal staff, but instead of placing it in Jesus' hands, they used it to strike Him on His head. They spat on Him, and they kneeled in mock obeisance.

— 15:20-21 —

By this time, Jesus was an unrecognizable mass of blood and pulp, His flesh flayed by the whip. According to Mark, once the soldiers were tired of mocking Jesus, they put his clothes back on him and took him away to be crucified.[13]

Standard procedure called for Him to be handed over to an *exactor mortis*, a man trained in the macabre art of crucifixion, usually a centurion in rank given command of a squad of four soldiers (called a *quaternion*). The soldiers laid the crossbeam on Jesus' shoulders to carry. Prisoners would not have carried the entire cross. The weight would have exceeded 250 pounds. A healthy man would struggle to carry—or even drag—that much weight more than a few hundred yards, to say nothing of someone scourged nearly to death. Jesus carried the horizontal crossbeam portion known as the *patibulum*.

Ordinarily, the prisoner would be forced to carry the crossbeam to the place of execution, but trembling with shock and teetering on the edge of consciousness, Jesus couldn't carry it far. The soldiers grabbed a random man from the crowd to bear the crossbeam for Him. All three

Synoptic Gospels name the man as Simon, who had traveled to Jerusalem from Cyrene, a city on the coast of present-day Libya. The Gospels name him most likely because he would have been well-known to first-century Christians by the time Matthew, Mark, and Luke published their accounts.

— 15:22-25 —

As mentioned earlier, "Golgotha" is a translation of the Aramaic word for "skull." Locals may have chosen this name because the outcropping of rock resembled a skull from a distance. When the prisoner arrived, the *patibulum* was placed on top of a vertical member called the *stipes* and secured by a mortise-and-tenon joint. The "cross" most likely looked like a large capital *T*. The soldiers placed Jesus on the face of the *T* with His arms outstretched and feet flat against the *stipes*. Most often, a victim was tied in place to prolong his death, but they nailed the hands and feet of Jesus so that He would die within hours instead of lingering for days. Pilate undoubtedly ordered this in view of the Passover feast. He could not afford more complaints against him in Rome.

In keeping with Roman practice, Jesus was stripped for crucifixion, adding to the humiliation of the experience (15:24). Artists don't generally depict this. They almost always cover Him out of a sense of modesty. But the soldiers didn't care about modesty. In fact, they did everything possible to bring shame upon their victim.

Then came the nailing. Combining history with a little imagination, I would suggest that one soldier lay

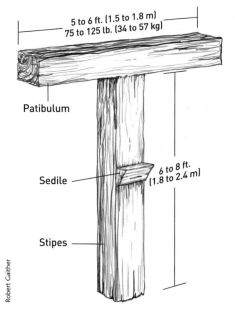

Illustration of Cross. The Romans wasted nothing during execution, including wood and nails. Everything would be used again. Therefore, the *patibulum* (crossbeam) was attached to the top of the *stipes* (vertical member) with a mortise and tenon joint, which allowed them to dismantle the cross for the next victim more easily. Sometimes, to delay death and to prolong the victim's agony, the executioner attached a *sedile* (seat) between the victim's legs.

Figure labels: 5 to 6 ft. (1.5 to 1.8 m) / 75 to 125 lb. (34 to 57 kg); Patibulum; Sedile; 6 to 8 ft. (1.8 to 2.4 m); Stipes; Robert Gaither across His chest while another pinned His legs. Two others stretched His arms across the beam and drove a five-inch-long, three-eighths-of-an-inch-wide, square nail through the base of each palm, angled inward to exit the wrist. They bent His knees, placed His feet flat against the *stipes*, and drove a nail through each foot. (Several years ago, archaeologists found a man's bones with a nail still lodged in one ankle, suggesting that his feet had been nailed to the side of the *stipes*.[14]) The soldiers then tilted the cross up and guided the base into a hole. The cross suddenly stood vertical and was then dropped to the bottom with a jarring thud. By nine o'clock in the morning, the soldiers had finished driving wedges between the beam and the sides of the hole to keep the cross firmly upright.

— 15:26-27 —

The religious leaders had forced Pilate's hand, compelling him to execute an innocent man. As a taunt to the religious leaders, he ordered the *titulus* above Jesus' head to read "THE KING OF THE JEWS" (15:26). The Lord was one of three men condemned to die that morning. He had taken the place of Barabbas, a notorious brigand guilty of murder. The other two men may have been accomplices of Barabbas. If so, they would have been surprised to see someone hanging in his place.

Jim Bishop combined science, historical information, and his imagination to describe what Jesus' experience must have been like:

> His arms were now in a *V* position, and Jesus became conscious of two unendurable circumstances: the first was that the pain in his wrists was beyond bearing, and that muscle cramps knotted his forearms and upper arms and the pads of His shoulders; the second was that his pectoral muscles at the sides of his chest were momentarily paralyzed. This induced in him an involuntary panic; for he found that while he could draw air into his lungs, he was powerless to exhale.
>
> At once, Jesus raised himself on his bleeding feet. As the weight of his body came down on the insteps, the single nail pressed hard against the top of the wound. Slowly, steadily, Jesus was forced to raise himself higher and higher until, for the moment, his head hid the sign which told of his crime. When his shoulders were on a level with his hands, breathing was rapid and easier. Like the other two, he fought the pain in his feet in order to breathe rapidly for a few moments. Then, unable to bear the pain below, which cramped legs and thighs and wrung

moans from the strongest, he let his torso sag lower and lower, and His knees projected a little at a time until, with a deep sigh, he felt himself to be hanging by His wrists. And this process must have been repeated again and again.[15]

— 15:28 —

The earliest and best manuscripts of the Gospel of Mark do not have this verse. It's likely that a later scribe copying Mark's Gospel jotted down a comment based on Luke 22:37 in the margin of his manuscript and later copyists moved the comment into the text, believing it to be an overlooked line from the original. Nevertheless, the statement is completely accurate. To His right and to His left, the only completely innocent man in history was numbered with sinners who deserved their punishment.

— 15:29-32 —

While Jesus agonized on the cross, His enemies came to taunt Him. The Greek word for "hurling abuse" (15:29) is *blasphemeō* [987], which means "to slander or disparage someone unfairly." Mark specifically highlights an earlier half-truth used against Jesus at His trial (see 14:58). When the temple authorities had challenged Jesus on His "authority for doing these things"—that is, cleansing the temple of money changers—He replied, "Destroy this temple, and in three days I will raise it up" (John 2:18-19). The religious elite in Jerusalem had turned the temple into a fetish; they served the house of God while rejecting the God of the house.

A common theme to the various taunts was the challenge for Jesus to save Himself. They failed to recognize that it was necessary for the Messiah to die for the sins of the people (cf. Luke 24:26). At any moment, Jesus could reclaim the divine attribute of omnipotence He had laid aside, return to His privileged place in heaven, reduce the earth to a cinder, and then call all of humanity to stand before Him for judgment—including His pugnacious enemies. Years later, Paul the apostle used Jesus' voluntary sacrifice as an illustration of self-denying sacrifice:

> Do nothing from selfishness or empty conceit, but with humility of mind regard one another as more important than yourselves; do not merely look out for your own personal interests, but also for the interests of others. Have this attitude in yourselves which was also in Christ Jesus, who, although He existed in the form of God, did not regard equality with God a thing to be grasped, but

emptied Himself, taking the form of a bond-servant, and being made in the likeness of men. Being found in appearance as a man, He humbled Himself by becoming obedient to the point of death, even death on a cross. (Phil. 2:3-8)

Jesus could have saved Himself; He chose, instead, to sacrifice Himself to save the world from sin.

— 15:33-35 —

"The sixth hour" (15:33) by our reckoning of time would be noon. When the sun had reached its highest point in the day, darkness enveloped the region. Old Testament prophets had used the image of supernatural darkness as a sign of God's judgment (Amos 8:9-10; Mic. 3:5-7; Zeph. 1:14-15). At Jesus' birth, the light of God's glory had overwhelmed the night sky, turning normal darkness to supernatural light (Luke 2:9). At His death, the noonday sky turned black. It's as if nature could not bear to look at its Creator dying. In a manner of speaking, heaven held its breath.

At three o'clock in the afternoon, Jesus cried out a personal lament drawn from David's prophetic Psalm 22. When Jesus called, in Aramaic, "Eloi, Eloi . . ." (Mark 15:34), the Gentiles thought this was a reference to the Old Testament prophet—"Behold, He is calling for Elijah" (15:35). His Jewish enemies knew better. They must have found David's lament eerily prophetic.

> My God, my God, why have You forsaken me?
> Far from my deliverance are the words of my groaning. . . .
>
> I am poured out like water,
> And all my bones are out of joint;
> My heart is like wax;
> It is melted within me.
> My strength is dried up like a potsherd,
> And my tongue cleaves to my jaws;
> And You lay me in the dust of death.
> For dogs have surrounded me;
> A band of evildoers has encompassed me;
> They pierced my hands and my feet.
> I can count all my bones.
> They look, they stare at me;
> They divide my garments among them,
> And for my clothing they cast lots. (Ps. 22:1, 14-18)

This is the most epochal moment in the history of time. At this time your sins and my sins and those sins of our forefathers and those sins of our progeny and those who will live in the future were all laid on Jesus at one awful moment. So overwhelming was this experience, He literally screamed.

— 15:36-38 —

Someone put on the end of a stick a sponge dipped in a jar of "sour wine" (15:36), a beverage consumed by soldiers and workers as an aid in reducing fever and giving refreshment.[16] After drinking from the sponge, Jesus cried out one last time, dismissed His spirit, and then breathed His last.

Mark notes that the veil separating humanity from the most holy place was torn (cf. Exod. 26:31-33). This thick tapestry kept people from approaching the ark of the covenant, above which—during Old Testament times—the supernatural glow of God's presence had rested. To make contact with the ark improperly was known to result in immediate death (cf. Num. 4:15; 1 Sam. 6:19; 2 Sam. 6:6-7). Because of the atoning death of the Lamb of God, the long-standing separation between humanity and God was rendered obsolete (cf. Rom. 5:1-2).

— 15:39 —

Matthew, Mark, and Luke note the response of the centurion in charge of the crucifixion *quaternion*. Remember, this is the man known as the *exactor mortis*. He had taken charge of Jesus after His scourging and final appearance before Pilate and the crowd. He had stripped the Savior naked, laid the *patibulum* on His shoulders, hung the *titulus* above his head, prodded Him along the Way of Suffering, conscripted Simon the Cyrene to carry His burden, supervised the hammering of nails and the erecting of the cross, witnessed the taunting of Jesus, and studied the Lord's response. When Jesus died, the man who had seen hundreds die by crucifixion exclaimed, "Truly this man was the Son of God!"

Notably, the soldier recognized what the experts in the Law did not. Moreover, he saw the truth about Jesus before the Resurrection.

— 15:40-41 —

As the darkest day in history slipped into night, Mark notes the presence of several women standing at a distance from the cross, who become particularly important to the story a little later. They had been faithful followers of Jesus for years, tending to His physical needs out of their own resources. The women included Mary the mother of James and Joses, Mary Magdalene, and Salome. Matthew adds the mother of the disciples James and John (Matt. 27:56). John adds Mary the mother of Jesus, the Lord's aunt, and Mary the wife of Clopas (John 19:25).

These women had remained as close to the cross as the soldiers would allow. Meanwhile, all but one of His disciples had scattered and left Him to die alone. The one who had sold his Messiah for the price of a common slave had hanged himself. The one who had denied any association with his Messiah shamefully lay weeping uncontrollably in a hiding place. The others—all except John—had scurried away to cower in their own private corners of the darkness. The women, however, continued to support their Master as they had since the early days in Galilee.

APPLICATION: MARK 15:16-41

The Scapegoat

You probably know the word "scapegoat" from popular culture. In modern terms, it refers to someone who is unfairly punished for the misdeeds or mistakes of another. Synonyms include "fall guy" and "patsy." This person is the one "left holding the bag." Usually that person is innocent of everything except the sin of being naïve, too foolish to avoid being blamed.

The term actually comes from the Old Testament, which commands a yearly ritual to be performed on Yom Kippur, the Day of Atonement. On that solemn day, the high priest would carry out the instructions given by God to Moses and Aaron. The Lord had commanded,

> He shall take the two goats and present them before the LORD at the doorway of the tent of meeting. Aaron shall cast lots for the two goats, one lot for the LORD and the other lot for the scapegoat. Then Aaron shall offer the goat on which the lot for the LORD fell, and make it a sin offering. But the goat on which the lot for the scapegoat fell shall be presented alive before the LORD, to make atonement upon it, to send it into the wilderness as the scapegoat. (Lev. 16:7-10)

Since the beginning of Israel's history some fifteen hundred years prior, God's covenant people had watched this drama play out on the Day of Atonement. One goat became a substitutionary sacrifice, and the other goat became a picture of God sending away the sins of the nation. Both pointed forward to what we see played out vividly in the crucifixion of Jesus—one life substituted for many in order to pay the penalty of sin and to carry iniquity far away.

Though Christ's death atoned for all sinners, on the day Jesus died, one man in particular gained his freedom in a very tangible sense. Barabbas should have died on that cross to pay the penalty of his own sin. But he went free instead. One cannot help but wonder how Barabbas reacted when his cell door swung open and the guard shoved him into the bright light and fresh air of freedom. Did Barabbas ask any questions? Did he want to know who took his stripes from the *lictor*, who bore his cross to Golgotha, and who suffered his execution in his stead? Did Barabbas understand that Jesus was no "fall guy," no "patsy"? Did the convicted murderer recognize that Jesus suffered injustice willingly, that He took his place on the cross by choice? We don't know.

But that was then. This is now. What Barabbas experienced historically, we can experience spiritually. We are guilty of sin. Everyone deserves to pay the penalty of their own crimes against God. The Old Testament laws spell out in simple terms what God expects, and His demands are reasonable. They boil down to "Love Me" and "Be kind to others." The rest is simply details. Yet we fail at this daily.

As our internal love of justice tells us, wrongdoing demands a penalty. According to God, the penalty for rejecting His simple standard—which is the same as rejecting Him personally—is nothing short of eternal separation from God in a place of torment. And justice cannot be set aside. Fortunately, God's love and creativity know no limits. He found a solution to the problem of evil that would satisfy justice while granting us forgiveness for our sins: "God so loved the world, that He gave His only begotten Son, that whoever believes in Him shall not perish, but have eternal life" (John 3:16). Jesus, though innocent, took the place of someone who deserved to pay the penalty of death for wrongdoing. He took the place of another on the cross. Yes, Barabbas went free, but the grace he received is merely an illustration of a greater, more personal truth.

It was *your place* on the cross He took. Jesus died *for you.*

A Secret Too Wonderful to Keep
MARK 15:42–16:8

NASB

42 When evening had already come, because it was the preparation day, that is, the day before the Sabbath, 43 Joseph of Arimathea came, a prominent member of the Council, who himself was waiting for the kingdom of God; and he gathered up courage and went in before Pilate, and asked for the body of Jesus. 44 Pilate wondered if He was dead by this time, and summoning the centurion, he questioned him as to whether He was already dead. 45 And ascertaining this from the centurion, he granted the body to Joseph. 46 Joseph bought a linen cloth, took Him down, wrapped Him in the linen cloth and laid Him in a tomb which had been hewn out in the rock; and he rolled a stone against the entrance of the tomb. 47 Mary Magdalene and Mary the *mother* of Joses were looking on *to see* where He was laid.

16:1 When the Sabbath was over, Mary Magdalene, and Mary the *mother* of ªJames, and Salome, bought spices, so that they might come and anoint Him. 2 Very early on the first day of the week, they came to the tomb when the sun had risen. 3 They were saying to one another, "Who will roll away the stone for us from the entrance of the tomb?" 4 Looking up, they saw that the stone had been rolled away, ªalthough it was extremely large. 5 Entering the tomb, they saw a young man sitting at the right, wearing a white robe; and they were amazed. 6 And he said to them, "Do not be amazed; you are looking for Jesus the Nazarene, who has been crucified. He has risen; He is not here; behold, *here is* the place where

NLT

42 This all happened on Friday, the day of preparation,* the day before the Sabbath. As evening approached, 43 Joseph of Arimathea took a risk and went to Pilate and asked for Jesus' body. (Joseph was an honored member of the high council, and he was waiting for the Kingdom of God to come.) 44 Pilate couldn't believe that Jesus was already dead, so he called for the Roman officer and asked if he had died yet. 45 The officer confirmed that Jesus was dead, so Pilate told Joseph he could have the body. 46 Joseph bought a long sheet of linen cloth. Then he took Jesus' body down from the cross, wrapped it in the cloth, and laid it in a tomb that had been carved out of the rock. Then he rolled a stone in front of the entrance. 47 Mary Magdalene and Mary the mother of Joseph saw where Jesus' body was laid.

16:1 Saturday evening, when the Sabbath ended, Mary Magdalene, Mary the mother of James, and Salome went out and purchased burial spices so they could anoint Jesus' body. 2 Very early on Sunday morning,* just at sunrise, they went to the tomb. 3 On the way they were asking each other, "Who will roll away the stone for us from the entrance to the tomb?" 4 But as they arrived, they looked up and saw that the stone, which was very large, had already been rolled aside.

5 When they entered the tomb, they saw a young man clothed in a white robe sitting on the right side. The women were shocked, 6 but the angel said, "Don't be alarmed. You are looking for Jesus of Nazareth,* who was crucified. He isn't here! He is risen from the dead! Look, this is

they laid Him. ⁷But go, tell His disciples and Peter, 'He is going ahead of you to Galilee; there you will see Him, just as He told you.'" ⁸They went out and fled from the tomb, for trembling and astonishment had gripped them; and they said nothing to anyone, for they were afraid.

16:1 ªOr *Jacob* 16:4 ªLit *for*

where they laid his body. ⁷Now go and tell his disciples, including Peter, that Jesus is going ahead of you to Galilee. You will see him there, just as he told you before he died."

⁸The women fled from the tomb, trembling and bewildered, and they said nothing to anyone because they were too frightened.*

15:42 Greek *It was the day of preparation.*
16:2 Greek *on the first day of the week;* also in 16:9. 16:6 Or *Jesus the Nazarene.* 16:8 The most reliable early manuscripts of the Gospel of Mark end at verse 8. Other manuscripts include various endings to the Gospel. A few include both the "shorter ending" and the "longer ending." The majority of manuscripts include the "longer ending" immediately after verse 8.

Death is usually a topic we prefer to avoid. We don't talk about death at parties, at least not for very long before someone changes the subject or makes a joke. My friend Max Lucado writes,

> Make a list of depressing subjects, and burial garments is somewhere between IRS audits and long-term dental care.
>
> No one likes graveclothes. No one discusses graveclothes. Have you ever spiced up dinner-table chat with the question, "What are you planning to wear in your casket?" Have you ever seen a store specializing in burial garments? (If there is one, I have an advertising slogan to suggest: "Clothes to die for.")[17]

Thinking about death makes us uncomfortable, so we either avoid talking about it or we make jokes to feel more comfortable. But imagine how much worse this would be if Jesus hadn't come to earth. Because He died, we needn't fear death. Because He lives, we have hope beyond the finality of death. When Christians in the first century struggled with their fear of death or mourned the death of a fellow believer or began to feel hopeless about life in general, Paul the apostle reminded them that

> Christ died for our sins according to the Scriptures, and that He was buried, and that He was raised on the third day according to the Scriptures, and that He appeared to Cephas, then to the twelve. After that He appeared to more than five hundred brethren at one time, most of whom remain until now, but some have fallen asleep; then He appeared to James, then to all the apostles; and last of all, as to one untimely born, He appeared to me also. (1 Cor. 15:3-8)

He also wrote to Christians, "But we do not want you to be uninformed, brethren, about those who are asleep, so that you will not grieve as do the rest who have no hope. For if we believe that Jesus died and rose again, even so God will bring with Him those who have fallen asleep in Jesus" (1 Thes. 4:13-14).

Death will never be a comfortable or cheerful topic. It remains the greatest of all our sorrows on earth. But we need not fear the finality of death or despair in the hopelessness of the grave. Jesus changed all of that. Jesus removed the stinger from death when He died for us. And by His resurrection, we now have abundant life this side of the grave and eternal life beyond it.

The followers of Jesus didn't know this the day their Messiah died. Despite Jesus' best efforts to teach them otherwise, most of them held great hopes of a Hebrew renaissance in which Jesus would rise to power, take control of the temple, expel Rome from Judea, secure everlasting peace, revive their economy, extend the borders of Israel to encompass the whole earth, and rule over a worldwide Jewish empire. That, after all, had been the vision of the prophets. But as the sun began to set on the darkest day in human history, the disciples mourned their dead King. They had left all and followed for nothing. Despite His predictions of resurrection, all hope died when Jesus breathed His last. They grieved "as do the rest who have no hope" (1 Thes. 4:13).

We know the end of the story, but Jesus' followers didn't. When He breathed His last, some of those followers took on the difficult task of burying their only remaining hope.

— 15:42-43 —

Jesus died on Friday at about three o'clock in the afternoon. The Jewish Sabbath begins at sundown on Friday, around six o'clock, after which no one may work. The word "Sabbath" is based on the Hebrew word for "stop." The Sabbath calls for all Jews to cease everything, gather the family, share a meal, enjoy an extended time of rest, and celebrate the provision and protection of God. The time between sundown on Thursday and sundown on Friday is known as the "preparation day," during which the family prepares twice the amount of food as they normally would so that no cooking is necessary on the Sabbath. Everyone set out double the amount of feed for their animals. They stack double the amount of firewood they need.

The Jews also had a law concerning death on a Sabbath. Deuteronomy 21:22-23 required the body of someone who had been executed to be buried that same day. Moreover, it was an abomination to leave a body hanging after death; only the barbaric, filthy, ignorant Gentiles did such a thing. So the followers of Jesus found themselves pressed by time to take the body of Jesus down and prepare it before nightfall.

We learn from Mark that not all of the Sanhedrin hated Jesus or wanted Him dead. Joseph of Arimathea was "a good and righteous man" and "had not consented to their plan and action," according to Luke (Luke 23:50-51). He had become a disciple of Jesus, according to Matthew (Matt. 27:57), "but a secret one for fear of the Jews" according to John (John 19:38). In Mark's narrative, he suddenly emerges from the shadows. Too frightened to stand with Jesus before His death, he was now willing to risk rejection and reprisal, perhaps because something about the Lord's death had changed Joseph.

Regardless, this prominent member of the Sanhedrin approached Pilate and asked to take charge of Jesus' body. Pilate would have been sympathetic; he didn't believe Jesus to be guilty of anything. Furthermore, this Sabbath occurred during the Passover festival, so he was especially mindful of violating Jewish customs.

— **15:44-45** —

Pilate didn't want Jesus dead, but he wasn't about to release Him alive from the cross. To be certain of death, he called the *exactor mortis*, the centurion in charge of executing the three prisoners that day. Upon receiving confirmation, Pilate ordered the centurion to allow Jesus' followers to take charge of His body.

This was an important fact for Mark to include. The Romans had nothing to gain by lying about Jesus' death. In fact, Pilate's career depended upon the execution of Jesus. The centurion's *life* depended upon his skill as an executioner and his accurate report to Pilate. We know from John 19:34 that a soldier pierced Jesus with a spear to be certain of His death.

Why were these facts so important to Mark? First, the religious authorities would later propose alternate explanations for the Resurrection. They might claim that His body was stolen, or that the Romans had failed to execute their prisoner. Even today, cynics say, "Actually, He didn't really *die* on the cross. He slipped into a coma. When taken down from the cross, everyone thought He was dead, but in the tomb, He revived." After scourging and crucifixion and slipping into a coma, Jesus awoke, gathered the strength to move a two-ton bolder, slipped past the men guarding His tomb, and disappeared into a vast Christian conspiratorial underground network that later claimed He had risen from the dead.

Right.

The crucifixion expert certified the death of Jesus, and Pilate released His body to Joseph.

— 15:46-47 —

Joseph and a few other helpers (cf. John 19:39-42) watched as the soldiers removed the Lord's corpse from the cross. According to forensic scientists, the soft tissues of a dead body—beginning with the eyelids—stiffen from rigor mortis immediately. The process of rigor mortis accelerates if the individual had spent his or her last hours in strenuous physical activity. Jesus writhed on a cross for three hours, so His followers would have had to flex and massage His arms, which were set in an outstretched *V* position.

I include this detail to make the point that death was obvious.

With time running out, Joseph and the others rinsed the Lord's body, anointed it with oil and spiced resins, and then wrapped it in a linen cloth, all in keeping with Jewish burial customs. They hurried to move the body to a burial cave that Joseph had recently acquired for his own family. It was newly hewn from a limestone hill and had not yet been used (cf. Matt. 27:60; Luke 23:53; John 19:41). After placing Him inside,

Barry Beitzel

This **tomb**, hewn from a cave near Jerusalem, with a large cylindrical stone at the entrance, is similar to the one where Jesus would have been laid.

they rolled a large cylindrical stone in front of the entrance and departed, intending to return later to complete the burial process.

Mark notes that the Lord's female followers observed everything. The NASB rendering suggests they stood back and watched for the purpose of learning where He would be buried, but the Greek describes something different. In fact, Matthew states that after the tomb had been closed off, "Mary Magdalene was there, and the other Mary, sitting opposite the grave" (Matt. 27:61). Mark writes that they were looking at the tomb. He uses the verb *theōreō* [2334], one of at least three Greek terms describing visual observation. *Theōreō* means "to observe something with sustained attention"[18] or "to examine for the purpose of gaining understanding."

After the long, exhausting, traumatic day, the women sat before His tomb, staring, trying to make sense of it all.

— 16:1-3 —

The combined Gospel accounts reveal that several women came to the garden to complete the burial process after the Sabbath. They probably had arranged to meet at the same time, but they arrived separately. While John's narrative follows Mary Magdalene, the synoptic Gospels—Matthew, Mark, and Luke—trace the steps of the other women. Mark names the same women he mentioned at the crucifixion (15:40), probably because they were the most familiar to his audience in Rome.

The setting sun on Friday required Joseph and the other followers to act quickly; therefore, the women returned to complete the burial process. They would need to apply nearly 75 pounds of aromatic resins to neutralize the smell of decay. Naturally, they wondered how they would gain access to the body. Burial caves were designed to keep grave robbers and wild animals out, so the entrance of one like this would have been covered with a massive stone wheel weighing as much as a ton or more. The stone wheel rolled in a groove carved into the ground. To open the tomb, several men would need to use levers to roll the disk up an incline and then secure it with a wedge.

— 16:4-7 —

By the time the women reached the tomb, the stone had been rolled away. This would have been perplexing, perhaps even disconcerting. They may have assumed someone else had come to complete the burial ritual. But upon entering, they found no body. The tomb was empty.

According to John's Gospel, Mary Magdalene left immediately to find the apostles Peter and John (John 20:2). The other women remained behind.

Instead of the body of Jesus, the women saw "a young man" dressed in a white robe (Mark 16:5). Mark doesn't elaborate; he leaves it to the reader to interpret the information, but we are right to conclude that this is a supernatural presence, a heavenly messenger. To describe the women's reaction, Mark uses an emphatic form of the Greek term *ekthambeō* [1568], meaning "to be moved to a relatively intense emotional state because of something causing great surprise or perplexity" or to "be very excited."[19] Shocked. Amazed. Startled. Disturbed. Frightened. Certainly all of these emotions washed over the women.

The angel reassured them and explained the meaning of what they saw. No one had taken the body of Jesus—He had risen. *He is alive!*

He instructed the women to find the apostles, specifically mentioning Peter, who had denied Christ publicly but who would become the backbone of the early church. In fact, tradition holds that Peter was later martyred by Nero, which demonstrates a marked transformation from the cowardice he had displayed at Jesus' trial and crucifixion.

The women were told to summon the disciples and tell them to meet Jesus in Galilee, just as He had instructed them earlier (14:28). The program continues. Death had not interrupted the Lord's long-term plans. His agenda had not died. The plan of redemption, the restoration of Israel, the kingdom of God, the reign of the Messiah . . . all would still be accomplished!

— 16:8 —

These followers of Jesus, however, did not immediately do as they were instructed. They had been so faithful throughout His lifetime. They had tended to His physical needs. They had absorbed His teaching. They had remained close by His side during His crucifixion while the disciples fled. They had tended to Him to the very end, even placing His body in the grave. They had already risked their lives and reputations on the decision to follow Jesus. But ironically, they faltered when the victory had been won.

They fled the tomb in terror. Overcome by fear to the point of complete emotional collapse, beside themselves with consternation, they remained silent. Mark concludes his narrative with the haunting words, "They said nothing to anyone, for they were afraid." But anybody in the first century reading that ending would have known that those women—shaken by their circumstances—eventually found their voices. They overcame their initial fear.

The Gospel of Matthew tells the rest of the story: "And they left the tomb quickly with fear and great joy and ran to report it to His disciples" (Matt. 28:8). Before long, great joy overcame their fear, and they had to tell others about the glorious resurrection of their Lord and Savior, Jesus Christ.

It was a secret too wonderful to keep.

APPLICATION: MARK 15:42-16:8

Go and Tell

The original ending of Mark concluded the narrative on what seems to us to be a strange note: "Trembling and astonishment" took hold of the women, and their fear stifled their voices (16:8)—at least for a little while. I wonder what that muffled conversation would have sounded like as they made their way from the tomb.

"We can't tell anybody about this. They'll think we're crazy!"

"Nobody will ever believe us!"

"Are we sure that what we just saw and heard was real?"

"They might blame us and say we're making up excuses!"

Of course, Matthew's Gospel tells us that the women did eventually report what they saw and heard to the disciples (Matt. 28:8). Luke adds the detail that when the women told the eleven disciples the good news, "these words appeared to them as nonsense, and they would not believe them" (Luke 24:11). So the women's fears weren't without warrant. They knew the hardheadedness of the disciples. They knew the strangeness of the message. No wonder they were afraid to be the first emissaries of the gospel to those disinclined to believe in Jesus' miraculous resurrection!

The idea that the first witnesses of the Resurrection had been originally paralyzed by fear must have penetrated the hearts of the persecuted Christians in Rome, who were frightened by the terrifying deaths devised by the insane Emperor Nero. They were overcome by the temptation to deny their association with Christ, even to renounce Him as Savior and King. But they also knew the rest of the story. They knew by oral tradition, perhaps even from Peter himself, that the women did overcome their fear and they did indeed summon the disciples as they were instructed. They found the courage to stand boldly for Christ, His kingdom, and His gospel.

What about us? If the women could overcome their internal doubts and fears and tell the incredulous disciples about the Resurrection, why can't we tell our skeptical friends and relatives? And if the first-century Christians in Rome could conquer their reasonable fear of persecution, can't we get over our own hesitations, discomfort, and fears to go and tell others—even total strangers—the good news of the Resurrection?

I love the story of the little girl who kneels at the bed beside her father to say her scripted bedtime prayer. In a squeaky voice, she says, "Now I lay me down to sleep. I pray the Lord my soul to keep. If I should wake before I die—" Her eyes pop open and she has a look of embarrassment on her face. "Oh, Daddy, I messed it up!"

But her dad puts his arm around her and says, "No, you're right, honey. We all need to wake up before we die."

We can't ever forget this. It's the bad news about us that's answered by the good news about Jesus. Without the light of Christ, all are lost, dead in their sins, and desperately needing to hear the good news that Jesus saves all who come to Him in simple faith, trusting in His substitutionary death and miraculous resurrection as their only hope for forgiveness and new life. They won't awaken without Christ. So we need to overcome our fears.

Don't be afraid. Go and tell.

Postscripts and "Mark"
16:9-20

NASB

NLT

[*The most ancient manuscripts of Mark conclude with verse 16:8. Later manuscripts add one or both of the following endings.*]

[*Shorter Ending of Mark*]

Then they briefly reported all this to Peter and his companions. Afterward Jesus himself sent them out from east to west with the sacred and unfailing message of salvation that gives eternal life. Amen.

[Longer Ending of Mark]

⁹ After Jesus rose from the dead early on Sunday morning, the first person who saw him was Mary Magdalene, the woman from whom he had cast out seven demons. ¹⁰ She went to the disciples, who were grieving and weeping, and told them what had happened. ¹¹ But when she told them that Jesus was alive and she had seen him, they didn't believe her.

¹² Afterward he appeared in a different form to two of his followers who were walking from Jerusalem into the country. ¹³ They rushed back to tell the others, but no one believed them.

¹⁴ Still later he appeared to the eleven disciples as they were eating together. He rebuked them for their stubborn unbelief because they refused to believe those who had seen him after he had been raised from the dead.*

¹⁵ And then he told them, "Go into all the world and preach the Good News to everyone. ¹⁶ Anyone who believes and is baptized will be saved. But anyone who refuses to believe will be condemned. ¹⁷ These miraculous signs will accompany those who believe: They will cast out demons in my name, and they will speak in new languages.* ¹⁸ They will be able to handle snakes with safety, and if they drink anything poisonous, it won't hurt them. They will be able to place their hands on the sick, and they will be healed."

¹⁹ When the Lord Jesus had finished talking with them, he was taken up into heaven and sat down in the place of honor at God's right hand. ²⁰ And the disciples went everywhere and preached, and the

⁹ [ᵃNow after He had risen early on the first day of the week, He first appeared to Mary Magdalene, from whom He had cast out seven demons. ¹⁰ She went and reported to those who had been with Him, while they were mourning and weeping. ¹¹ When they heard that He was alive and had been seen by her, they refused to believe it.

¹² After that, He appeared in a different form to two of them while they were walking along on their way to the country. ¹³ They went away and reported it to the others, but they did not believe them either.

¹⁴ Afterward He appeared to the eleven themselves as they were reclining *at the table;* and He reproached them for their unbelief and hardness of heart, because they had not believed those who had seen Him after He had risen. ¹⁵ And He said to them, "Go into all the world and preach the gospel to all creation. ¹⁶ He who has believed and has been baptized shall be saved; but he who has disbelieved shall be condemned. ¹⁷ These ᵃsigns will accompany those who have believed: in My name they will cast out demons, they will speak with new tongues; ¹⁸ they will pick up serpents, and if they drink any deadly *poison,* it will not hurt them; they will lay hands on the sick, and they will recover."

¹⁹ So then, when the Lord Jesus had spoken to them, He was received up into heaven and sat down at the right hand of God. ²⁰ And they went out and preached everywhere, while

the Lord worked with them, and confirmed the word by the [a]signs that followed.]

[[b]*And they promptly reported all these instructions to Peter and his companions. And after that, Jesus Himself sent out through them from east to west the sacred and imperishable proclamation of eternal salvation.*]

16:9 [a]Later mss add vv 9-20 **16:17** [a]Or *attesting miracles* **16:20** [a]Or *attesting miracles* [b]A few late mss and versions contain this paragraph, usually after v 8; a few have it at the end of ch

Lord worked through them, confirming what they said by many miraculous signs.

16:14 Some early manuscripts add: *And they excused themselves, saying, "This age of lawlessness and unbelief is under Satan, who does not permit God's truth and power to conquer the evil [unclean] spirits. Therefore, reveal your justice now." This is what they said to Christ. And Christ replied to them, "The period of years of Satan's power has been fulfilled, but other dreadful things will happen soon. And I was handed over to death for those who have sinned, so that they may return to the truth and sin no more, and so they may inherit the spiritual, incorruptible, and righteous glory in heaven."* **16:17** Or *new tongues;* some manuscripts do not include *new.*

The NASB and most other English translations include a postscript, verses at the end of Mark (numbered 16:9-20) that are found in some ancient manuscripts but not in others. I noted a similar situation, albeit involving far fewer words, in the comments on Mark 7:16 and 11:26. The question is which, if any, of these verses were original to Mark's Gospel. To answer this question, scholars study the manuscripts and the text of Mark in an endeavor known as textual criticism.

I have always been uncomfortable with the term "textual criticism." It suggests that experts in the field have dedicated their lives to criticizing the Bible until the text of Scripture is either meaningless or untrustworthy. Undoubtedly, some scholars have attempted to do just that. But there are many fine men and women who pursue the true intent of textual criticism, which aims to ascertain which of the thousands of ancient manuscripts contain the original words the New Testament writers dutifully penned by the power of the Holy Spirit.

While Paul, Luke, James, Peter, John, and others in the first-century churches wrote, the Holy Spirit prompted them to include all the information we would need to believe and obey God, and He kept them from error as they wrote. What emerged was divine truth, preserved in ink on papyrus. And because these words were recognized as having divine authority, copyists made duplicates by hand for distribution to the other churches. Then copies were made of these copies, and more copies were later produced from those copies. Before long, hundreds of copies were circulating among the churches. Meanwhile, the papyrus of the original texts deteriorated.

The original scrolls are long gone now, and unfortunately, the process of copying was not perfect. An added word or phrase here, a dropped word there, some letters confused with others—those small errors in one manuscript would become a part of every copy created from it. Occasionally, a scribe would inadvertently create an error by trying to correct an earlier mistake—or what he *thought* to be a mistake—thus propagating another "variant." Many centuries later, there are more than five thousand manuscripts or fragments of manuscripts, all of them containing some portion of the original words of the New Testament.

A good example of this phenomenon today recently showed up on bulletin boards all over the United States. Years ago, someone copied what I had written in a piece I entitled "Attitudes." They typed it onto a sheet of paper in order to produce a rudimentary poster. Someone else liked it and copied it for a couple of friends, who displayed it on their bulletin boards. Later on, copies of those copies were handwritten or faxed and copied again. Before long, my original piece had been copied and faxed so many times that it was barely legible—the letters were blotched and smeared and faded. Yet very few people had difficulty reading the quote, even with missing letters and words.

Although there were of course no photocopiers, the original manuscripts of Scripture went through a similar process and were treated with the greatest of care. Scribes were famously diligent; nevertheless, after hundreds of copies, some errors were propagated. Fortunately, we have the dedication and expertise of textual critics to analyze and compare thousands of ancient copies in order to determine the original text of Scripture. The Bibles we have today are extremely reliable copies of the original texts—as close to accurate as any church would have had back in the first century—and all thanks to the efforts of diligent, godly scholars.

What does this have to do with the Gospel of Mark? As we approach the end of this masterpiece, we encounter a manuscript issue that's more significant than most. The earliest and best manuscripts end with 16:8. Manuscripts that do include further material show three very different endings. None of them bear the style or use the vocabulary of Mark's Gospel up to 16:8. The transition from 16:8 to 16:9 is awkward and forced. The women featured so prominently in 16:1-8 are suddenly gone; only Mary Magdalene remains. And the added material introduces very strange ideas. There's no reference in any other part of the Scriptures to people manipulating snakes or drinking deadly poison without being harmed (see 16:18).

I appreciate these words from the NET Bible:

Because of such problems regarding the authenticity of these alternative endings, 16:8 is usually regarded as the last verse of the Gospel of Mark. There are three possible explanations for Mark ending at 16:8: (1) The author intentionally ended the Gospel here in an open-ended fashion; (2) the Gospel was never finished; or (3) the last leaf of the ms was lost prior to copying. This first explanation is the most likely due to . . . the literary power of ending the Gospel so abruptly that the readers are now drawn into the story itself.[20]

So what are we to make of this? Is the Gospel of Mark suspect because of this added material?

Let me assure you that the Gospel of Mark is completely authentic Scripture, inerrant and infallible, just like the rest of the Old and New Testaments. While the manual copying system was less than perfect, it nevertheless has preserved divine truth over the span of some two thousand years. The vast majority of errors are small, so the meanings of the original text have very rarely been affected. In the rare cases in which the meanings have been impacted, the sheer number of manuscripts makes it very easy to note the scribe's mistake and correct it. And because most variants involve *additions* to the original text, the original wording is easy to spot. In the case of Mark's postscripts, I find the addition as obvious as a rubber nose on a movie star.

ENDNOTES

INTRODUCTION

1 Specifically the Anti-Marcionite Prologue, Irenaeus (*Against Heresies* 3.1.1), and Clement of Alexandria (as reported by Eusebius, *History of the Church* 6.14.6–7).
2 See, for example, Martin Hengel, *Studies in the Gospel of Mark*, trans. John Bowden (Eugene, OR: Wipf & Stock, 2003), 29.
3 Cornelius Tacitus, *The Annals of Tacitus* 15.44, trans. Alfred John Church and William Jackson Brodribb (London: MacMillan, 1921), 304–305.
4 Eusebius, *History of the Church*, trans. Arthur Cushman McGiffert, in *A Select Library of the Nicene and Post-Nicene Fathers of the Christian Church*, ed. Philip Schaff and Henry Wace (New York: Christian Literature Company, 1890), 1:172–173.
5 James R. Edwards, *The Gospel according to Mark*, The Pillar New Testament Commentary (Grand Rapids: Eerdmans, 2002), 13.

DISCIPLES CALLED (MARK 1:1–3:35)

1 L. Coenen, "Proclamation, Preach, Kerygma," in *New International Dictionary of New Testament Theology*, ed. Colin Brown (Grand Rapids: Zondervan, 1986), 3:56.
2 Paul O'Neil, quoted in Mike Wallace and Beth Knobel, *Heat & Light* (New York: Three Rivers Press, 2010), 101.
3 Pliny the Younger, "Letter 97," *The Selected Letters of Pliny: Pliny the Younger*, trans. William Melmoth, rev. F. C. T. Bosanquet (Lawrence, KS: Digireads Publishing, 2010), 136.
4 Wayne Grudem, *Systematic Theology: An Introduction to Biblical Doctrine* (Leicester, England: Inter-Varsity Press, 2000), 226.
5 Tacitus, *Annals* 15.44, 304–305.
6 Fyodor Dostoyevsky, *The Brothers Karamazov* (New York: Barnes & Noble Books, 1995), 235.
7 Edwards, *Mark*, 49.
8 Os Guiness, *The Call: Finding and Fulfilling the Central Purpose of Your Life* (Nashville: W Publishing Group, 1998), 6–7.
9 John Phillips, *Exploring the Gospel of Mark: An Expository Commentary* (Grand Rapids: Kregel Publications, 2004), 31.
10 William Barclay, *The Gospel of Mark*, rev. ed. (Philadelphia: Westminster John Knox Press, 1975), 30–31.
11 Henry George Liddell, Robert Scott, Henry Stuart Jones, and Roderick McKenzie, *A Greek-English Lexicon* (Oxford: Clarendon Press, 1996), 517.
12 See Josh. 22:24; Judg. 11:12; 2 Sam. 16:10; 19:22; 1 Kgs. 17:18; 2 Kgs. 3:13; Matt. 27:19; Mark 5:7; Luke 8:28; John 2:4.
13 Paul Brand and Philip Yancey, *Pain: The Gift Nobody Wants* (Grand Rapids: HarperCollins, 1993), 26.

14 Edwards, *Mark*, 72.
15 See Eph. 2:1.
16 R. Kent Hughes, *Mark: Jesus, Servant and Savior*, Preaching the Word (Wheaton, IL: Crossway, 1989), 1:62.
17 C. S. Lewis, *Mere Christianity*, rev. ed. (New York: MacMillan, 1965), 40.
18 S. Lewis Johnson, "The Paralysis of Legalism," *Bibliotheca Sacra* 120, no. 478 (April–June 1963): 109.
19 Jaroslav Pelikan, *The Vindication of Tradition* (New Haven, CT: Yale University Press, 1984), 65.
20 William Barclay, *The Gospel of Matthew* (Philadelphia: Westminster John Knox Press, 1958), 2:18.
21 Eugene Peterson, *Traveling Light: Modern Meditations on St. Paul's Letter of Freedom* (Colorado Springs: Helmers & Howard Publishers, 1988), 67.
22 Mishnah *Sotah* 9:14, *The Mishnah: A New Translation*, trans. Jacob Neusner (New Haven, CT: Yale University Press, 1988), 464–465.
23 J. C. McCann Jr., "Sabbath," in *The International Standard Bible Encyclopedia*, rev. ed., ed. Geoffrey W. Bromiley (Grand Rapids: Eerdmans, 1988), 4:251.
24 John F. Walvoord, Roy B. Zuck, and Dallas Theological Seminary, *The Bible Knowledge Commentary: An Exposition of the Scriptures* (Wheaton, IL: Victor Books, 1983), 2:45.
25 Martin Luther, quoted in Martin Brecht, *Oxford Encyclopedia of the Reformation*, trans. Wolfgang Katenz, ed. Hans J. Hillerbrand (New York: Oxford University Press, 1996), 1:460.
26 Mishnah *Shabbat* 22:6.
27 Gerhard Kittel and Gerhard Friedrich, eds., *Theological Dictionary of the New Testament: Abridged in One Volume*, trans. and ed. Geoffrey W. Bromiley (Grand Rapids: Eerdmans, 1985), 542.
28 J. Oswald Sanders, *Spiritual Leadership* (Chicago: Moody, 2007), 155–164.
29 Helmut Thielecke, *Encounter with Spurgeon*, trans. John W. Doberstein (Philadelphia: Fortress Press, 1963), 14.
30 Robert Coleman, *The Master Plan of Evangelism* (Grand Rapids: Revell, 2010), 21–22.
31 Richard J. Foster, foreword to *Ruthless Trust: The Ragamuffin's Path to God*, by Brennan Manning (New York: HarperCollins, 2002), ix.
32 Walter Bauer et al., *A Greek-English Lexicon of the New Testament and Other Early Christian Literature*, 3rd ed. (Chicago: University of Chicago Press, 2000), 564.
33 Walvoord, Zuck, and Dallas, *Bible Knowledge Commentary*, Mark 3:23-27.

DISCIPLES CULLED (MARK 4:1–8:38)

1 B. C. Crisler, "The Acoustics and Crowd Capacity of Natural Theaters in Palestine," *Biblical Archaeologist* 39, no. 4 (December 1976): 128–141.
2 Robert R. Stein, *An Introduction to the Parables of Jesus* (Philadelphia: Westminster John Knox Press, 1981), 15.
3 Bauer, *Greek-English Lexicon*, 384.
4 Pliny, *Natural History*, 16:74.
5 Bauer, *Greek-English Lexicon*, 765.
6 Kittel and Friedrich, eds., *Dictionary: Abridged*, 219.
7 C. S. Lewis, *The Problem of Pain*, rev. ed. (New York: HarperOne, 2001), 94.
8 D. Edmond Hiebert, *Mark: A Portrait of the Servant* (Chicago: Moody Press, 1974), 139.
9 Elton Trueblood, *The Company of the Committed* (New York: Harper, 1961).
10 Henryk Sienkiewicz, *Quo Vadis: A Tale of the Time of Nero* (Mineola, NY: Dover), 130–131.

11 Martin Luther, quoted in Ernest Gordon Rupp, *Luther's Progress to the Diet of Worms* (New York: Harper & Row, 1965), 99.
12 Macrobius, *The Saturnalia*, trans. Percival Vaughan Davies (New York: Columbia University Press, 1969); 171.
13 Phillips, *Exploring the Gospel of Mark*, 142.
14 *Merriam-Webster's Collegiate Dictionary*, 11th ed., s.v. "rationalize."
15 Spiros Zodhiates, *The Complete Word Study Dictionary: New Testament* (Chattanooga, TN: AMG Publishers, 2000), s.v. 2894.
16 Gerald L. Borchert, *John 1–11*, The New American Commentary (Nashville: Broadman & Holman, 1996), 258.
17 Bauer, *Greek-English Lexicon*, 444.
18 Alfred Edersheim, *The Life and Times of Jesus the Messiah* (Bellingham, WA: Logos Research Systems, 1896), 2:11.
19 Kittel and Friedrich, eds., *Dictionary: Abridged*, 1236.
20 Philip Yancey, *What Good Is God?: In Search of a Faith That Matters* (New York: FaithWords, 2010), 119.
21 James Moffatt, *The Bible: James Mofatt Translation* (1922; repr., San Francisco: Harper Collins, 1994).
22 Bauer, *Greek-English Lexicon*, 942.
23 John Milton Gregory, *The Seven Laws of Teaching* (Boston: The Pilgrim Press, 1886), vii.
24 Ibid., 119.
25 Hughes, *Mark*, 1:185.
26 Bauer, *Greek-English Lexicon*, 391.
27 Edwards, *Mark*, 203, 234.
28 Flavius Josephus, *Antiquities of the Jews* 15.10.3; 17.8.1, in *The Works of Josephus: Complete and Unabridged*, trans. William Whiston (Peabody, MA: Hendrickson, 1996).
29 Ray C. Stedman, *Expository Studies in Mark 1–8: The Servant Who Rules* (Waco, TX: Word, 1976), 221.
30 Bauer, *Greek-English Lexicon*, 36.
31 A. W. Tozer, *The Pursuit of God*, ed. James L. Snyder (Ventura, CA: Regal Books, 2013), 36–37.

DISCIPLES CULTIVATED (MARK 9:1–13:37)

1 Kittel and Friedrich, eds., *Dictionary: Abridged*, 316.
2 Luke reports eight days, most likely because he used an inclusive reckoning of time. By this method, which is common in the East, the first and last days are included, whereas the exclusive reckoning counts only the full days in between. For example, the Gospels use the inclusive method when stating that Jesus was raised on the third day after His crucifixion. Good Friday is day one, Saturday is day two, and Sunday is day three.
3 Henri Nouwen, *The Genesee Diary* (New York: Doubleday, 1989), 14.
4 Bauer, *Greek-English Lexicon*, 954.
5 Ibid., 816–818.
6 R. T. France, *The Gospel of Mark: A Commentary on the Greek Text*, The New International Greek Testament Commentary (Grand Rapids: Eerdmans, 2002), 370.
7 Edwards, *Mark*, 281.
8 David McKenna, *Mark*, The Preacher's Commentary, ed. Lloyd J. Ogilvie (Nashville: Thomas Nelson, 1982), 25:186.
9 Edwards, *Mark*, 289.
10 Hughes, *Mark*, 2:30.
11 Mishnah *Gittin* 9:10A–F.

12 David Instone-Brewer, *Divorce and Remarriage in the Church: Biblical Solutions for Pastoral Realities* (Downers Grove, IL: InterVarsity Press, 2003), 55.

13 Later, Paul addressed the circumstance when one becomes the victim of an unjust divorce. If someone is abandoned, he or she is "not under bondage," the same way a widow is not bound to a dead spouse (1 Cor. 7:15, 39-40).

14 See Bauer, *Greek-English Lexicon*, 949.

15 Ibid.

16 Samuel Rocca, *Herod's Judea: A Mediterranean State in the Classic World* (Eugene, OR: Wipf & Stock, 2008), 282.

17 Bauer, *Greek-English Lexicon*, 229.

18 Edwards, *Mark*, 325.

19 This expositor is here quoting from John R. W. Stott, *The Cross of Christ* (Downers Grove, IL: InterVarsity Press, 1986), 286–287.

20 David E. Garland, *Mark*, NIV Application Commentary (Grand Rapids: Zondervan, 1996), 415–416.

21 Flavius Josephus, *Wars of the Jews* 1.138, in *The Works of Josephus: Complete and Unabridged*, trans. William Whiston (Peabody, MA: Hendrickson, 1996).

22 Ibid., 4.469.

23 Bauer, *Greek-English Lexicon*, 563.

24 Charles R. Swindoll, *Insights on Luke* (Grand Rapids: Zondervan, 2012), 434.

25 Robert Payne, *The Roman Triumph* (London: Abalard-Schuman, 1962), 41.

26 See Josephus, *Wars of the Jews* 5.465–470; 7.3.

27 Yehiel Dinur, interview by Mike Wallace, *60 Minutes*, CBS, February 6, 1983.

28 Ibid.

29 C. S. Lewis, *The Lion, the Witch and the Wardrobe* (New York: HarperCollins, 1950), 80–81.

30 Bauer, *Greek-English Lexicon*, 684.

31 *Merriam-Webster's Collegiate Dictionary*, 11th ed., s.v. "arrogance."

32 Gilbert K. Chesterton, *Orthodoxy* (New York: John Lane Company, 1909), 56.

33 Martin Luther, *Martin Luther's Basic Theological Writings*, ed. Timothy F. Lull (Minneapolis: Augsburg Fortress Press, 2005), 388.

34 Warren W. Wiersbe, *The Wiersbe Bible Commentary: The Complete New Testament* (Colorado Springs: David C. Cook, 2007), 162.

35 Bauer, *Greek-English Lexicon*, 341.

36 Psalm 90 is taken from Deuteronomy 33.

37 Josephus, *Wars of the Jews* 2.164–166.

38 Josephus, *Antiquities* 18.16.

39 Bauer, *Greek-English Lexicon*, 821.

40 John D. Grassmick, "Mark," in *Bible Knowledge Commentary*, ed. Walvoord, Zuck, and Dallas, Mark 11:12-13.

DISCIPLES CHALLENGED (MARK 14:1–16:20)

1 W. Phillip Keller, *Rabboni: Which Is to Say, Master* (Grand Rapids: Kregel Publications, 1977), 222–223.

2 Bauer, *Greek-English Lexicon*, 303.

3 Ibid., 685.

4 C.J. Wright, *Jesus the Revelation of God: His Mission and Message According to St. John* (London: Hodder & Stoughton, 1950), 164.

5 Adapted from Charles R. Swindoll, *Jesus: The Greatest Life of All* (Nashville: Thomas Nelson, 2008), 184–185.

6 Mishnah *Sanhedrin* 4:1E, 4:1H.

7 Philo of Alexandria, *The Works of Philo: Complete and Unabridged*, trans. Charles Duke Yonge (Peabody, MA: Hendrickson, 1993), 784.

8 Josephus, *Antiquities* 18.3.1.

9   A detailed discussion of the effects of crucifixion can be found in Frederick T. Zugibe, *The Crucifixion of Jesus: A Forensic Inquiry*, 2nd ed. (New York: Evans, 2005).

10 Josephus, *Wars of the Jews* 5.238.

11 W. D. Edwards, W. J. Gabel, and F. E. Hosmer, "On the Physical Death of Jesus Christ," *Journal of the American Medical Association* 255, no. 11 (March 21, 1986): 1457.

12 Zugibe, *Crucifixion of Jesus*, 22.

13 John's Gospel adds the detail that after the brutal scourging, the soldiers returned Jesus to Pilate, who tried one last time to reason with the mob (John 19:4). When the religious leaders persisted and threatened Pilate (John 19:12), Jesus was sent to take the place of Barabbas on the cross.

14 This was a rare find. Because nails were expensive, soldiers usually reclaimed the hardware for repeated use. In this case, they couldn't remove the nail from the wood, so they buried the poor man with the hardware and part of the cross.

15 Jim Bishop, *The Day Christ Was Born* and *The Day Christ Died* (New York: Galahad, 1993), 491–492.

16 Gerhard Kittel, Geoffrey W. Bromiley, and Gerhard Friedrich, eds., *Theological Dictionary of the New Testament* (Grand Rapids: Eerdmans, 1964), 5:288.

17 Max Lucado, *He Chose the Nails* (Nashville: Thomas Nelson, 2000), 119.

18 Bauer, *Greek-English Lexicon*, 454.

19 Ibid., 303.

20 *The NET Bible First Edition Notes* (Peabody, MA: Biblical Studies Press, 2006, available at bible.org), note on Mark 16:9.